P9-DDR-003

Betty Crocker

Mix It Up DESSERTS

COOKIES, CAKES, BROWNIES, and MORE

RODALE

Mention of specific companies, organizations, or authorities in this book does not imply endorsement by the author or publisher, nor does mention of specific companies, organizations, or authorities imply that they endorse this book, its author, or the publisher.

Internet addresses and telephone numbers given in this book were accurate at the time it went to press.

© 2012 by General Mills, Minneapolis, Minnesota

All rights reserved. No part of this publication may be reproduced or transmitted in any form or by any means, electronic or mechanical, including photocopying, recording, or any other information storage and retrieval system, without the written permission of the publisher.

Betty Crocker is a registered trademark of General Mills, Inc.

Printed in the United States of America
Rodale Inc. makes every effort to use acid-free ♾, recycled paper ♻.

Front Cover Recipes: (*center*) Banana Turtle Torte, page 60; (*top left*) Chocolate Cupcakes with Penuche Filling, page 154; (*middle left*) Creamy Fruit Tarts, page 296; and (*bottom left*) Carrot-Spice Cookies, page 256
Back Cover Recipes: (*left*) Lemon-Ginger Bundt Cake, page 88; (*center*) Chocolate-Marshmallow Pillows, page 205 and page 376; and (*right*) Happy Birthday Marshmallow Cupcakes, page 140

Interior and Cover Photography © General Mills Photography Studios and Image Library

Library of Congress Cataloging-in-Publication Data is on file with the publisher.

ISBN 978-1-60961-783-7 hardcover

2 4 6 8 10 9 7 5 3 1 hardcover

We inspire and enable people to improve their lives and the world around them.

www.rodalebooks.com

dear friends,

There's nothing like a home-baked dessert to make any occasion special. And with *Betty Crocker Mix It Up Desserts,* it's never been easier. Simply start out with your favorite Betty Crocker mix, add a few simple ingredients and—voilà!—you have a fabulous dessert that tastes terrific and looks sensational.

What can you make with a mix? A lot more than you may have guessed! Start with cookie mix to whip up fabulously flavored cookies and bars like Chocolate-Marshmallow Pillows and Almond Streusel–Cherry Cheesecake Bars, or use it to create delicious fruit desserts like Southern Apple Crumble. Turn cake mix into decadent layer cakes like Chocolate Mousse–Raspberry Cake, adorable cupcakes and even cheesecake! Don't miss the bite-size desserts sprinkled throughout that add a touch of fun to any occasion.

In this exclusive, expanded edition, get timeless tips and smart solutions in each chapter for cakes, cookies, crumbles and cupcakes that taste—and look—perfect, every time. Also be sure to visit our bonus chapter on gluten-free desserts. It features 50 gluten-free treats from a mix that make serving up dessert sweet for *everyone* at the table.

So whip up a delicious dessert today with an easy mix at your fingertips. No one will guess your secret ingredient!

happy baking!

Betty Crocker®

contents

chapter one

cakes

Perfect Cakes Every Time

Any occasion can call for cake, from birthdays to weddings to just surprising the family with a homemade treat. There are almost as many cakes as there are days to celebrate with them. Here's everything you'll need to know to bake, frost and store your cakes.

Mixing Cakes

Portable or standard electric mixers both work well for beating cake batter. Standard mixers are the more powerful of the two, so when using one, reduce the speed to low during the first step of beating to prevent spattering.

You can also mix cake batter by hand. Stir the ingredients to moisten and blend, then beat 150 strokes for every minute of beating time (i.e., 3 minutes equal 450 strokes).

Baking Cakes

- Turn the oven on 10 to 15 minutes before you plan to use it so it can heat to the baking temperature.
- Check your oven control for accuracy. Here are some tips:
    - If your cakes are already golden brown at the minimum bake time in a recipe, your oven may run high.
    - If your cakes are not done at the maximum bake time, your oven may run low.
    - Purchase an inexpensive oven thermometer to check the accuracy of your oven temperature.
- Measure liquid by placing a standard liquid-ingredient measuring cup on your counter. Pour the liquid into the cup and check the measurement at eye level.
- Beat the batter for the time specified by the cake recipe, using low or medium speed on an electric mixer. If mixing by hand, beat at the rate of 150 strokes per minute. Do not overbeat. Overbeating breaks down the cake structure and causes low volume and shrinkage as the cake cools.
- Bake cakes on the oven rack placed in the center of the oven, unless noted otherwise in a recipe.
- Follow the test for doneness indicated in the recipe.

Choosing Pans

- **Pan Size** Use the size of pan called for in the recipe. To verify pan size, measure the length and width from inside edge to inside edge. If the pan is too big, your cake will be flat and dry. If it's too small, your cake will bulge or overflow out of the pan.
- **Metal, Nonstick and Glass Pans** Shiny metal pans are the first choice for baking cakes. They reflect heat away from the cake for a tender, light brown crust. If you use dark nonstick metal or glass baking pans, follow the manufacturer's directions. You may need to reduce the baking temperature by 25°F because these pans absorb heat, which causes cakes to bake and brown faster.

Removing Cake Layers from Pans

1. Cool cake layers in pans on wire cooling racks for 10 minutes.
2. Run a dinner knife around the side of each pan to loosen the cake.
3. Cover a rack with a towel, then place it, towel side down, on top of the cake layer; turn upside down as a unit. Remove the pan.

4. Place a rack, top side down, on the bottom of the cake layer.
5. Turn over both racks so the layer is right side up.
6. Remove the towel.
7. Let the layers cool completely on racks.

Splitting Cake Layers

1. Mark middle points on the sides of the cake layer with toothpicks.
2. Using picks as a guide, cut through the layer with a long, thin, sharp knife.
3. Or try the thread trick: Split the cake layer by pulling a piece of heavy sewing thread horizontally, back and forth, through the layer.

Layer Cake Frosting

1. Place 4 strips of waxed paper around the edge of a cake plate. The waxed paper will protect the plate as you frost and can be removed later.
2. Brush away any loose crumbs from the cooled cake layer.
3. Place the layer, rounded side down, on the plate.
4. Spread about ⅓ cup creamy frosting or ½ cup fluffy frosting over the top of the first layer to within about ¼ inch of the edge.
5. Place the second layer, rounded side up, on the first layer. The two flat sides of the layers should be together with frosting in between.
6. Coat the side of the cake with a very thin layer of frosting to seal in the crumbs.
7. Frost the side of the cake in swirls, making a rim about ¼-inch high above the top of the cake to prevent the top from appearing sloped.
8. Spread the remaining frosting on top, filling in the built-up rim.

Number of Servings by Cake Type

SIZE AND KIND	SERVINGS
8- or 9-inch one-layer round cake	8
8- or 9-inch two-layer round cake	12–16
8- or 9-inch square cake	9
13 × 9 × 2-inch rectangular cake	12–16
10 × 4-inch angel food or chiffon cake	12–16
12-cup bundt cake or pound cake	16–24

Tips for Storing Cakes

At Room Temperature

- Store cakes loosely covered at room temperature for up to 2 days. To loosely cover, place aluminum foil, plastic wrap or waxed paper over the cake without sealing the edges so air can circulate.
- Cool unfrosted cakes completely before covering and storing to keep the top from getting sticky. Store cakes with a creamy frosting loosely covered with aluminum foil, plastic wrap or waxed paper or under a cake safe or a large inverted bowl.
- Serve a cake with fluffy frosting the same day you make it. Put leftovers in a cake safe or under an inverted bowl with a knife slipped under the edge to let in air.

In the Refrigerator

- Store cakes with whipped cream toppings, cream fillings or cream cheese frostings in the refrigerator.
- Put cakes containing very moist ingredients such as chopped apples, applesauce, shredded carrots or zucchini, mashed bananas or pumpkin in the refrigerator during humid weather or in humid climates. If stored at room temperature, these cakes tend to mold quickly.

In the Freezer

To freeze cake, tightly cover and place in the freezer for up to 2 months. Loosen the wrap on frozen unfrosted cakes and thaw at room temperature for 2 to 3 hours. Loosen the wrap on frozen frosted cakes and thaw overnight in the refrigerator.

cutting frosted cakes

Follow these tips for perfect cake servings every time.

- **Use a sharp, thin knife** to cut most cakes.
- **Use a long serrated knife** for angel food cakes.
- **If frosting sticks,** dip the knife in hot water; wipe with a damp paper towel after cutting each piece.

honey bun cake

PREP TIME: 15 minutes *START TO FINISH:* 2 hours 5 minutes [12 SERVINGS]

1 box Betty Crocker® SuperMoist® yellow cake mix

⅔ cup vegetable oil

4 eggs

1 container (8 oz) sour cream (1 cup)

1 cup packed brown sugar

⅓ cup chopped pecans

2 teaspoons ground cinnamon

1 cup powdered sugar

1 tablespoon milk

1 teaspoon vanilla

1 Heat oven to 350°F (325°F for dark or nonstick pan). Grease with shortening and lightly flour 13 × 9-inch pan, or spray with baking spray with flour.

2 In large bowl, beat cake mix, oil, eggs and sour cream with electric mixer on low speed 30 seconds, then on medium speed 2 minutes, scraping bowl occasionally. Spread half of the batter in pan.

3 In small bowl, stir together brown sugar, pecans and cinnamon; sprinkle over batter in pan. Carefully spread remaining batter evenly over pecan mixture.

4 Bake 44 to 48 minutes or until deep golden brown. In another small bowl, stir powdered sugar, milk and vanilla until thin enough to spread. Prick surface of warm cake several times with fork. Spread powdered sugar mixture over cake. Cool completely, about 1 hour. Store covered at room temperature.

1 SERVING: Calories 480; Total Fat 23g (Saturated Fat 6g; Trans Fat 1g); Cholesterol 85mg; Sodium 320mg; Total Carbohydrate 65g (Dietary Fiber 0g); Protein 4g EXCHANGES: 1 Starch; 3½ Other Carbohydrate; 4 Fat CARBOHYDRATE CHOICES: 4

sweet note Tackle spreading the batter over the pecan mixture with ease! Simply drizzle the batter over the pecans from one end of the pan to the other, then spread to fill in uncovered spaces.

fruit-topped almond cake

PREP TIME: 15 minutes *START TO FINISH:* 1 hour 50 minutes [8 SERVINGS]

Cake

½ box Betty Crocker® SuperMoist® yellow cake mix (1⅔ cups)

½ cup water

½ cup slivered almonds, finely ground

3 tablespoons vegetable oil

½ teaspoon almond extract

2 eggs

Topping

3 cups assorted fresh berries (such as raspberries, blueberries and blackberries)

¾ cup apricot preserves

3 tablespoons apple juice

3 tablespoons sliced almonds, toasted, if desired

1 Heat oven to 350°F (325°F for dark or nonstick pan). Generously spray bottom and side of 8- or 9-inch round cake pan with baking spray with flour.

2 In large bowl, beat cake ingredients with electric mixer on low speed until moistened, then on medium speed 2 minutes, scraping bowl occasionally. Pour into pan.

3 Bake and cool as directed on box for 8- or 9-inch rounds.

4 Place berries in medium bowl. In 1-quart saucepan, heat preserves and apple juice to boiling, stirring frequently. Pour over berries; toss berries until coated with preserves mixture. Let stand 5 minutes.

5 Gently cut off any dome from top of cake, using serrated knife, to make top level. On serving plate, place cake, sliced side down. Arrange berries on cake; drizzle with syrup remaining in bowl. Sprinkle with sliced almonds. Store leftover cake covered in refrigerator.

1 SERVING: Calories 320; Total Fat 11g (Saturated Fat 2g; Trans Fat 0g); Cholesterol 55mg; Sodium 220mg; Total Carbohydrate 52g (Dietary Fiber 4g); Protein 4g EXCHANGES: 1 Starch; ½ Fruit; 2 Other Carbohydrate; 2 Fat CARBOHYDRATE CHOICES: 3½

sweet note Grind the slivered almonds in a small food processor, or very finely chop them with a knife.

luscious mandarin orange cake

PREP TIME: 10 minutes *START TO FINISH:* 1 hour 50 minutes [20 SERVINGS]

1 box Betty Crocker® SuperMoist® yellow cake mix

½ cup vegetable oil

½ cup chopped walnuts, if desired

1 can (11 oz) mandarin orange segments, undrained

4 eggs

1 can (20 oz) crushed pineapple, undrained

1 box (4-serving size) vanilla instant pudding and pie filling mix

½ to 1 teaspoon grated orange peel, if desired

1 cup frozen (thawed) whipped topping

1 Heat oven to 350°F (325°F for dark or nonstick pan). Grease bottom only of 13 × 9-inch pan with shortening or cooking spray.

2 In large bowl, beat cake mix, oil, walnuts, orange segments, reserved ⅓ cup orange liquid and eggs with electric mixer on low speed 30 seconds, then on medium speed 2 minutes. Pour into pan.

3 Bake 35 to 40 minutes or until toothpick inserted in center comes out clean. Cool completely, about 1 hour.

4 To make pineapple frosting, stir together pineapple, dry pudding mix and orange peel. Gently stir in whipped topping. Spread on cake. Store tightly covered in refrigerator.

1 SERVING: Calories 200; Total Fat 8g (Saturated Fat 2½g; Trans Fat 0g); Cholesterol 40mg; Sodium 240mg; Total Carbohydrate 30g (Dietary Fiber 0g); Protein 2g EXCHANGES: ½ Starch; 0 Fruit; 1½ Other Carbohydrate; 1½ Fat CARBOHYDRATE CHOICES: 2

caramel-apple sundae cake

PREP TIME: 10 minutes *START TO FINISH:* 1 hour 20 minutes [15 SERVINGS]

1 box Betty Crocker® SuperMoist® yellow cake mix

1 cup chopped nuts

⅓ cup packed brown sugar

¼ cup butter or margarine, softened

1 teaspoon cinnamon

⅓ cup water

2 tablespoons vegetable oil

2 eggs

3 medium cooking apples, peeled and sliced

½ cup caramel topping

Ice cream, if desired

Additional caramel topping, if desired

1 Heat oven to 350°F (325°F for dark or nonstick pan). Grease bottom and sides of 13 × 9-inch pan with shortening; lightly flour.

2 Mix 1 cup of the cake mix, the nuts, brown sugar, butter and cinnamon in small bowl with fork until crumbly; set aside.

3 Mix remaining cake mix, ⅓ cup water, the oil and eggs in medium bowl with spoon (batter will be lumpy). Spread in pan. Arrange apple slices on top. Sprinkle with half of the crumbly mixture. Drizzle with ½ cup caramel topping. Sprinkle with remaining crumbly mixture.

4 Bake 45 to 50 minutes or until cake is golden brown and pulls away from the sides of pan. Cool about 30 minutes. Serve warm with ice cream and additional caramel topping. Store covered in refrigerator.

1 SERVING: Calories 279; Total Fat 13g (Saturated Fat 4g; Trans Fat 1g); Cholesterol 36mg; Sodium 259mg; Total Carbohydrate 40g (Dietary Fiber 1g); Protein 3g EXCHANGES: 2 Other Carbohydate; 2 Fat CARBOHYDRATE CHOICES: 2½

sweet note Be picky when picking your apples for this recipe. Cooking apples, such as Rome Beauty, Granny Smith and Greening, have a firm texture and will hold their shape when baked in this dessert.

ooey-gooey caramel cake

PREP TIME: 20 minutes *START TO FINISH:* 2 hours 5 minutes [15 SERVINGS]

- 1 box Betty Crocker® SuperMoist® yellow cake mix
- ⅓ cup Gold Medal® all-purpose flour
- 1 cup water
- ⅓ cup vegetable oil
- 3 eggs
- 1 bag (8 oz) milk chocolate-coated toffee bits
- 1 can (13.4 oz) dulce de leche (caramelized sweetened condensed milk)
- Sweetened whipped cream, if desired
- Caramel topping, if desired

1. Heat oven to 350°F (325°F for dark or nonstick pan). Spray bottom and sides of 13 × 9-inch pan with baking spray with flour.
2. In large bowl, beat cake mix, flour, water, oil and eggs with electric mixer on low speed 30 seconds, then on medium speed 2 minutes, scraping bowl occasionally. Stir in ½ cup of the toffee bits. Pour into pan.
3. Reserve ½ cup dulce de leche. Spoon remaining dulce de leche by teaspoonfuls onto batter.
4. Bake 34 to 42 minutes or until toothpick inserted in center comes out clean. Cool 5 minutes. In small microwavable bowl, microwave reserved dulce de leche on High 10 to 15 seconds or until softened; spread evenly over top of cake. Sprinkle with remaining toffee bits. Cool about 1 hour before serving. Top each serving with whipped cream and caramel topping.

1 SERVING: Calories 340; Total Fat 13g (Saturated Fat 4½g; Trans Fat 0g); Cholesterol 50mg; Sodium 290mg; Total Carbohydrate 51g (Dietary Fiber 0g); Protein 4g EXCHANGES: 1½ Starch; 2 Other Carbohydrate; 2½ Fat CARBOHYDRATE CHOICES: 3½

sweet note You can substitute crushed chocolate-covered English toffee candy bars for the toffee bits.

dulce de leche cake

PREP TIME: 30 minutes *START TO FINISH:* 2 hours 10 minutes [12 SERVINGS]

Cake

⅓ cup butter (do not use margarine)

1 box Betty Crocker® SuperMoist® butter recipe yellow cake mix

1 cup water

2 teaspoons vanilla

3 eggs

Frosting

1 can (13.4 oz) dulce de leche (caramelized sweetened condensed milk)

1 package (8 oz) cream cheese, softened

½ cup whipping cream

1 Heat oven to 350°F (325°F for dark or nonstick pan). Grease bottom only of 13 × 9-inch pan with shortening or cooking spray.

2 In 1-quart saucepan, heat butter over medium heat 4 to 6 minutes, stirring frequently, just until golden brown. Remove from heat. Cool 15 minutes.

3 In large bowl, beat cake mix, browned butter, water, vanilla and eggs with electric mixer on low speed 30 seconds. Beat on medium speed 2 minutes (brown flecks from butter will appear in batter). Pour into pan.

4 Bake as directed on box for 13 × 9-inch pan. Cool completely, about 1 hour.

5 Meanwhile, in large bowl, beat dulce de leche and cream cheese with electric mixer on high speed about 2 minutes or until blended and smooth. Beat in whipping cream until stiff peaks form. Spread frosting over cooled cake. Serve immediately, or refrigerate until serving.

1 SERVING: Calories 400; Total Fat 20g (Saturated Fat 11g; Trans Fat ½g); Cholesterol 110mg; Sodium 400mg; Total Carbohydrate 51g (Dietary Fiber 0g); Protein 5g
EXCHANGES: 1 Starch; 2½ Other Carbohydrate; 4 Fat CARBOHYDRATE CHOICES: 3½

sweet note You won't want to substitute margarine or vegetable oil spreads for the butter in this richly flavored recipe. Because those products don't contain the milk proteins found in butter, they will not brown and will burn instead.

premium tres leches cake

PREP TIME: 15 minutes *START TO FINISH:* 1 hour 55 minutes [15 SERVINGS]

1 box Betty Crocker® SuperMoist® yellow cake mix

1¼ cups water

1 tablespoon vegetable oil

2 teaspoons vanilla

4 eggs

1 can (14 oz) sweetened condensed milk (not evaporated)

1 cup whole milk or evaporated milk

1 cup whipping cream

1 container (12 oz) Betty Crocker® Whipped fluffy white frosting

1 Heat oven to 350°F (325°F for dark or nonstick pan). Grease and flour or spray bottom and sides of 13 × 9-inch pan.

2 In large bowl, beat cake mix, water, oil, vanilla and eggs with electric mixer on low speed 30 seconds, then on medium speed 2 minutes, scraping bowl occasionally. Pour into pan.

3 Bake as directed on box for 13 × 9-inch pan. Let stand 5 minutes. Poke top of hot cake every ½ inch with long-tined fork, wiping fork occasionally to reduce sticking.

4 In large bowl, stir together sweetened condensed milk, whole milk and whipping cream. Carefully pour evenly over top of cake. Cover; refrigerate about 1 hour or until mixture is absorbed into cake. Frost with frosting.

1 SERVING: Calories 390; Total Fat 17g (Saturated Fat 8g; Trans Fat 1½g); Cholesterol 90mg; Sodium 290mg; Total Carbohydrate 54g (Dietary Fiber 0g); Protein 5g EXCHANGES: ½ Starch; 2½ Other Carbohydrate; ½ Milk; 2½ Fat CARBOHYDRATE CHOICES: 3½

sweet note

Tres leches is the Spanish term for three milks. The three types of milk create this cake's signature indulgence and moistness.

peanut butter silk cake

PREP TIME: 15 minutes *START TO FINISH:* 2 hours 10 minutes [12 SERVINGS]

- 1 box Betty Crocker® SuperMoist® yellow cake mix
- 1¼ cups water
- ½ cup creamy peanut butter
- ⅓ cup vegetable oil
- 3 eggs
- ¼ cup butter or margarine
- ¼ cup packed brown sugar
- 1 cup whipping cream
- ½ cup creamy peanut butter
- 1 container (1 lb) Betty Crocker® Rich & Creamy chocolate frosting
- 1 cup chopped peanuts, if desired

1. Heat oven to 350°F (325°F for dark or nonstick pans). Generously grease bottoms only of two 8- or 9-inch round cake pans with shortening or cooking spray.
2. In large bowl, beat cake mix, water, ½ cup peanut butter, the oil and eggs with electric mixer on low speed 30 seconds. Beat on medium speed 2 minutes, scraping bowl occasionally. Pour into pans.
3. Bake 30 to 35 minutes or until toothpick inserted in center comes out clean. Cool 10 minutes. Run knife around sides of pans to loosen cakes; remove from pans to cooling rack. Cool completely, about 1 hour.
4. In 2-quart saucepan, melt butter over medium heat; stir in brown sugar. Heat to boiling; boil and stir 1 minute. Remove from heat. Refrigerate 10 minutes.
5. In chilled medium bowl, beat whipping cream on high speed until soft peaks form; set aside. In another medium bowl, beat ½ cup peanut butter and the brown sugar mixture on medium speed until smooth and creamy. Add whipped cream to peanut butter mixture; beat on medium speed until mixture is smooth and creamy.
6. Split each cake layer horizontally to make 2 layers. Fill each layer with about ⅔ cup peanut butter mixture to within ½ inch of edge. Stack 4 layers on top of one another and frost side and top of cake with frosting. Press peanuts onto frosting on side of cake. Store covered in refrigerator.

1 SERVING: Calories 610; Total Fat 36g (Saturated Fat 13g; Trans Fat 2½g); Cholesterol 90mg; Sodium 510mg; Total Carbohydrate 62g (Dietary Fiber 1g); Protein 8g EXCHANGES: 2½ Starch; 1½ Other Carbohydrate; 7 Fat CARBOHYDRATE CHOICES: 4

sweet note For a fun garnish, top this cake with coarsely cut-up chocolate-covered peanut butter cups. Or dot the top with mini cups that have been cut in half crosswise.

praline mini cakes

PREP TIME: 20 minutes *START TO FINISH:* 1 hour 55 minutes [12 CAKES]

Cakes

1 box Betty Crocker® SuperMoist® yellow cake mix

1¼ cups water

⅓ cup vegetable oil

3 eggs

½ cup chopped pecans

½ cup toffee bits

Glaze and Garnish

¼ cup butter (do not use margarine)

½ cup packed brown sugar

2 tablespoons corn syrup

2 tablespoons milk

1 cup powdered sugar

1 teaspoon vanilla

¼ cup toffee bits

1 Heat oven to 350°F (325°F for dark or nonstick pans). Generously grease 12 mini fluted tube cake pans or 12 jumbo muffin cups with shortening (do not spray with cooking spray); lightly flour.

2 In large bowl, beat cake mix, water, oil and eggs with electric mixer on low speed 30 seconds. Beat on medium speed 2 minutes, scraping bowl occasionally. Fold in pecans and ½ cup toffee bits. Divide batter evenly among mini pans.

3 Bake 18 to 23 minutes or until toothpick inserted in center of cake comes out clean. Cool 10 minutes; remove from pans to cooling rack. Cool completely, about 1 hour.

4 In 1-quart saucepan, melt butter over medium-high heat. Stir in brown sugar, corn syrup and milk. Heat to rolling boil over medium-high heat, stirring frequently; remove from heat. Immediately beat in powdered sugar and vanilla with wire whisk until smooth. Immediately drizzle about 1 tablespoon glaze over each cake; sprinkle each with 1 teaspoon toffee bits. Store loosely covered at room temperature.

1 MINI CAKE: Calories 470; Total Fat 24g (Saturated Fat 8g; Trans Fat 0g); Cholesterol 65mg; Sodium 310mg; Total Carbohydrate 62g (Dietary Fiber 1g); Protein 3g EXCHANGES: 1 Starch; 3 Other Carbohydrate; 4½ Fat CARBOHYDRATE CHOICES: 4

sweet note To keep the cakes from sticking to the cake pans, be sure to grease and flour the pans generously.

raspberry crumb cake

PREP TIME: 20 minutes *START TO FINISH:* 1 hour 30 minutes [9 SERVINGS]

Cake

½ box Betty Crocker® SuperMoist® yellow cake mix (1⅔ cups)

¼ cup sour cream

3 tablespoons vegetable oil

3 tablespoons water

1 egg

¾ cup fresh raspberries

Topping

½ cup sugar

⅓ cup sliced almonds

3 tablespoons Gold Medal® all-purpose flour

3 tablespoons butter or margarine, softened

Garnish

Fresh raspberries, if desired

Fresh mint leaves, if desired

1 Heat oven to 350°F (325°F for dark or nonstick pan). Spray bottom and sides of 8- or 9-inch square pan with baking spray with flour.

2 In large bowl, beat cake mix, sour cream, oil, water and egg with electric mixer on low speed 30 seconds, then on medium speed 2 minutes, scraping bowl occasionally. Spread in pan. Place raspberries on top of batter.

3 In small bowl, stir topping ingredients until well mixed. Sprinkle evenly over batter and raspberries.

4 Bake 9-inch pan 30 to 40 minutes, 8-inch pan 35 to 45 minutes, or until toothpick inserted in center comes out clean. Cool at least 30 minutes before serving. Garnish with fresh raspberries and mint leaves.

1 SERVING: Calories 270; Total Fat 13g (Saturated Fat 4½g; Trans Fat 0g); Cholesterol 35mg; Sodium 210mg; Total Carbohydrate 35g (Dietary Fiber 1g); Protein 2g EXCHANGES: ½ Starch; 2 Other Carbohydrate; 2½ Fat CARBOHYDRATE CHOICES: 2

sweet note Frozen berries (not packed in any syrup), thawed and drained, can be used in place of the fresh raspberries.

mini sunflower cakes

PREP TIME: 20 minutes *START TO FINISH:* 45 minutes [12 CAKES]

1 box Betty Crocker® SuperMoist® yellow cake mix

Water, vegetable oil and eggs called for on cake mix box

Yellow food color, if desired

¾ cup miniature semisweet chocolate chips

1 Heat oven to 325°F. Grease and lightly flour cups of sunflower mini pan, or spray pan with baking spray with flour.

2 Make cake batter as directed on box, adding food color to batter. Pour batter into pan, filling each cup about three-fourths full.

3 Bake 18 to 25 minutes or until toothpick inserted in center comes out clean. Cool 10 minutes. Remove cakes from pan to cooling rack, placing sunflower side up. Spoon about 1 tablespoon of the chocolate chips onto center of each cake. After chips melt slightly, spread chocolate with knife. Cool completely, about 30 minutes. Store loosely covered.

1 MINI CAKE: Calories 368; Total Fat 18g (Saturated Fat 7g; Trans Fat 1g); Cholesterol 35mg; Sodium 264mg; Total Carbohydrate 49g (Dietary Fiber 0g); Protein 5g EXCHANGES: 3 Other Carbohydrate; 3 Fat CARBOHYDRATE CHOICES: 3

sweet note Look for the sunflower mini pans at specialty cookware stores. You can add a few drops of yellow food color to cake mix batter to create a sunny color.

blueberry–cream cheese coffee cake

PREP TIME: 15 minutes *START TO FINISH:* 55 minutes [9 SERVINGS]

1 Heat oven to 425°F. Grease bottom and sides of 8-inch square pan.

2 In medium bowl, beat cream cheese and sugar with electric mixer on medium speed; beat in 1 egg and lemon juice until smooth. Set aside.

3 In a second medium bowl, stir muffin mix, water, oil, remaining 1 egg and the lemon peel just until blended. Spread half of the batter in pan. Spread cream cheese mixture over batter. Spread remaining batter over cream cheese mixture.

4 Bake 35 to 40 minutes or until golden brown.

1 SERVING: Calories 350; Total Fat 16g (Saturated Fat 8g; Trans Fat 0g); Cholesterol 75mg; Sodium 370mg; Total Carbohydrate 45g (Dietary Fiber 0g); Protein 6g EXCHANGES: 2½ Starch; 3 Other Carbohydrate; 2½ Fat CARBOHYDRATE CHOICES: 3

1 package (8 oz) cream cheese

¼ cup sugar

2 eggs

1 teaspoon lemon juice

1 package (1 lb 2.25 oz) Betty Crocker® wild blueberry muffin mix

1 cup water

3 tablespoons vegetable oil

1 teaspoon grated lemon peel, if desired

sweet note For extra flavor and a healthy boost, mix fresh blueberries in gently with the batter mixture before spreading in the pan.

chocolate chip cookie surprise cake

PREP TIME: 20 minutes *START TO FINISH:* 2 hours [15 SERVINGS]

1 box Betty Crocker® SuperMoist® yellow cake mix

1 cup milk

½ cup vegetable oil

4 eggs

1 pouch (1 lb 1.5 oz) Betty Crocker® chocolate chip cookie mix

Butter and egg called for on cookie mix pouch

1 container (1 lb) Betty Crocker® Rich & Creamy chocolate frosting

1 Heat oven to 350°F (325°F for dark or nonstick pan). Generously grease and lightly flour, or spray with baking spray with flour, bottom only of 13 × 9-inch pan.

2 In large bowl, beat cake mix, milk, oil and 4 eggs with electric mixer on low speed 30 seconds, then on medium speed 2 minutes. Pour into pan.

3 Make cookie dough as directed on pouch. Drop dough by teaspoonfuls evenly over batter in pan.

4 Bake 54 to 59 minutes or until toothpick inserted in center comes out clean. Run knife around sides of pan to loosen cake. Cool completely, about 1 hour. Spread frosting over top of cake. Store loosely covered at room temperature.

1 SERVING: Calories 510; Total Fat 24g (Saturated Fat 10g; Trans Fat 2g); Cholesterol 90mg; Sodium 490mg; Total Carbohydrate 68g (Dietary Fiber 0g); Protein 4g
EXCHANGES: 1½ Starch; 3 Other Carbohydrate; 4½ Fat CARBOHYDRATE CHOICES: 4½

sweet note Need ice cream with your cake and cookies? Skip the frosting, and serve with spoonfuls of ice cream and topping for an indulgent treat.

chocolate chip marble cake

PREP TIME: 15 minutes *START TO FINISH:* 1 hour 55 minutes [15 SERVINGS]

¾ cup miniature semisweet chocolate chips (do not use regular-size chips)

1 box Betty Crocker® SuperMoist® vanilla cake mix

Water, vegetable oil and eggs called for on cake mix box

¼ cup chocolate-flavor syrup

1 container (1 lb) Betty Crocker® Rich & Creamy vanilla frosting

Additional chocolate-flavor syrup, if desired

1 Heat oven to 350°F (325°F for dark or nonstick pan). Generously grease bottom only of 13 × 9-inch pan with cooking spray or shortening.

2 In small bowl, toss ½ cup of the chocolate chips with 1 tablespoon of the dry cake mix. Make cake batter as directed on box—except stir in the coated chocolate chips. Reserve 1 cup of the batter. Pour remaining batter into pan. Stir chocolate syrup into reserved batter. Drop by tablespoonfuls randomly in 8 mounds in pan. Cut through batters in S-shaped curves. Turn pan one-fourth turn; repeat.

3 Bake 33 to 38 minutes or until toothpick inserted in center of chocolate portion of cake comes out clean. Run knife around sides of pan to loosen cake. Cool completely, about 1 hour.

4 Stir remaining ¼ cup chocolate chips into frosting. Spread frosting on cake. Drizzle additional chocolate syrup over top. Store loosely covered at room temperature.

1 SERVING: Calories 370; Total Fat 16g (Saturated Fat 4½g; Trans Fat 2g); Cholesterol 40mg; Sodium 290mg; Total Carbohydrate 53g (Dietary Fiber 1g); Protein 2g
EXCHANGES: 1 Starch; 2½ Other Carbohydrate; 3 Fat CARBOHYDRATE CHOICES: 3½

sweet note Miniature chocolate chips are scattered throughout the swirled batter of this delicious cake.

caramel latte cake

PREP TIME: 30 minutes *START TO FINISH:* 3 hours 15 minutes [16 SERVINGS]

Cake

- 1 box Betty Crocker® SuperMoist® yellow cake mix
- 1 cup warm water
- 1 tablespoon instant espresso coffee granules
- ⅓ cup butter, melted
- 3 eggs

Filling

- 1 can (13.4 oz) dulce de leche (caramelized sweetened condensed milk)
- ½ cup hot water
- 3 tablespoons instant espresso coffee granules
- 1 tablespoon dark rum or 1 teaspoon rum extract plus 2 teaspoons water

Frosting and Garnish

- 1 cup whipping cream
- ¼ cup powdered sugar
- 2 oz semisweet baking chocolate, chopped, or 1 teaspoon unsweetened baking cocoa

1 Heat oven to 350°F (325°F for dark or nonstick pan). Spray bottom only of 13 × 9-inch pan with baking spray with flour.

2 In large bowl, place cake mix. In 1-cup glass measuring cup, stir 1 cup warm water and 1 tablespoon espresso granules until granules are dissolved. Add espresso mixture, butter and eggs to cake mix. Beat with electric mixer on low speed 30 seconds; scrape bowl. Beat on medium speed 2 minutes longer. Pour batter into pan.

3 Bake as directed on box for 13 × 9-inch pan. Cool in pan on cooling rack 15 minutes.

4 Meanwhile, spoon dulce de leche into medium microwavable bowl. In small bowl, mix ½ cup hot water, 3 tablespoons espresso granules and the rum; stir into dulce de leche until smooth. Microwave uncovered on High 2 to 3 minutes, stirring after about 1 minute with whisk, until pourable. Set aside while cake cools.

5 Poke cooled cake every ½ inch with handle end of wooden spoon. Pour dulce de leche mixture evenly over cake; spread mixture over top of cake with metal spatula to fill holes. Run knife around sides of pan to loosen cake. Cover; refrigerate 2 hours.

6 In medium bowl, beat whipping cream and powdered sugar on high speed until stiff. Spread whipped cream evenly over chilled cake. Sprinkle with chopped chocolate. Store covered in refrigerator.

1 SERVING: Calories 510; Total Fat 14g (Saturated Fat 9g; Trans Fat 2g); Cholesterol 75mg; Sodium 260mg; Total Carbohydrate 41g (Dietary Fiber 1g); Protein 4g EXCHANGES: 1½ Starch; 1 Other Carbohydrate; 2½ Fat CARBOHYDRATE CHOICES: 3

sweet note Place the cocoa in a tea strainer and lightly shake over the frosting to "dust" the top of the cake.

apricot petits fours

PREP TIME: 1 hour 20 minutes *START TO FINISH:* 4 hours 20 minutes [54 SERVINGS]

Cake

1 box Betty Crocker® SuperMoist® yellow cake mix

1 cup apricot nectar or juice

⅓ cup vegetable oil

1 teaspoon grated orange peel

2 eggs

2 tablespoons orange-flavored liqueur or apricot nectar

Icing

9 cups powdered sugar

¾ cup apricot nectar or water

½ cup corn syrup

⅓ cup butter or margarine, melted

2 teaspoons almond extract

Decorations, if desired

Sliced almonds

Orange peel

1 Heat oven to 350°F (325°F for dark or nonstick pan). Spray bottom and sides of 15 × 10-inch pan with baking spray with flour.

2 In large bowl, beat all cake ingredients except liqueur with electric mixer on low speed 30 seconds, then on medium speed 2 minutes, scraping bowl occasionally. Pour batter into pan.

3 Bake 22 to 28 minutes or until cake springs back when touched lightly in center. Brush liqueur over top of cake. Cool completely, about 20 minutes. To avoid cake crumbs when adding icing, freeze cake 1 hour before cutting.

4 In large bowl, beat icing ingredients on low speed until powdered sugar is moistened. Beat on high speed until smooth. If necessary, add 2 to 3 teaspoons more apricot nectar until icing is pourable.

5 Place cooling rack on cookie sheet or waxed paper to catch icing drips. Cut cake into 9 rows by 6 rows. Working with 6 pieces at a time, remove cake pieces from pan and place on cooling rack. Spoon icing evenly over top and sides of cake pieces, letting icing coat sides. (Icing that drips off can be reused.) Let stand until icing is set, about 2 hours.

6 Decorate with almonds and orange peel as desired. Store in single layer in airtight plastic container.

1 PETIT FOUR: Calories 150; Total Fat 3g (Saturated Fat 1g; Trans Fat 0g); Cholesterol 10mg; Sodium 70mg; Total Carbohydrate 30g (Dietary Fiber 0g); Protein 0g EXCHANGES: 2 Other Carbohydrate; ½ Fat CARBOHYDRATE CHOICES: 2

sweet note You can make the cakes up to 2 weeks earlier and freeze, but wait to add the icing until shortly before you serve them.

almond cheesecake

PREP TIME: 40 minutes *START TO FINISH:* 7 hours 45 minutes [16 SERVINGS]

Crust

1 box Betty Crocker® SuperMoist® yellow cake mix

½ cup butter or margarine, softened

Filling

3 packages (8 oz each) cream cheese, softened

¾ cup sugar

1 cup whipping cream

1 teaspoon almond extract

3 eggs

Garnish

¼ cup sliced almonds

4 teaspoons sugar

Fresh raspberries, if desired

1 Heat oven to 350°F (325°F for dark or nonstick pan). Spray bottom and side of 10-inch springform pan with baking spray with flour. Wrap outside of side and bottom of pan with foil.

2 Reserve ½ cup of the cake mix; set aside. In large bowl, beat remaining cake mix and butter with electric mixer on low speed until crumbly. Press in bottom and 1½ inches up side of pan. Bake about 15 minutes or until edges are golden brown. Reduce oven temperature to 325°F (300°F for dark or nonstick pan).

3 In same large bowl, beat reserved ½ cup cake mix and the cream cheese on medium speed until well blended. Beat in ¾ cup sugar, the whipping cream and almond extract on medium speed until smooth and creamy. On low speed, beat in eggs, one at a time, until well blended. Pour batter over crust. Place springform pan in large roasting pan on oven rack. Pour boiling water into roasting pan halfway up side of springform pan.

4 Bake 55 to 60 minutes or until edge is set but center jiggles slightly when moved. Cool in pan (in water bath) on cooling rack 20 minutes. Remove pan from water bath. Carefully run knife around side of pan to loosen, but do not remove side of pan. Cool 1 hour 30 minutes at room temperature.

5 Cover loosely; refrigerate at least 4 hours or overnight.

6 Meanwhile, in 1-quart saucepan, cook almonds and 4 teaspoons sugar over low heat about 10 minutes, stirring constantly, until sugar is melted and almonds are coated. Cool on waxed paper; break apart.

7 Remove side of pan before serving. Garnish cheesecake with sugared almonds and raspberries. Store covered in refrigerator.

1 SERVING: Calories 420; Total Fat 28g (Saturated Fat 16g; Trans Fat 1g); Cholesterol 120mg; Sodium 390mg; Total Carbohydrate 36g (Dietary Fiber 0g); Protein 5g EXCHANGES: 1½ Starch; 1 Other Carbohydrate; 5½ Fat CARBOHYDRATE CHOICES: 2½

sweet note Yellow cake mix is a deliciously different crust for creamy cheesecake flavored with almonds.

banana-cinnamon cake

PREP TIME: 15 minutes *START TO FINISH:* 3 hours 20 minutes [16 SERVINGS]

1 box Betty Crocker® SuperMoist® yellow cake mix

½ cup water

1 cup mashed very ripe bananas (2 medium)

½ cup butter or margarine, softened

2 teaspoons ground cinnamon

3 eggs

½ cup chopped walnuts

Cinnamon Glaze

½ cup Betty Crocker® Rich & Creamy cream cheese frosting (from 1-lb container)

2 to 3 teaspoons milk

¼ teaspoon ground cinnamon

1 Heat oven to 350°F (325°F for dark or nonstick pan). Grease and lightly flour 12-cup fluted tube cake pan, or spray with baking spray with flour.

2 In large bowl, beat cake mix, water, bananas, butter, cinnamon and eggs with electric mixer on low speed 30 seconds, then on medium speed 2 minutes, scraping bowl occasionally. Stir in walnuts. Pour into pan.

3 Bake 47 to 57 minutes or until toothpick inserted in center comes out clean. Cool in pan 10 minutes. Turn pan upside down onto cooling rack or heatproof serving plate; remove pan. Cool completely, about 2 hours. In small bowl, stir glaze ingredients until thin enough to drizzle. Drizzle over cake. Store loosely covered.

1 SERVING: Calories 240; Total Fat 11g (Saturated Fat 5g; Trans Fat ½g); Cholesterol 55mg; Sodium 260mg; Total Carbohydrate 32g (Dietary Fiber 1g); Protein 2g EXCHANGES: 1 Starch; 1 Other Carbohydrate; 2 Fat CARBOHYDRATE CHOICES: 2

sweet note Have too many perfectly ripe bananas? Toss them in the freezer, unpeeled. When you're ready for them, just thaw, cut off the top of the peel, then squeeze the banana straight into your mixing bowl.

banana split cake

PREP TIME: 15 minutes *START TO FINISH:* 1 hour 5 minutes [16 SERVINGS]

Cake and Frosting

1 box Betty Crocker® SuperMoist® white cake mix

Water, vegetable oil and whole eggs called for on cake mix box

1 cup mashed bananas (2 medium)

¾ cup miniature semisweet chocolate chips

1 container (1 lb) Betty Crocker® Rich & Creamy chocolate frosting

Garnishes, as desired

Banana slices

Whipped topping

Betty Crocker® rainbow mix decorating decors

Cherries

1 Heat oven to 350°F (325°F for dark or nonstick pan). Grease bottom only of 13 × 9-inch pan. In large bowl, beat cake mix, water, oil, whole eggs and bananas with electric mixer on low speed 30 seconds, then on medium speed 2 minutes, scraping bowl occasionally. Stir in chocolate chips. Pour into pan.

2 Bake 38 to 42 minutes or until toothpick inserted in center comes out clean. Cool 15 minutes.

3 In small microwavable bowl, microwave frosting uncovered on High 20 seconds; stir. Microwave 5 to 10 seconds longer or until very soft and smooth; spread evenly over cake. Garnish as desired. Store loosely covered.

1 SERVING: Calories 320; Total Fat 13g (Saturated Fat 4½g; Trans Fat 1½g); Cholesterol 40mg; Sodium 290mg; Total Carbohydrate 48g (Dietary Fiber 1g); Protein 3g
EXCHANGES: 1 Starch; 2 Other Carbohydrate; 2½ Fat CARBOHYDRATE CHOICES: 3

sweet note Bananas that are turning brown and soft are just right for using in recipes like this cake.

cashew lover's cake

PREP TIME: 30 minutes *TOTAL TIME:* 3 hours 55 minutes [20 SERVINGS]

1 can (9.5 oz) honey-roasted whole cashews

1 box Betty Crocker® SuperMoist® yellow cake mix

Water, vegetable oil and eggs called for on cake mix box

2 packages (3 oz each) cream cheese, softened

¾ cup butterscotch caramel topping

2 cups whipping cream

1 Heat oven to 350°F (325°F for dark or nonstick pan). Grease bottom only of 15 × 10-inch pan with shortening or cooking spray.

2 Reserve ⅔ cup cashews for garnish. Place remaining cashews in food processor or blender; cover and process until finely ground.

3 Make cake batter as directed on box. Stir in ground cashews. Pour into pan.

4 Bake 18 to 23 minutes (20 to 27 minutes for dark or nonstick pan) or until toothpick inserted in center comes out clean. Run knife around sides of pan to loosen cake. Cool completely in pan on cooling rack, about 1 hour. Cut cake crosswise into 3 pieces; freeze pieces in pan 1 hour.

5 In medium bowl, beat cream cheese and butterscotch caramel topping on low speed until well blended. Gradually beat in whipping cream on low speed. Beat on high speed about 4 minutes or until mixture thickens and soft peaks form.

6 Remove 1 cake piece from pan, using wide spatula; place on serving plate. Spread ¾ cup caramel mixture over cake piece. Top with second cake piece; spread with ¾ cup caramel mixture. Top with third cake piece. Frost sides and top of cake with remaining caramel mixture. Sprinkle reserved whole cashews over top of cake. Cover; refrigerate about 1 hour or until ready to serve. Store covered in refrigerator.

1 SERVING: Calories 370; Total Fat 24g (Saturated Fat 10g; Trans Fat 0g); Cholesterol 75mg; Sodium 280mg; Total Carbohydrate 32g (Dietary Fiber 0g); Protein 4g EXCHANGES: 1½ Starch; ½ Other Carbohydrate; 4½ Fat CARBOHYDRATE CHOICES: 2

sweet note The easiest way to cut this cake into 20 serving pieces is to slice it lengthwise in half with a sharp knife, then cut it crosswise 9 times to make 20 pieces.

chocolate checkerboard cake

PREP TIME: 25 minutes *TOTAL TIME:* 2 hours 5 minutes [16 SERVINGS]

1 box Betty Crocker® SuperMoist® yellow cake mix

1 cup milk

1 package (3 oz) cream cheese, softened

1 teaspoon vanilla

3 eggs

¼ cup unsweetened baking cocoa

1 container (1 lb) Betty Crocker® Rich & Creamy chocolate frosting

1 Heat oven to 350°F. Grease bottoms and sides of three 9-inch round pans of checkerboard cake set with shortening; lightly flour. Place divider ring in one of the pans, following manufacturer's directions.

2 In medium bowl, beat cake mix, milk, cream cheese, vanilla and eggs with electric mixer on low speed 30 seconds, scraping bowl constantly. Beat on medium speed 2 minutes. Divide batter in half; stir cocoa into half of the batter.

3 Spoon batter into pan with divider ring, following manufacturer's directions.

4 Bake 20 to 25 minutes or until toothpick inserted in center comes out clean. Cool 10 minutes. Loosen side of cake from pan with metal spatula; turn upside down onto cooling rack. Cool completely, about 1 hour.

5 Using a thin layer of frosting between layers, stack cake layers so outside colors of cake alternate. Place cake on serving plate; frost side and top of cake with frosting.

1 SERVING: Calories 250; Total Fat 8g (Saturated Fat 3½g; Trans Fat 1½g); Cholesterol 45mg; Sodium 310mg; Total Carbohydrate 41g (Dietary Fiber 0g); Protein 3g
EXCHANGES: 1 Starch; 1½ Other Carbohydrate; 1½ Fat CARBOHYDRATE CHOICES: 3

sweet note "Check" out this classic patterned cake. It's the pan that makes the magic!

coconut-carrot cake

PREP TIME: 20 minutes *START TO FINISH:* 2 hours 18 minutes [16 SERVINGS]

1 cup flaked coconut

1 box Betty Crocker® SuperMoist® carrot cake mix

Water, vegetable oil and eggs called for on cake mix box

½ cup Betty Crocker® Rich & Creamy vanilla frosting (from 1-lb container)

1 Heat oven to 325°F. Grease and flour 12-cup fluted tube cake pan, or spray with baking spray with flour. In ungreased shallow pan, spread coconut. Bake uncovered 5 to 7 minutes, stirring occasionally, until golden brown. Reserve 2 tablespoons toasted coconut for garnish.

2 Make cake batter as directed on box. Fold remaining toasted coconut into batter. Pour into pan.

3 Bake as directed on box for fluted tube pan. Cool 15 minutes; remove from pan to cooling rack. Cool completely, about 1 hour.

4 In small microwavable bowl, microwave frosting uncovered on Medium (50%) 15 seconds. Drizzle frosting over top of cake. Sprinkle with reserved toasted coconut. Cut cake with serrated knife. Store loosely covered.

1 SERVING: Calories 260; Total Fat 14g (Saturated Fat 4½g; Trans Fat ½g); Cholesterol 40mg; Sodium 240mg; Total Carbohydrate 30g (Dietary Fiber 0g); Protein 2g EXCHANGES: 1 Starch; 1 Other Carbohydrate; 2½ Fat CARBOHYDRATE CHOICES: 2

sweet note For extra coconut flavor, stir ½ teaspoon coconut extract into the frosting.

caramel-carrot cake

PREP TIME: 10 minutes *START TO FINISH:* 3 hours [15 SERVINGS]

- 1 package Betty Crocker® SuperMoist® carrot cake mix
- 1 cup water
- ½ cup butter or margarine, melted
- 3 eggs
- 1 jar (16 to 17.5 oz) caramel or butterscotch topping
- 1 container (1 lb) Betty Crocker® Rich & Creamy vanilla frosting

1 Heat oven to 350°F (325°F for dark or nonstick pan). Grease bottom only of 13 × 9-inch pan with shortening or cooking spray.

2 In large bowl, beat cake mix, water, butter and eggs with electric mixer on low speed 30 seconds, then on medium speed 2 minutes. Pour into pan.

3 Bake 31 to 36 minutes or until toothpick inserted in center comes out clean. Cool 15 minutes. Poke top of warm cake every ½ inch with handle of wooden spoon, wiping handle occasionally to reduce sticking. Reserve ½ cup caramel topping. Drizzle remaining caramel topping evenly over top of cake; let stand about 15 minutes or until caramel topping has been absorbed into cake. Run knife around side of pan to loosen cake. Cover and refrigerate about 2 hours or until chilled.

4 Set aside 2 tablespoons of the reserved ½ cup caramel topping. Stir remaining topping into frosting; spread over top of cake. Drizzle with reserved 2 tablespoons caramel topping. Store covered in refrigerator.

1 SERVING: Calories 380; Total Fat 13g (Saturated Fat 6g; Trans Fat 2g); Cholesterol 60mg; Sodium 430mg; Total Carbohydrate 63g (Dietary Fiber 0g); Protein 3g EXCHANGES: 1 Starch; 3 Other Carbohydrate; 2½ Fat CARBOHYDRATE CHOICES: 4

sweet note Some caramel toppings are thicker and stickier than others. If the type you purchased is too thick to pour, warm it in the microwave just until it can be poured.

turtle tart

PREP TIME: 25 minutes *START TO FINISH:* 3 hours 15 minutes [16 SERVINGS]

Cookie Base

1 pouch (1 lb 1.5 oz) Betty Crocker® oatmeal cookie mix

½ cup butter or margarine, softened

1 tablespoon water

1 egg

1 cup chopped pecans

Filling

40 caramels, unwrapped

⅓ cup whipping cream

¾ cup chopped pecans

Topping

1 bag (11.5 oz) milk chocolate chips (2 cups)

⅓ cup whipping cream

¼ cup chopped pecans

1 Heat oven to 350°F.

2 In large bowl, stir cookie mix, butter, water and egg until soft dough forms. Stir in 1 cup pecans. Press dough in bottom and up sides of ungreased 9-inch tart pan with removable bottom.

3 Bake 19 to 21 minutes or until light golden brown. Cool 10 minutes.

4 Meanwhile, in medium microwavable bowl, microwave caramels and ⅓ cup cream on High 2 to 4 minutes, stirring twice, until caramels are melted. Stir in ¾ cup pecans. Spread over cooled crust. Refrigerate 15 minutes.

5 In another medium microwavable bowl, microwave chocolate chips and ⅓ cup cream on High 1 to 2 minutes, stirring every 30 seconds, until chocolate is smooth. Pour over filling. Sprinkle with ¼ cup pecans. Refrigerate 2 hours or until set.

6 To serve, let stand at room temperature 10 minutes before cutting. Store covered in refrigerator.

1 SERVING: Calories 530; Total Fat 29g (Saturated Fat 10g; Trans Fat 0g); Cholesterol 45mg; Sodium 240mg; Total Carbohydrate 59g (Dietary Fiber 3g); Protein 7g EXCHANGES: 4 Other Carbohydrate; 1 High-Fat Meat; 4 Fat CARBOHYDRATE CHOICES: 4

sweet note If you don't have a tart pan, just use a 13 × 9-inch pan, and cut into squares instead of wedges.

chocolate-caramel-nut cake

PREP TIME: 15 minutes *START TO FINISH:* 2 hours 57 minutes [16 SERVINGS]

1 box Betty Crocker® SuperMoist® butter recipe chocolate cake mix

1 box (4-serving size) chocolate instant pudding and pie filling mix

1 cup water

½ cup butter or margarine, softened

4 eggs

1 cup semisweet chocolate chips (6 oz)

⅓ cup caramel topping

2 tablespoons chopped nuts

1 Heat oven to 350°F (325°F for fluted tube, dark or nonstick pan). Grease and flour 12-cup fluted tube cake pan or 10-inch angel food (tube) cake pan, or spray with baking spray with flour.

2 In large bowl, beat cake mix, dry pudding mix, water, butter and eggs with electric mixer on low speed 30 seconds, then on medium speed 2 minutes, scraping bowl occasionally. Stir in chocolate chips. Pour into pan.

3 Bake 46 to 54 minutes or until toothpick inserted in center comes out clean. Cool 15 minutes in pan. Remove from pan to plate. Cool 10 minutes. Prick top of warm cake several times with fork; spread caramel topping over top of cake. Sprinkle with nuts. Cool completely, about 1 hour. Store covered.

1 SERVING: Calories 270; Total Fat 12g (Saturated Fat 7g; Trans Fat 0g); Cholesterol 70mg; Sodium 380mg; Total Carbohydrate 38g (Dietary Fiber 1g); Protein 3g EXCHANGES: 1 Starch; 1½ Other Carbohydrate; 2½ Fat CARBOHYDRATE CHOICES: 2½

sweet note Can't get enough of the good stuff? Pass bowls of caramel topping and extra chopped nuts for an extra-rich hit!

chocolate lover's dream cake

PREP TIME: 20 minutes *START TO FINISH:* 3 hours 35 minutes [16 SERVINGS]

Cake

1 box Betty Crocker® SuperMoist® butter recipe chocolate cake mix

¾ cup chocolate milk

⅓ cup butter or margarine, melted

3 eggs

1 container (8 oz) sour cream

1 package (4-serving size) chocolate fudge instant pudding and pie filling mix

1 bag (12 oz) semisweet chocolate chips (2 cups)

Rich Chocolate Glaze

¾ cup semisweet chocolate chips

3 tablespoons butter or margarine

3 tablespoons light corn syrup

1½ teaspoons water

1 Heat oven to 350°F (325°F for dark or nonstick pan). Generously grease and lightly flour 12-cup fluted tube cake pan, or spray with baking spray with flour.

2 In large bowl, mix cake mix, chocolate milk, butter, eggs, sour cream and dry pudding mix with spoon until well blended (batter will be very thick). Stir in chocolate chips. Spoon into pan.

3 Bake 56 to 64 minutes or until top springs back when touched lightly in center. Cool 10 minutes in pan. Turn pan upside down onto cooling rack or heatproof serving plate; remove pan. Cool completely, about 2 hours.

4 In 1-quart saucepan, heat glaze ingredients over low heat, stirring frequently, until chocolate chips are melted and mixture is smooth. Drizzle over cake. Store loosely covered.

1 SERVING: Calories 400; Total Fat 20g (Saturated Fat 12g; Trans Fat 0g); Cholesterol 65mg; Sodium 390mg; Total Carbohydrate 50g (Dietary Fiber 2g); Protein 4g
EXCHANGES: 1 Starch; 2½ Other Carbohydrate; 4 Fat CARBOHYDRATE CHOICES: 3

sweet note You don't want to lose even a drop of this divine batter, so measure the volume of your bundt cake pan using water to make sure it holds 12 cups. If the pan is smaller than 12 cups, the batter will overflow during baking.

mint-chocolate ice cream cake

PREP TIME: 25 minutes *START TO FINISH:* 5 hours 50 minutes [16 SERVINGS]

Cake

1 box Betty Crocker® SuperMoist® butter recipe chocolate cake mix

Water, butter and eggs called for on cake mix box

Filling

6 cups green mint-flavored ice cream with chocolate chips or chocolate swirl, slightly softened

Frosting

1½ cups whipping cream

2 tablespoons powdered sugar

4 drops green food color

1 Heat oven to 350°F (325°F for dark or nonstick pans). Grease bottoms only of two 9-inch round cake pans; line bottoms with waxed paper. Make cake batter as directed on box. Spoon evenly into pans.

2 Bake as directed on box for 9-inch rounds. Cool in pans 10 minutes. Remove from pans to cooling racks. Remove waxed paper. Cool completely, about 30 minutes.

3 Line 9-inch round cake pan with foil. Spoon and spread ice cream evenly in pan. Cover with foil; freeze until completely frozen, about 2 hours.

4 On serving plate, place 1 cake layer with rounded side down. Remove ice cream from pan; peel off foil. Place on top of cake. Top with remaining cake layer, rounded side up.

5 In medium bowl, beat whipping cream, powdered sugar and food color on high speed until stiff peaks form. Frost side and top of cake with whipped cream. Freeze about 2 hours or until firm. Let stand at room temperature 10 minutes before serving.

1 SERVING: Calories 330; Total Fat 19g (Saturated Fat 12g; Trans Fat ½g); Cholesterol 100mg; Sodium 310mg; Total Carbohydrate 35g (Dietary Fiber 1g); Protein 4g
EXCHANGES: 1½ Starch; 1 Other Carbohydrate; 3½ Fat CARBOHYDRATE CHOICES: 2

sweet note This dessert, wrapped with foil, will keep up to a month in the freezer. You can also make the ice cream layer ahead of time and freeze it. For a restaurant-fancy finish, heat hot fudge topping as directed on the label and drizzle onto individual serving plates.

chocolate mousse–raspberry cake

PREP TIME: 25 minutes *START TO FINISH:* 2 hours 45 minutes [16 SERVINGS]

- 1 box Betty Crocker® SuperMoist® devil's food cake mix
- Water, vegetable oil and eggs called for on cake mix box
- 1 cup semisweet chocolate chips (6 oz)
- 1½ cups whipping cream
- ⅓ cup powdered sugar
- 2 tablespoons seedless raspberry jam
- 1 container (6 oz) fresh raspberries
- White chocolate truffle candies, if desired
- Unsweetened baking cocoa, if desired

1 Heat oven to 350°F (325°F for dark or nonstick pans). Grease two 8- or 9-inch round cake pans, or spray with baking spray with flour.

2 Make and bake cake as directed on box for 8- or 9-inch round cake pans. Cool in pans 10 minutes. Remove from pans to cooling racks. Cool completely, about 30 minutes.

3 Meanwhile, in medium microwavable bowl, microwave chocolate chips and ½ cup of the whipping cream uncovered on High 45 to 60 seconds; stir until smooth and melted. Refrigerate 15 to 30 minutes or until cool.

4 In large bowl, beat remaining 1 cup whipping cream and the powdered sugar with electric mixer on high speed until mixture starts to thicken. Add melted chocolate. Beat until stiff peaks form (do not overbeat or mixture will begin to look curdled).

5 On serving plate, place 1 cake layer, rounded side down. Spread raspberry jam over cake layer. Spread ½-inch-thick layer of chocolate mixture over jam. Cut ½ cup of the raspberries in half; press into chocolate mixture. Top with other cake layer, rounded side up; press lightly. Frost side and top of cake with remaining chocolate mixture. Refrigerate about 1 hour or until firm.

6 To serve, let stand at room temperature about 10 minutes before serving. Garnish with remaining raspberries and candies. Sprinkle with cocoa. Store loosely covered in refrigerator.

1 SERVING: Calories 340; Total Fat 20g (Saturated Fat 9g; Trans Fat 0g); Cholesterol 70mg; Sodium 250mg; Total Carbohydrate 35g (Dietary Fiber 2g); Protein 3g EXCHANGES: 1 Starch; 1½ Other Carbohydrate; 4 Fat CARBOHYDRATE CHOICES: 2

sweet note You could simply garnish the cake with the remaining raspberries and fresh mint leaves if you prefer.

chocolate-mint swirl cake

PREP TIME: 20 minutes *START TO FINISH:* 2 hours 30 minutes [16 SERVINGS]

Filling

2 packages (3 oz each) cream cheese, softened

¼ cup granulated sugar

1 egg

⅛ teaspoon peppermint extract

3 drops green food color

Cake

1 box Betty Crocker® SuperMoist® devil's food cake mix

⅓ cup Gold Medal® all-purpose flour

1 cup water

½ cup butter or margarine, melted

2 eggs

Chocolate and Mint Glaze

2 tablespoons semisweet chocolate chips

1 teaspoon shortening

1 cup powdered sugar

¼ teaspoon peppermint extract

1 or 2 drops green food color

1 tablespoon corn syrup

3 to 4 teaspoons water

1 Heat oven to 325°F. Grease and flour 12-cup fluted tube cake pan, or spray with baking spray with flour. In small bowl, beat cream cheese with electric mixer on high speed until smooth and fluffy. Beat in granulated sugar, 1 egg, ⅛ teaspoon peppermint extract and 3 drops food color until smooth; set aside.

2 In large bowl, beat cake mix, flour, 1 cup water, the butter and 2 eggs on low speed 30 seconds; beat on medium speed 2 minutes. Pour into pan. Spoon cream cheese filling over batter.

3 Bake 42 to 48 minutes or until toothpick inserted in center of cake comes out clean. Cool in pan 15 minutes. Turn pan upside down onto cooling rack or heatproof plate; remove pan. Cool completely, about 1 hour.

4 In 1-quart saucepan, heat chocolate chips and shortening over low heat, stirring frequently, until melted; set aside. For glaze, mix powdered sugar, ¼ teaspoon peppermint extract, 1 or 2 drops food color, the corn syrup and enough of the 3 to 4 teaspoons water to make a thick glaze that can be easily drizzled. Drizzle over cake. Immediately spoon melted chocolate over glaze in ½-inch-wide ring. Working quickly, pull toothpick through chocolate to make swirls. Refrigerate until serving time. Store in refrigerator.

1 SERVING: Calories 270; Total Fat 12g (Saturated Fat 7g; Trans Fat 0g); Cholesterol 65mg; Sodium 310mg; Total Carbohydrate 37g (Dietary Fiber 0g); Protein 3g EXCHANGES: 1 Starch; 1½ Other Carbohydrate; 2½ Fat CARBOHYDRATE CHOICES: 2½

sweet note The shortening keeps the melted chocolate chips smooth. Butter and margarine contain more water than shortening, so they can't be substituted.

chocolate chai latte cake

PREP TIME: 15 minutes *START TO FINISH:* 1 hour 55 minutes [15 SERVINGS]

Cake

1 cup miniature semisweet chocolate chips

1 box Betty Crocker® SuperMoist® devil's food cake mix

¼ cup chai latte–flavored international instant coffee mix (from 9.7-oz container)

Water, vegetable oil and eggs called for on cake mix box

Frosting

2½ cups powdered sugar

2 tablespoons butter or margarine, softened

3 tablespoons milk

1 tablespoon chai latte–flavored international instant coffee mix (from 9.7-oz container)

Ground cinnamon, if desired

1 Heat oven to 350°F (325°F for dark or nonstick pan). Grease or spray bottom only of 13 × 9-inch pan with baking spray with flour.

2 In small bowl, toss chocolate chips with 1 tablespoon of the cake mix. In large bowl, beat remaining cake mix, ¼ cup dry chai latte mix, the water, oil and eggs with electric mixer on low speed 30 seconds, then on medium speed 2 minutes, scraping bowl occasionally. Stir in coated chocolate chips. Pour into pan.

3 Bake as directed on box for 13 × 9-inch pan. Cool completely, about 1 hour.

4 In medium bowl, mix powdered sugar and butter until smooth; set aside. In small microwavable bowl, microwave milk on High 10 to 15 seconds or until very warm. Stir in 1 tablespoon dry chai latte mix until dissolved; stir into powdered sugar mixture until smooth and spreadable. Spread over cake. Just before serving, sprinkle with cinnamon. Store loosely covered.

1 SERVING: Calories 360; Total Fat 15g (Saturated Fat 5g; Trans Fat 0g); Cholesterol 45mg; Sodium 290mg; Total Carbohydrate 53g (Dietary Fiber 1g); Protein 3g EXCHANGES: 1 Starch; 2½ Other Carbohydrate; 3 Fat CARBOHYDRATE CHOICES: 3½

sweet note Look for the chai latte mix near the coffee at the grocery store. Dry instant espresso coffee can be substituted for the chai latte mix.

café au lait cake

PREP TIME: 20 minutes *START TO FINISH:* 4 hours 5 minutes [12 SERVINGS]

1 tablespoon instant espresso coffee (dry)

1¼ cups water

1 box Betty Crocker® SuperMoist® devil's food cake mix

Vegetable oil and eggs called for on cake mix box

2 teaspoons instant espresso coffee (dry)

1 tablespoon cool water

1 container (12 oz) Betty Crocker® Whipped milk chocolate frosting

1½ cups frozen (thawed) whipped topping

Chocolate-covered espresso beans, if desired

1 Heat oven to 350°F (325°F for dark or nonstick pans). Grease two 8- or 9-inch round cake pans, or spray with baking spray with flour. Dissolve 1 tablespoon coffee in 1¼ cups water. Make cake batter as directed on box, using coffee mixture in place of the water. Bake and cool as directed.

2 Dissolve 2 teaspoons coffee in 1 tablespoon cool water. Stir 2 teaspoons of the coffee mixture into frosting. In medium bowl, stir together whipped topping and remaining coffee mixture; gently stir in ¼ cup of the frosting mixture.

3 On serving plate, place 1 cake layer, rounded side down. Spread with half of the whipped topping mixture (about ¾ cup) to within ¼ inch of edge. Top with second layer, rounded side up. Frost side and top of cake with frosting. Pipe remaining whipped topping mixture around top of cake. Refrigerate 1 to 2 hours or until chilled. Garnish top of cake with espresso beans. Store covered in refrigerator.

1 SERVING: Calories 370; Total Fat 19g (Saturated Fat 6g; Trans Fat 1g); Cholesterol 55mg; Sodium 380mg; Total Carbohydrate 48g (Dietary Fiber 1g); Protein 3g EXCHANGES: 1 Starch; 2 Other Carbohydrate; 3½ Fat CARBOHYDRATE CHOICES: 3

sweet note If the cake is served just after chilling, the espresso flavor will be mild. The flavor develops more fully as it continues to chill, and if served the next day, the flavor will be stronger.

marble cheesecake

PREP TIME: 20 minutes *START TO FINISH:* 6 hours [15 SERVINGS]

1 box Betty Crocker® SuperMoist® devil's food cake mix

3 tablespoons butter or margarine, melted

3 eggs

⅓ cup sugar

1 package (8 oz) cream cheese, softened

¾ teaspoon vanilla

1 container (8 oz) sour cream

¾ cup whipping cream

1 Heat oven to 350°F (325°F for dark or nonstick pans). Grease bottom and sides of 13 × 9-inch pan with shortening, or spray with cooking spray.

2 Reserve 1 cup dry cake mix for filling. Beat remaining cake mix, the butter and 1 egg in large bowl with electric mixer on low speed just until dough forms. Press on bottom of pan.

3 Beat sugar, cream cheese and vanilla in large bowl with electric mixer on medium speed until smooth. Beat in remaining 2 eggs, the sour cream and ¼ cup of the whipping cream on low speed until smooth; reserve 1 cup cream cheese mixture. Pour remaining cream cheese mixture over crust.

4 Beat reserved 1 cup cake mix, reserved 1 cup cream cheese mixture and remaining ½ cup whipping cream in same bowl on low speed until smooth. Drop chocolate cream cheese mixture by spoonfuls over cream cheese mixture in pan. Cut chocolate mixture through plain mixture with knife in S-shaped curves in one continuous motion. Turn pan ¼ turn, and repeat for marbled design. Tap bottom of pan sharply on counter to level cream cheese mixtures.

5 Bake 32 to 40 minutes or until sharp knife inserted 1 inch from side of pan comes out clean (center will not be set). Cool 30 minutes on wire rack. Refrigerate 30 minutes. Run knife around side of pan to loosen cheesecake. Refrigerate at least 4 hours or until chilled. Store covered in refrigerator.

1 SERVING: Calories 290; Total Fat 18g (Saturated Fat 10g; Trans Fat 1g); Cholesterol 92mg; Sodium 337mg; Total Carbohydrate 28g (Dietary Fiber 1g); Protein 4g
EXCHANGES: 2 Other Carbohydrate; 3 Fat CARBOHYDRATE CHOICES: 2

sweet note For Chocolate Chip Marble Cheesecake, stir ¼ cup miniature semisweet chocolate chips into the plain cream cheese mixture in step 3.

chocolate ganache mini cakes

PREP TIME: 45 minutes *START TO FINISH:* 1 hour 55 minutes [60 SERVINGS]

Mini Cakes

1 box Betty Crocker® SuperMoist® devil's food cake mix

Water, vegetable oil and eggs called for on cake mix box

Filling

⅔ cup raspberry jam

Glaze and Garnish

6 oz dark baking chocolate, chopped

⅔ cup whipping cream

1 tablespoon raspberry-flavored liqueur, if desired

Fresh raspberries, if desired

1 Heat oven to 350°F (325°F for dark or nonstick pans). Place miniature paper baking cup in each of 60 mini muffin cups. Make cake mix as directed on box, using water, oil and eggs. Fill muffin cups three-fourths full (about 1 heaping tablespoon each).

2 Bake 10 to 15 minutes or until toothpick inserted in center comes out clean. Cool in pans 5 minutes. Remove from pans to cooling racks. Cool completely, about 30 minutes.

3 By slowly spinning end of round handle of wooden spoon back and forth, make deep, ½-inch-wide indentation in center of top of each cupcake, not quite to bottom (wiggle end of spoon in cupcake to make opening large enough).

4 Spoon jam into small resealable food-storage plastic bag; seal bag. Cut ⅜-inch tip off 1 bottom corner of bag. Insert tip of bag into opening in each cupcake; squeeze bag to fill opening.

5 Place chocolate in medium bowl. In 1-quart saucepan, heat whipping cream just to boiling; pour over chocolate. Let stand 3 to 5 minutes until chocolate is melted and smooth when stirred. Stir in liqueur. Let stand 15 minutes, stirring occasionally, until mixture coats a spoon.

6 Spoon about 1 teaspoon chocolate glaze onto each mini cake. Garnish each with a raspberry.

1 MINI CAKE: Calories 80; Total Fat 5g (Saturated Fat 2g; Trans Fat 0g); Cholesterol 15mg; Sodium 65mg; Total Carbohydrate 9g (Dietary Fiber 0g); Protein 1g EXCHANGES: ½ Starch; 1 Fat CARBOHYDRATE CHOICES: ½

sweet note If you refrigerate these mini cakes, let them stand at room temperature for at least 20 minutes before serving.

chocolate rum cake

PREP TIME: 15 minutes *START TO FINISH:* 4 hours [15 SERVINGS]

Cake

1 box Betty Crocker® SuperMoist® devil's food or dark chocolate cake mix

1 cup water

⅓ cup vegetable oil

3 eggs

1 cup whipping cream

1 cup whole milk

1 can (14 oz) sweetened condensed milk

⅓ cup rum

Topping

1 cup whipping cream

2 tablespoons rum or 1 teaspoon rum extract

½ teaspoon vanilla

1 cup flaked coconut, toasted

½ cup chopped pecans, toasted

1 Heat oven to 350°F (325°F for dark or nonstick pan). Grease bottom only of 13 × 9-inch pan with shortening or cooking spray.

2 In large bowl, beat cake mix, water, oil and eggs with electric mixer on low speed 30 seconds, then on medium speed 2 minutes. Pour into pan.

3 Bake 30 to 38 minutes or until toothpick inserted in center comes out clean. Let stand 5 minutes. In large bowl, mix 1 cup whipping cream, the whole milk, condensed milk and ⅓ cup rum. Pierce top of hot cake every ½ inch with long-tined fork, wiping fork occasionally to reduce sticking. Carefully pour whipping cream mixture evenly over top of cake. Cover and refrigerate about 3 hours or until chilled and most of whipping cream mixture has been absorbed into cake.

4 In chilled large bowl, beat 1 cup whipping cream, 2 tablespoons rum and the vanilla on high speed until soft peaks form. Frost cake with whipped cream mixture. Sprinkle with coconut and pecans. Store covered in refrigerator.

1 SERVING: Calories 430; Total Fat 24g (Saturated Fat 12g; Trans Fat 0g); Cholesterol 90mg; Sodium 330mg; Total Carbohydrate 43g (Dietary Fiber 1g); Protein 6g
EXCHANGES: 1½ Starch; 1½ Other Carbohydrate; 4½ Fat CARBOHYDRATE CHOICES: 3

sweet note Instead of rum in the cake, use 1 tablespoon rum extract plus enough water to measure ⅓ cup. In the topping, substitute 1 teaspoon rum extract for the rum.

triple-chocolate torte

PREP TIME: 15 minutes *START TO FINISH:* 5 hours 5 minutes [16 SERVINGS]

1 box (1 lb 2.3 oz) Betty Crocker® fudge brownie mix

Water, vegetable oil and eggs called for on brownie mix box

1¼ cups milk

1 box (4-serving size) white chocolate pudding and pie filling mix

1 container (8 oz) frozen whipped topping, thawed (3½ cups)

⅓ cup miniature semisweet chocolate chips

1 pint (2 cups) raspberries or strawberries, if desired

1 Heat oven to 325°F. Spray bottom only of 9-inch springform pan with cooking spray. Make brownie mix as directed on box, using water, oil and eggs. Spread in pan.

2 Bake 38 to 40 minutes or until toothpick inserted in center comes out clean. Cool completely. (Do not remove side of pan.)

3 In large bowl, beat milk and pudding mix with wire whisk about 2 minutes or until thickened. Fold in whipped topping and chocolate chips. Pour over brownie.

4 Cover and freeze at least 4 hours before serving. Remove side of pan. Serve with raspberries. Store covered in freezer.

1 SERVING: Calories 205; Total Fat 11g (Saturated Fat 3g; Trans Fat 0g); Cholesterol 20mg; Sodium 210mg; Total Carbohydrate 25g (Dietary Fiber 1g); Protein 2g EXCHANGES: 1 Starch; 1 Fruit; 1½ Fat CARBOHYDRATE CHOICES: 0

sweet note For a spectacular presentation, drizzle chocolate topping on dessert plates before adding the torte. Or drizzle chocolate topping over the top of the torte, and garnish with chocolate-dipped strawberries or raspberries.

chocolate turtle cake

PREP TIME: 25 minutes *START TO FINISH:* 1 hour 50 minutes [20 SERVINGS]

1 box Betty Crocker® SuperMoist® devil's food cake mix

Water, vegetable oil and eggs called for on cake mix box

1 bag (14 oz) caramels

½ cup evaporated milk

1 cup chopped pecans

1 cup semisweet chocolate chips (6 oz)

Ice cream or whipped cream, if desired

Caramel and chocolate topping, if desired

Chopped pecans, if desired

1 Heat oven to 350°F (325°F for dark or nonstick pan). Grease bottom only of 13 × 9-inch pan with shortening or cooking spray.

2 Make cake batter as directed on box. Pour half of the batter into pan. Bake 22 minutes. Refrigerate remaining batter.

3 Meanwhile, in 1-quart saucepan, heat caramels and evaporated milk over medium heat, stirring frequently, until caramels are melted. Stir in pecans. Pour caramel mixture over warm cake in pan. Sprinkle with chocolate chips. Spread with remaining batter. Bake 25 to 28 minutes or until cake springs back when lightly touched. Run knife around sides of pan to loosen cake. Cool at least 30 minutes. Serve with ice cream, drizzle with toppings and sprinkle with pecans. Store loosely covered.

1 SERVING: Calories 310; Total Fat 15g (Saturated Fat 4g; Trans Fat 0g); Cholesterol 35mg; Sodium 250mg; Total Carbohydrate 40g (Dietary Fiber 1g); Protein 4g EXCHANGES: 1 Starch; 1½ Other Carbohydrate; 3 Fat CARBOHYDRATE CHOICES: 2½

sweet note No wonder this is a bake sale winner! Devil's food cake sandwiches caramel, pecans and, yes, more chocolate in the middle. Yum.

triple-fudge cake

PREP TIME: 15 minutes *START TO FINISH:* 3 hours 5 minutes [15 SERVINGS]

⅓ cup sweetened condensed milk (not evaporated)

1 cup semisweet chocolate chips (6 oz)

1 box Betty Crocker® SuperMoist® chocolate fudge cake mix

½ cup vegetable oil

¾ cup applesauce

2 eggs

½ cup chopped pecans

1 Heat oven to 350°F (325°F for dark or nonstick pan). Grease and lightly flour bottom only of 13 × 9-inch pan.

2 In small microwavable bowl, microwave condensed milk and ½ cup of the chocolate chips uncovered on Medium (50%) about 1 minute or until chocolate is softened; stir until smooth, and set aside.

3 In large bowl, beat dry cake mix and oil with electric mixer on low speed about 15 seconds or until crumbly; reserve ¾ cup. Add applesauce and eggs to remaining mixture; beat on low speed 30 seconds, scraping bowl occasionally (batter will be thick and grainy). Beat on medium speed 2 minutes, scraping bowl occasionally. Spread batter in pan.

4 Drop melted chocolate mixture by teaspoonfuls over batter, dropping more around edge than in center. Stir remaining ½ cup chocolate chips and the pecans into reserved cake mixture; crumble over batter.

5 Bake 37 to 43 minutes or until center is set. Run knife around sides of pan to loosen cake. Cool completely, about 2 hours. Store covered.

1 SERVING: Calories 300; Total Fat 16g (Saturated Fat 4½g; Trans Fat 0g); Cholesterol 30mg; Sodium 270mg; Total Carbohydrate 36g (Dietary Fiber 2g); Protein 3g
EXCHANGES: 1 Starch; 1½ Other Carbohydrate; 3 Fat CARBOHYDRATE CHOICES: 2½

sweet note If you have milk chocolate or white baking chips on hand, you can use them as part of the ½ cup chocolate chips stirred into the reserved cake mixture.

deep dark mocha torte

PREP TIME: 50 minutes *START TO FINISH:* 2 hours 40 minutes [21 SERVINGS]

Torte

1 box Betty Crocker® SuperMoist® chocolate fudge cake mix

Water, vegetable oil and eggs called for on cake mix box

⅓ cup granulated sugar

⅓ cup rum or water

1¼ teaspoons instant espresso coffee granules

Filling

2 packages (8 oz each) cream cheese, softened

1 cup powdered sugar

1 teaspoon vanilla

2 to 3 teaspoons milk

Ganache

1½ cups semisweet chocolate chips

6 tablespoons butter (do not use margarine)

⅓ cup whipping cream

1 Heat oven to 350°F (325°F for dark or nonstick pans). Grease and lightly flour two 8- or 9-inch round cake pans, or spray with baking spray with flour. Make, bake and cool cakes as directed on box for 8- or 9-inch rounds. Refrigerate layers about 45 minutes for easier handling.

2 Meanwhile, in 1-quart saucepan, stir granulated sugar, rum and coffee granules until coffee is dissolved. Heat to boiling, stirring occasionally; remove from heat. Cool completely.

3 In medium bowl, beat filling ingredients with electric mixer on low speed just until blended, adding enough milk for spreading consistency; set aside.

4 In 1-quart saucepan, heat ganache ingredients over low heat, stirring frequently, until chips are melted and mixture is smooth. Refrigerate about 30 minutes, stirring occasionally, until slightly thickened.

5 Cut each cake layer horizontally to make 2 layers. (To cut, mark side of cake with toothpicks and cut with long, thin knife.) Brush about 1 tablespoon of the rum mixture over cut side of each layer; let stand 1 minute to soak into cake. Fill each layer with about ⅔ cup filling. Spread ganache over side and top of torte. Store loosely covered in refrigerator.

1 SERVING: Calories 600; Total Fat 39g (Saturated Fat 19g; Trans Fat 1g); Cholesterol 120mg; Sodium 500mg; Total Carbohydrate 54g (Dietary Fiber 2g); Protein 6g EXCHANGES: 2 Starch; 1½ Other Carbohydrate; 7½ Fat CARBOHYDRATE CHOICES: 3½

sweet note If the ganache becomes too thick to spread, let it stand at room temperature for a few minutes, then stir to soften.

fudge lover's strawberry truffle cake

PREP: 25 minutes *START TO FINISH:* 2 hours 50 minutes [12 SERVINGS]

Cake

1 box Betty Crocker® SuperMoist® chocolate fudge cake mix

Water, vegetable oil and eggs called for on cake mix box

Ganache Filling and Topping

2 packages (8 oz each) semisweet baking chocolate, finely chopped

1⅓ cups whipping cream

¼ cup butter (do not use margarine)

2 cups cut-up fresh strawberries

Garnish

6 fresh strawberries, cut in half lengthwise through stem

¼ cup white vanilla baking chips

½ teaspoon vegetable oil

sweet note Impress your friends with this decadent chocolate and strawberry dessert. Save the six prettiest strawberries for the garnish.

1 Heat oven to 350°F (325°F for dark or nonstick pan). Make and bake cake as directed on box for 13 × 9-inch pan. Cool completely, about 1 hour.

2 Meanwhile, in large bowl, place chopped chocolate; set aside. In 2-quart saucepan, heat whipping cream and butter over medium heat, stirring occasionally, until butter is melted and mixture comes to a boil. Pour cream mixture over chocolate; stir until smooth.

3 Line bottom of 9-inch springform pan with waxed paper. Cut cake into 1-inch cubes. In large bowl, beat half of the cake cubes on low speed until cake is crumbly. Add remaining cake cubes and 1¾ cups of the ganache (reserve remaining ganache for topping). Beat on low speed 30 seconds, then on medium speed until well combined (mixture will look like fudge). Fold in 2 cups cut-up strawberries. Spoon mixture into springform pan; smooth top. Cover with plastic wrap; freeze about 45 minutes or until firm enough to unmold.

4 Run knife around side of pan to loosen cake mixture. Place serving plate upside down on pan; turn pan and plate over. Frost side and top of cake with reserved ganache. Arrange strawberry halves on top of cake.

5 In small microwavable bowl, microwave baking chips and ½ teaspoon oil uncovered on High 45 seconds, stirring every 15 seconds, until melted. Place in small resealable food-storage plastic bag; cut off tiny corner of bag. Drizzle over top of cake. Refrigerate until ready to serve. Best served the same day.

1 SERVING: Calories 546; Total Fat 35g (Saturated Fat 18g; Trans Fat 1g); Cholesterol 83mg; Sodium 346mg; Total Carbohydrate 56g (Dietary Fiber 3g); Protein 6g
EXCHANGES: ½ Starch; 4 Other Carbohydrate; 6 Fat CARBOHYDRATE CHOICES: 4

mini hot fudge cakes and strawberry hearts

PREP TIME: 15 minutes *START TO FINISH:* 45 minutes [12 CAKES]

1 box Betty Crocker® Complete Desserts® triple chocolate hot fudge cake mix

About 1 quart strawberries

Ice cream, if desired

1 Make, bake and cool Mini Hot Fudge Cakes as directed on side of cake mix box.

2 Place each cake on dessert plate. For each dessert, slice 2 or 3 strawberries. To make slices look like hearts, cut small "V" at rounded end of each slice, using small sharp knife. Randomly place strawberry slices around cakes. Serve warm with ice cream.

1 SERVING: Calories 230; Total Fat 7g (Saturated Fat 2½g; Trans Fat ½g); Cholesterol 0mg; Sodium 260mg; Total Carbohydrate 41g (Dietary Fiber 3g); Protein 3g EXCHANGES: ½ Starch; 2 Other Carbohydrate; 1½ Fat CARBOHYDRATE CHOICES: 3

sweet note Double the strawberry amount for lots of "hearts." Alternately, raspberries make a flavorful stand-in for the strawberries.

chocolate-orange truffle cake

PREP TIME: 15 minutes *START TO FINISH:* 3 hours 3 minutes [16 SERVINGS]

1 box Betty Crocker® SuperMoist® chocolate fudge cake mix

Water, vegetable oil and eggs called for on cake mix box

1 tablespoon grated orange peel

1 container (1 lb) Betty Crocker® Rich & Creamy chocolate frosting

⅓ cup whipping cream

½ cup semisweet chocolate chips

1 Heat oven to 350°F (325°F for dark or nonstick pans). Make, bake and cool cake as directed on box for two 8- or 9-inch round pans—except add orange peel to batter.

2 Fill layers and frost side and top of cake with frosting. In 1-quart saucepan, heat whipping cream over medium heat until hot (do not boil); remove from heat. Stir in chocolate chips until melted and smooth. Let stand 5 minutes.

3 Carefully pour chocolate mixture on top center of cake; spread to edge, allowing some to drizzle down side. Refrigerate about 1 hour or until chocolate is set. Store covered in refrigerator.

1 SERVING: Calories 330; Total Fat 16g (Saturated Fat 5g; Trans Fat 1½g); Cholesterol 45mg; Sodium 330mg; Total Carbohydrate 43g (Dietary Fiber 1g); Protein 2g EXCHANGES: 1 Starch; 2 Other Carbohydrate; 3 Fat CARBOHYDRATE CHOICES: 3

sweet note To keep the edge of the plate clean while frosting the cake, place several strips of waxed paper around the edge of the plate, place the cake on the paper, frost the cake, then carefully remove and discard the strips.

mud slide ice cream cake

PREP TIME: 30 minutes *START TO FINISH:* 6 hours [15 SERVINGS]

- 1 box Betty Crocker® SuperMoist® chocolate fudge cake mix
- ½ cup butter or margarine, melted
- 1 egg
- 2 tablespoons milk
- 2 tablespoons coffee-flavored liqueur or strong coffee
- 4 cups vanilla ice cream
- 1 container (12 oz) Betty Crocker® Whipped chocolate frosting
- 2 tablespoons coffee-flavored liqueur, if desired

1 Heat oven to 350°F (325°F for dark or nonstick pan). Grease bottom only of 13 9-inch pan with shortening or cooking spray. In large bowl, beat cake mix, butter, egg and milk with spoon or electric mixer on low speed until well blended. Spread batter in pan.

2 Bake 16 to 18 minutes or until center is set (top may appear dry and cracked). Cool completely, about 1 hour.

3 Brush 2 tablespoons liqueur over cake. Let ice cream stand about 15 minutes at room temperature to soften. Spread ice cream over cake. Freeze about 3 hours or until firm.

4 In medium bowl, mix frosting and 2 tablespoons liqueur; spread over ice cream. Freeze at least 1 hour. Store covered in freezer.

1 SERVING: Calories 340; Total Fat 16g (Saturated Fat 8g; Trans Fat 1½g); Cholesterol 45mg; Sodium 390mg; Total Carbohydrate 46g (Dietary Fiber 1g); Protein 3g EXCHANGES: 1 Starch; 2 Other Carbohydrate; 3 Fat CARBOHYDRATE CHOICES: 3

sweet note This yummy dessert has a fudgy brownie base. Coffee lovers can substitute coffee-flavored ice cream for the vanilla.

mocha mousse cake

PREP TIME: 20 minutes *START TO FINISH:* 4 hours [12 SERVINGS]

Cake

1 box Betty Crocker® SuperMoist® chocolate fudge cake mix

1¼ cups water

⅓ cup vegetable oil

2 tablespoons coffee-flavored liqueur or cold brewed coffee

4 eggs

Mocha Mousse

¾ cup whipping cream

2 tablespoons granulated sugar

⅓ cup coffee-flavored liqueur or cold brewed coffee

1 cup semisweet chocolate chips (6 oz)

2 teaspoons vanilla

Chocolate Whipped Cream Topping

1 cup whipping cream

¾ cup powdered sugar

¼ cup Dutch processed unsweetened baking cocoa

½ teaspoon vanilla

1 Heat oven to 350°F (325°F for dark or nonstick pans). Grease and lightly flour bottoms and sides of two 8- or 9-inch round cake pans. In large bowl, beat cake mix, water, oil, 2 tablespoons liqueur and the eggs with electric mixer on low speed 30 seconds, then on medium speed 2 minutes, scraping bowl occasionally. Pour into pans.

2 Bake 8-inch pans 34 to 40 minutes, 9-inch pans 31 to 37 minutes, or until toothpick inserted in center comes out clean. Cool 10 minutes. Run knife around sides of pans to loosen cakes; remove from pans to cooling rack. Cool completely, about 1 hour. Refrigerate layers 45 minutes for easier handling.

3 Meanwhile, to make mousse, in 2-quart saucepan, mix ¼ cup of the whipping cream, the granulated sugar and ⅓ cup liqueur. Cook over medium heat, stirring constantly, until sugar is dissolved and mixture simmers; remove from heat. Stir in chocolate chips with whisk until chips are melted. Stir in 2 teaspoons vanilla. Pour into large bowl; cool to room temperature, about 10 minutes.

4 In chilled medium bowl, beat remaining ½ cup whipping cream on high speed just until soft peaks form. Fold whipped cream into chocolate mixture. Cover and refrigerate 30 minutes.

5 In another chilled medium bowl, beat topping ingredients on high speed until soft peaks form.

6 Trim off rounded top of one cake layer. Cut each cake layer horizontally to make 2 layers. (To cut, mark side of cake with toothpicks and cut with long, thin knife.) Place 1 layer, cut side up, on serving plate; spread with one-third of the mousse. Repeat with second and third layers. Top with fourth layer, cut side down. Spread topping over side and top of cake. Cover; refrigerate at least 1 hour before serving. Store covered in refrigerator.

1 SERVING: Calories 470; Total Fat 26g (Saturated Fat 13g; Trans Fat 0g); Cholesterol 120mg; Sodium 350mg; Total Carbohydrate 51g (Dietary Fiber 2g); Protein 5g EXCHANGES: 1½ Starch; 2 Other Carbohydrate; 5 Fat CARBOHYDRATE CHOICES: 3½

sweet note In a hurry? You can use 1 container (1 lb) Betty Crocker® Whipped chocolate frosting instead of the Chocolate Whipped Cream Topping.

banana turtle torte

PREP TIME: 30 minutes *START TO FINISH:* 5 hours 15 minutes [16 SERVINGS]

- 1 box Betty Crocker® SuperMoist® German chocolate cake mix
- Water, vegetable oil and eggs called for on cake mix box
- 1½ cups whipping cream
- 3 bananas
- 1 cup butterscotch caramel topping
- 6 tablespoons chopped pecans, toasted

1 Heat oven to 350°F (325°F for dark or nonstick pans). Grease two 9-inch round cake pans with shortening or cooking spray.

2 Make and bake cake as directed on box for 9-inch rounds. Cool 10 minutes. Run knife around sides of pans to loosen cakes; remove from pans to cooling racks. Cool completely, about 30 minutes. Refrigerate layers about 45 minutes for easier handling. Trim off rounded top of one layer. Slice each cake in half horizontally to make a total of 4 layers. Reserve untrimmed cake layer top.

3 In chilled medium bowl, beat whipping cream with electric mixer on high speed until stiff peaks form. Place 1 cake layer bottom, cut side up, on serving plate. Spread ⅔ cup whipped cream over layer to within ¼ inch of edge. Slice 1 banana; arrange on whipped cream, overlapping slices if necessary. Drizzle ¼ cup butterscotch caramel topping over banana, spreading to coat slices. Sprinkle with 2 tablespoons pecans.

4 Repeat with second and third layers. Top with reserved cake layer, rounded side up. Frost top of cake with remaining whipped cream. Spoon remaining butterscotch caramel topping over whipped cream. Swirl caramel into whipped cream with tip of knife.

5 Cover; refrigerate about 2 hours or until ready to serve. For best results, serve cake the same day. Store covered in refrigerator.

1 SERVING: Calories 250; Total Fat 18g (Saturated Fat 7g; Trans Fat 0g); Cholesterol 70mg; Sodium 115mg; Total Carbohydrate 20g (Dietary Fiber 1g); Protein 2g EXCHANGES: ½ Starch; 1 Other Carbohydrate; 3½ Fat CARBOHYDRATE CHOICES: 1

sweet note For a pretty serving presentation, drizzle caramel topping in a pretty pattern on each plate. Center a slice of torte on the plate, then place a dollop of whipped cream topped with a pecan half next to it.

easy red velvet cake

PREP TIME: 15 minutes *START TO FINISH:* 1 hour 50 minutes [12 SERVINGS]

Cake

1 box Betty Crocker® SuperMoist® German chocolate cake mix

1 cup buttermilk or water

½ cup vegetable oil

3 eggs

1 bottle (1 oz) red food color

1 tablespoon unsweetened baking cocoa

Frosting

2 oz cream cheese, softened

2 teaspoons milk

1½ cups whipping cream

½ cup powdered sugar

1 Heat oven to 350°F (325°F for dark or nonstick pans). Grease bottom and sides of 13 × 9-inch pan or two 9-inch round cake pans and lightly flour, or spray with baking spray with flour.

2 In large bowl, beat cake ingredients with electric mixer on low speed 30 seconds, then on medium speed 2 minutes, scraping bowl occasionally. Pour into pan(s).

3 Bake as directed on box. Cool rounds 10 minutes; remove from pans. Cool completely.

4 In chilled large bowl, mix cream cheese and milk until smooth. Beat in whipping cream and powered sugar with electric mixer on high speed, scraping bowl occasionally, until soft peaks form. Frost top of 13 × 9-inch cake or fill and frost cake layers. Store loosely covered in refrigerator.

1 SERVING: Calories 150; Total Fat 4½g (Saturated Fat 2g; Trans Fat 1g); Cholesterol 10mg; Sodium 150mg; Total Carbohydrate 27g (Dietary Fiber 0g); Protein 1g EXCHANGES: 2 Other Carbohydrate; 1 Fat CARBOHYDRATE CHOICES: 2

sweet note You will need the whole 1-ounce bottle of red food color to achieve the intense red color that is characteristic of this special cake. For a classic red velvet cake, add ¾ cup buttermilk, reduce water to ¼ cup and reduce oil to ¼ cup. All other ingredients remain the same. (Do not use a dark or nonstick 13 × 9-inch pan.)

chocolate-covered strawberry cake

PREP TIME: 15 minutes *START TO FINISH:* 2 hours [16 SERVINGS]

Cake

1 box Betty Crocker® SuperMoist® white cake mix

1 box (4-serving size) strawberry-flavored gelatin

Water, vegetable oil and whole eggs called for on cake mix box

Dipped Strawberries

1 pint (2 cups) medium-large strawberries (18 to 20 strawberries)

½ cup white vanilla baking chips

1 teaspoon shortening or vegetable oil

Filling and Frosting

1 cup seedless strawberry jam

1 container (1 lb) Betty Crocker® Rich & Creamy milk chocolate frosting

1 Heat oven to 350°F (325°F for dark or nonstick pans). Grease and lightly flour bottoms and sides of two 9-inch round cake pans, or spray with baking spray with flour. In large bowl, mix cake mix and gelatin. Beat in water, oil and whole eggs with electric mixer on low speed 30 seconds, then on medium speed 2 minutes, scraping bowl occasionally. Pour into pans.

2 Bake 28 to 33 minutes or until toothpick inserted in center comes out clean. Cool 10 minutes. Remove from pans to cooling racks. Cool completely, about 1 hour.

3 Meanwhile, gently rinse strawberries and dry on paper towels (berries must be completely dry). Line cookie sheet with waxed paper. In 1-quart saucepan, melt vanilla baking chips and shortening over low heat, stirring frequently. Remove from heat.

4 Dip lower half of each strawberry into vanilla chip mixture; allow excess to drip back into saucepan. Place on waxed paper–lined cookie sheet. Refrigerate until coating is firm, about 30 minutes, or until serving time.

5 Split each cake layer horizontally into 2 layers. On serving plate, place top of 1 layer, cut side up; spread with ⅓ cup of the jam. Add bottom half of layer, cut side down; spread with ⅓ cup jam. Add top of second layer, cut side up; spread with remaining ⅓ cup jam. Add bottom of remaining layer. Frost side and top of cake with frosting. Arrange dipped strawberries around top of cake. Store covered in refrigerator.

1 SERVING: Calories 390; Total Fat 13g (Saturated Fat 4½g; Trans Fat 1g); Cholesterol 40mg; Sodium 330mg; Total Carbohydrate 64g (Dietary Fiber 0g); Protein 3g
EXCHANGES: 1 Starch; 3½ Other Carbohydrate; 2½ Fat CARBOHYDRATE CHOICES: 4

sweet note For a tangy shortcut, skip the dipped strawberries and just serve a fresh strawberry with each cake serving.

berry cream torte

PREP TIME: 25 minutes *START TO FINISH:* 2 hours 10 minutes [16 SERVINGS]

- 1 box Betty Crocker® SuperMoist® white cake mix
- Water, vegetable oil and egg whites called for on cake mix box
- 2 containers (12 oz each) Betty Crocker® Whipped fluffy white frosting
- 1 container (8 oz) frozen whipped topping, thawed
- 1 cup fresh raspberries
- 1 cup fresh blueberries
- 1 cup sliced fresh strawberries
- ¼ cup seedless strawberry jam
- 1 tablespoon orange juice

1. Heat oven to 350°F (325°F for dark or nonstick pans). Make, bake and cool cake as directed on box for two 8- or 9-inch round cake pans.
2. In large bowl, mix frosting and whipped topping until well blended. To assemble cake, cut each layer in half horizontally. Place 1 layer half on serving plate; spread with 1 cup of the frosting mixture. Repeat 3 more times. Arrange berries on top of cake.
3. In small microwavable bowl, microwave jam uncovered on High about 20 seconds or until warm. Stir in orange juice; mix well with fork. Brush over berries. Store covered in refrigerator.

1 SERVING: Calories 410; Total Fat 18g (Saturated Fat 7g; Trans Fat 2½g); Cholesterol 0mg; Sodium 260mg; Total Carbohydrate 59g (Dietary Fiber 1g); Protein 2g EXCHANGES: 1 Starch; 3 Other Carbohydrate; 3½ Fat CARBOHYDRATE CHOICES: 4

sweet note If you don't have a cake dome to store the cake, use plastic wrap; but first insert toothpicks all over the cake to keep the wrap from sticking to the frosting.

cherry mini cakes

PREP TIME: 45 minutes *START TO FINISH:* 1 hour 50 minutes [58 SERVINGS]

Mini Cakes

1 box Betty Crocker® SuperMoist® white cake mix

Water, vegetable oil and egg whites called for on cake mix box

1 package (0.14 oz) cherry-flavored unsweetened soft drink mix

1 teaspoon almond extract

Glaze

1 bag (2 lb) powdered sugar (8 cups)

½ cup water

½ cup corn syrup

2 teaspoons almond extract

2 to 3 teaspoons hot water

Decoration

Miniature red candy hearts

1 Heat oven to 375°F (350°F for dark or nonstick pans). Grease bottoms only of about 58 mini muffin cups. In large bowl, beat mini cakes ingredients with electric mixer on low speed 30 seconds, then on medium speed 2 minutes, scraping bowl occasionally.

2 Divide batter evenly among muffin cups, filling each about half full. (If using 1 pan, refrigerate batter while baking other cakes; wash pan before filling with additional batter.)

3 Bake 10 to 13 minutes or until toothpick inserted in center comes out clean. Cool 5 minutes. Remove cakes from muffin cups to cooling rack. Cool completely, about 30 minutes.

4 Place cooling rack on cookie sheet or waxed paper to catch glaze drips. In 3-quart saucepan, mix all glaze ingredients except hot water. Heat over low heat, stirring frequently, until sugar is dissolved. Remove from heat. Stir in 2 teaspoons hot water. If necessary, stir in up to 1 teaspoon more water so glaze will just coat cakes.

5 Turn each cake so top side is down on cooling rack. Pour about 1 tablespoon glaze over each cake, letting glaze coat sides. Let stand until glaze is set, about 15 minutes.

6 Top each cake with candy hearts. Store loosely covered.

1 MINI CAKE: Calories 110; Total Fat 1½g (Saturated Fat 0g; Trans Fat 0g); Cholesterol 0mg; Sodium 60mg; Total Carbohydrate 24g (Dietary Fiber 0g); Protein 0g EXCHANGES: 1½ Other Carbohydrate; ½ Fat CARBOHYDRATE CHOICES: 1½

sweet note Mini cakes are great for themed parties. Pipe letters on the cakes to spell out "Congratulations" or "Bon Voyage."

strawberries 'n cream cake

PREP TIME: 15 minutes *START TO FINISH:* 1 hour 35 minutes [15 SERVINGS]

1 box Betty Crocker® SuperMoist® white cake mix

1¼ cups half-and-half

1 tablespoon vegetable oil

4 eggs

½ cup strawberry syrup

1 container (8 oz) frozen whipped topping, thawed

3 cups fresh whole strawberries, sliced

¼ cup strawberry jam

2 tablespoons sugar

1 Heat oven to 350°F (325°F for dark or nonstick pan). Spray bottom and sides of 13 × 9-inch pan with baking spray with flour.

2 In large bowl, beat cake mix, half-and-half, oil and eggs with electric mixer on low speed 30 seconds. Beat on medium speed 2 minutes, scraping bowl occasionally. Pour into pan.

3 Bake 25 to 30 minutes or until toothpick inserted in center comes out clean. Cool 20 minutes. Poke cake every inch with tines of meat fork or a table knife. Pour syrup slowly over cake, allowing syrup to fill holes in cake. Cool completely, about 35 minutes longer.

4 Spread whipped topping over cake. In medium bowl, gently mix strawberries, jam and sugar. Top each serving with strawberry mixture. Store covered cake and strawberry mixture separately in refrigerator.

1 SERVING: Calories 280; Total Fat 9g (Saturated Fat 5g; Trans Fat 0g); Cholesterol 65mg; Sodium 240mg; Total Carbohydrate 44g (Dietary Fiber 1g); Protein 4g EXCHANGES: 1 Starch; 2 Other Carbohydrate; 1½ Fat CARBOHYDRATE CHOICES: 3

sweet note Using a meat fork to poke the cake works well because the tines are longer and larger, ensuring better saturation of the syrup in the cake. Be sure to take your time pouring the syrup over the cake, letting it seep down into the holes.

easy tiramisu

PREP TIME: 25 minutes *START TO FINISH:* 2 hours 10 minutes [15 SERVINGS]

Cake

1 box Betty Crocker® SuperMoist® white cake mix

1 cup water

⅓ cup vegetable oil

¼ cup brandy

3 egg whites

Espresso Syrup

¼ cup instant espresso coffee granules

½ cup boiling water

2 tablespoons corn syrup

Topping

1 package (8 oz) cream cheese, softened

½ cup powdered sugar

2 cups whipping cream

1 tablespoon unsweetened baking cocoa, if desired

1 Heat oven to 350°F (325°F for dark or nonstick pan). Grease bottom only of 13 × 9-inch pan. In large bowl, beat cake ingredients with electric mixer on low speed 30 seconds, then on medium speed 2 minutes, scraping bowl occasionally. Pour into pan.

2 Bake as directed on box for 13 × 9-inch pan. Cool 15 minutes.

3 In small bowl, mix espresso granules and ½ cup boiling water. Stir in corn syrup. Pierce top of cake every ½ inch with long-tined fork. Brush top of cake with espresso syrup. Cool completely, about 1 hour.

4 In medium bowl, beat cream cheese and powdered sugar with electric mixer on low speed until mixed. Beat on high speed until smooth. Gradually beat in whipping cream, beating on high speed about 2 minutes or until stiff peaks form. Spread cream mixture over top of cake; sprinkle with cocoa. Store covered in refrigerator.

1 SERVING: Calories 150; Total Fat 4½g (Saturated Fat 2g; Trans Fat 1g); Cholesterol 10mg; Sodium 150mg; Total Carbohydrate 27g (Dietary Fiber 0g); Protein 1g EXCHANGES: 2 Other Carbohydrate; 1 Fat CARBOHYDRATE CHOICES: 2

sweet note Instead of brandy, you can use 1½ teaspoons of brandy extract plus ¼ cup water. Keep the topping smooth and creamy by adding the whipping cream gradually to the cream cheese mixture.

ambrosia cake

PREP TIME: 25 minutes *START TO FINISH:* 2 hours 10 minutes [12 SERVINGS]

Cake

1 box Betty Crocker® SuperMoist® white cake mix

Water, vegetable oil and egg whites called for on cake mix box

Orange-Coconut Filling

¼ cup sugar

2 teaspoons cornstarch

⅓ cup water

1 teaspoon grated orange peel

2 teaspoons orange juice

2 tablespoons flaked coconut

Frosting

1 container (12 oz) Betty Crocker® Whipped fluffy white frosting

½ cup flaked coconut

1 Heat oven to 350°F (325°F for dark or nonstick pans). Make, bake and cool cake as directed on box for two 8- or 9-inch round pans.

2 To make orange-coconut filling, in small microwavable bowl, mix sugar and cornstarch. Gradually stir in ⅓ cup water. Stir in orange peel and orange juice. Microwave uncovered on High about 1 minute or until mixture thickens and boils; stir. Microwave 30 seconds longer, stirring every 15 seconds. Stir in 2 tablespoons coconut; cool.

3 Fill cake layers with orange-coconut filling. Frost side and top of cake with frosting. Sprinkle ½ cup coconut over top. Store loosely covered.

1 SERVING: Calories 370; Total Fat 15g (Saturated Fat 5g; Trans Fat 2g); Cholesterol 0mg; Sodium 320mg; Total Carbohydrate 55g (Dietary Fiber 0g); Protein 2g EXCHANGES: 1 Starch; 2½ Other Carbohydrate; 3 Fat CARBOHYDRATE CHOICES: 3½

sweet note If you love the warm, nutty flavor of toasted coconut, you can toast it before sprinkling on top. To toast coconut, sprinkle it in an ungreased heavy skillet and cook over medium-low heat 6 to 14 minutes, stirring frequently until browning begins, then stirring constantly until golden brown.

coconut cake with white chocolate frosting

PREP TIME: 25 minutes *START TO FINISH:* 2 hours [15 SERVINGS]

- 1 can (14 oz) coconut milk (not cream of coconut)
- 1 box Betty Crocker® SuperMoist® white cake mix
- ¼ cup water
- 3 egg whites
- ½ cup flaked coconut
- 1 cup white vanilla baking chips (6 oz)
- 1¾ cups powdered sugar
- ⅓ cup butter or margarine, softened
- ½ teaspoon vanilla
- ¼ cup coconut

1 Heat oven to 350°F (325°F for dark or nonstick pan). Spray bottom only of 13 × 9-inch pan with baking spray with flour. Reserve ⅓ cup coconut milk for frosting.

2 In large bowl, beat cake mix, remaining coconut milk (1⅓ cups), the water and egg whites with electric mixer on low speed 30 seconds, then on medium speed 2 minutes, scraping bowl occasionally. Stir in ½ cup coconut until well combined. Pour into pan.

3 Bake as directed on box for 13 × 9-inch pan. Cool completely; about 1 hour.

4 Meanwhile, in 2-quart bowl, microwave vanilla baking chips uncovered on High about 30 seconds or until melted. Stir; if chips are not completely melted, microwave 15 seconds longer, then stir until all chips are melted. Stir in powdered sugar, butter, reserved ⅓ cup coconut milk and the vanilla. Cover; refrigerate 30 to 60 minutes. (If frosting becomes too firm to spread, microwave uncovered on High 10 to 15 seconds to soften; stir until smooth.)

5 Spread frosting over cake. Immediately sprinkle top with ¼ cup coconut. Store loosely covered.

1 SERVING: Calories 330; Total Fat 13g (Saturated Fat 10g; Trans Fat 0g); Cholesterol 10mg; Sodium 310mg; Total Carbohydrate 51g (Dietary Fiber 0g); Protein 3g
EXCHANGES: 1 Starch; 2½ Other Carbohydrate; 2½ Fat CARBOHYDRATE CHOICES: 3½

sweet note The larger flaked coconut is great for this cake, but you can use regular flaked or shredded coconut instead.

key lime pie poke cake

PREP TIME: 20 minutes *START TO FINISH:* 1 hour 55 minutes [15 SERVINGS]

Cake

1 box Betty Crocker® SuperMoist® white cake mix

1¼ cups water

1 tablespoon vegetable oil

4 eggs

Key Lime Filling

1 can (14 oz) sweetened condensed milk (not evaporated)

¾ cup whipping cream

½ cup Key lime juice or regular lime juice

1 teaspoon grated lime peel

4 drops yellow food color

1 drop green food color

Frosting

1 container (12 oz) Betty Crocker® Whipped vanilla frosting

2 teaspoons grated lime peel

Garnish, if desired

Fresh strawberries

Key lime slices

Lemon leaves

1 Heat oven to 350°F (325°F for dark or nonstick pan). Spray bottom only of 13 × 9-inch pan with baking spray with flour.

2 In large bowl, beat cake ingredients with electric mixer on low speed 30 seconds, then on medium speed 2 minutes, scraping bowl occasionally. Pour into pan.

3 Bake 27 to 33 minutes or until toothpick inserted in center comes out clean. Cool 5 minutes. With handle of wooden spoon (¼ to ½ inch in diameter), poke holes almost to bottom of cake every ½ inch, wiping spoon handle occasionally to reduce sticking.

4 In medium bowl, stir together filling ingredients (mixture will thicken). Pour over cake; spread evenly over surface, working back and forth to fill holes. (Some filling should remain on top of cake.) Refrigerate 1 hour.

5 Spread frosting over cake; sprinkle with lime peel. Garnish as desired. Store loosely covered in refrigerator.

1 SERVING: Calories 370; Total Fat 15g (Saturated Fat 7g; Trans Fat 1½g); Cholesterol 80mg; Sodium 290mg; Total Carbohydrate 54g (Dietary Fiber 0g); Protein 5g EXCHANGES: 1½ Starch; 2 Other Carbohydrate; 3 Fat CARBOHYDRATE CHOICES: 3½

sweet note Key lime juice is not green, so if you'd prefer a greener filling in this cake, add a couple drops of green food color to the filling before pouring it over the cake. You'll find key lime juice near the other bottled lime juices in the grocery store.

lemon-orange cake

PREP TIME: 25 minutes *START TO FINISH:* 3 hours 50 minutes [16 SERVINGS]

- 1 box Betty Crocker® SuperMoist® white cake mix
- Juice from 1 orange, plus water to measure 1¼ cups
- Vegetable oil and egg whites called for on cake mix box
- 1½ teaspoons grated orange peel
- 1 can (15¾ oz) lemon pie filling
- 1 container (12 oz) Betty Crocker® Whipped fluffy white frosting
- Grated orange peel, if desired

1 Heat oven to 350°F (325°F for dark or nonstick pans). Make, bake and cool cake as directed on box for two 8- or 9-inch round pans—except use 1¼ cups of orange juice mixture in place of the water and add 1½ teaspoons orange peel along with egg whites. Chill completely cooled layers 45 minutes before cutting.

2 Cut each cake layer horizontally in half to make 2 layers. Fill layers with generous ½ cup pie filling. Frost side and top of cake with frosting. Garnish with orange peel. Refrigerate about 1 hour or until chilled. Store loosely covered in refrigerator.

1 SERVING: Calories 310; Total Fat 12g (Saturated Fat 3g; Trans Fat 2g); Cholesterol 0mg; Sodium 330mg; Total Carbohydrate 46g (Dietary Fiber 0g); Protein 3g EXCHANGES: 1 Starch; 2 Other Carbohydrate; 2½ Fat CARBOHYDRATE CHOICES: 3

sweet note For a touch of elegance, scatter a few fragrant rose petals (just make sure they're pesticide free) on top of the frosted cake.

strawberry yogurt cake

PREP TIME: 20 minutes *START TO FINISH:* 2 hours 2 minutes [12 SERVINGS]

1 Heat oven to 350°F (325°F for dark or nonstick pans). Generously grease and lightly flour two 8- or 9-inch round pans, or spray with baking spray with flour.

2 In large bowl, beat cake ingredients with electric mixer on low speed 30 seconds, then on medium speed 2 minutes. Pour into pans.

3 Bake as directed on box for 8- or 9-inch rounds. Cool 10 minutes. Run knife around sides of pans to loosen cakes; remove from pans to cooling rack. Cool completely, about 1 hour.

4 Spread ⅓ cup frosting over 1 cake layer to within ¼ inch of edge. Cut about 10 strawberries into ¼-inch slices; arrange on frosted layer. Top with second layer. Frost side and top of cake with remaining frosting. Cut remaining strawberries in half; arrange on top of cake. Store loosely covered in refrigerator.

1 SERVING: Calories 360; Total Fat 14g (Saturated Fat 3½g; Trans Fat 2g); Cholesterol 0mg; Sodium 320mg; Total Carbohydrate 55g (Dietary Fiber 1g); Protein 3g EXCHANGES: 1 Starch; 2½ Other Carbohydrate; 2½ Fat CARBOHYDRATE CHOICES: 3½

Cake

- 1 box Betty Crocker® SuperMoist® white cake mix
- ¾ cup water
- ⅓ cup vegetable oil
- 3 egg whites
- 1 container (6 oz) Yoplait® Original 99% Fat Free strawberry yogurt

Frosting and Fruit

- 1 container (12 oz) Betty Crocker® Whipped vanilla frosting
- 1 quart (4 cups) strawberries

sweet note Try other Yoplait® fruit yogurts in place of the strawberry for adventures in flavor! Match the fresh fruit with the yogurt flavor.

mango-strawberry sorbet torte

PREP TIME: 35 minutes *START TO FINISH:* 5 hours 25 minutes [16 SERVINGS]

Cake

1 box Betty Crocker® SuperMoist® white cake mix

Water, vegetable oil and egg whites called for on cake mix box

1 pint (2 cups) mango sorbet, softened

1 pint (2 cups) strawberry sorbet, softened

Frosting

1½ cups whipping cream

½ cup powdered sugar

1 teaspoon grated lime peel

2 tablespoons lime juice

Garnish, if desired

Lime peel twists

Fresh strawberries

1 Heat oven to 350°F (325°F for dark or nonstick pan). Spray bottom only of 15 × 10-inch pan with baking spray with flour. Line bottom of pan with waxed paper; spray waxed paper.

2 Make cake batter as directed on box. Pour into pan. Bake 21 to 27 minutes or until toothpick inserted in center comes out clean. Cool in pan 10 minutes. Remove from pan to cooling rack; remove waxed paper. Cool completely, about 1 hour.

3 Cut cake crosswise into 3 equal sections. On long serving platter, place 1 section, rounded side down. Spread mango sorbet evenly over top. Place another cake section onto the sorbet; press down. Spread with strawberry sorbet. Top with remaining cake section; press down. Cover lightly; freeze about 2 hours or until firm.

4 In large bowl, beat frosting ingredients with electric mixer on high speed until stiff peaks form. Frost sides and top of torte. Freeze about 1 hour or until firm. Just before serving, garnish top with lime peel and strawberries. To serve, let stand at room temperature 10 minutes. Cut torte in half lengthwise, then cut crosswise 7 times to make a total of 16 slices.

1 SERVING: Calories 300; Total Fat 13g (Saturated Fat 6g; Trans Fat 0g); Cholesterol 25mg; Sodium 220mg; Total Carbohydrate 45g (Dietary Fiber 0g); Protein 2g EXCHANGES: 1 Starch; 2 Other Carbohydrate; 2½ Fat CARBOHYDRATE CHOICES: 3

sweet note To make the white chocolate–dipped strawberries, melt 4 ounces chopped vanilla candy coating and 1 teaspoon vegetable oil. Dip strawberries in melted coating and place on waxed paper to set.

white chocolate–cherry chip ice cream cake

PREP TIME: 25 minutes *START TO FINISH:* 4 hours 55 minutes [16 SERVINGS]

- 1 box Betty Crocker® SuperMoist® white cake mix
- 1 box (4-serving size) white chocolate instant pudding and pie filling mix
- 1 cup water
- ⅓ cup vegetable oil
- 4 egg whites
- 6 cups cherry–chocolate chip ice cream
- 1 cup whipping cream
- 1 package (6 oz) white chocolate baking bars, chopped
- ¼ cup hot fudge topping

1 Heat oven to 350°F (325°F for dark or nonstick pan). Spray bottom only of 13 × 9-inch pan with baking spray with flour. In large bowl, beat cake mix, dry pudding mix, water, oil and egg whites with electric mixer on low speed 30 seconds, then on medium speed 2 minutes (batter will be very thick). Pour into pan.

2 Bake 29 to 35 minutes or until toothpick inserted in center comes out clean. Cool completely, about 1 hour. Meanwhile, place ice cream in refrigerator 1 hour to soften.

3 Cut cake into 1- to 1½-inch squares with serrated knife. In very large bowl, stir ice cream until very soft. Add cake squares; stir until cake is coated (cake pieces will break up). Spoon mixture back into pan. Smooth top. Freeze about 3 hours or until firm.

4 Meanwhile, in 1-quart saucepan, heat whipping cream until hot but not boiling. Stir in chopped white chocolate until melted and smooth. Pour mixture into small bowl. Refrigerate 1 hour 30 minutes to 2 hours or until cold.

5 Beat white chocolate mixture on high speed until soft peaks form (do not overbeat or mixture will look curdled). Spread over ice cream cake.

6 In microwavable food-storage plastic bag, place hot fudge topping; seal bag. Microwave on High about 15 seconds or until melted; squeeze bag until topping is smooth. Cut off tiny corner of bag; squeeze bag to drizzle topping over cake. Serve immediately, or cover and freeze.

1 SERVING: Calories 400; Total Fat 20g (Saturated Fat 10g; Trans Fat 0g); Cholesterol 40mg; Sodium 370mg; Total Carbohydrate 50g (Dietary Fiber 0g); Protein 5g EXCHANGES: 1½ Starch; 2 Other Carbohydrate; 3½ Fat CARBOHYDRATE CHOICES: 3

sweet note Experiment with other flavors of ice cream.

margarita cake

PREP TIME: 20 minutes *START TO FINISH:* 3 hours [15 SERVINGS]

Crust

1½ cups coarsely crushed pretzels

½ cup sugar

½ cup butter or margarine, melted

Cake

1 box Betty Crocker® SuperMoist® white cake mix

¾ cup bottled nonalcoholic margarita mix

½ cup water

⅓ cup vegetable oil

1 tablespoon grated lime peel

3 egg whites

Topping

1 container (8 oz) frozen whipped topping, thawed

Additional grated lime peel, if desired

1 Heat oven to 350°F (325°F for dark or nonstick pan). Grease bottom only and lightly flour 13 × 9-inch pan, or spray bottom with baking spray with flour. In medium bowl, mix crust ingredients. Sprinkle evenly on bottom of pan; press gently.

2 In large bowl, beat cake ingredients with electric mixer on low speed 30 seconds, then on medium speed 2 minutes, scraping bowl occasionally. Pour batter over crust.

3 Bake 34 to 39 minutes or until light golden brown and top springs back when touched lightly in center. Cool completely, about 2 hours. Frost with whipped topping; sprinkle with additional lime peel. Store loosely covered in refrigerator.

1 SERVING: Calories 330; Total Fat 16g (Saturated Fat 8g; Trans Fat 0g); Cholesterol 15mg; Sodium 350mg; Total Carbohydrate 45g (Dietary Fiber 0g); Protein 3g EXCHANGES: 1 Starch; 2 Other Carbohydrate; 3 Fat CARBOHYDRATE CHOICES: 3

sweet note Look for the bottled pale green nonalcoholic margarita mix in the soft drink section of the supermarket. It is usually on the shelf with club soda, tonic water and other mixers.

neapolitan cake

PREP TIME: 20 minutes *START TO FINISH:* 2 hours 15 minutes [12 SERVINGS]

- 1 box Betty Crocker® SuperMoist® white cake mix
- 1 cup water
- ¼ cup vegetable oil
- 3 egg whites
- ¼ teaspoon almond extract
- 10 drops red food color
- ¼ cup chocolate-flavored syrup
- ½ cup Betty Crocker® Rich & Creamy chocolate frosting (from 1-lb container)

1 Heat oven to 325°F. Grease and lightly flour 12-cup fluted tube cake pan, or spray with baking spray with flour.

2 In large bowl, beat cake mix, water, oil and egg whites with electric mixer on low speed 30 seconds, then on medium speed 2 minutes, scraping bowl occasionally. Pour about 1⅔ cups batter into pan.

3 Into small bowl, pour 1⅓ cups batter; stir in almond extract and food color. Carefully pour pink batter over white batter in pan. Stir chocolate syrup into remaining batter. Carefully pour chocolate batter over pink batter.

4 Bake 40 to 45 minutes or until toothpick inserted 1½ inches from side of cake comes out clean. Cool 10 minutes. Turn pan upside down onto cooling rack or heatproof serving plate; remove pan. Cool completely, about 1 hour.

5 In microwavable bowl, microwave frosting uncovered on High about 15 seconds or until frosting can be stirred smooth and is thin enough to drizzle. Spread over top of cake, allowing some to drizzle down side. Store loosely covered.

1 SERVING: Calories 250; Total Fat 8g (Saturated Fat 2g; Trans Fat ½g); Cholesterol 0mg; Sodium 320mg; Total Carbohydrate 42g (Dietary Fiber 0g); Protein 2g EXCHANGES: 1 Starch; 2 Other Carbohydrate; 1½ Fat CARBOHYDRATE CHOICES: 3

sweet note Serve with Neapolitan ice cream, of course!

mini pumpkin cakes

PREP TIME: 45 minutes *START TO FINISH:* 1 hour [48 CAKES]

1 box Betty Crocker® SuperMoist® white cake mix

Water, vegetable oil and egg whites called for on cake mix box

2 teaspoons grated orange peel

Red and yellow food colors

1 container (1 lb) Betty Crocker® Rich & Creamy vanilla frosting

3 tubes (0.68 oz each) Betty Crocker® black decorating gel

3 rolls Betty Crocker® Fruit by the Foot® chewy fruit snack, any green variety (from 4.5-oz box), or small green candies

1 Heat oven to 350°F (325°F for dark or nonstick pans). Place mini paper baking cup in each of 48 mini muffin cups. Make cake batter as directed on box—except stir in orange peel and 6 to 8 drops each red and yellow food colors. Divide batter evenly among cups, about 1 heaping tablespoonful each. Bake 14 to 18 minutes or until toothpick inserted in center comes out clean. Cool in pan 5 minutes; remove from pan and cool completely, about 10 minutes.

2 In medium bowl, stir together frosting, 6 drops red food color and 8 drops yellow food color. Frost top of each cupcake. Using black gel, draw 2 triangles on each cupcake to look like pumpkin eyes, and draw a circle to look like a mouth.

3 Cut fruit snack into 48 (1-inch) pieces; tightly roll each piece to make a stem for each pumpkin. Place stem at top of each pumpkin. Store loosely covered.

1 MINI CAKE: Calories 100; Total Fat 3½g (Saturated Fat ½g; Trans Fat ½g); Cholesterol 0mg; Sodium 95mg; Total Carbohydrate 16g (Dietary Fiber 0g); Protein 0g EXCHANGES: ½ Starch; ½ Other Carbohydrate; ½ Fat CARBOHYDRATE CHOICES: 1

sweet note Colorful dessert ready in an hour! Enjoy these mini cupcakes made using Betty Crocker® SuperMoist® white cake mix and fruit snacks.

winter fruit and nut cake

PREP TIME: 20 minutes *START TO FINISH:* 2 hours 30 minutes [15 SERVINGS]

Cake

½ cup chopped dates

½ cup sweetened dried cranberries

½ cup chopped pecans

1 box Betty Crocker® SuperMoist® yellow cake mix

1 teaspoon pumpkin pie spice

2 tablespoons water

⅓ cup vegetable oil

3 eggs

1 cup chunky applesauce

Topping

⅓ cup butter or margarine, melted

¾ cup packed brown sugar

¾ cup chopped pecans

3 tablespoons milk

1 Heat oven to 375°F (350°F for dark or nonstick pan). Grease bottom only of 13 × 9-inch pan with shortening or cooking spray. In medium bowl, toss dates, cranberries and ½ cup pecans with ¼ cup cake mix. In large bowl, beat remaining cake mix, pumpkin pie spice, water, oil, eggs and applesauce with electric mixer on low speed 30 seconds, then on medium speed 2 minutes. Stir in date mixture. Spread in pan.

2 Bake 34 to 39 minutes (37 to 43 minutes for dark or nonstick pan) or until toothpick inserted in center comes out clean. Meanwhile, in small bowl, mix butter, brown sugar, ¾ cup pecans and the milk. Spread over top of warm cake.

3 Set oven control to broil. Broil cake with top 4 inches from heat about 1 minute or until bubbly. (Watch carefully to prevent burning.) Cool completely, about 1½ hours. Store loosely covered.

1 SERVING: Calories 360; Total Fat 18g (Saturated Fat 5g; Trans Fat 0g); Cholesterol 55mg; Sodium 250mg; Total Carbohydrate 46g (Dietary Fiber 2g); Protein 3g EXCHANGES: 1 Starch; 2 Other Carbohydrate; 3½ Fat CARBOHYDRATE CHOICES: 3

sweet note For a special treat, top each serving with a dollop of whipped cream.

candy cane cake

PREP TIME: 20 minutes *START TO FINISH:* 2 hours 20 minutes [12 SERVINGS]

Cake

1 box Betty Crocker® SuperMoist® white cake mix

Water, vegetable oil and egg whites called for on cake mix box

½ teaspoon red food color

½ teaspoon peppermint extract

White Icing

1 cup powdered sugar

1 tablespoon milk or water

½ teaspoon vanilla, if desired

Decoration

Crushed candy canes or crushed hard peppermint candies, if desired

1 Heat oven to 350°F (325°F for dark or nonstick pan). Generously grease and flour 12-cup fluted tube cake pan. Make cake batter as directed on box. Pour about 2 cups batter into pan. In small bowl, pour about ¾ cup batter; stir in food color and peppermint extract. Carefully pour pink batter over white batter in pan. Carefully pour remaining white batter over pink batter.

2 Bake and cool cake as directed on box.

3 In small bowl, mix white icing ingredients. If necessary, stir in additional milk, 1 teaspoon at a time, until smooth and spreadable. Spread over cake. Sprinkle crushed candy on top. Store loosely covered.

1 SERVING: Calories 240; Total Fat 8g (Saturated Fat 2g; Trans Fat 0g); Cholesterol 0mg; Sodium 280mg; Total Carbohydrate 41g (Dietary Fiber 0g); Protein 2g EXCHANGES: 1 Starch; 1½ Other Carbohydrate; 1½ Fat CARBOHYDRATE CHOICES: 3

sweet note Fluted tube cake pans can be a challenge to grease. Try this: Place a dab of shortening on the outside of a small food-storage plastic bag. Slip the bag on your hand and rub shortening on the inside of the pan. Repeat with more shortening until every nook and cranny is greased. Give the inside of the pan a good sprinkling with flour, shake excess from pan, and your baked cake will slip right out!

orange crunch cake

PREP TIME: 40 minutes *TOTAL TIME:* 2 hours 45 minutes [12 SERVINGS]

Cake

1 cup graham cracker crumbs (15 squares)

½ cup packed brown sugar

½ cup chopped pecans

1 teaspoon ground cinnamon

½ cup butter or margarine, melted

1 box Betty Crocker® SuperMoist® yellow cake mix

Grated peel from 2 oranges (about 2 tablespoons)

Juice from 2 oranges, plus water to measure 1 cup

⅓ cup vegetable oil

3 eggs

Frosting

1 container (12 oz) Betty Crocker® Whipped vanilla frosting

2 cups frozen (thawed) whipped topping

1 to 2 tablespoons grated orange peel

Orange slices, if desired

1 Heat oven to 350°F (dark or nonstick pans are not recommended). Grease bottoms only of two 8- or 9-inch round cake pans. Line bottoms of pans with waxed paper, then grease and flour entire pans.

2 In medium bowl, mix cracker crumbs, brown sugar, pecans, cinnamon and butter. Sprinkle 1 cup pecan mixture evenly into bottom of each pan; press gently.

3 In large bowl, beat cake mix, orange peel, orange juice mixture, oil and eggs with electric mixer on low speed 30 seconds, then on medium speed 2 minutes, scraping bowl occasionally. Pour evenly into pans.

4 Bake 8-inch rounds 34 to 41 minutes, 9-inch rounds 30 to 37 minutes, or until toothpick inserted in center comes out clean and tops are rich golden brown. Cool in pans 15 minutes. Carefully run sharp knife around sides of pans to loosen cakes. Remove from pans to cooling rack, placing crumb mixture side up. Cool completely, about 1 hour.

5 In large bowl, stir frosting ingredients until well blended. Place 1 layer, crumb side up, on serving plate. Spread with 1 cup frosting to within ¼ inch of edge. Add second layer, crumb side up. Frost side and top of cake with remaining frosting. Garnish with orange slices. To serve, cut cake with serrated knife. Store covered in refrigerator.

1 SERVING: Calories 540; Total Fat 28g (Saturated Fat 11g; Trans Fat 2g); Cholesterol 75mg; Sodium 410mg; Total Carbohydrate 67g (Dietary Fiber 1g); Protein 3g
EXCHANGES: 1 Starch; 3½ Other Carbohydrate; 5½ Fat CARBOHYDRATE CHOICES: 4½

sweet note For the freshest orange flavor, grate only the bright orange part of the peel. Stop at the bitter-tasting pith, the white portion directly under the bright orange part.

lemon mousse cake

PREP TIME: 15 minutes *START TO FINISH:* 1 hour 3 minutes [16 SERVINGS]

1 box Betty Crocker® SuperMoist® lemon cake mix

Water, vegetable oil and eggs called for on cake mix box

¾ cup lemon pie filling (from 15- to 16-oz can)

2 containers (12 oz each) Betty Crocker® Whipped vanilla frosting

1 Heat oven to 350°F (325°F for dark or nonstick pans). Make, bake and cool cake as directed on box for two 8- or 9-inch rounds.

2 In medium bowl, gently stir pie filling into frosting.

3 Place 1 cake layer, rounded side down, on serving plate. Spread with 1 cup of the lemon mixture to within ¼ inch of edge. Top with second layer. Frost side and top of cake with remaining lemon mixture. Store loosely covered.

1 SERVING: Calories 370; Total Fat 18g (Saturated Fat 5g; Trans Fat ½g); Cholesterol 40mg; Sodium 300mg; Total Carbohydrate 52g (Dietary Fiber 0g); Protein 2g
EXCHANGES: 1 Starch; 2½ Other Carbohydrate; 3½ Fat CARBOHYDRATE CHOICES: 3½

sweet note Leftover pie filling? Layer it with vanilla yogurt in dessert dishes, or mix it with an equal amount of whipped topping and serve over pancakes or waffles.

lemon-ginger bundt cake

PREP TIME: 25 minutes *START TO FINISH:* 2 hours 20 minutes [16 SERVINGS]

Cake

1 box Betty Crocker® SuperMoist® lemon cake mix

¾ cup water

½ cup vegetable oil

½ cup sour cream

1 teaspoon ground ginger

3 eggs

½ cup finely chopped crystallized ginger (about 2½ oz)

Frosting

1 cup powdered sugar

½ teaspoon grated fresh lemon peel

4 teaspoons fresh lemon juice

1 Heat oven to 325°F. Generously spray 12-cup fluted tube cake pan with baking spray with flour.

2 In large bowl, beat cake mix, water, oil, sour cream, ground ginger and eggs with electric mixer on low speed 30 seconds, then on medium speed 2 minutes, scraping bowl occasionally. Stir in crystallized ginger. Pour batter into pan.

3 Bake 43 to 48 minutes or until toothpick inserted in center comes out clean. Cool 10 minutes. Place cooling rack or heatproof serving plate upside down on pan; turn rack and pan over. Remove pan. Cool completely, about 1 hour.

4 In small bowl, stir frosting ingredients until well blended. Spoon over cake. Store loosely covered.

1 SERVING: Calories 240; Total Fat 10g (Saturated Fat 3g; Trans Fat 0g); Cholesterol 45mg; Sodium 220mg; Total Carbohydrate 35g (Dietary Fiber 0g); Protein 2g EXCHANGES: ½ Starch; 2 Other Carbohydrate; 2 Fat CARBOHYDRATE CHOICES: 2

sweet note Look for the crystallized ginger in clear plastic bags in the produce department. Buying ginger this way is less expensive than buying it in a jar from the spice section and it tastes the same. If you purchase a 3-ounce package, you'll have enough left over to garnish the cake.

lemon-raspberry cake

PREP TIME: 10 minutes *START TO FINISH:* 1 hour 45 minutes [16 SERVINGS]

1 box Betty Crocker® SuperMoist® lemon cake mix

Water, vegetable oil and eggs called for on cake mix box

6 tablespoons raspberry preserves

1¼ cups butter or margarine, softened

2 teaspoons grated lemon peel

3 tablespoons lemon juice

3 cups powdered sugar

1 Heat oven to 350°F (325°F for dark or nonstick pans). Grease bottoms only of three 9-inch round cake pans with shortening or cooking spray.

2 In large bowl, beat cake mix, water, oil and eggs with electric mixer on low speed 2 minutes (do not overbeat). Pour into pans.

3 Bake 15 to 22 minutes or until toothpick inserted in center comes out clean. Cool 10 minutes; remove from pans. Cool completely, about 1 hour.

4 Fill layers with raspberry preserves. To make frosting, in medium bowl, beat butter, lemon peel and lemon juice on medium speed 30 seconds. Gradually beat in powdered sugar. Beat 2 to 3 minutes longer or until light and fluffy. Frost side and top of cake with frosting. Store covered in refrigerator.

1 SERVING: Calories 420; Total Fat 23g (Saturated Fat 11g; Trans Fat ½g); Cholesterol 80mg; Sodium 320mg; Total Carbohydrate 50g (Dietary Fiber 0g); Protein 2g EXCHANGES: ½ Starch; 3 Other Carbohydrate; 4½ Fat CARBOHYDRATE CHOICES: 3

sweet note For a great twist, try strawberry or apricot preserves instead of raspberry. Top the cake with fresh raspberries, lemon peel curls or edible flowers.

lemon–poppy seed cake

PREP TIME: 20 minutes *START TO FINISH:* 2 hours 5 minutes [16 SERVINGS]

1 box Betty Crocker® SuperMoist® lemon cake mix

Water, vegetable oil and eggs called for on cake mix box

2 tablespoons poppy seed

½ cup Betty Crocker® Rich & Creamy lemon frosting (from 1-lb container)

1 Heat oven to 325°F. Grease and flour 12-cup fluted tube cake pan, or spray with baking spray with flour.

2 Make cake batter as directed on box—except stir poppy seed into batter. Pour into pan.

3 Bake as directed on box for fluted tube pan. Cool in pan 15 minutes; turn upside down onto heatproof serving plate. Remove pan; cool cake completely, about 1 hour.

4 In microwavable bowl, microwave frosting uncovered on Medium (50%) 15 seconds. Spread over top of cake, allowing some to drizzle down side. Store loosely covered.

1 SERVING: Calories 220; Total Fat 10g (Saturated Fat 2½g; Trans Fat ½g); Cholesterol 40mg; Sodium 230mg; Total Carbohydrate 29g (Dietary Fiber 0g); Protein 2g EXCHANGES: ½ Starch; 1½ Other Carbohydrate; 2 Fat CARBOHYDRATE CHOICES: 2

sweet note Each poppy seed measures less than 1⁄16 inch in diameter. It takes about 900,000 of them to make 1 pound!

lemonade party cake

PREP TIME: 20 minutes *START TO FINISH:* 3 hours 10 minutes [12 SERVINGS]

- 1 box Betty Crocker® SuperMoist® lemon or yellow cake mix
- Water, vegetable oil and eggs called for on cake mix box
- 1 can (6 oz) frozen lemonade concentrate, thawed
- ¾ cup powdered sugar
- 1 container (12 oz) Betty Crocker® Whipped fluffy white or fluffy lemon frosting
- Yellow colored sugar, if desired

1 Heat oven to 350°F (325°F for dark or nonstick pan). Make cake as directed on box for 13 × 9-inch pan. Cool 15 minutes.

2 Mix lemonade concentrate and powdered sugar. Pierce top of warm cake every ½ inch with long-tined fork, wiping fork occasionally to reduce sticking. Drizzle lemonade mixture evenly over top of cake. Run knife around sides of pan to loosen cake. Cover and refrigerate about 2 hours or until chilled.

3 Spread frosting over top of cake. Sprinkle with colored sugar. Store covered in refrigerator.

1 SERVING: Calories 410; Total Fat 18g (Saturated Fat 4½g; Trans Fat 2g); Cholesterol 55mg; Sodium 310mg; Total Carbohydrate 62g (Dietary Fiber 0g); Protein 2g EXCHANGES: 1 Starch; 3 Other Carbohydrate; 3½ Fat CARBOHYDRATE CHOICES: 4

sweet note A fun way to enjoy Lemonade Party Cake is at a Lemon Party. Make lemon the flavor and decoration theme for your next get-together, and serve up lemon-inspired dishes such as this cake along with plenty of ice-cold lemonade.

rainbow angel birthday cake

PREP TIME: 20 minutes *START TO FINISH:* 3 hours [12 SERVINGS]

1 box Betty Crocker® white angel food cake mix

1¼ cups cold water

1 teaspoon grated lemon or orange peel

Red, yellow and green food colors

1 cup Betty Crocker® Rich & Creamy vanilla frosting (from 1-lb container)

12 to 15 square candy fruit chews

1 Move oven rack to lowest position (remove other racks). Heat oven to 350°F. In extra-large glass or metal bowl, beat cake mix, water and lemon peel with electric mixer on low speed 30 seconds; beat on medium speed 1 minute.

2 Divide batter evenly among 3 bowls. Gently stir 6 to 8 drops of one food color into each of the batters. Pour red batter into ungreased 10-inch angel food (tube) cake pan. (Do not use fluted tube cake pan or 9-inch angel food pan or batter will overflow.) Spoon yellow batter over red batter. Spoon green batter over top.

3 Bake 37 to 47 minutes or until top is dark golden brown and cracks feel very dry and not sticky. Do not underbake. Immediately turn pan upside down onto glass bottle until cake is completely cool, about 2 hours. Run knife around edges of cake; remove from pan to serving plate.

4 Spoon ½ cup of the frosting into microwavable bowl. Microwave uncovered on High about 15 seconds or until frosting can be stirred smooth and is thin enough to drizzle. (Or spoon frosting into 1-quart saucepan and heat over low heat, stirring constantly, until thin enough to drizzle.) Drizzle over cake.

5 Place remaining frosting in decorating bag with writing tip. Pipe a ribbon and bow on each candy square to look like a wrapped package. Arrange packages on top of cake. Store loosely covered at room temperature.

1 SERVING: Calories 240; Total Fat 5g (Saturated Fat 2g; Trans Fat 0g); Cholesterol 0mg; Sodium 370mg; Total Carbohydrate 45g (Dietary Fiber 0g); Protein 3g EXCHANGES: 1 Starch; 2 Other Carbohydrate; 1 Fat CARBOHYDRATE CHOICES: 3

sweet note Add a scoop of rainbow sherbet to each serving for more rainbow fun.

cookies ’n cream angel cake

PREP TIME: 15 minutes *START TO FINISH:* 3 hours 2 minutes [12 SERVINGS]

- 1 box Betty Crocker® white angel food cake mix
- 1¼ cups cold water
- 3 reduced-fat chocolate sandwich cookies, finely crushed
- 1 package Betty Crocker® fluffy white frosting mix
- ½ cup boiling water
- 6 reduced-fat chocolate sandwich cookies, cut in half

1 Move oven rack to lowest position (remove other racks). Heat oven to 350°F.

2 Beat cake mix and cold tap water in large (4-quart) glass or metal bowl on low speed 30 seconds. Beat on medium speed 1 minute. Carefully fold crushed cookies into batter. Pour into ungreased angel food (tube) cake pan. Gently cut through batter in pan using metal spatula or knife.

3 Bake 37 to 47 minutes or until top is dark golden brown and cracks feel very dry and not sticky. Do not underbake. Immediately turn pan upside down onto glass bottle, or rest edges on 2 to 4 cans of equal height. Let stand 2 hours or until completely cool. Remove from pan by gently pulling cake away from side of pan, using fingers, taking care not to tear cake (cake will spring back to original shape). Turn pan over; press on removable bottom of pan, or shake pan gently to remove cake.

4 Beat frosting mix and boiling water in small glass or metal bowl on low speed 30 seconds, scraping bowl constantly. Beat on high speed 5 to 7 minutes, scraping bowl occasionally, until stiff peaks form.

5 Frost cake, and garnish with sandwich cookie halves.

1 SERVING: Calories 241; Total Fat 1g (Saturated Fat 0g; Trans Fat 0g); Cholesterol 0mg; Sodium 300mg; Total Carbohydrate 55g (Dietary Fiber 0g); Protein 4g EXCHANGES: 3 Starch CARBOHYDRATE CHOICES: 3½

sweet note This cake is just as delicious without the frosting! Simply top each slice with a dollop of whipped topping and a sandwich cookie.

orange cream angel food cake

PREP TIME: 35 minutes *START TO FINISH:* 5 hours 25 minutes [12 SERVINGS]

Cake

1 box Betty Crocker® white angel food cake mix

1¼ cups cold water

Orange Cream

6 egg yolks

1 cup sugar

2 teaspoons cornstarch

⅔ cup orange juice

Pinch salt

¾ cup butter or margarine, cut into pieces

1 cup whipping cream

1 tablespoon grated orange peel

Orange peel twists, if desired

sweet note When frosting this cake, first seal in the crumbs by spreading a thin layer of orange cream around the side of the cake. Then frost the top and go back over the side for complete coverage.

1 Move oven rack to lowest position (remove other racks). Heat oven to 350°F. In extra-large glass or metal bowl, beat cake mix and cold water with electric mixer on low speed 30 seconds. Beat on medium speed 1 minute. Pour into ungreased 10-inch angel food (tube) cake pan. (Do not use fluted tube cake pan or 9-inch angel food pan or batter will overflow.)

2 Bake 37 to 47 minutes or until top is dark golden brown and cracks feel very dry and not sticky. Do not underbake. Immediately turn pan upside down onto glass bottle until cake is completely cool, about 2 hours.

3 Meanwhile, in 2-quart saucepan, beat egg yolks, sugar, cornstarch, orange juice and salt with wire whisk until blended. Add butter; cook 2 to 3 minutes over medium heat, stirring frequently, until boiling. Boil 3 to 5 minutes, stirring constantly, until thickened and mixture coats the back of a spoon. Immediately pour orange mixture (orange curd) through fine-mesh strainer into medium bowl. Cover with plastic wrap, pressing wrap directly onto surface of orange curd. Refrigerate about 1 hour or until completely chilled.

4 In medium bowl, beat whipping cream on high speed until stiff peaks form. Fold whipped cream and grated orange peel into orange curd.

5 On serving plate, place cake with browned side down. Cut off top third of cake, using long, sharp knife; set aside. Scoop out 1-inch-wide and 1-inch-deep tunnel around cake. Set aside scooped-out cake for another use. Spoon 1⅓ cups orange cream into tunnel. Replace top of cake to seal filling. Frost top and side of cake with remaining orange cream. Refrigerate at least 2 hours before serving. Garnish with orange twists. Store covered in refrigerator.

1 SERVING: Calories 420; Total Fat 21g (Saturated Fat 13g; Trans Fat ½g); Cholesterol 160mg; Sodium 410mg; Total Carbohydrate 51g (Dietary Fiber 0g); Protein 5g EXCHANGES: 3½ Other Carbohydrate; ½ High-Fat Meat; 3½ Fat CARBOHYDRATE CHOICES: 3½

strawberry-rhubarb angel cake

PREP TIME: 25 minutes *START TO FINISH:* 3 hours 10 minutes [12 SERVINGS]

Cake

1 box Betty Crocker® white angel food cake mix

1¼ cups cold water

2 teaspoons grated orange peel

Filling

2 cups sliced rhubarb

½ cup granulated sugar

2 tablespoons orange juice

1½ cups sliced strawberries

Red food color, if desired

Frosting

1½ cups whipping (heavy) cream

3 tablespoons granulated or powdered sugar

1 container (15 oz) ricotta cheese

¼ cup powdered sugar

Garnish

½ cup sliced strawberries

1 Move oven rack to lowest position (remove other racks). Heat oven to 350°F. In extra-large glass or metal bowl, beat cake mix, water and orange peel with electric mixer on low speed 30 seconds; beat on medium speed 1 minute. Pour into ungreased 10-inch angel food (tube) cake pan. (Do not use fluted tube cake pan or 9-inch angel food pan or batter will overflow.)

2 Bake 37 to 47 minutes or until top is dark golden brown and cracks feel very dry and not sticky. Do not underbake. Immediately turn pan upside down onto glass bottle until cake is completely cool, about 2 hours.

3 Meanwhile, in 2-quart saucepan, mix rhubarb, ½ cup granulated sugar and the orange juice. Cook over medium heat 10 minutes, stirring occasionally. Cool 15 minutes. Stir in 1½ cups strawberries. Stir in 4 drops food color if deeper red color is desired. Refrigerate about 1 hour.

4 In chilled medium bowl, beat whipping cream and 3 tablespoons sugar on high speed until soft peaks form. In large bowl, beat ricotta cheese and ¼ cup powdered sugar on medium speed until fluffy. Fold in whipped cream.

5 Run knife around edges of cake; remove from pan. Cut cake horizontally to make 3 layers. Fill layers with filling. Frost side and top of cake with frosting. Arrange ½ cup strawberries over top of cake. Store covered in refrigerator.

1 SERVING: Calories 350; Total Fat 12g (Saturated Fat 8g; Trans Fat 0g); Cholesterol 45mg; Sodium 380mg; Total Carbohydrate 51g (Dietary Fiber 0g); Protein 8g EXCHANGES: 2½ Starch; 1 Other Carbohydrate; 2 Fat CARBOHYDRATE CHOICES: 3½

sweet note If fresh rhubarb is out of season, use frozen rhubarb instead. Be sure to thaw and drain well before making the filling.

rainbow sherbet roll

PREP TIME: 15 minutes *START TO FINISH:* 7 hours 50 minutes [12 SERVINGS]

1 package Betty Crocker® white angel food cake mix (only half the mix is used for this cake)

1¼ cups cold water

Powdered sugar

1½ cups raspberry sherbet, softened

1½ cups orange sherbet, softened

1½ cups lime sherbet, softened

1 Preheat oven to 350°F. Line 15½ × 10½-inch jelly roll pan with waxed paper.

2 Beat cake mix and cold water in extra-large glass or metal bowl on low speed 30 seconds; beat on medium speed 1 minute. Spread half of the batter in pan. Spread remaining batter in ungreased 9 × 5-inch loaf pan.

3 Bake jelly roll pan 20 to 25 minutes, loaf pan 35 to 45 minutes, or until top springs back when touched lightly in center. Reserve loaf pan for another use. Cool jelly roll pan 10 minutes. Loosen cake from edges of pan; turn upside down onto towel sprinkled with powdered sugar. Carefully remove waxed paper. Trim off stiff edges of cake if necessary. Carefully roll hot cake and towel from narrow end. Cool completely on wire rack, about 1 hour.

4 Unroll cake; remove towel. Beginning at a narrow end, spread raspberry sherbet on one-third of cake, orange sherbet on next third of cake and lime sherbet on remaining cake. Roll up carefully. Place roll, seam side down, on 18 × 12-inch piece of aluminum foil. Wrap in foil; freeze at least 6 hours until firm. Remove from freezer 15 minutes before serving. Cut roll into ¾-inch slices. Store wrapped in freezer.

1 SERVING: Calories 164; Total Fat 1g (Saturated Fat ½g; Trans Fat 0g); Cholesterol 3mg; Sodium 185mg; Total Carbohydrate 36g (Dietary Fiber 0g); Protein 2g EXCHANGES: 2 Starch CARBOHYDRATE CHOICES: 2½

sweet note Rolling is easy if you have the right towel. Use a clean, low-lint cotton kitchen towel with a tight broadcloth or flour-sack weave.

lemon chiffon dessert

PREP TIME: 25 minutes *START TO FINISH:* 7 hours 12 minutes [15 SERVINGS]

1 package Betty Crocker® white angel food cake mix

2 cups boiling water

1 package (8-serving size) lemon-flavored gelatin

1 can (6 oz) frozen lemonade concentrate, thawed

1½ cups whipping (heavy) cream

1 Heat oven to 350°F. Bake and cool cake as directed on package for angel food (tube) pan.

2 Pour boiling water on gelatin in large bowl; stir until gelatin is dissolved. Refrigerate about 15 minutes or until thickened but not set.

3 Add enough cold water to lemonade concentrate to measure 2 cups; stir into gelatin. Beat with electric mixer on medium speed until foamy.

4 Beat whipping cream in chilled medium bowl on high speed until stiff; fold into gelatin.

5 Tear cake into about 1-inch pieces. Fold cake pieces into gelatin mixture. Spread in ungreased 13 × 9–inch baking dish.

6 Cover and refrigerate at least 4 hours until firm but no longer than 24 hours. Cut into squares. Store covered in refrigerator.

1 SERVING: Calories 240; Total Fat 9g (Saturated Fat 6g; Trans Fat 0g); Cholesterol 33mg; Sodium 304mg; Total Carbohydrate 38g (Dietary Fiber 0g); Protein 4g EXCHANGES: 2 Starch; ½ Fruit; 2 Fat CARBOHYDRATE CHOICES: 2½

sweet note This refreshing do-ahead dessert is perfect for a springtime luncheon or bridal shower. Serve with small scoops of vanilla sorbet drizzled with chocolate ice-cream topping. A garnish of fresh mint sprigs completes the sunshiny look!

cream cheese pound cake

PREP TIME: 15 minutes *TOTAL TIME:* 1 hour 15 minutes [16 SERVINGS]

- 3 cups Original Bisquick® mix
- 1½ cups granulated sugar
- ½ cup Gold Medal® all-purpose flour
- ¾ cup butter or margarine
- 1 teaspoon vanilla
- ⅛ teaspoon salt
- 6 eggs
- 1 package (8 oz) cream cheese, softened
- Powdered sugar, if desired

1 Heat oven to 350°F. Grease and flour 10-inch angel food (tube) cake pan, 12-cup fluted tube cake pan or two 9 × 5-inch loaf pans.

2 Beat all ingredients except powdered sugar in large bowl on low speed 30 seconds, scraping bowl frequently. Beat on medium speed 4 minutes, scraping bowl occasionally. Pour into pan(s).

3 Bake 55 to 60 minutes or until toothpick inserted near center comes out clean. Cool 5 minutes; turn pan upside down onto wire rack or heatproof serving plate. Remove pan; cool cake completely. Sprinkle with powdered sugar.

1 SERVING: Calories 331; Total Fat 19g (Saturated Fat 10g; Trans Fat 1g); Cholesterol 118mg; Sodium 429mg; Total Carbohydrate 37g (Dietary Fiber 0g); Protein 5g
EXCHANGES: 1 Starch; 3 Fat CARBOHYDRATE CHOICES: 2½

sweet note For a hint of lemon, use lemon extract instead of the vanilla.

impossibly easy toffee bar cheesecake

PREP TIME: 10 minutes *START TO FINISH:* 5 hours 45 minutes [8 SERVINGS]

¼ cup milk
2 teaspoons vanilla
2 eggs
¾ cup packed brown sugar
¼ cup Original Bisquick® mix
2 packages (8 oz each) cream cheese, cut into 16 pieces, softened
3 bars (1.4 oz each) chocolate-covered English toffee candy, coarsely chopped
½ cup caramel topping

1 Heat oven to 325°F. Spray bottom only of 9-inch glass pie plate with cooking spray.

2 In blender, place milk, vanilla, eggs, brown sugar and Bisquick mix. Cover; blend on high speed 15 seconds. Add cream cheese. Cover; blend 2 minutes. Pour into pie plate.

3 Sprinkle candy over top; swirl gently with table knife to evenly distribute candy.

4 Bake 30 to 35 minutes or until about 2 inches of edge of pie are set and center is still soft and wiggles slightly. Cool completely, about 1 hour.

5 Refrigerate at least 4 hours. Serve with caramel topping. Store in refrigerator.

1 SERVING: Calories 460; Total Fat 27g (Saturated Fat 16g; Trans Fat 1g); Cholesterol 125mg; Sodium 360mg; Total Carbohydrate 47g (Dietary Fiber 0g); Protein 7g EXCHANGES: 3 Other Carbohydrate; 1 High-Fat Meat; 4 Fat CARBOHYDRATE CHOICES: 3

sweet note If you love nuts, sprinkle a few over the batter with the chopped candy. Or pass the nuts with a pitcher of caramel topping, and let guests top their own desserts.

impossibly easy banana custard pie

PREP TIME: 15 minutes *START TO FINISH:* 4 hours [8 SERVINGS]

- 1 cup mashed ripe bananas (2 medium)
- 2 teaspoons lemon juice
- ½ cup Original Bisquick® mix
- ¼ cup sugar
- 1 tablespoon butter or margarine, softened
- ½ teaspoon vanilla
- 2 eggs
- 1 can (14 oz) sweetened condensed milk
- ¾ cup frozen (thawed) whipped topping
- ¼ cup coarsely chopped walnuts, if desired
- Caramel topping, warmed, if desired

1. Heat oven to 350°F. Grease 9-inch glass pie plate with shortening or spray with cooking spray. In small bowl, mix bananas and lemon juice; set aside.
2. In medium bowl, stir remaining ingredients except whipped topping, walnuts and caramel topping until blended. Add banana mixture; stir until blended. Pour into pie plate.
3. Bake 40 to 45 minutes or until golden brown and knife inserted in center comes out clean. Cool completely, about 1 hour. Cover and refrigerate about 2 hours or until chilled.
4. Spread pie with whipped topping; sprinkle with walnuts. Drizzle with caramel topping before serving. Store covered in refrigerator.

1 SERVING: Calories 300; Total Fat 10g (Saturated Fat 5g; Trans Fat 0g); Cholesterol 75mg; Sodium 200mg; Total Carbohydrate 46g (Dietary Fiber 0g); Protein 6g EXCHANGES: 1½ Starch; 1½ Other Carbohydrate; 2 Fat CARBOHYDRATE CHOICES: 3

sweet note Don't throw away those old speckled brown bananas! Their sweet flavor and soft texture make this easy pie so delicious.

cinnamon streusel coffee cake

PREP TIME: 10 minutes *START TO FINISH:* 35 minutes [6 SERVINGS]

Streusel Topping

- 1/3 cup Original Bisquick® mix
- 1/3 cup packed brown sugar
- 1/2 teaspoon ground cinnamon
- 2 tablespoons firm butter or margarine

Coffee Cake

- 2 cups Original Bisquick® mix
- 2/3 cup milk or water
- 2 tablespoons granulated sugar
- 1 egg

1 Heat oven to 375°F. Grease bottom and side of 9-inch round pan with shortening or cooking spray. In small bowl, mix 1/3 cup Bisquick mix, the brown sugar and cinnamon. With fork or pastry blender, cut in butter until mixture is crumbly; set aside.

2 In medium bowl, stir all coffee cake ingredients until blended. Spread in pan. Sprinkle with topping.

3 Bake 18 to 22 minutes or until golden brown. Serve warm or cool.

1 SERVING: Calories 310; Total Fat 12g (Saturated Fat 4½g; Trans Fat 1½g); Cholesterol 50mg; Sodium 720mg; Total Carbohydrate 46g (Dietary Fiber 0g); Protein 5g EXCHANGES: 1½ Starch; 1½ Other Carbohydrate; 2 Fat CARBOHYDRATE CHOICES: 3

sweet note This coffee cake is best served warm, but you can microwave a piece for 10 to 15 seconds on High to bring back that fresh-from-the-oven taste.

chapter two

cupcakes

Perfect Cupcakes Every Time

What's great about cupcakes is that a few basic skills, tools and ingredients are all you need to make them for any occasion, whether they're for a party that's a month away or you're in the mood for a spur-of-the-moment batch.

Cupcake Baker's Pantry

With these basic items, you can make and decorate a batch of cupcakes in a snap.

Equipment:

- Cupcake pans (mini and regular).
- Paper baking cups available in a variety of colors and prints. Find them in supermarkets and party, craft or specialty cake decorating stores.
- Resealable food-storage plastic bags for piping icings and glazes.

Staples:

- Boxed cake mixes in a variety of flavors.
- Ready-to-spread frostings.
- Decorating icing, assorted colors.
- Decorating gels, assorted colors.
- Food colors (liquid, gel or paste). Try paste food color for more vivid color frosting.
- Assorted colored sugars and edible glitters.
- Assorted candy sprinkles.

Baking Pans

A box of cake mix makes 24 to 30 cupcakes in a regular-size cupcake pan. There are also pans that have mini, large and jumbo cups.

Pan Size	Cup Size
Mini	1¾ × 1 inches
Regular	2½ × 1¼ inches
Large	2¾ × 1¼ inches
Jumbo	3½ × 1¾ inches

If you have only one pan and a recipe calls for more cupcakes than your pan will make, just cover and refrigerate the rest of the batter while baking the first batch. Cool the pan about 15 minutes, then bake the rest of the batter, adding 1 to 2 minutes to the bake time.

An easy way to fill baking cups is to use an ice cream scoop. Use one that measures out ⅓ cup batter when filling regular-size cups. Use one that measures out 2 tablespoons batter when filling mini cups.

Frosting Tips

- Carefully dip top of cupcake into the frosting, give a slight twist and remove. Finish off with a swirl of a knife, if needed.
- Dip frosted cupcakes into bowls of nuts, colored sugar, sprinkles or other decors for easy decorating.

How to Store Cupcakes

1. Cool cupcakes completely before covering to keep tops from becoming sticky (about 30 minutes).

2. Cover cupcakes that will be frosted later loosely so the tops stay dry. If covered tightly, they become sticky and difficult to frost.
3. Store cupcakes with a creamy-type frosting loosely covered with foil, plastic wrap or waxed paper or under a cake safe or inverted bowl.
4. Refrigerate cupcakes with whipped cream toppings or cream fillings.
5. Frost cupcakes with fluffy frosting on the day they are to be served.
6. Freeze cupcakes 2 to 3 months, tightly wrapped.
7. To prevent frosting on frosted cupcakes from sticking, freeze cupcakes uncovered 1 hour, then insert a toothpick in the top of the cupcake, and tightly wrap.
8. Thaw cupcakes in the refrigerator or on the countertop.
9. When thawing on the countertop, loosen or remove wrapping to prevent condensation.
10. Decorating gel, hard candies and colored sugars do not freeze well because they tend to run during thawing.

freezing cupcakes

Unfrosted cupcakes freeze best. Plan to frost them when you remove them from the freezer.

- Cool cupcakes 30 minutes before covering and freezing.
- Freeze tightly wrapped or in tightly covered container for up to 3 months.
- Frost cupcakes frozen or thaw at room temperature and then frost.
- If you do freeze them frosted (creamy frosting works best), freeze uncovered for 1 hour, then cover tightly.

chai latte cupcakes

PREP TIME: 25 minutes *START TO FINISH:* 1 hour 50 minutes [24 CUPCAKES]

Cake

1 box Betty Crocker® SuperMoist® French vanilla cake mix

Water, vegetable oil and eggs called for on cake mix box

1 package (1.1 oz) instant chai tea latte mix (or 3 tablespoons from larger container)

Frosting and Garnish

1 cup white vanilla baking chips

1 container (1 lb) Betty Crocker® Rich & Creamy vanilla frosting

Ground cinnamon, if desired

1 Heat oven to 350°F (325°F for dark or nonstick pans). Place paper baking cup in each of 24 regular-size muffin cups.

2 Make and bake cake mix as directed on box for 24 cupcakes, adding chai tea latte mix to batter. Cool in pans 10 minutes; remove from pans to cooling rack. Cool completely, about 30 minutes.

3 In medium microwavable bowl, microwave baking chips on High 30 seconds; stir until melted. If necessary, microwave 15 seconds longer. Stir until smooth; cool 5 minutes. Stir in frosting until well blended.

4 Immediately spread or pipe frosting mixture on cupcakes. Sprinkle with cinnamon. Store loosely covered.

1 CUPCAKE: Calories 250; Total Fat 11g (Saturated Fat 4g; Trans Fat 1g); Cholesterol 25mg; Sodium 200mg; Total Carbohydrate 34g (Dietary Fiber 0g); Protein 2g EXCHANGES: ½ Starch; 2 Other Carbohydrate; 2 Fat CARBOHYDRATE CHOICES: 2

sweet note ***Chai*** **is the Hindi word for a tea made with milk and spices such as cardamom, cinnamon, cloves, ginger, nutmeg and pepper. Instant chai tea mix comes in a variety of flavors. Experiment to find your favorite.**

double-coconut cupcakes

PREP TIME: 35 minutes *START TO FINISH:* 1 hour 45 minutes [24 CUPCAKES]

Cupcakes

2 cups flaked coconut

½ cup sweetened condensed milk (from 14-oz can)

1 box Betty Crocker® SuperMoist® yellow cake mix

Water, vegetable oil and eggs called for on cake mix box

Coconut Cream Frosting

3 cups powdered sugar

⅓ cup butter or margarine, softened

¼ teaspoon salt

1 teaspoon coconut extract

1 to 3 tablespoons milk

Garnish

1 cup flaked coconut, toasted

1 Heat oven to 350°F (325°F for dark or nonstick pans). Place paper baking cup in each of 24 regular-size muffin cups.

2 In medium bowl, stir 2 cups coconut and the condensed milk; set aside.

3 Make cake batter as directed on box. Divide batter evenly among muffin cups, filling each about two-thirds full. Top each with about 1 heaping teaspoonful coconut mixture.

4 Bake as directed on box for 24 cupcakes. Cool in pans 5 minutes; remove from pans to cooling rack. Cool completely, about 30 minutes.

5 In medium bowl, beat powdered sugar, butter and salt with spoon or with electric mixer on low speed until well blended. Beat in coconut extract and 1 tablespoon of the milk. Gradually beat in just enough remaining milk to make frosting smooth and spreadable. Immediately frost cupcakes. Dip tops of cupcakes into toasted coconut. Store loosely covered.

1 CUPCAKE: Calories 280; Total Fat 13g (Saturated Fat 7g; Trans Fat 0g); Cholesterol 35mg; Sodium 220mg; Total Carbohydrate 39g (Dietary Fiber 0g); Protein 2g
EXCHANGES: ½ Starch; 2 Other Carbohydrate; 2½ Fat CARBOHYDRATE CHOICES: 2½

sweet note To toast the coconut, bake in a shallow pan at 350°F for 5 to 7 minutes, stirring occasionally, until golden brown.

piña colada cupcakes

PREP TIME: 20 minutes *START TO FINISH:* 1 hour 50 minutes [24 CUPCAKES]

1 box Betty Crocker® SuperMoist® yellow cake mix

⅓ cup vegetable oil

¼ cup water

1 teaspoon rum extract

1 can (8 oz) crushed pineapple in juice, undrained

3 eggs

1 teaspoon coconut extract

1 teaspoon rum extract

1 container (12 oz) Betty Crocker® Whipped vanilla frosting

¾ cup shredded coconut

1 Heat oven to 375°F (350°F for dark or nonstick pans). Place paper baking cup in each of 24 regular-size muffin cups. In large bowl, beat cake mix, oil, water, 1 teaspoon rum extract, the pineapple and eggs with electric mixer on low speed 30 seconds. Beat on medium speed 2 minutes, scraping bowl occasionally. Divide batter evenly among muffin cups.

2 Bake 15 to 20 minutes or until toothpick inserted in center comes out clean. Cool 10 minutes; remove from pan to cooling rack. Cool completely, about 30 minutes.

3 Stir coconut extract and 1 teaspoon rum extract into frosting. Spread frosting on cupcakes. Dip tops of frosted cupcakes in coconut. Store loosely covered at room temperature.

1 CUPCAKE: Calories 190; Total Fat 8g (Saturated Fat 3g; Trans Fat 1g); Cholesterol 25mg; Sodium 160mg; Total Carbohydrate 27g (Dietary Fiber 0g); Protein 1g EXCHANGES: ½ Starch; 1½ Other Carbohydrate; 1½ Fat CARBOHYDRATE CHOICES: 2

sweet note For very white-on-white cupcakes, use Betty Crocker® Whipped whipped cream frosting instead of the vanilla frosting.

banana toffee cupcakes

PREP TIME: 15 minutes *START TO FINISH:* 1 hour 12 minutes [24 CUPCAKES]

1 box Betty Crocker® SuperMoist® yellow cake mix

1 cup mashed very ripe bananas (2 medium)

⅓ cup water

⅓ cup vegetable oil

½ teaspoon almond extract

3 eggs

½ cup toffee bits

1 Heat oven to 350°F (325°F for dark or nonstick pans). Place paper baking cup in each of 24 regular-size muffin cups.

2 In large bowl, beat cake mix, bananas, water, oil, almond extract and eggs with electric mixer on low speed 30 seconds, then on medium speed 2 minutes. Stir in toffee bits. Divide batter evenly among muffin cups.

3 Bake 18 to 25 minutes or until golden brown and toothpick inserted in center comes out clean. Immediately remove from pans to cooling rack. Cool completely, about 30 minutes. Store loosely covered.

1 CUPCAKE: Calories 140; Total Fat 6g (Saturated Fat 2g; Trans Fat 0g); Cholesterol 25mg; Sodium 135mg; Total Carbohydrate 20g (Dietary Fiber 0g); Protein 1g EXCHANGES: ½ Starch; 1 Other Carbohydrate; 1 Fat CARBOHYDRATE CHOICES: 1

sweet note Stir in ½ cup miniature semisweet chocolate chips in place of the toffee bits, or to be really indulgent, toss in a half cup of both! If your bananas aren't ripe enough, speed the process by placing bananas in a perforated brown paper bag with a ripe apple.

s'mores cupcakes

PREP TIME: 45 minutes *START TO FINISH:* 2 hours 20 minutes [26 CUPCAKES]

Cupcakes

1 box Betty Crocker® SuperMoist® yellow cake mix

Water, vegetable oil and eggs called for on cake mix box

1 cup graham cracker crumbs

4 bars (1.55 oz each) milk chocolate candy, finely chopped

Frosting

1 jar (7 oz) marshmallow creme

½ cup butter or margarine, softened

2 cups powdered sugar

1 to 2 teaspoons milk

1 bar (1.55 oz) milk chocolate candy, if desired

26 teddy-bear-shaped graham crackers, if desired

1 Heat oven to 350°F (325°F for dark or nonstick pans). Place paper baking cup in each of 26 regular-size muffin cups. Make cake batter as directed on box; fold in graham cracker crumbs and chopped chocolate bars. Divide batter evenly among muffin cups.

2 Bake 18 to 23 minutes or until toothpick inserted in center comes out clean. Cool in pans 10 minutes; remove from pans to cooling rack. Cool completely, about 30 minutes.

3 In large bowl, beat marshmallow creme, butter and powdered sugar on low speed until blended. Beat in enough milk, ½ teaspoon at a time, to make frosting spreadable. Spread over tops of cupcakes. Divide chocolate bar into rectangles. Cut each rectangle diagonally in half and place on top of each cupcake. Top each cupcake with bear-shaped cracker. After frosting has set, store loosely covered.

1 CUPCAKE: Calories 240; Total Fat 10g (Saturated Fat 4½g; Trans Fat 0g); Cholesterol 35mg; Sodium 180mg; Total Carbohydrate 36g (Dietary Fiber 0g); Protein 2g
EXCHANGES: ½ Starch; 2 Other Carbohydrate; 2 Fat CARBOHYDRATE CHOICES: 2

sweet note To keep the chocolate from sinking into the cake batter, chop it finely. Try chocolate-flavored graham crackers instead of regular graham crackers for more chocolate taste.

pb & j cupcakes

PREP TIME: 30 minutes *START TO FINISH:* 1 hour 40 minutes [24 CUPCAKES]

Cupcakes

1 box Betty Crocker® SuperMoist® yellow cake mix

1¼ cups water

¾ cup creamy peanut butter

¼ cup vegetable oil

3 eggs

PB & J Frosting

1 container (12 oz) Betty Crocker® Whipped vanilla frosting

½ cup creamy peanut butter

2 to 4 tablespoons grape jelly

1 Heat oven to 350°F (325°F for dark or nonstick pans). Place paper baking cup in each of 24 regular-size muffin cups.

2 In large bowl, beat cupcake ingredients with electric mixer on low speed 30 seconds, then on medium speed 2 minutes, scraping bowl occasionally. Divide batter evenly among muffin cups, filling each about two-thirds full.

3 Bake 18 to 23 minutes or until toothpick inserted in center comes out clean. Remove from pan to cooling rack. Cool completely, about 30 minutes.

4 In medium bowl, mix frosting and ½ cup peanut butter. Frost cupcakes with frosting. Make a small indentation in center of frosting on each cupcake with back of spoon. Just before serving, spoon ¼ to ½ teaspoon jelly into each indentation. Store loosely covered.

1 CUPCAKE: Calories 250; Total Fat 13g (Saturated Fat 3½g; Trans Fat 1g); Cholesterol 25mg; Sodium 210mg; Total Carbohydrate 28g (Dietary Fiber 1g); Protein 4g EXCHANGES: 1½ Starch; ½ Other Carbohydrate; 2½ Fat CARBOHYDRATE CHOICES: 2

sweet note No grape jelly on the shelf? Substitute your favorite flavor of jam, preserves or jelly. Jelly or jam from a squeezable container makes quick work of topping the cupcakes.

peanut butter cupcakes with chocolate frosting

PREP TIME: 40 minutes *START TO FINISH:* 1 hour 35 minutes [24 CUPCAKES]

- 1 box Betty Crocker® SuperMoist® yellow cake mix
- 1¼ cups water
- ¼ cup vegetable oil
- 3 eggs
- ¾ cup creamy peanut butter
- 1 container (1 lb) Betty Crocker® Rich & Creamy chocolate frosting
- ¼ cup creamy peanut butter
- ⅓ cup chopped peanuts

1 Heat oven to 350°F (325°F for dark or nonstick pans). Place paper baking cup in each of 24 regular-size muffin cups.

2 In large bowl, beat cake mix, water, oil, eggs and ¾ cup peanut butter with electric mixer on low speed 30 seconds, then on medium speed 2 minutes, scraping bowl occasionally. Divide batter evenly among muffin cups, filling each about two-thirds full.

3 Bake 18 to 23 minutes or until toothpick inserted in center comes out clean. Remove from pan to cooling rack. Cool completely, about 30 minutes.

4 In medium bowl, stir together frosting and ¼ cup peanut butter. Frost cupcakes with frosting mixture. Sprinkle with peanuts; press lightly into frosting.

1 CUPCAKE: Calories 250; Total Fat 13g (Saturated Fat 3g; Trans Fat 1g); Cholesterol 25mg; Sodium 240mg; Total Carbohydrate 29g (Dietary Fiber 1g); Protein 4g EXCHANGES: 1 Starch; 1 Other Carbohydrate; 2½ Fat CARBOHYDRATE CHOICES: 2

sweet note If you don't want to chop peanuts, look for chopped nuts mix in the baking section of the supermarket. The package size is usually ½ cup and contains a mix of nuts including peanuts.

brownie cupcakes with peanut butter frosting

PREP TIME: 30 minutes *START TO FINISH:* 1 hour [12 CUPCAKES]

Brownies

1 box Betty Crocker® fudge brownie mix

Water, vegetable oil and eggs called for on brownie mix box

Peanut Butter Frosting, if desired

1 cup Betty Crocker® Rich & Creamy vanilla frosting (from 1-lb container)

⅓ cup peanut butter

2 to 3 teaspoons milk

Betty Crocker® Decor Selects candy sprinkles, nonpareils or colored sugars, if desired

1 Heat oven to 350°F. Place paper baking cup in each of 12 regular-size muffin cups. Make brownie batter as directed on box. Fill cups about three-fourths full (about ¼ cup each).

2 Bake 25 to 28 minutes or until toothpick inserted near edge comes out almost clean. Cool 5 minutes; remove from pan. Cool completely.

3 In small bowl, mix all frosting ingredients until smooth and spreadable. Spread frosting over brownies; sprinkle with candy sprinkles. Store tightly covered.

1 CUPCAKE: Calories 310; Total Fat 13g (Saturated Fat 3½g; Trans Fat ½g); Cholesterol 20mg; Sodium 210mg; Total Carbohydrate 45g (Dietary Fiber 2g); Protein 3g EXCHANGES: 1 Starch; 2 Other Carbohydrate; 2½ Fat CARBOHYDRATE CHOICES: 3

sweet note Decorative baking cups, found at cake decorating stores, will make these mouthwatering cupcakes a hit at any party!

strawberry–cream cheese cupcakes

PREP TIME: 20 minutes *START TO FINISH:* 1 hour 25 minutes [24 CUPCAKES]

1 box Betty Crocker® SuperMoist® yellow cake mix

⅔ cup water

½ cup sour cream

⅓ cup vegetable oil

2 eggs

3 tablespoons strawberry preserves

1 package (3 oz) cream cheese, cut into 24 pieces

1 container (1 lb) Betty Crocker® Rich & Creamy cream cheese frosting

Sliced fresh small strawberries, if desired

1 Heat oven to 350°F (325°F for dark or nonstick pans). Place paper baking cup in each of 24 regular-size muffin cups. In large bowl, mix cake mix, water, sour cream, oil and eggs with spoon until well blended (batter will be thick). Divide batter evenly among muffin cups.

2 In small bowl, stir preserves until smooth. Place 1 piece of cream cheese on top of each cupcake; press into batter slightly. Spoon ¼ teaspoon preserves on top of cream cheese in each cupcake.

3 Bake 20 to 25 minutes or until tops are golden brown and spring back when touched lightly in center (some preserves may show in tops of cupcakes). Cool 10 minutes in pans; remove from pans to cooling rack. Cool completely, about 30 minutes.

4 Spread frosting over cupcakes. Just before serving, garnish each cupcake with strawberry slices. Store covered in refrigerator.

1 CUPCAKE: Calories 200; Total Fat 9g (Saturated Fat 3g; Trans Fat 1g); Cholesterol 25mg; Sodium 190mg; Total Carbohydrate 30g (Dietary Fiber 0g); Protein 1g EXCHANGES: ½ Starch; 1½ Other Carbohydrate; 1½ Fat CARBOHYDRATE CHOICES: 2

sweet note Turn these tasty treasures into yummy raspberry cupcakes. Just substitute raspberry preserves for the strawberry preserves and garnish with fresh raspberries.

spiced pumpkin cupcakes

PREP TIME: 40 minutes *START TO FINISH:* 1 hour 35 minutes [24 CUPCAKES]

½ cup finely chopped pecans

3 tablespoons sugar

1 box Betty Crocker® SuperMoist® yellow cake mix

1 cup (from 15-oz can) pumpkin (not pumpkin pie mix)

½ cup water

⅓ cup vegetable oil

4 eggs

1½ teaspoons pumpkin pie spice

1 container (1 lb) Betty Crocker® Rich & Creamy cream cheese frosting

1 Heat oven to 350°F (325°F for dark or nonstick pans). Place paper baking cup in each of 24 regular-size muffin cups.

2 In heavy 8-inch nonstick skillet, cook pecans and 2 tablespoons of the sugar over low heat about 8 minutes, stirring constantly, until sugar is melted. Spoon and spread pecans onto sheet of waxed paper. Sprinkle with remaining 1 tablespoon sugar; toss.

3 In large bowl, beat cake mix, pumpkin, water, oil, eggs and pumpkin pie spice with electric mixer on low speed 30 seconds, then on medium speed 2 minutes, scraping bowl occasionally. Divide batter evenly among muffin cups, filling each about two-thirds full.

4 Bake 19 to 24 minutes or until toothpick inserted in center comes out clean. Cool in pans 10 minutes; remove from pans to cooling rack. Cool completely, about 30 minutes.

5 Frost cupcakes with frosting. Sprinkle edge of frosted cupcakes with pecans; press lightly into frosting. Store loosely covered.

1 CUPCAKE: Calories 210; Total Fat 9g (Saturated Fat 2g; Trans Fat 1g); Cholesterol 35mg; Sodium 180mg; Total Carbohydrate 30g (Dietary Fiber 0g); Protein 1g EXCHANGES: 2 Other Carbohydrate; 2 Fat CARBOHYDRATE CHOICES: 2

sweet note Use a heavy skillet, low heat and a constant eye to cook the sugar and nuts to ensure no burning.

spiced apple cupcakes with salted caramel frosting

PREP TIME: 30 minutes *START TO FINISH:* 1 hour 30 minutes [12 CUPCAKES]

Cupcakes

1½ cups Original Bisquick® mix

½ cup sugar

1 teaspoon apple pie spice

½ cup apple cider or juice

2 tablespoons butter or shortening, softened

1 teaspoon vanilla

1 egg

1¼ cups chopped peeled apple (about 1 medium)

Salted Caramel Frosting

¾ cup Betty Crocker® Rich & Creamy vanilla frosting (from 1-lb container)

¼ cup caramel topping

¼ teaspoon kosher (coarse) salt

1 Heat oven to 375°F. Place paper baking cup in each of 12 regular-size muffin cups.

2 In large bowl, beat all cupcake ingredients except apple with electric mixer on low speed 30 seconds, scraping bowl constantly. Beat on medium speed 4 minutes, scraping bowl occasionally. Fold in apple. Fill muffin cups about three-fourths full.

3 Bake 17 to 22 minutes or until toothpick inserted in center comes out clean. Immediately remove cupcakes from pan to cooling rack; cool completely.

4 In small bowl, mix frosting and caramel topping until smooth and spreadable. Frost cupcakes. Sprinkle with kosher salt.

1 CUPCAKE: Calories 220; Total Fat 7g (Saturated Fat 2½g; Trans Fat 1½g); Cholesterol 25mg; Sodium 310mg; Total Carbohydrate 37g (Dietary Fiber 0g); Protein 1g
EXCHANGES: 1 Starch; 1½ Other Carbohydrate; 1½ Fat CARBOHYDRATE CHOICES: 2½

sweet note Try a Braeburn apple in this cupcake recipe, or another crisp, sweet-tart apple such as Gala or Cortland.

malted milk ball cupcakes

PREP TIME: 25 minutes *START TO FINISH:* 2 hours [24 CUPCAKES]

1 Heat oven to 350°F (325°F for dark or nonstick pans). Place paper baking cup in each of 24 regular-size muffin cups.

2 In large bowl, stir together cake mix, 1 cup malted milk balls and ¼ cup malted milk powder. Add water, oil and eggs. Beat with electric mixer on low speed 2 minutes. Divide batter evenly among muffin cups.

3 Bake 21 to 26 minutes or until toothpick inserted in center comes out clean. Cool 10 minutes; remove from pan. Cool completely, about 1 hour.

4 In medium bowl, beat frosting ingredients on medium speed until smooth. Frost cupcakes. Sprinkle with 1⅔ cups malted milk balls. Store loosely covered.

1 CUPCAKE: Calories 240; Total Fat 9g (Saturated Fat 4½g; Trans Fat ½g); Cholesterol 30mg; Sodium 190mg; Total Carbohydrate 36g (Dietary Fiber 0g); Protein 2g EXCHANGES: ½ Starch; 2 Other Carbohydrate; 2 Fat CARBOHYDRATE CHOICES: 2½

sweet note The malted milk balls will be easier to crush if they are frozen. Freeze them in a food-storage plastic bag for about 30 minutes. Then tap the bag with a rolling pin or meat mallet until the balls are coarsely crushed.

Cupcakes

1 box Betty Crocker® SuperMoist® yellow cake mix

1 cup malted milk balls, coarsely crushed

¼ cup natural-flavor malted milk powder

Water, vegetable oil and eggs called for on cake mix box

Malted Milk Frosting

¼ cup butter or margarine, softened

2 cups powdered sugar

2 tablespoons natural-flavor malted milk powder

1 tablespoon unsweetened baking cocoa

2 tablespoons milk

Garnish

1⅔ cups malted milk balls, coarsely crushed

lucky charms® cupcakes

PREP TIME: 35 minutes *START TO FINISH:* 1 hour 40 minutes [24 CUPCAKES]

- 1 box Betty Crocker® SuperMoist® yellow or devil's food cake mix
- Water, vegetable oil and eggs called for on cake mix box
- 1 container (1 lb) Betty Crocker® Rich & Creamy vanilla frosting
- 3 cups Lucky Charms® cereal
- Green edible glitter

1 Heat oven to 350°F (325°F for dark or nonstick pans). Place paper baking cup in each of 24 regular-size muffin cups.

2 Make and bake cake mix as directed on box for 24 cupcakes. Cool in pans 10 minutes; remove from pans to cooling rack. Cool completely, about 30 minutes.

3 Frost cupcakes with frosting. Top each cupcake with 2 tablespoons cereal; sprinkle with glitter. Store loosely covered.

1 CUPCAKE: Calories 210; Total Fat 9g (Saturated Fat 2g; Trans Fat 1g); Cholesterol 25mg; Sodium 210mg; Total Carbohydrate 31g (Dietary Fiber 0g); Protein 1g EXCHANGES: 2 Other Carbohydrate; 2 Fat CARBOHYDRATE CHOICES: 2

sweet note Be sure to serve and savor these cupcakes within a few days of baking—before the marshmallows get stale!

birthday cupcakes

PREP TIME: 10 minutes *START TO FINISH:* 1 hour 40 minutes [24 CUPCAKES]

- 1 box Betty Crocker® SuperMoist® yellow cake mix
- Water, vegetable oil and eggs called for on cake mix box
- 1 container (1 lb) Betty Crocker® Rich & Creamy frosting (any flavor)
- 24 ring-shaped hard candies or jelly bean candies, if desired

1 Heat oven to 350°F (325°F for dark or nonstick pans). Make, bake and cool cake as directed on box for 24 cupcakes.

2 Frost with frosting. Decorate with candies. Store loosely covered at room temperature.

1 CUPCAKE: Calories 210; Total Fat 9g (Saturated Fat 2½g; Trans Fat 2g); Cholesterol 25mg; Sodium 190mg; Total Carbohydrate 30g (Dietary Fiber 0g); Protein 1g EXCHANGES: ½ Starch; 1½ Other Carbohydrate; 2 Fat CARBOHYDRATE CHOICES: 2

sweet note Chocoholics will want to use chocolate cake mix and chocolate frosting. Sprinkling with miniature chocolate chips and drizzling with melted white chocolate turn these simple cupcakes into bakery delights!

confetti party cake

PREP TIME: 30 minutes *START TO FINISH:* 1 hour 45 minutes [12 CUPCAKES]

1 box Betty Crocker® SuperMoist® cake mix (any flavor)

Water, vegetable oil and eggs called for on cake mix box

1 container (12 oz or 1 lb) Betty Crocker® Whipped fluffy white or Rich & Creamy vanilla frosting

Yellow, red and blue food colors

Betty Crocker® candy sprinkles or decors, as desired

1 Heat oven to 350°F (325°F for dark or nonstick pans). Grease bottom and side of 9-inch round cake pan and lightly flour, or spray with baking spray with flour. Place paper baking cup in each of 12 regular-size muffin cups.

2 Make cake mix as directed on box, using water, oil and eggs. Pour half of batter in round pan; spoon remaining batter into muffin cups. Bake as directed on box. Cool completely, about 1 hour.

3 In small bowl, place 1 tablespoon of the frosting; stir in 1 drop yellow food color. In another small bowl, place ¼ cup frosting; stir in 2 drops red food color. In third small bowl, place ½ cup frosting; stir in 4 drops blue food color.

4 On serving plate, place cake layer with rounded side down. Frost top and side with white frosting. Frost 7 cupcakes with blue frosting, 4 cupcakes with pink frosting and 1 cupcake with yellow frosting. Place 1 blue cupcake on center of white frosted cake. Place remaining blue cupcakes, sides touching, in circle around center cupcake. Place 2 rows of 2 pink cupcakes on top center of blue cupcakes. Place yellow cupcake on top center. Sprinkle with candy sprinkles. Store loosely covered at room temperature.

1 CUPCAKE: Calories 360; Total Fat 17g (Saturated Fat 4½g; Trans Fat 2g); Cholesterol 55mg; Sodium 300mg; Total Carbohydrate 48g (Dietary Fiber 0g); Protein 2g
EXCHANGES: ½ Starch; 2½ Other Carbohydrate; 3½ Fat CARBOHYDRATE CHOICES: 3

sweet note Celebrate with an easy and delicious stacked cupcake extravaganza.

mr. sun cupcakes

PREP TIME: 1 hour 15 minutes *START TO FINISH:* 2 hours 20 minutes [24 CUPCAKES]

Cupcakes

1 box Betty Crocker® SuperMoist® butter recipe yellow or yellow cake mix

Water, vegetable oil and eggs called for on cake mix box

Frosting and Decorations

Yellow food color

1 container (1 lb) Betty Crocker® Rich & Creamy vanilla frosting

Powdered sugar

48 large yellow, orange and/or red gumdrops

1 tube (4.25 oz) Betty Crocker® black decorating icing

1 tube (0.68 oz) Betty Crocker® red decorating gel

1 Heat oven to 350°F (325°F for dark or nonstick pans). Place paper baking cup in each of 24 regular-size muffin cups. Make and bake cake mix as directed on box for 24 cupcakes. Cool in pans 10 minutes. Remove from pans to cooling racks. Cool completely, about 30 minutes.

2 Stir 15 drops food color into frosting until bright yellow. Frost cupcakes.

3 Lightly sprinkle powdered sugar on work surface and rolling pin. Roll 4 gumdrops at a time into flat ovals about ⅛ inch thick. Cut thin sliver off top and bottom of each oval to make rectangles. Cut each rectangle in half crosswise to make 2 squares; cut each square diagonally in half to make 2 triangles.

4 Arrange 8 gumdrop triangles around edge of each cupcake for sun rays. Using small writing tip on black icing tube, pipe sunglasses on each cupcake. Using red gel, pipe smiling mouth on each cupcake. Refrigerate until ready to serve. Store covered in refrigerator.

1 CUPCAKE (CAKE AND FROSTING ONLY): Calories 170; Total Fat 7g (Saturated Fat 3g; Trans Fat 1g); Cholesterol 35mg; Sodium 190mg; Total Carbohydrate 28g (Dietary Fiber 0g); Protein 1g EXCHANGES: 2 Other Carbohydrate; 1½ Fat CARBOHYDRATE CHOICES: 2

sweet note Roll and cut sun rays ahead of time so kids can easily assemble the cupcakes. For brighter yellow frosting, use gel food color instead of liquid.

hot chocolate cupcakes

PREP TIME: 20 minutes *START TO FINISH:* 1 hour 25 minutes [12 CUPCAKES]

½ box Betty Crocker® SuperMoist® devil's food cake mix (about 1⅔ cups)

½ cup water

¼ cup vegetable oil

1 egg

1 cup Betty Crocker® Whipped vanilla frosting (from 12-oz container)

½ cup marshmallow creme

¼ teaspoon unsweetened baking cocoa

6 miniature pretzel twists, broken in half

1 Heat oven to 350°F (325°F for dark or nonstick pans). Place paper baking cup in each of 12 regular-size muffin cups.

2 In large bowl, beat cake mix, water, oil and egg with electric mixer on low speed 30 seconds, then on medium speed 2 minutes, scraping bowl occasionally. Divide batter evenly among muffin cups.

3 Bake 17 to 22 minutes or until toothpick inserted in center comes out clean. Cool in pan 10 minutes; remove from pan to cooling rack. Cool completely, about 30 minutes.

4 In small bowl, mix frosting and marshmallow creme. Spoon into small resealable food-storage plastic bag; seal bag. Cut ⅜-inch tip off 1 corner of bag. (Or spoon mixture onto cupcakes instead of piping.)

5 Pipe 3 small dollops of frosting mixture on top of each cupcake to look like melted marshmallows. Sprinkle with cocoa. Press pretzel half into side of each cupcake for cup handle. Store loosely covered.

1 CUPCAKE: Calories 200; Total Fat 9g (Saturated Fat 2½g; Trans Fat 1g); Cholesterol 20mg; Sodium 180mg; Total Carbohydrate 28g (Dietary Fiber 0g); Protein 1g
EXCHANGES: ½ Starch; 1½ Other Carbohydrate; 1½ Fat CARBOHYDRATE CHOICES: 2

sweet note If you like peppermint, frost these fun cupcakes with the frosting mixture, and sprinkle the tops with crushed candy canes.

snowball cupcakes

PREP TIME: 40 minutes *START TO FINISH:* 1 hour 30 minutes [24 CUPCAKES]

Cupcakes

1 box Betty Crocker® Super Moist® devil's food cake mix

⅔ cup water

⅓ cup vegetable oil

½ cup sour cream

2 eggs

1 package (3 oz) cream cheese, cut into 24 cubes

Frosting

½ cup sugar

2 tablespoons water

2 egg whites

1 jar (7 oz) marshmallow creme

1 teaspoon vanilla

2 cups coconut

1 Heat oven to 350°F (325°F for dark or nonstick pans). Place paper baking cup in each of 24 regular-size muffin cups. In large bowl, beat cake mix, water, oil, sour cream and eggs with electric mixer on low speed 30 seconds, then on medium speed 2 minutes, scraping bowl occasionally.

2 Spoon batter into muffin cups. Place 1 cube cream cheese in center of each cupcake; press down into batter almost to center (top of cream cheese will still show).

3 Bake 21 to 27 minutes or until toothpick inserted near center of cupcake comes out clean (test between cream cheese and edge). Remove cupcakes from pan to cooling racks. Cool completely, about 30 minutes.

4 In 2-quart stainless steel or other noncoated saucepan, mix sugar, water and egg whites. Cook over low heat, beating continuously with electric hand mixer at high speed until soft peaks form, about 4 minutes. Add marshmallow creme; beat until stiff peaks form. Remove saucepan from heat. Beat in vanilla.

5 Spread frosting evenly over cupcakes; sprinkle each with generous tablespoonful of coconut. Store loosely covered in refrigerator.

1 CUPCAKE: Calories 200; Total Fat 9g (Saturated Fat 4½g; Trans Fat 0g); Cholesterol 25mg; Sodium 200mg; Total Carbohydrate 29g (Dietary Fiber 0g); Protein 2g
EXCHANGES: 1 Starch; 1 Other Carbohydrate; 1½ Fat CARBOHYDRATE CHOICES: 2

sweet note Add sparkle to each snowball by sprinkling with edible glitter or decorating sugar.

dreamy cream-filled cupcakes

PREP TIME: 30 minutes *START TO FINISH:* 1 hour 15 minutes [24 CUPCAKES]

1 box Betty Crocker® SuperMoist® devil's food cake mix

Water, vegetable oil and eggs called for on cake mix box

1½ containers (12 oz each) Betty Crocker® Whipped fluffy white frosting

½ cup miniature semisweet chocolate chips

1 Heat oven to 350°F (325°F for dark or nonstick pans). Make and bake cake mix as directed on box for 24 cupcakes. Cool 10 minutes; remove from pan to cooling racks. Cool completely, about 30 minutes.

2 Spoon frosting into corner of resealable heavy-duty food-storage plastic bag. Cut about ¼ inch off corner of bag. Gently push cut corner of bag into center of cupcake. Squeeze about 2 teaspoons frosting into center of each cupcake for filling, being careful not to split cupcake. Frost tops of cupcakes with remaining frosting.

3 Sprinkle chocolate chips on top of each cupcake. Store loosely covered.

1 CUPCAKE: Calories 230; Total Fat 11g (Saturated Fat 3½g; Trans Fat 1½g); Cholesterol 25mg; Sodium 180mg; Total Carbohydrate 30g (Dietary Fiber 0g); Protein 1g EXCHANGES: ½ Starch; 1½ Other Carbohydrate; 2 Fat CARBOHYDRATE CHOICES: 2

sweet note Instead of sprinkling with chocolate chips, drizzle with melted chocolate. In small microwavable bowl, microwave ¼ cup miniature semisweet chocolate chips and ½ teaspoon shortening uncovered on High just until mixture can be stirred smooth. Place in small food-storage plastic bag; cut off small corner of bag. Drizzle over frosted cupcakes.

"from the heart" cupcakes

PREP TIME: 35 minutes *START TO FINISH:* 1 hour 55 minutes [24 CUPCAKES]

Cupcakes

1 box Betty Crocker® SuperMoist® devil's food cake mix

Water, vegetable oil and eggs called for on cake mix box

Frosting

1 cup white vanilla baking chips (6 oz)

1 container (1 lb) Betty Crocker® Rich & Creamy vanilla frosting

Chocolate Hearts

½ cup semisweet chocolate chips

½ teaspoon shortening

1 Heat oven to 350°F (325°F for dark or nonstick pans). Place paper baking cup in each of 24 regular-size muffin cups. Make and bake cake mix as directed on box for cupcakes, using water, oil and eggs.

2 In medium microwavable bowl, microwave white baking chips uncovered on High 45 seconds. Stir; if necessary, microwave in 15-second increments, stirring after each, until chips are melted and smooth. Cool 5 minutes. Stir in frosting until well blended. Immediately frost cupcakes, or pipe frosting on cupcakes.

3 Line cookie sheet with waxed paper. In 1-cup microwavable measuring cup, microwave chocolate chips and shortening uncovered on Medium (50%) 30 seconds. Stir; microwave in 10-second increments, stirring after each, until melted and smooth. Place chocolate in small resealable food-storage plastic bag; seal bag. Cut off tiny corner of bag. Squeeze bag to pipe 24 heart shapes on waxed paper. Refrigerate 10 minutes to set chocolate. Garnish each cupcake with a chocolate heart.

1 CUPCAKE: Calories 260; Total Fat 12g (Saturated Fat 5g; Trans Fat 1g); Cholesterol 25mg; Sodium 210mg; Total Carbohydrate 35g (Dietary Fiber 0g); Protein 2g
EXCHANGES: ½ Starch; 2 Other Carbohydrate; 2½ Fat CARBOHYDRATE CHOICES: 2

sweet note For a touch that's "from the heart," place melted and cooled dark or white chocolate in a resealable food-storage plastic bag. Cut the tip off one corner and pipe heart shapes onto waxed paper. Refrigerate to harden, then carefully place on cupcakes.

teddy-at-the-beach cupcakes

PREP TIME: 30 minutes *START TO FINISH:* 1 hour 35 minutes [12 CUPCAKES]

1 box Betty Crocker® SuperMoist® cake mix (any flavor)

Water, vegetable oil and eggs called for on cake mix box

2 drops blue food color

1 cup Betty Crocker® Whipped vanilla frosting (from 12-oz container)

1 roll (from 4.5-oz box) Betty Crocker® Fruit by the Foot® chewy fruit snack (any flavor)

½ cup teddy-bear-shaped graham snacks, crushed, or brown sugar

1 tablespoon blue sugar or edible glitter, if desired

12 teddy-bear-shaped graham crackers

6 paper drink umbrellas or small plastic umbrellas, if desired

6 ring-shaped gummy candies

6 multicolored fish-shaped crackers

1 Heat oven to 350°F (325°F for dark or nonstick pans). Place paper baking cup in each of 24 regular-size muffin cups. Make and bake cake mix as directed on box for 24 cupcakes. Cool in pans 10 minutes; remove from pans to cooling rack. Cool completely, about 30 minutes. Tightly wrap 12 cupcakes; freeze for a later use.

2 Stir blue food color into frosting until blended. Frost remaining 12 cupcakes with frosting.

3 Cut six 1½-inch pieces from fruit snack roll; peel off paper backing. Use fruit snack and remaining ingredients to decorate cupcakes as shown in photo or as desired.

1 CUPCAKE (CAKE AND FROSTING ONLY): Calories 190; Total Fat 9g (Saturated Fat 2½g; Trans Fat 1g); Cholesterol 25mg; Sodium 150mg; Total Carbohydrate 25g (Dietary Fiber 0g); Protein 1g EXCHANGES: 1½ Other Carbohydrate; 2 Fat CARBOHYDRATE CHOICES: 1½

sweet note If you have Betty Crocker® decorating icing (in 4.25-oz tubes), use the writing tip to pipe swimsuits on the bears. The small plastic umbrellas can be found at www.fancyflours.com.

red velvet cupcakes with cream cheese frosting

PREP TIME: 20 minutes *START TO FINISH:* 2 hours [24 CUPCAKES]

1 teaspoon water

1 bottle (1 oz) red food color

1 box Betty Crocker® SuperMoist® German chocolate cake mix

1 cup water

½ cup vegetable oil

3 eggs

1 container (1 lb) Betty Crocker® Rich & Creamy cream cheese frosting

1 Heat oven to 350°F (325°F for dark or nonstick pans). Place paper baking cup in each of 24 regular-size muffin cups. To make red food color paint, in small bowl, mix 1 teaspoon water and 3 to 4 drops of the food color; set aside.

2 In large bowl, beat cake mix, 1 cup water, the oil, eggs and remaining food color from bottle with electric mixer on low speed 30 seconds, then on medium speed 2 minutes, scraping bowl occasionally. Divide batter evenly among muffin cups.

3 Bake and cool completely as directed on box for cupcakes.

4 Frost tops of cupcakes with frosting. Using a fine-tip brush, paint cupcakes with red food color paint, swirling paint to create design. Store loosely covered at room temperature.

1 CUPCAKE: Calories 130; Total Fat 8g (Saturated Fat 1½g; Trans Fat 1g); Cholesterol 25mg; Sodium 60mg; Total Carbohydrate 13g (Dietary Fiber 0g); Protein 1g EXCHANGES: 1 Other Carbohydrate; 1½ Fat CARBOHYDRATE CHOICES: 1

sweet note

Red velvet cake has been popular in the southern United States since the early 1900s. Try serving with vanilla ice cream and red candy sprinkles or a drizzle of grenadine syrup.

chocolate velvet cupcakes

PREP TIME: 20 minutes *START TO FINISH:* 1 hour 20 minutes [24 CUPCAKES]

Cupcakes

1 box Betty Crocker® SuperMoist® devil's food cake mix

1 cup sour cream

¾ cup milk

⅓ cup vegetable oil

3 eggs

1 to 2 teaspoons butter flavor or vanilla

2 heaping tablespoons unsweetened baking cocoa

1 cup chocolate chips (6 oz)

Cream Cheese Icing

1 package (8 oz) cream cheese, softened

½ cup butter or margarine, softened

3½ to 4 cups powdered sugar

1 to 2 teaspoons butter flavor or vanilla

24 chocolate curls

1 Heat oven to 350°F (325°F for dark or nonstick pans). Place paper baking cup in each of 24 regular-size muffin cups.

2 In large bowl, beat all cupcake ingredients except chocolate chips with electric mixer on medium speed about 2 minutes, or until well blended. Stir in chocolate chips. Divide batter evenly among muffin cups.

3 Bake 18 to 24 minutes or until toothpick inserted in center of cupcake comes out almost clean. Cool 10 minutes; remove from muffin pans. Cool completely.

4 In medium bowl, beat cream cheese and butter with electric mixer on medium speed until well blended. Beat in powdered sugar until smooth. Beat in butter flavor until icing is creamy. Place in decorating bag fitted with tip; pipe large swirls on tops of cupcakes. Top with chocolate curls. Store covered in refrigerator.

1 CUPCAKE: Calories 310; Total Fat 16g (Saturated Fat 8g; Trans Fat 0g); Cholesterol 55mg; Sodium 230mg; Total Carbohydrate 39g (Dietary Fiber 1g); Protein 3g EXCHANGES: 1 Starch; 1½ Other Carbohydrate; 3 Fat CARBOHYDRATE CHOICES: 2½

sweet note Using a scoop makes spooning cupcake batter quick and less messy, and it also ensures cupcakes will be the same size. Use a #70 or small-size spring-loaded ice cream scoop that is equal to about 1 tablespoon.

happy birthday marshmallow cupcakes

PREP TIME: 25 minutes *START TO FINISH:* 1 hour 25 minutes [24 CUPCAKES]

1 box Betty Crocker® SuperMoist® white cake mix

Water, vegetable oil and egg whites called for on cake mix box

2 containers (1 lb each) Betty Crocker® Rich & Creamy creamy white frosting

24 to 30 large marshmallows

Betty Crocker® colored sugar or candy sprinkles

White or colored birthday candles

1 Heat oven to 350°F (325°F for dark or nonstick pans).

2 Make, bake and cool cake mix as directed on box for 24 cupcakes. Frost cupcakes with frosting.

3 Spray blades of kitchen scissors with cooking spray. Cut marshmallows crosswise into slices; sprinkle with colored sugar. Arrange on cupcakes in flower shape. Place candle in center of each flower. Store loosely covered.

1 CUPCAKE: Calories 250; Total Fat 9g (Saturated Fat 2g; Trans Fat 0g); Cholesterol 0mg; Sodium 220mg; Total Carbohydrate 40g (Dietary Fiber 0g); Protein 1g EXCHANGES: ½ Starch; 2 Other Carbohydrate; 2 Fat CARBOHYDRATE CHOICES: 2½

sweet note

Use edible glitter in place of the colored sugar or candy sprinkles. It adds sparkle to cake decorations. Also, be sure to check out party-supply or cake-decorating stores for fun birthday candles. Lots of new and unique shapes are available.

candy-sprinkled cupcakes

PREP TIME: 20 minutes *START TO FINISH:* 1 hour 30 minutes [24 CUPCAKES]

1 box Betty Crocker® SuperMoist® yellow or white cake mix

Water, vegetable oil and eggs or egg whites called for on cake mix box

1 container (12 oz) Betty Crocker® Whipped fluffy white frosting

Pastel candy sprinkles

1 Heat oven to 350°F (325°F for dark or nonstick pans). Place paper baking cup in each of 24 regular-size muffin cups. Make and bake cake mix as directed on box for 24 cupcakes. Cool in pans 10 minutes; remove from pans to cooling rack.

2 Frost cupcakes with frosting.

3 To decorate, roll edge of each cupcake in candy sprinkles. Store loosely covered.

1 CUPCAKE (CAKE AND FROSTING ONLY): Calories 180; Total Fat 9g (Saturated Fat 2g; Trans Fat 1g); Cholesterol 25mg; Sodium 150mg; Total Carbohydrate 24g (Dietary Fiber 0g); Protein 1g EXCHANGES: 1½ Other Carbohydrate; 2 Fat CARBOHYDRATE CHOICES: 1½

strawberry and cream cupcakes

PREP TIME: 30 minutes *START TO FINISH:* 1 hour 30 minutes [24 CUPCAKES]

1 box Betty Crocker® SuperMoist® white cake mix

1¼ cups strawberry-flavored soda pop

Vegetable oil and egg whites called for on cake mix box

Red food color

1 container (1 lb) Betty Crocker® Rich & Creamy cream cheese frosting

½ cup Betty Crocker® white candy sprinkles

Fresh strawberries, if desired

1 Heat oven to 350°F (325°F for dark or nonstick pans). Make, bake and cool cake mix as directed on box for 24 cupcakes, substituting soda pop for the water.

2 Stir 1 or 2 drops food color into frosting. Frost cupcakes.

3 In small resealable food-storage plastic bag, place sprinkles and 1 drop food color; seal bag. Gently shake and massage sprinkles until mixture is various shades of pink; sprinkle around edges of frosted cupcakes. Garnish with fresh strawberries. Store loosely covered in refrigerator.

1 CUPCAKE: Calories 200; Total Fat 8g (Saturated Fat 2½g; Trans Fat 1g); Cholesterol 0mg; Sodium 180mg; Total Carbohydrate 32g (Dietary Fiber 0g); Protein 1g EXCHANGES: ½ Starch; 1½ Other Carbohydrate; 1½ Fat CARBOHYDRATE CHOICES: 2

toasted almond cupcakes with caramel frosting

PREP TIME: 25 minutes *START TO FINISH:* 2 hours 5 minutes [24 CUPCAKES]

Cupcakes

1½ cups sliced almonds

1 box Betty Crocker® SuperMoist® white cake mix

Water, vegetable oil and whole eggs called for on cake mix box

1 teaspoon almond extract

Caramel Frosting

½ cup butter or margarine

1 cup packed brown sugar

¼ cup milk

2 cups powdered sugar

1 Heat oven to 350°F (325°F for dark or nonstick pans). Place paper baking cup in each of 24 regular-size muffin cups. In shallow baking pan, toast almonds 6 to 10 minutes, stirring occasionally, until golden brown. Cool 15 minutes. Reserve 1 cup almonds for garnish. In food processor, grind remaining almonds until finely ground.

2 In large bowl, beat cake mix, water, oil, whole eggs and almond extract with electric mixer on low speed 30 seconds, then on medium speed 2 minutes, scraping bowl occasionally. Fold in ground almonds. Divide batter evenly among muffin cups.

3 Bake and cool as directed on box for cupcakes.

4 In 2-quart saucepan, melt butter over medium heat. Stir in brown sugar. Heat to boiling, stirring constantly. Reduce heat to low; boil and stir 2 minutes. Stir in milk. Heat to boiling. Remove from heat. Cool to lukewarm, about 30 minutes.

5 Gradually stir powdered sugar into brown sugar mixture. Place saucepan of frosting in bowl of cold water. Beat with spoon until smooth and spreadable. If frosting becomes too stiff, stir in additional milk, 1 teaspoon at a time. Frost a few cupcakes at a time with 1 tablespoon frosting each; press reserved almonds lightly into frosting. Store loosely covered.

1 CUPCAKE: Calories 260; Total Fat 11g (Saturated Fat 4g; Trans Fat 0g); Cholesterol 35mg; Sodium 170mg; Total Carbohydrate 36g (Dietary Fiber 1g); Protein 3g
EXCHANGES: 1 Starch; 1½ Other Carbohydrate; 2 Fat CARBOHYDRATE CHOICES: 2½

sweet note Try this recipe with other favorite nuts, like hazelnuts or pecans, instead of the almonds. For the richest and most intense caramel flavor, use real butter and dark brown sugar.

Six
cupcakes

"you're a star!" cupcakes

PREP TIME: 40 minutes *START TO FINISH:* 1 hour 40 minutes [24 CUPCAKES]

Cupcakes

1 box Betty Crocker® SuperMoist® white cake mix

Water, vegetable oil and egg whites called for on cake mix box

½ teaspoon almond extract

Frosting and Decorations

1 container (1 lb) Betty Crocker® Rich & Creamy vanilla frosting

Blue paste food color

¼ cup blue candy sprinkles

2 oz vanilla-flavored candy coating (almond bark), chopped

1 Heat oven to 350°F (325°F for dark or nonstick pans). Make, bake and cool cake mix as directed on box for 24 cupcakes, adding almond extract with the water.

2 Meanwhile, on sheet of paper, draw five-pointed star (about 2 inches wide) to use as pattern.

3 In small bowl, place half of frosting. Dip toothpick into paste food color; stir food color into frosting in bowl until color is evenly distributed and desired shade. Frost 12 cupcakes with blue frosting. Frost remaining 12 cupcakes with white frosting; sprinkle blue candy sprinkles over white cupcakes.

4 In small microwavable bowl, place candy coating. Microwave uncovered on High 30 seconds; stir until melted and smooth. If necessary, microwave 10 seconds longer. Place in heavy-duty food-storage plastic bag; seal bag and cut tiny hole in one bottom corner of bag.

5 Place paper star pattern under large sheet of waxed paper. Squeezing bag of candy coating, trace the star on waxed paper; move pattern under waxed paper to make 12 stars. Let stars cool until set, about 5 minutes. Remove stars from waxed paper; insert 1 star in each of 12 cupcakes. Store loosely covered.

1 CUPCAKE: Calories 200; Total Fat 8g (Saturated Fat 2½g; Trans Fat 1g); Cholesterol 0mg; Sodium 180mg; Total Carbohydrate 31g (Dietary Fiber 0g); Protein 1g EXCHANGES: ½ Starch; 1½ Other Carbohydrate; 1½ Fat CARBOHYDRATE CHOICES: 2

sweet note Wow friends and family with beautiful cupcakes that get a jump start from cake mix and ready-to-spread frosting.

black and white rum cakes

PREP TIME: 55 minutes *START TO FINISH:* 2 hours [24 CUPCAKES]

Cupcakes

- 1 box Betty Crocker® SuperMoist® white cake mix
- 1¼ cups water
- ⅓ cup vegetable oil
- 3 eggs
- 3 oz unsweetened baking chocolate, melted, cooled
- 2 teaspoons rum extract

Rum Frosting

- 2 egg whites
- ½ cup sugar
- ¼ cup light corn syrup
- 2 tablespoons water
- 2 teaspoons rum extract
- Betty Crocker® chocolate sprinkles, if desired

1 Heat oven to 375°F. Place paper baking cup in each of 24 regular-size muffin cups. In large bowl, beat cake mix, 1¼ cups water, the oil and 3 eggs with electric mixer on low speed 30 seconds. Beat on medium speed 2 minutes, scraping bowl occasionally.

2 In small bowl, place 2 cups of the batter; stir in chocolate. Into remaining batter, stir 2 teaspoons rum extract. Into bottom of each muffin cup, spoon about 1½ tablespoons chocolate batter. Top each with about 1½ tablespoons rum batter.

3 Bake 15 to 20 minutes or until toothpick inserted in center comes out clean. Cool 10 minutes; remove from pan to cooling rack. Cool completely, about 30 minutes.

4 In medium bowl, beat 2 egg whites with electric mixer on high speed just until stiff peaks form; set aside.

5 In 1-quart saucepan, stir sugar, corn syrup and 2 tablespoons water until well mixed. Cover and heat to rolling boil over medium heat. Uncover and boil 4 to 8 minutes, without stirring, to 242°F on candy thermometer or until small amount of mixture dropped into cup of very cold water forms a firm ball that holds its shape until pressed. For an accurate temperature reading, tilt the saucepan slightly so mixture is deep enough for thermometer.

6 Pour hot syrup very slowly in thin stream into egg whites, beating constantly on medium speed. Add 2 teaspoons rum extract. Beat on high speed about 10 minutes or until stiff peaks form. Immediately spread frosting on cupcakes. Sprinkle with chocolate sprinkles. Store in refrigerator.

1 CUPCAKE: Calories 180; Total Fat 8g (Saturated Fat 2½g; Trans Fat ½g); Cholesterol 25mg; Sodium 160mg; Total Carbohydrate 25g (Dietary Fiber 0g); Protein 3g
EXCHANGES: 1 Starch; ½ Other Carbohydrate; 1½ Fat CARBOHYDRATE CHOICES: 1½

sweet note Punch up these rum-flavored treats with a scoop of rum-raisin ice cream.

mini candy bar cupcakes

PREP TIME: 20 minutes *START TO FINISH:* 1 hour 10 minutes [70 MINI CUPCAKES]

5 bars (2.1 oz each) chocolate-covered crispy peanut-buttery candy

1 box Betty Crocker® SuperMoist® white cake mix

Water, vegetable oil and egg whites called for on cake mix box

1 container (12 oz) Betty Crocker® Whipped milk chocolate frosting

1 Heat oven to 350°F (325°F for dark or nonstick pans). Place mini paper baking cup in each of 70 mini muffin cups. Finely chop enough candy to equal ¾ cup (about 2 bars).

2 In large bowl, beat cake mix, water, oil and egg whites with electric mixer on low speed 30 seconds, then on medium speed 2 minutes, scraping bowl occasionally. On low speed, beat in chopped candy just until blended. Divide batter evenly among muffin cups, filling each about two-thirds full. Refrigerate any remaining cake batter until ready to use.

3 Bake 12 to 16 minutes or until toothpick inserted in center comes out clean. Cool 5 minutes; remove from pan to cooling rack. Cool completely, about 30 minutes.

4 Frost cupcakes with frosting. Coarsely chop remaining candy. Place candy pieces on frosting, pressing down slightly. Store loosely covered.

1 MINI CUPCAKE: Calories 80; Total Fat 3½g (Saturated Fat 1½g; Trans Fat 0g); Cholesterol 0mg; Sodium 75mg; Total Carbohydrate 10g (Dietary Fiber 0g); Protein 1g EXCHANGES: ½ Starch; ½ Other Carbohydrate; ½ Fat CARBOHYDRATE CHOICES: ½

sweet note Bake these cupcakes, but don't frost them. Place in an airtight container and freeze. A few hours before serving, remove them from the freezer, frost and decorate.

lemon cupcakes with strawberry frosting

PREP TIME: 40 minutes *START TO FINISH:* 1 hour 45 minutes [24 CUPCAKES]

Cupcakes

1 box Betty Crocker® SuperMoist® white cake mix

Water, vegetable oil and egg whites called for on cake mix box

3 tablespoons grated lemon peel

Frosting

4 to 6 medium strawberries (about 4 oz), hulled

1 container (12 oz) Betty Crocker® Whipped fluffy white frosting

Garnish, if desired

12 strawberries, sliced

Lemon peel curls

1 Heat oven to 350°F (325°F for dark or nonstick pans). Make, bake and cool cake mix as directed on box for 24 cupcakes, adding grated lemon peel with the water.

2 Place 4 oz strawberries in blender. Cover; pulse 20 seconds to puree strawberries. Pour ¼ cup of the strawberry puree into medium bowl. Stir in fluffy white frosting until well mixed.

3 Generously frost cupcakes. Garnish with sliced strawberries and lemon peel curls. Store loosely covered in refrigerator.

1 CUPCAKE: Calories 80; Total Fat 3½g (Saturated Fat 1½g; Trans Fat 1g); Cholesterol 0mg; Sodium 75mg; Total Carbohydrate 10g (Dietary Fiber 0g); Protein 1g EXCHANGES: ½ Starch; ½ Other Carbohydrate; ½ Fat CARBOHYDRATE CHOICES: ½

sweet note

An easy way to hull strawberries is to push one end of a plastic drinking straw into the point of the berry and push it through to pop off the green cap.

spring polka dot cupcakes

PREP TIME: 40 minutes *START TO FINISH:* 1 hour 45 minutes [24 CUPCAKES]

Cupcakes

1 box Betty Crocker® SuperMoist® white cake mix

Water, vegetable oil and egg whites called for on cake mix box

1 box (4-serving size) orange-flavored gelatin

Bright Buttercream Frosting

3 cups powdered sugar

⅓ cup butter or margarine, softened

1 teaspoon vanilla

2 to 3 tablespoons milk

Yellow, red and blue food colors

⅓ cup white baking chips

1 Heat oven to 350°F (325°F for dark or nonstick pans). Place paper baking cup in each of 24 regular-size muffin cups.

2 Make cake batter as directed on cake mix box, adding gelatin with the water. Divide batter evenly among muffin cups, filling each about two-thirds full.

3 Bake 22 to 27 minutes or until toothpick inserted in center comes out clean. Cool 10 minutes; remove from pan to cooling rack. Cool completely, about 30 minutes.

4 Meanwhile, in medium bowl, beat powdered sugar and butter with spoon or with electric mixer on low speed until well blended. Beat in vanilla and 2 tablespoons of the milk. Gradually beat in just enough of the remaining milk to make frosting smooth and spreadable. Divide frosting among 4 small bowls. Stir 6 drops yellow food color into frosting in one bowl. Stir 4 drops red food color into frosting in second bowl. Stir 6 to 8 drops blue food color into frosting in third bowl. Stir 4 drops yellow and 2 drops red food color into frosting in fourth bowl.

5 Frost 6 cupcakes with each color of frosting. Poke 4 or 5 white vanilla baking chips, flat side up, into frosting on each cupcake to look like polka dots. Store loosely covered.

1 CUPCAKE: Calories 220; Total Fat 7g (Saturated Fat 3½g; Trans Fat 0g); Cholesterol 5mg; Sodium 180mg; Total Carbohydrate 36g (Dietary Fiber 0g); Protein 2g EXCHANGES: ½ Starch; 2 Other Carbohydrate; 1½ Fat CARBOHYDRATE CHOICES: 2½

sweet note Have fun making other colors and flavors of cupcakes by using lemon, lime, strawberry, raspberry or watermelon gelatin.

wedding cupcakes

PREP TIME: 1 hour *START TO FINISH:* 1 hour 25 minutes [24 CUPCAKES]

Cupcakes

White paper baking cups

1 box Betty Crocker® SuperMoist® white cake mix

Water, vegetable oil and egg whites called for on cake mix box

2 containers (1 lb each) Betty Crocker® Rich & Creamy creamy white frosting

Decorating Options

White chocolate curls

Pink rose petals

Handmade paper, cut into 8 × 1¼-inch strips

Decorator sugar crystals or edible glitter

Ribbon

1 Heat oven to 350°F (325°F for dark or nonstick pans). Place white paper baking cup in each of 24 regular-size muffin cups. Make, bake and cool cake mix as directed on box for 24 cupcakes.

2 Frost cupcakes with frosting. Choose from these decorating options: • Top cupcakes with white chocolate curls (see below) or rose petals. • Wrap handmade paper around each cupcake; attach permanent double-stick tape. • Sprinkle decorator sugar crystals or edible glitter over frosting. • Wrap ribbon around each cupcake and tie in a bow. Store loosely covered.

White chocolate curls: Place a bar of room-temperature white chocolate on waxed paper. Make curls by pulling a vegetable peeler toward you in long, thin strokes while pressing firmly against the chocolate. (If curls crumble or stay too straight, chocolate may be too cold; placing the heel of your hand on the chocolate will warm it enough to get good curls.) Transfer each curl carefully with a toothpick directly onto a frosted cupcake or to a waxed paper–lined cookie sheet.

1 CUPCAKE: Calories 370; Total Fat 20g (Saturated Fat 10g; Trans Fat ½g); Cholesterol 95mg; Sodium 300mg; Total Carbohydrate 45g (Dietary Fiber 0g); Protein 2g EXCHANGES: ½ Starch; 2½ Other Carbohydrate; 4 Fat CARBOHYDRATE CHOICES: 3

sweet note

Look for edible flowers and/or rose petals in the produce department of the grocery store. Edible flowers have not been treated with chemicals, so they're safe to eat.

white-on-white wedding cupcakes

PREP TIME: 30 minutes *START TO FINISH:* 1 hour 45 minutes [24 CUPCAKES]

- 1 box Betty Crocker® SuperMoist® natural vanilla or white cake mix
- Water, vegetable oil and eggs called for on cake mix box
- 1 package (4 oz) white chocolate baking bar
- 1 container (12 oz) Betty Crocker® Whipped fluffy white frosting
- 1 tablespoon powdered sugar

1 Heat oven to 350°F (325°F for dark or nonstick pans). Make, bake and cool cake mix as directed on box for 24 cupcakes, using water, oil and eggs.

2 To make chocolate curls, pull a swivel-bladed vegetable peeler down the edge of white chocolate bar, using long, thin strokes. Frost cupcakes with frosting. Sprinkle each with about 2 teaspoons white chocolate curls, using toothpick to lift curls.

3 Lightly sprinkle powdered sugar through small strainer over cupcakes. Store loosely covered.

1 CUPCAKE: Calories 200; Total Fat 9g (Saturated Fat 3g; Trans Fat 1g); Cholesterol 25mg; Sodium 160mg; Total Carbohydrate 27g (Dietary Fiber 0g); Protein 2g EXCHANGES: ½ Starch; 1½ Other Carbohydrate; 1½ Fat CARBOHYDRATE CHOICES: 2

sweet note Try a practice run well in advance of the wedding; then you'll know exactly what to expect. You can make the cupcakes up to 2 weeks ahead of time. Wrap unfrosted cupcakes well with plastic wrap; freeze. Six hours before frosting, remove from the freezer and loosely cover. Frost, loosely cover and serve within 24 hours.

pink champagne cupcakes

PREP TIME: 25 minutes *START TO FINISH:* 1 hour 15 minutes [24 CUPCAKES]

Champagne Cupcakes

1 box Betty Crocker® SuperMoist® white cake mix

1¼ cups champagne

⅓ cup vegetable oil

3 egg whites

4 to 5 drops red food color

Champagne Frosting

½ cup butter or margarine, softened

4 cups powdered sugar

¼ cup champagne

1 teaspoon vanilla

4 to 5 drops red food color

Garnish

Pink decorator sugar crystals

Edible pink pearls

1 Heat oven to 350°F (325°F for dark or nonstick pans). Place paper baking cup in each of 24 regular-size muffin cups.

2 In large bowl, mix dry cake mix and 1¼ cups champagne. Add oil, egg whites and food color. Beat with electric mixer on medium speed 2 minutes. Divide batter evenly among muffin cups.

3 Bake 17 to 22 minutes or until toothpick inserted in center comes out clean. Cool 10 minutes; remove from pan to cooling rack. Cool completely, about 30 minutes.

4 In medium bowl, beat frosting ingredients with electric mixer on medium speed until smooth. Frost cupcakes. Sprinkle with garnishes. Store loosely covered.

1 CUPCAKE (CAKE AND FROSTING ONLY): Calories 250; Total Fat 8g (Saturated Fat 3½g; Trans Fat 0g); Cholesterol 10mg; Sodium 170mg; Total Carbohydrate 40g (Dietary Fiber 0g); Protein 1g EXCHANGES: 3 Other Carbohydrate; 1½ Fat CARBOHYDRATE CHOICES: 2½

sweet note Champagne is a sparkling wine, and while many expensive champagnes are available, this is one time you might choose less expensive champagne. Have the champagne at room temperature when preparing the cupcakes. For pink decorator sugar crystals, edible pink pearls and decorative cupcake liners, check out www.fancyflours.com.

engagement ring mini cupcakes

PREP TIME: 20 minutes *START TO FINISH:* 1 hour [58 MINI CUPCAKES]

1 box Betty Crocker® SuperMoist® white cake mix

Water, vegetable oil and egg whites called for on cake mix box

2 cups powdered sugar

3 to 4 tablespoons milk

Assorted colored rock candy

1 Heat oven to 350°F (325°F for dark or nonstick pans). Place mini paper baking cup in each of 58 mini muffin cups.

2 Make cake batter as directed on box. Divide batter evenly among muffin cups, filling each about two-thirds full. If necessary, refrigerate any remaining batter until ready to use.

3 Bake 11 to 14 minutes or until toothpick inserted in center comes out clean. Cool 5 minutes; remove from pan to cooling rack. Cool completely, about 30 minutes.

4 In small bowl, stir powdered sugar and 3 tablespoons milk until smooth. Add additional milk 1 teaspoon at a time, until desired spreading consistency. Frost cupcakes. Top with rock candy pieces. Store loosely covered.

1 MINI CUPCAKE: Calories 70; Total Fat 1½g (Saturated Fat 0g; Trans Fat 0g); Cholesterol 0mg; Sodium 60mg; Total Carbohydrate 13g (Dietary Fiber 0g); Protein 0g EXCHANGES: ½ Starch; ½ Other Carbohydrate CARBOHYDRATE CHOICES: 1

sweet note Colorful rock candy embellishes these bite-size treats with a nod to Princess Kate's sapphire engagement ring.

chocolate cupcakes with penuche filling

PREP TIME: 40 minutes *START TO FINISH:* 2 hours 40 minutes [24 CUPCAKES]

Cupcakes

1 box Betty Crocker® SuperMoist® chocolate fudge cake mix

Water, oil and eggs called for on cake mix box

1 teaspoon vanilla

Filling and Garnish

1 cup butter or margarine

2 cups packed brown sugar

½ cup milk

4 cups powdered sugar

1 oz grated semisweet baking chocolate, if desired

sweet note A layer of penuche creates frosted chocolate cupcakes reminiscent of a delicious mini layered cake.

1 Heat oven to 350°F (325°F for dark or nonstick pans). Place paper baking cup in each of 24 regular-size muffin cups. Make, bake and cool cupcakes as directed on box for 24 cupcakes—except add vanilla to batter.

2 Meanwhile, in 2-quart saucepan, melt butter over medium heat. Stir in brown sugar. Heat to boiling, stirring constantly; reduce heat to low. Boil and stir 2 minutes. Stir in milk. Heat to boiling; remove from heat. Pour mixture into medium bowl; refrigerate 1 hour or until lukewarm, about 90°F.

3 Beat powdered sugar into cooled brown sugar mixture with electric mixer on low speed until smooth. If filling becomes too stiff, stir in additional milk, 1 teaspoon at a time. If filling is too soft, cover; return to refrigerator 15 minutes to firm up.

4 Remove paper baking cups from cupcakes. Using serrated knife, cut each cupcake in half horizontally, being careful not to break either half. Place heaping 1 tablespoon filling on each cupcake base. Replace rounded cupcake tops. Pipe or spoon rounded 1 tablespoon frosting onto cupcake tops. Garnish with grated chocolate. Store in airtight container at room temperature.

1 CUPCAKE: Calories 340; Total Fat 14g (Saturated Fat 6g; Trans Fat 0g); Cholesterol 45mg; Sodium 230mg; Total Carbohydrate 53g (Dietary Fiber 0g); Protein 2g EXCHANGES: 1 Starch; 2½ Other Carbohydrate; 2½ Fat CARBOHYDRATE CHOICES: 3½

the scoop on penuche filling

The word *penuche* comes from a Mexican word meaning "raw sugar" or "brown sugar." It is used to describe a fudgelike candy made from brown sugar, butter, milk or cream and vanilla. It's important to refrigerate the brown sugar mixture to lukewarm (90°F). This will give you the proper consistency for the penuche when powdered sugar is beaten in.

truffle lover's cupcakes

PREP TIME: 35 minutes *START TO FINISH:* 1 hour 50 minutes [24 CUPCAKES]

Cupcakes

¾ cup miniature semisweet chocolate chips

1 box Betty Crocker® SuperMoist® chocolate fudge cake mix

1 cup water

½ cup vegetable oil

3 eggs

3 tablespoons hazelnut or orange-flavored liqueur

Ganache

⅓ cup whipping cream

½ cup miniature semisweet chocolate chips

Garnish

Miniature semisweet chocolate chips

Grated orange peel

Ground hazelnuts

1 Heat oven to 350°F (325°F for dark or nonstick pans). Place paper baking cup in each of 24 regular-size muffin cups. In small bowl, toss chocolate chips with 1 tablespoon of the cake mix. In large bowl, beat remaining cake mix, the water, oil and eggs with electric mixer on low speed 30 seconds, then on medium speed 2 minutes, scraping bowl occasionally. Stir in coated chocolate chips. Divide batter evenly among muffin cups.

2 Bake as directed on box for 24 cupcakes. Cool 10 minutes; remove from pan to cooling rack. Immediately prick holes in tops of cupcakes with toothpick. Brush about ½ teaspoon liqueur over each cupcake. Cool completely, about 30 minutes.

3 In heavy 1-quart saucepan, heat whipping cream over medium-high heat until hot but not boiling; remove from heat. Stir in ½ cup chocolate chips until melted. Let stand 10 minutes. Dip tops of cupcakes in ganache. Top with miniature chocolate chips, grated orange peel or ground hazelnuts, if desired. Store loosely covered.

1 CUPCAKE: Calories 180; Total Fat 10g (Saturated Fat 3½g; Trans Fat 0g); Cholesterol 30mg; Sodium 170mg; Total Carbohydrate 20g (Dietary Fiber 1g); Protein 2g
EXCHANGES: ½ Starch; 1 Other Carbohydrate; 2 Fat CARBOHYDRATE CHOICES: 1

sweet note To toast hazelnuts, bake uncovered in ungreased shallow pan in a 350°F oven 6 to 10 minutes, stirring occasionally, until light brown. Rub the nuts with a towel to remove skins. Place nuts in food processor or blender; cover and process until ground.

espresso cupcakes

PREP TIME: 40 minutes *START TO FINISH:* 1 hour 45 minutes [24 CUPCAKES]

Cupcakes

1 box Betty Crocker® SuperMoist® chocolate fudge cake mix

Water, vegetable oil and eggs called for on cake mix box

1 tablespoon instant espresso coffee powder

Filling

1 container (8 oz) mascarpone cheese

2 teaspoons milk

2 teaspoons instant espresso coffee powder

1 cup powdered sugar

Frosting and Garnish

1 teaspoon instant espresso coffee powder

1 container (12 oz) Betty Crocker® Whipped milk chocolate frosting

Chocolate-covered espresso beans, if desired

1 Heat oven to 350°F (325°F for dark or nonstick pans). Place paper baking cup in each of 24 regular-size muffin cups.

2 Make batter as directed on box; gently stir in 1 tablespoon espresso powder just until blended. Divide batter evenly among muffin cups. Bake and cool as directed on box for cupcakes.

3 In medium bowl, beat mascarpone cheese, milk, 2 teaspoons espresso powder and the powdered sugar with electric mixer on medium speed until smooth. Spoon mixture into decorating bag fitted with ¼-inch (#9) writing tip.

4 To fill each cupcake, insert tip of bag into center of cooled cupcake; gently squeeze bag until cupcake expands slightly but does not burst (each cupcake should be filled with about 1 tablespoon filling).

5 Stir 1 teaspoon espresso powder into the frosting. Spoon frosting mixture into decorating bag fitted with ¾-inch (#824) star tip. Pipe over tops of cupcakes. Garnish with espresso beans. Store covered in refrigerator.

1 CUPCAKE: Calories 210; Total Fat 10g (Saturated Fat 3½g; Trans Fat ½g); Cholesterol 35mg; Sodium 200mg; Total Carbohydrate 28g (Dietary Fiber 0g); Protein 1g
EXCHANGES: ½ Starch; 1½ Other Carbohydrate; 2 Fat CARBOHYDRATE CHOICES: 2

sweet note Instant coffee granules can be substituted for the instant espresso coffee powder. The flavor will probably not be as intense.

midnight molten brownie cupcakes

PREP TIME: 10 minutes *START TO FINISH:* 30 minutes [12 CUPCAKES]

- ½ cup semisweet chocolate chips
- ½ cup butter or margarine
- 3 eggs
- 3 egg yolks
- 1 box (1 lb 2.4 oz) Betty Crocker® Original Supreme Premium brownie mix
- About ½ cup Betty Crocker® stars, confetti or critters decors, if desired

sweet note

These brownies are "fork food." Place them on the individual plates right side up or upside down before drizzling with chocolate.

1 Heat oven to 400°F. Generously grease 12 muffin cups (2¾ × 1¼ inches). In medium microwavable bowl, microwave chocolate chips and butter uncovered on High 45 to 60 seconds or until melted and mixture can be stirred smooth.

2 In large bowl, beat eggs and egg yolks with wire whisk or electric mixer until foamy. Reserve chocolate syrup pouch from brownie mix. Gradually beat dry brownie mix into egg mixture until well blended. Gently stir in melted chocolate mixture. Fill muffin cups half full of brownie mixture; top each with ½ teaspoon decors. Top with remaining brownie mixture.

3 Bake 10 to 12 minutes or until edges are set and internal temperature is at least 160°F. Do not overbake. Centers will be soft. Cool 2 minutes.

4 Loosen each cupcake with knife; turn upside down onto heatproof tray or cookie sheet. To serve, place cupcake on plate; drizzle with reserved chocolate syrup and top with additional decors.

1 CUPCAKE: Calories 310; Total Fat 14g (Saturated Fat 8g; Trans Fat 0g); Cholesterol 125mg; Sodium 210mg; Total Carbohydrate 41g (Dietary Fiber 1g); Protein 4g
EXCHANGES: 1 Starch; 2 Other Carbohydrate; 2½ Fat CARBOHYDRATE CHOICES: 3

heart brownie cupcakes

PREP TIME: 30 minutes *START TO FINISH:* 1 hour 30 minutes [24 CUPCAKES]

1 box Betty Crocker® fudge brownie mix

Water, vegetable oil and eggs called for on brownie mix box (for fudge- or cakelike brownies)

1 to 2 tablespoons powdered sugar

1 Heat oven to 350°F. Place paper baking cup in each of 24 regular-size muffin cups. Make brownie batter as directed. Fill each baking cup with about 2 level measuring tablespoonfuls of batter.

2 Bake 18 to 22 minutes or until toothpick inserted in center comes out almost clean. Do not overbake. Cool in pan 20 minutes. Carefully remove paper baking cups from muffins; cool upside down about 15 minutes or until completely cool.

3 Cut small heart out of paper. Place on bottom of cupcake. Sprinkle with powdered sugar. Carefully remove heart. Repeat with remaining cupcakes.

1 CUPCAKE: Calories 110; Total Fat 4g (Saturated Fat 1g; Trans Fat 0g); Cholesterol 20mg; Sodium 80mg; Total Carbohydrate 18g (Dietary Fiber 0g); Protein 1g EXCHANGES: 1 Other Carbohydrate; 1 Fat CARBOHYDRATE CHOICES: 1

sweet note Wow! Brownie mix baked in muffin cups and sprinkled with powdered sugar. You can do it!

key lime cupcakes

PREP TIME: 30 minutes *START TO FINISH:* 1 hour 35 minutes [24 CUPCAKES]

Cupcakes

1 box Betty Crocker® SuperMoist® lemon cake mix

1 box (4-serving size) lime-flavored gelatin

¾ cup water

⅓ cup Key lime juice

⅓ cup vegetable oil

3 eggs

2 or 3 drops green food color, if desired

Glaze

1 cup powdered sugar

2 to 2½ tablespoons Key lime juice

Frosting

1 package (8 oz) cream cheese, softened

¼ cup butter or margarine, softened

1 teaspoon vanilla

3½ cups powdered sugar

Grated lime peel, if desired

1 Heat oven to 350°F (325°F for dark or nonstick pans). Place paper baking cup in each of 24 regular-size muffin cups. In large bowl, beat cupcake ingredients with electric mixer on low speed 30 seconds, then on medium speed 2 minutes, scraping bowl occasionally. Divide batter evenly among muffin cups, filling each about two-thirds full.

2 Bake 19 to 24 minutes or until toothpick inserted in center comes out clean. Cool in pan 10 minutes. Remove from pan to cooling rack. With toothpick or wooden skewer, pierce tops of cupcakes in several places.

3 In small bowl, mix 1 cup powdered sugar and enough of the 2 to 2½ tablespoons lime juice until glaze is smooth and thin enough to drizzle. Drizzle and spread glaze over cupcakes. Cool completely, about 30 minutes.

4 In large bowl, beat cream cheese and butter on medium speed until light and fluffy. On low speed, beat in vanilla and 3½ cups powdered sugar until mixed; beat on medium speed until fluffy. Frost cupcakes, mounding and swirling frosting in center. Garnish with lime peel. Store covered in refrigerator.

1 CUPCAKE: Calories 260; Total Fat 9g (Saturated Fat 4g; Trans Fat 0g); Cholesterol 40mg; Sodium 200mg; Total Carbohydrate 41g (Dietary Fiber 0g); Protein 2g EXCHANGES: 1½ Starch; 1 Other Carbohydrate; 1½ Fat CARBOHYDRATE CHOICES: 3

sweet note Garnish each cupcake with a small piece of jellied lime candy slice instead of the lime peel.

lemon-blueberry cupcakes

PREP TIME: 25 minutes *START TO FINISH:* 1 hour 55 minutes [24 CUPCAKES]

Cupcakes

1 box Betty Crocker® SuperMoist® lemon cake mix

1½ cups fresh blueberries

¾ cup water

⅓ cup vegetable oil

1 tablespoon grated lemon peel

2 eggs

1 package (3 oz) cream cheese, softened

Frosting and Garnish

2½ cups powdered sugar

¾ cup unsalted butter, softened

1 teaspoon grated lemon peel

½ teaspoon kosher (coarse) salt

1¼ teaspoons vanilla

1 tablespoon milk

1 cup fresh blueberries

Lemon peel, if desired

Fresh mint leaves, if desired

1 Heat oven to 375°F (350°F for dark or nonstick pans). Place paper baking cup in each of 24 regular-size muffin cups.

2 In small bowl, gently toss 2 tablespoons of the dry cake mix with 1½ cups blueberries to coat; set aside.

3 In large bowl, beat remaining cake mix, water, oil, lemon peel, eggs and cream cheese with electric mixer on low speed 30 seconds. Beat on medium speed 2 minutes, scraping bowl occasionally. Fold blueberry mixture into batter. Divide batter evenly among muffin cups.

4 Bake 18 to 22 minutes or until tops are light golden brown. Cool 5 minutes; remove from pan to cooling rack. Cool completely, about 1 hour.

5 In medium bowl, beat powdered sugar, butter, 1 teaspoon lemon peel, the salt, vanilla and 1 tablespoon milk on high speed about 4 minutes or until smooth and well blended, adding more milk by teaspoonfuls if needed. Frost cupcakes with frosting. Garnish with 1 cup blueberries, the lemon peel and mint leaves. Store in airtight container at room temperature.

1 CUPCAKE: Calories 230; Total Fat 11g (Saturated Fat 5g; Trans Fat 0g); Cholesterol 35mg; Sodium 180mg; Total Carbohydrate 30g (Dietary Fiber 0g); Protein 1g EXCHANGES: ½ Starch; 1½ Other Carbohydrate; 2 Fat CARBOHYDRATE CHOICES: 2

sweet note Unsalted butter tastes a little sweeter than the more common salted butter. We added the coarse salt for small bursts of saltiness to complement the sweetness of the other ingredients and to bring out the lemon flavor. If you don't have unsalted butter, use salted butter and omit the kosher salt.

chapter three

cookies, brownies & bars

Perfect Cookies, Brownies and Bars Every Time

The right pan, oven temperature and pan treatment are a few brownie baking basics good to know. Who knew there were tricks of the trade for something this easy to bake!

Mix and bake easy cookies, brownies and bars while making dinner for warm-from-the-oven weeknight treats. Dress them up for favorite pack-and-go potluck treats or sweets to share. Whatever you choose, discover these tips and techniques for cookies and brownies baked just right.

Cookie Success Tips

- To make drop cookies uniform in size and shape, use a spring-handled cookie scoop. Look for scoops at the grocery store or kitchen specialty shops. Select the size of the scoop based on how large or small you like your cookies.
- Have three or four cookie sheets on hand, so as you bake one sheet, you can get another one ready to go.
- Use cookie sheets that are at least 2 inches narrower and shorter than the inside dimensions of your oven, so heat circulates around them.
- Shiny aluminum cookie sheets (both smooth and textured) give best results for evenly baked and browned cookies.
- It's best to bake only one cookie sheet at a time, using the middle oven rack. If you want to bake two sheets at once, put one on the oven rack in the upper third of the oven and one on the oven rack in the lower third. Switch their positions halfway through the baking time.
- Use shortening or cooking spray to grease cookie sheets and baking pans, but only when the recipe specifies greasing. Butter, margarine and vegetable oil are not recommended—they can burn and stick to metal surfaces, making cleanup very difficult.
- Check cookies at the minimum bake time. Even 1 minute can make a difference with cookies, especially those high in sugar and fat. The longer cookies bake, the more brown, crisp or hard they become.
- Always put cookie dough on completely cooled cookie sheets. Cookies spread too much if put on a hot, or even a warm, cookie sheet. Cool cookie sheets quickly by popping them in the refrigerator or freezer or by running cold water over them (dry completely and grease again if needed).

Brownie and Bar Success Tips

- Use the pan size and baking time called for in the bar or brownie recipe for best results.
- Shiny aluminum baking pans are best for baking bars, because they reflect heat and prevent bars from overbrowning and becoming hard.
- Use shortening or cooking spray to grease baking pans, but only when the recipe says it's needed. Butter, margarine and vegetable oil aren't recommended—they can burn and stick to metal surfaces, making cleanup difficult.
- Line your pan with heavy-duty foil when making several batches of bars or brownies. Grease only the bottom of the foil. Brownies are easy to lift from the pan and cut on the foil when cool. And your pan is ready to line and bake the next batch!

- Spread or press dough for bars and brownies evenly to the sides of the pan. For dough that is sticky, try one of these methods:
    - Wet your hands or spray them with cooking spray.
    - Place a piece of plastic wrap directly on top of the dough and smooth out the top of the dough with your hands.
    - Place your hands in plastic bags.
- Be sure to follow your recipe's "doneness test." When a toothpick inserted 2 inches from the side of the pan comes out clean or almost clean, brownies are ready.
- For easier cutting, cool brownies and bars completely and use a plastic knife.

How to Store Cookies and Bars

- Store crisp cookies at room temperature in a loosely covered container.
- Store chewy and soft cookies at room temperature in resealable food-storage plastic bags or tightly covered containers. Do not store crisp cookies and soft cookies together, or crisp cookies will become soft.
- Let frosted or decorated cookies set or harden before storing; store them between layers of waxed paper, plastic wrap or foil.
- Store different flavors of cookies in separate containers, or they will pick up the flavors of the other cookies.
- Most bars can be stored tightly covered, but check the recipe to be sure; some may need to be loosely covered and others need to be refrigerated.
- To freeze cookies and bars, tightly wrap and label; freeze unfrosted cookies up to 3 months. Do not freeze meringue, custard-filled or cream-filled cookies. Put delicate frosted or decorated cookies in single layers in freezer containers and cover with waxed paper before adding another layer. Thaw most cookies, covered, in the container at room temperature for 1 to 2 hours. For crisp cookies, remove from the container to thaw.

So Many Flavors

- For time-saving, delicious results, try any of the Betty Crocker® Supreme Brownie mixes or the Betty Crocker Sunkist® Lemon Bar mix.
- Think of favorite flavors or items you have on hand; then "search" those words on BettyCrocker.com. We've enough recipes for you to try from now until next year! Enjoy.

crisp chocolate-espresso ribbon cookies

PREP TIME: 1 hour 20 minutes *START TO FINISH:* 3 hours 20 minutes [48 SERVINGS]

1 pouch (1 lb 1.5 oz) Betty Crocker® sugar cookie mix

1 tablespoon Gold Medal® all-purpose flour

½ cup butter or margarine, softened

1 teaspoon almond extract

1 egg, slightly beaten

⅓ cup bittersweet chocolate chips, melted

½ cup coarsely to finely crushed chocolate-covered espresso coffee beans

⅓ cup coarsely chopped toasted almonds

1 Line bottom and sides of 9 × 5-inch loaf pan with plastic wrap. In large bowl, stir cookie mix, flour, butter, almond extract and egg until soft dough forms. Divide dough in half; place half of dough in another bowl. Stir melted chocolate into half of dough. To remaining half of dough, mix in espresso beans and almonds.

2 Firmly press half of chocolate dough evenly in bottom of loaf pan. Evenly press half of espresso dough over chocolate dough in pan. Repeat with remaining chocolate dough and espresso dough. Fold plastic wrap over dough to cover. Refrigerate about 2 hours or until firm.

3 Heat oven to 350°F. Remove dough from pan; unwrap. Place dough on cutting board. Cut dough crosswise into 4 equal pieces. Cut each piece crosswise into ¼-inch slices. On ungreased cookie sheets, place slices 2 inches apart.

4 Bake 9 to 10 minutes or until edges are light golden brown. Cool 1 minute; remove from cookie sheets to cooling rack.

1 SERVING: Calories 80; Total Fat 4½g (Saturated Fat 2g; Trans Fat 0g); Cholesterol 10mg; Sodium 45mg; Total Carbohydrate 10g (Dietary Fiber 0g); Protein 1g EXCHANGES: ½ Starch; 1 Fat CARBOHYDRATE CHOICES: ½

sweet note To toast nuts, heat oven to 350°F. Spread nuts in ungreased shallow pan. Bake uncovered 6 to 10 minutes, stirring occasionally, until light brown.

aloha paradise bars

PREP TIME: 25 minutes *START TO FINISH:* 1 hour 15 minutes [36 SERVINGS]

1 pouch (1 lb 1.5 oz) Betty Crocker® sugar cookie mix

½ cup butter or margarine, softened

1 egg

2 cups white vanilla baking chips

1 cup coarsely chopped dried pineapple

1 cup flaked coconut

1 cup chopped macadamia nuts

1 can (14 oz) sweetened condensed milk (not evaporated)

1 Heat oven to 350°F. Spray bottom only of 13 × 9-inch pan with cooking spray. In large bowl, stir cookie mix, butter and egg until soft dough forms. Press dough in bottom of pan.

2 Bake 15 minutes. Sprinkle with baking chips, pineapple, coconut and nuts. Drizzle evenly with sweetened condensed milk.

3 Bake 30 to 35 minutes longer or until light golden brown. Cool completely. For bars, cut into 9 rows by 4 rows. Store covered in refrigerator.

1 BAR: Calories 230; Total Fat 12g (Saturated Fat 6g; Trans Fat ½g); Cholesterol 15mg; Sodium 100mg; Total Carbohydrate 29g (Dietary Fiber 0g); Protein 3g EXCHANGES: 1 Starch; 1 Other Carbohydrate; 2 Fat CARBOHYDRATE CHOICES: 2

sweet note Skip the cooking spray, and instead line the pan with quick-release foil for quick cleanup and easy removal of bars.

super-easy macaroon chewies

PREP TIME: 1 hour 15 minutes *START TO FINISH:* 3 hours 15 minutes [36 SERVINGS]

1 pouch (1 lb 1.5 oz) Betty Crocker® sugar cookie mix

1 bag (14 oz) flaked coconut

¼ cup milk

1 can (14 oz) sweetened condensed milk (not evaporated)

½ cup semisweet chocolate chips

1 teaspoon butter or margarine

1 In large bowl, stir together cookie mix and coconut. Stir in milk and sweetened condensed milk until well blended. Cover; refrigerate 2 hours.

2 Heat oven to 375°F. Line cookie sheets with cooking parchment paper or use ungreased cookie sheets. Using 1-tablespoon-size cookie scoop, scoop dough onto cookie sheets 2 inches apart.

3 Bake 12 to 14 minutes or until edges are light golden brown. Cool 5 minutes; remove from cookie sheets to cooling racks. Cool completely.

4 In small microwavable bowl, microwave chocolate chips and butter on High 1 to 1½ minutes, stirring every 30 seconds, until melted and stirred smooth. Using fork, drizzle chocolate in lines over cookies. Store loosely covered.

1 COOKIE: Calories 170; Total Fat 7g (Saturated Fat 5g; Trans Fat ½g); Cholesterol 0mg; Sodium 75mg; Total Carbohydrate 24g (Dietary Fiber 0g); Protein 2g EXCHANGES: ½ Starch; 1 Other Carbohydrate; 1½ Fat CARBOHYDRATE CHOICES: 1

sweet note Use a #70 (1-tablespoon-size) ice cream scoop to make quick work out of dropping cookie dough. The cookies will be exactly the same size, which means they'll bake for the same time.

cran-orange 'n date-nut cookies

PREP TIME: 1 hour *START TO FINISH:* 1 hour [42 SERVINGS]

- ⅓ cup dried cranberries
- ¼ cup chopped orange slice candy
- ¼ cup coarsely chopped dates
- 2 tablespoons fresh orange juice
- 1 pouch (1 lb 1.5 oz) Betty Crocker® sugar cookie mix
- 2 tablespoons Gold Medal® all-purpose flour
- ½ teaspoon ground cinnamon
- ¼ teaspoon ground ginger
- ⅓ cup butter or margarine, softened
- 1 teaspoon grated orange peel
- 1 egg
- 1 cup chopped pistachio nuts
- ½ cup flaked coconut

1 Heat oven to 375°F. In small bowl, stir together cranberries, chopped candy, dates and orange juice; set aside.

2 In large bowl, stir together cookie mix, flour, cinnamon and ginger. Stir in butter, orange peel and egg until dough forms. Stir in cranberry mixture, pistachio nuts and coconut until thoroughly mixed. On ungreased cookie sheets, drop dough by teaspoonfuls 2 inches apart.

3 Bake 10 to 12 minutes or until edges are light golden brown. Cool 5 minutes; remove from cookie sheets to cooling racks. Store in tightly covered container.

1 COOKIE: Calories 100; Total Fat 4½g (Saturated Fat 1½g; Trans Fat ½g); Cholesterol 10mg; Sodium 45mg; Total Carbohydrate 15g (Dietary Fiber 0g); Protein 1g EXCHANGES: ½ Starch; ½ Other Carbohydrate; 1 Fat CARBOHYDRATE CHOICES: 1

orange-spice drops

PREP TIME: 1 hour 5 minutes *START TO FINISH:* 2 hours 5 minutes [36 SERVINGS]

- 1 pouch (1 lb 1.5 oz) Betty Crocker® sugar cookie mix
- ⅓ cup mascarpone cheese or 1 package (3 oz) cream cheese
- ¼ cup butter or margarine, softened
- 1 tablespoon grated orange peel
- 1 tablespoon fresh orange juice
- ¼ teaspoon pumpkin pie spice
- 1 egg
- 1 cup finely chopped pecans
- 2 cups white candy melts, coating wafers or white vanilla baking chips (12 oz)
- Edible orange glitter, if desired

1 Heat oven to 375°F. In large bowl, beat cookie mix, cheese and butter with electric mixer on low speed until well mixed. Add orange peel, orange juice, pumpkin pie spice and egg; beat until thoroughly mixed.

2 Using small cookie scoop, shape dough into 1-inch balls. Roll balls in pecans. On ungreased cookie sheets, place balls 2 inches apart.

3 Bake 11 to 13 minutes or until edges are light golden brown. Cool 5 minutes. Remove from cookie sheets to cooling racks. Cool completely.

4 In small microwavable bowl, microwave candy melts uncovered on High 1 to 2 minutes, stirring every 30 seconds, until melted and stirred smooth. Dip each cookie halfway into melted candy, letting excess drip off. Place on waxed paper until almost set. Sprinkle dipped half of each cookie with edible glitter. Let cookies stand until candy coating is completely set, about 1 hour. Store between sheets of waxed paper in tightly covered container.

1 COOKIE: Calories 150; Total Fat 8g (Saturated Fat 3½g; Trans Fat ½g); Cholesterol 10mg; Sodium 65mg; Total Carbohydrate 18g (Dietary Fiber 0g); Protein 2g EXCHANGES: 1 Starch; 1½ Fat CARBOHYDRATE CHOICES: 1

sweet note Find edible glitter in the baking section of craft stores or specialty kitchen stores.

apple cheddar-n-spice cookie tart

PREP TIME: 15 minutes *START TO FINISH:* 2 hours [16 SERVINGS]

1 pouch (1 lb 1.5 oz) Betty Crocker® sugar cookie mix

1 teaspoon apple pie spice

½ cup cold butter or margarine, cut into pieces

¾ cup chopped pecans

½ cup finely shredded Cheddar cheese

1 egg white

1 can (21 oz) apple pie filling with more fruit

1 Heat oven to 350°F. Place cookie sheet in oven. Spray 10-inch tart pan with removable bottom with cooking spray. In large bowl, stir cookie mix and apple pie spice until blended. Cut in butter using pastry blender or fork until mixture is crumbly. Reserve 1 cup of the crumb mixture in a small bowl; stir in pecans and cheese.

2 To remaining crumb mixture in large bowl, stir in egg white until soft dough forms. Press dough in bottom and up sides of tart pan.

3 Place apple pie filling in medium bowl. Using knife, cut apples into small pieces. Spoon apple mixture evenly over cookie dough crust. Sprinkle reserved crumb mixture over apples.

4 Place tart pan on cookie sheet in oven. Bake 40 to 45 minutes or until edges are golden brown and topping is set. Cool completely, about 1 hour. To serve, remove sides of pan; cut into wedges. Store covered at room temperature.

1 SERVING: Calories 270; Total Fat 13g (Saturated Fat 5g; Trans Fat 1½g); Cholesterol 20mg; Sodium 160mg; Total Carbohydrate 35g (Dietary Fiber 1g); Protein 3g
EXCHANGES: ½ Starch; 2 Other Carbohydrate; 2½ Fat CARBOHYDRATE CHOICES: 2

sweet note If you don't have apple pie spice, use ½ teaspoon ground cinnamon, ¼ teaspoon ground nutmeg, ⅛ teaspoon ground allspice and ⅛ teaspoon ground cardamom. Serve with a scoop of ice cream or a dollop of whipped cream.

candy corn cookies

PREP TIME: 1 hour *START TO FINISH:* 2 hours 30 minutes [114 COOKIES]

1 pouch (1 lb 1.5 oz) Betty Crocker® sugar cookie mix

⅓ cup butter or margarine, melted

1 egg

Orange paste food color

2 oz semisweet chocolate, melted, cooled

1 Line 8 × 4-inch loaf pan with waxed paper, extending paper over sides of pan. In medium bowl, stir cookie mix, butter and egg until soft dough forms.

2 On work surface, place ¾ cup dough. Knead desired amount of food color into dough until color is uniform. Press dough evenly in bottom of pan.

3 Divide remaining dough in half. Gently press one half of remaining dough into pan on top of orange dough. On work surface, knead chocolate into remaining dough until color is uniform. Press over plain dough in pan, pressing gently to edge of pan. Refrigerate 1½ to 2 hours or until firm.

4 Heat oven to 375°F. Remove dough from pan. Cut crosswise into ¼-inch-thick slices. Cut each slice into 5 wedges. On ungreased cookie sheet, place wedges 1 inch apart.

5 Bake 7 to 9 minutes or until cookies are set and edges are very light golden brown. Cool 1 minute; remove from cookie sheet. Cool completely. Store in tightly covered container.

1 COOKIE: Calories 25; Total Fat 1g (Saturated Fat ½g; Trans Fat 0g); Cholesterol 0mg; Sodium 15mg; Total Carbohydrate 4g (Dietary Fiber 0g); Protein 0g EXCHANGES: ½ Other Carbohydrate CARBOHYDRATE CHOICES: 0

sweet note Cookie dough can be frozen in an airtight container for up to 9 months. Thaw just until soft enough to cut. To keep cookies longer, wrap tightly, label and freeze up to 6 months.

lemon dream tassies

PREP TIME: 40 minutes *START TO FINISH:* 2 hours 10 minutes [36 COOKIE CUPS]

1 pouch (1 lb 1.5 oz) Betty Crocker® sugar cookie mix

½ cup whole almonds, ground

6 tablespoons butter or margarine, melted

1 package (3 oz) cream cheese, softened

1 jar (12 oz) lemon curd

⅔ cup Betty Crocker® Whipped fluffy white frosting (from 12-oz container)

½ cup frozen (thawed) whipped topping

1 teaspoon grated lemon peel

2 tablespoons sliced almonds

1 Heat oven to 375°F. Spray 36 mini muffin cups with cooking spray.

2 In large bowl, stir cookie mix, ground almonds, butter and cream cheese until soft dough forms.

3 Shape dough into thirty-six 1¼-inch balls. Press each ball in bottom and up side of muffin cup.

4 Bake 12 to 15 minutes or until golden brown. Cool completely in pan, about 30 minutes.

5 Remove cookie cups from pan. Fill each with about 1½ teaspoons lemon curd.

6 In small bowl, mix frosting and whipped topping until well blended. Pipe or spoon 1 rounded teaspoon frosting mixture on top of each filled cookie cup. Top each with lemon peel and almonds. Store covered in refrigerator.

1 COOKIE CUP: Calories 140; Total Fat 6g (Saturated Fat 2½g; Trans Fat 1g); Cholesterol 15mg; Sodium 65mg; Total Carbohydrate 21g (Dietary Fiber 0g); Protein 1g EXCHANGES: 1½ Other Carbohydrate; 1 Fat CARBOHYDRATE CHOICES: 1½

sweet note To add a greater variety of flavors, try lime or raspberry curd.

lemon linzer bars

PREP TIME: 20 minutes *START TO FINISH:* 5 hours 15 minutes [24 BARS]

Cookie Base

1 pouch (1 lb 1.5 oz) Betty Crocker® sugar cookie mix

⅓ cup butter or margarine, softened

2 oz cream cheese, softened

4½ teaspoons frozen (thawed) lemonade concentrate

¾ teaspoon almond extract

1 egg

Filling

⅔ cup seedless raspberry jam

1 package (8 oz) cream cheese, softened

½ cup lemon curd (from 10- to 12-oz jar)

2 cups frozen (thawed) whipped topping or 2 cups sweetened whipped cream

Topping

⅓ cup sliced almonds, toasted

24 fresh or frozen (thawed and drained) raspberries

1 Heat oven to 350°F. Spray bottom and sides of 13 × 9-inch pan with cooking spray.

2 In large bowl, stir cookie base ingredients until soft dough forms. Spread dough in bottom of pan.

3 Bake 20 to 23 minutes or until golden brown. Cool completely, about 30 minutes.

4 Spread raspberry jam over cooled base. In large bowl, beat cream cheese and lemon curd with electric mixer on medium speed until smooth. Fold in whipped topping. Drop lemon mixture by teaspoonfuls over jam layer; spread gently and evenly over jam.

5 Sprinkle toasted almonds over top. Refrigerate at least 4 hours or overnight. For bars, cut into 6 rows by 4 rows. To serve, top each bar with 1 raspberry, gently pressing into lemon mixture. Store covered in refrigerator.

1 BAR: Calories 230; Total Fat 11g (Saturated Fat 6g; Trans Fat 1g); Cholesterol 35mg; Sodium 115mg; Total Carbohydrate 30g (Dietary Fiber 0g); Protein 2g EXCHANGES: 2 Other Carbohydrate; 1½ Fat CARBOHYDRATE CHOICES: 2

sweet note Lemon curd is a lovely, thick, not-too-sweet product that you'll find next to the jams and jellies at the grocery store.

cinna-spin cookies

PREP TIME: 1 hour 10 minutes *START TO FINISH:* 1 hour 10 minutes [30 SERVINGS]

Cookies

1 pouch (1 lb 1.5 oz) Betty Crocker® sugar cookie mix

½ teaspoon ground cinnamon

½ cup butter or margarine, softened

1 egg, slightly beaten

1 tablespoon ground cinnamon

Glaze

1 cup powdered sugar

2 tablespoons milk

¼ teaspoon vanilla

1 Heat oven to 375°F. In large bowl, mix cookie mix and ½ teaspoon cinnamon. Stir in butter and egg until soft dough forms.

2 On piece of waxed paper, shape 1 tablespoon cinnamon into a line about 5 inches long. Using floured fingers, shape 1 tablespoon of dough into a rope 5 inches long. Press one side of dough rope into cinnamon.

3 On ungreased cookie sheet, coil dough rope tightly, cinnamon side facing center, into cinnamon-roll shape. Press end of rope into roll to seal. Repeat with remaining dough. Place cookies 2 inches apart on cookie sheets.

4 Bake 7 to 10 minutes or until edges are light golden brown. Cool 1 minute; remove from cookie sheets to cooling rack. Cool completely, about 15 minutes.

5 In small bowl, mix glaze ingredients until smooth. Drizzle over cookies.

1 COOKIE: Calories 110; Total Fat 5g (Saturated Fat 2½g; Trans Fat ½g); Cholesterol 15mg; Sodium 70mg; Total Carbohydrate 17g (Dietary Fiber 0g); Protein 1g EXCHANGES: ½ Starch; ½ Other Carbohydrate; 1 Fat CARBOHYDRATE CHOICES: 1

sweet note Serve these fun cookies as an after-school snack with a glass of milk.

mini burger cookies

PREP TIME: 40 minutes *START TO FINISH:* 1 hour 40 minutes [8 SANDWICH COOKIES]

1 pouch (1 lb. 1.5 oz) Betty Crocker® sugar cookie mix

3 tablespoons Gold Medal® all-purpose flour

⅓ cup butter or margarine, softened

1 egg

½ cup Betty Crocker® Rich & Creamy vanilla frosting (from 1-lb container)

16 chocolate-covered peppermint patties (1.5 oz each), unwrapped

2 tablespoons green-tinted flaked coconut (see Sweet Note)

1 can (6.4 oz) each Betty Crocker® red and yellow decorating icing

1 teaspoon honey

1 teaspoon water

2 teaspoons sesame seeds

1 Heat oven to 375°F. In medium bowl, combine cookie mix, flour, butter, and egg until soft dough forms. Shape dough into sixteen 1-inch balls. On ungreased cookie sheets, place balls 1 inch apart.

2 Bake 10 to 12 minutes or until set and edges are light golden brown. Cool 1 minute; remove to cooling rack. Cool completely.

3 Spread about ½ teaspoon vanilla frosting on bottom of each cookie. Top 1 cookie, frosted side up, with 1 peppermint pattie and ½ teaspoon green coconut. Pipe red and yellow icing on peppermint pattie for mustard and ketchup; top with another cookie, frosting side down. Repeat with remaining cookies.

4 In small bowl, combine honey and water. Brush on top of each cookie; sprinkle with sesame seeds.

1 SANDWICH COOKIE: Calories 410; Total Fat 14g (Saturated Fat 6g; Trans Fat 2g); Cholesterol 25mg; Sodium 160mg; Total Carbohydrate 69g (Dietary Fiber 1g); Protein 2g EXCHANGES: 1 Starch; 3½ Other Carbohydrate; 2½ Fat CARBOHYDRATE CHOICES: 4½

sweet note To tint coconut, shake coconut and a few drops green food color in tightly covered jar or resealable food-storage plastic bag.

baklava bars

PREP TIME: 25 minutes *START TO FINISH:* 2 hours 50 minutes [24 BARS]

1 Heat oven to 350°F. Spray bottom only of 13 × 9-inch pan with cooking spray.

2 In large bowl, stir cookie base ingredients until soft dough forms. Press dough in bottom of pan. Bake 15 minutes.

3 Meanwhile, in medium bowl, stir walnuts, granulated sugar, ¼ cup butter, 1 teaspoon cinnamon and the salt with fork until mixture is well mixed and crumbly.

4 Sprinkle nut mixture evenly over partially baked base. With hands, crumble frozen phyllo shells evenly over nut mixture. Bake 18 to 20 minutes longer or until golden brown.

5 Meanwhile, in small microwavable bowl, microwave ⅓ cup honey, 2 tablespoons butter, the brown sugar, lemon juice and ¼ teaspoon cinnamon uncovered on High 1 minute or until bubbly. Stir in vanilla.

6 Drizzle honey mixture evenly over phyllo. Cool completely, about 2 hours.

7 For bars, cut into 6 rows by 4 rows. Before serving, drizzle ½ teaspoon honey over each bar. Store covered at room temperature.

1 BAR: Calories 250; Total Fat 14g (Saturated Fat 5g; Trans Fat 1g); Cholesterol 25mg; Sodium 115mg; Total Carbohydrate 29g (Dietary Fiber 0g); Protein 2g EXCHANGES: 2 Other Carbohydrate; 2 Fat CARBOHYDRATE CHOICES: 2

Cookie Base

1 pouch (1 lb 1.5 oz) Betty Crocker® sugar cookie mix

½ cup butter or margarine, softened

½ teaspoon grated lemon peel

1 egg

Filling

1½ cups chopped walnuts

⅓ cup granulated sugar

¼ cup butter or margarine, softened

1 teaspoon ground cinnamon

⅛ teaspoon salt

8 frozen mini phyllo shells (from 2.1-oz package)

Glaze

⅓ cup honey

2 tablespoons butter or margarine, softened

1 tablespoon packed brown sugar

½ teaspoon lemon juice

¼ teaspoon ground cinnamon

1 teaspoon vanilla

Garnish

5 tablespoons honey

sweet note Baklava is a sweet dessert made with layers of butter-drenched pastry, spices and nuts. A honey-lemon syrup is poured over the baked warm pastry and left to soak. The dessert is traditionally cut into triangles. You can find mini phyllo shells in the freezer section of your supermarket.

almond, apricot and white chocolate decadence bars

PREP TIME: 35 minutes *START TO FINISH:* 3 hours 35 minutes [36 BARS]

Cookie Base

1 pouch (1 lb 1.5 oz) Betty Crocker® sugar cookie mix

½ cup butter or margarine, melted

½ teaspoon almond extract

1 egg, slightly beaten

Filling

1 package (7 or 8 oz) almond paste (not marzipan)

½ cup sugar

1 cup finely chopped dried apricots (6 oz)

6 oz cream cheese, softened

2 eggs

1 teaspoon lemon juice

Topping

1 bag (12 oz) white vanilla baking chips (2 cups)

⅔ cup whipping cream

½ cup sliced almonds

1 Heat oven to 375°F. In large bowl, stir cookie base ingredients until soft dough forms. Spread dough in bottom of ungreased 13 × 9-inch pan. Bake 10 to 15 minutes or until set. Cool 10 minutes.

2 Meanwhile, in large bowl, beat almond paste and sugar with electric mixer on low speed until crumbly but blended. Add apricots; beat on low speed just until combined. Add cream cheese, 2 eggs and the lemon juice; beat on medium speed until well blended. Pour over warm cookie base.

3 Bake 20 to 25 minutes or until set. Cool 30 minutes.

4 Place baking chips in small bowl. In 1-quart saucepan, heat whipping cream just to boiling over low heat, stirring occasionally; pour over baking chips. Let stand 1 minute. Stir until chips are melted and mixture is smooth. Pour and spread over filling. Sprinkle with almonds. Refrigerate about 2 hours or until set. For bars, cut into 9 rows by 4 rows. Store covered in refrigerator.

1 BAR: Calories 220; Total Fat 12g (Saturated Fat 6g; Trans Fat ½g); Cholesterol 35mg; Sodium 100mg; Total Carbohydrate 25g (Dietary Fiber 0g); Protein 3g EXCHANGES: ½ Starch; 1 Other Carbohydrate; 2½ Fat CARBOHYDRATE CHOICES: 1½

sweet note Look for the almond paste in the baking aisle of the grocery store. It should be fresh and fairly pliable, so check the freshness date on the package.

strawberry cheesecake bars

PREP TIME: 15 minutes *START TO FINISH:* 3 hours [32 BARS]

- 1 pouch (1 lb 1.5 oz) Betty Crocker® sugar cookie mix
- ⅓ cup butter or margarine, melted
- 2 tablespoons Gold Medal® all-purpose flour
- 1 egg
- 2 packages (8 oz each) cream cheese, softened
- ¾ cup sugar
- 1 teaspoon vanilla
- 2 eggs
- ¾ cup strawberry spreadable fruit

sweet note To make extra tiny treats and add a new shape to your cookie tray, cut bars diagonally in half to make triangles.

1. Heat oven to 350°F. Spray bottom of 13 × 9-inch pan with cooking spray.
2. In medium bowl, stir cookie mix, butter, flour and 1 egg until soft dough forms. Press evenly in pan. Bake 15 to 18 minutes or until light golden brown. Cool 15 minutes.
3. In large bowl, beat cream cheese, sugar, vanilla and 2 eggs with electric mixer on medium speed until smooth. Spread evenly over crust in pan.
4. Place spreadable fruit in small resealable food-storage plastic bag; seal bag. Cut off tiny corner of bag. Squeeze spreadable fruit in 3 lines the length of the pan. Use knife to pull spread from side to side through cream cheese mixture at 1-inch intervals. Bake 25 to 30 minutes longer or until filling is set. Refrigerate until chilled, about 2 hours. For bars, cut into 8 rows by 4 rows. Store covered in refrigerator.

1 BAR: Calories 180; Total Fat 9g (Saturated Fat 5g; Trans Fat 1g); Cholesterol 40mg; Sodium 100mg; Total Carbohydrate 22g (Dietary Fiber 0g); Protein 2g EXCHANGES: ½ Starch;1 Other Carbohydrate; 2 Fat CARBOHYDRATE CHOICES: 1½

boston cream dessert cups

PREP TIME: 45 minutes *START TO FINISH:* 2 hours 45 minutes [23 DESSERT CUPS]

Cookie Crust

1 pouch (1 lb 1.5 oz) Betty Crocker® sugar cookie mix

½ cup butter or margarine, softened

1 egg

2 tablespoons sugar

Filling

2 packages (8 oz each) cream cheese, softened

½ cup sugar

1 tablespoon Gold Medal® all-purpose flour

1 tablespoon milk

½ cup sour cream

2 eggs

1 box (4-serving size) vanilla instant pudding and pie filling mix

Topping

1 container (1 lb) Betty Crocker® Rich & Creamy chocolate frosting

1 Heat oven to 350°F. Place paper baking cup in each of 23 regular-size muffin cups. Lightly spray baking cups with cooking spray.

2 In large bowl, stir cookie mix, butter and 1 egg until dough forms. Shape dough into twenty-three 1½-inch balls. Place 1 ball in each baking cup. Moisten bottom of small flat-bottomed glass with drop of water, then dip into 2 tablespoons sugar. Press glass on dough balls to flatten slightly, dipping glass in sugar after each dough ball.

3 In same large bowl, beat cream cheese, ½ cup sugar, the flour and milk with electric mixer on medium speed until smooth. Beat in sour cream. On low speed, beat in 2 eggs, one at a time, just until blended. Stir in dry pudding mix until well blended. Spoon about 2 tablespoons filling over dough in each cup.

4 Bake 25 to 30 minutes or until set. Cool 30 minutes; remove from pan.

5 Open container of frosting; remove foil lid. Microwave uncovered on High 30 seconds to soften frosting; stir until smooth. Spoon about 1 tablespoon frosting onto center of each cookie cup. Refrigerate about 1 hour or until set. Store covered in refrigerator. If desired, remove from paper baking cups to serve.

1 DESSERT CUP: Calories 330; Total Fat 18g (Saturated Fat 9g; Trans Fat 2½g); Cholesterol 65mg; Sodium 280mg; Total Carbohydrate 39g (Dietary Fiber 0g); Protein 3g EXCHANGES: 1 Starch; 1½ Other Carbohydrate; 3½ Fat CARBOHYDRATE CHOICES: 2½

sweet note Here's a mini version of Boston cream pie made with cookie mix.

almond streusel–cherry cheesecake bars

PREP TIME: 45 minutes *START TO FINISH:* 4 hours [24 BARS]

Cookie Base and Topping

1 pouch (1 lb 1.5 oz) Betty Crocker® sugar cookie mix

¼ cup cold butter or margarine

4 oz (half of 8-oz package) cream cheese

½ cup sliced almonds

Filling

2½ packages (8 oz each) cream cheese (20 oz), softened

½ cup sugar

2 tablespoons Gold Medal® all-purpose flour

1 teaspoon almond extract

2 eggs

1 can (21 oz) cherry pie filling

1 Heat oven to 350°F. Spray bottom and sides of 13 × 9-inch pan with cooking spray. Place cookie mix in large bowl. Cut in butter and 4 oz cream cheese, using pastry blender or fork, until mixture is crumbly. Reserve 1½ cups mixture for topping. Press remaining mixture in bottom of pan. Bake 12 minutes.

2 Meanwhile, in large bowl, beat 20 oz cream cheese, the sugar, flour, almond extract and eggs with electric mixer on medium speed until smooth.

3 Spread cream cheese mixture evenly over partially baked cookie base. Spoon pie filling evenly over cream cheese mixture. Sprinkle with reserved topping and almonds.

4 Bake 40 to 45 minutes or until light golden brown. Cool 30 minutes. Refrigerate about 2 hours or until chilled. For bars, cut into 6 rows by 4 rows. Store covered in refrigerator.

1 BAR: Calories 270; Total Fat 15g (Saturated Fat 8g; Trans Fat 1g); Cholesterol 55mg; Sodium 160mg; Total Carbohydrate 28g (Dietary Fiber 0g); Protein 4g EXCHANGES: 1 Starch; 1 Other Carbohydrate; 3 Fat CARBOHYDRATE CHOICES: 2

sweet note Cheesecake in an easy bar—yum! You'll need a total of three 8-ounce packages of cream cheese for this recipe.

fiesta fudge cookies

PREP TIME: 1 hour *START TO FINISH:* 1 hour [60 COOKIES]

1 Heat oven to 350°F. In large microwavable bowl, microwave butter and chocolate on High 1 minute. Stir; microwave on High 1 minute longer or until butter is melted and chocolate can be stirred smooth.

2 Stir condensed milk into chocolate mixture. Stir in cookie mix and cinnamon until well blended.

3 Using 1 level tablespoonful of dough for each cookie, shape into 60 balls. Place 2 inches apart on ungreased cookie sheets.

4 Bake 6 to 7 minutes or until edges lose their shiny look (do not overbake). Immediately press 1 candy into center of each cookie. Cool cookies on cookie sheet 5 minutes; remove from cookie sheets. To get candy to spread slightly on top of cookie, tap edge of each cookie lightly. Cool completely. Store covered at room temperature.

1 COOKIE: Calories 100; Total Fat 4½g (Saturated Fat 2½g; Trans Fat 0g); Cholesterol 5mg; Sodium 45mg; Total Carbohydrate 13g (Dietary Fiber 0g); Protein 1g EXCHANGES: 1 Other Carbohydrate; 1 Fat CARBOHYDRATE CHOICES: 1

⅓ cup butter or margarine

6 oz unsweetened chocolate

1 can (14 oz) sweetened condensed milk (not evaporated)

1 pouch (1 lb 1.5 oz) Betty Crocker® sugar cookie mix

1 teaspoon ground cinnamon

60 white and chocolate-striped candy drops or pieces, unwrapped

sweet note You can substitute milk chocolate candy drops for the striped candy.

turtle tassies

PREP TIME: 1 hour 40 minutes *START TO FINISH:* 1 hour 40 minutes [48 COOKIES]

1 pouch (1 lb 1.5 oz) Betty Crocker® sugar cookie mix

Butter and egg called for on cookie mix pouch

2 bags (14 oz each) caramels, unwrapped

⅓ cup whipping cream

¾ cup dark chocolate chips

½ cup chopped pecans

1 Heat oven to 375°F. Lightly spray 48 mini muffin cups with cooking spray.

2 Make dough as directed on cookie pouch. Shape dough into forty-eight 1-inch balls. Press 1 ball into bottom of each muffin cup, pressing up sides to fill cups.

3 Bake 8 to 9 minutes or until edges begin to brown. Meanwhile, in 3-quart saucepan, heat caramels and whipping cream over medium heat, stirring frequently, until melted. Reduce heat to low.

4 Remove pans from oven; gently press end of wooden spoon into bottoms and against sides of cookie cups to flatten, being careful not to make holes in dough.

5 Bake 2 to 3 minutes longer or until edges are light golden brown. Immediately spoon ½ teaspoon (about 4) chocolate chips into each cookie cup.

6 Spoon about 1 tablespoon caramel mixture into each cookie cup. Immediately top with chopped pecans. Cool 5 minutes; remove from pans with narrow spatula.

1 COOKIE: Calories 150; Total Fat 6g (Saturated Fat 2½g; Trans Fat 0g); Cholesterol 15mg; Sodium 85mg; Total Carbohydrate 22g (Dietary Fiber 0g); Protein 1g EXCHANGES: ½ Starch; 1 Other Carbohydrate; 1 Fat CARBOHYDRATE CHOICES: 1½

sweet note Store tassies in an airtight container in the freezer for up to 1 month.

chocolate chip truffle bars

PREP TIME: 35 minutes *START TO FINISH:* 2 hours [35 BARS]

½ cup butter or margarine, softened

1 egg

1 pouch (1 lb 1.5 oz) Betty Crocker® chocolate chip cookie mix

1 cup semisweet chocolate chips (6 oz)

1 container (1 lb) Betty Crocker® Rich & Creamy chocolate frosting

1 can (6.4 oz) Betty Crocker® Easy Flow pink decorating icing

35 yogurt-covered miniature pretzels

1 Heat oven to 350°F. Spray bottom of 13 × 9-inch pan with cooking spray. In medium bowl, stir together softened butter and egg. Stir in cookie mix until soft dough forms. Press mixture in bottom of pan, using floured fingers.

2 Bake 19 to 21 minutes or until golden brown. Cool 30 minutes.

3 In medium microwavable bowl, microwave chocolate chips on High 1 to 2 minutes, stirring every 30 seconds, until melted. Stir in frosting. Spread evenly over bars. Cool completely, about 30 minutes. For bars, cut into 7 rows by 5 rows.

4 Using star tip on pink decorating icing, fill in each hole of each pretzel, forming a heart in center of each. Place decorated pretzel on each bar.

1 BAR: Calories 190; Total Fat 10g (Saturated Fat 5g; Trans Fat 0g); Cholesterol 15mg; Sodium 150mg; Total Carbohydrate 25g (Dietary Fiber 0g); Protein 1g EXCHANGES: ½ Starch; 1 Other Carbohydrate; 2 Fat CARBOHYDRATE CHOICES: 1½

sweet note For easy removal, line your pan with foil, then spray the foil with cooking spray. When the bars are cooled, you can easily lift them from the pan for cutting.

caramel s'mores cups

PREP TIME: 30 minutes *START TO FINISH:* 1 hour 30 minutes [36 CUPS]

1 pouch (1 lb 1.5 oz) Betty Crocker® chocolate chip cookie mix

½ cup butter or margarine, softened

1 egg

36 round chewy caramels in milk chocolate, from 5 rolls (1.91 oz each), unwrapped

108 mini marshmallows (1 cup)

½ cup semisweet chocolate chips

1 Heat oven to 375°F. Spray 36 mini muffin cups with cooking spray.

2 Make cookie dough as directed on package, using butter and egg. Shape dough into thirty-six 1-inch balls. Place 1 ball into each muffin cup.

3 Bake 8 to 9 minutes or until edges begin to brown. Remove from oven; firmly press 1 candy into center of each cookie until flush with cookie top. Top each with 3 marshmallows. Bake 2 to 4 minutes longer or until marshmallows are puffed. Cool 30 minutes. Loosen edges of cookie with small metal spatula and remove to cooling racks. Cool completely.

4 Place chocolate chips in small resealable freezer plastic bag. Microwave on High about 1 minute or until softened. Gently squeeze bag until chocolate is smooth; cut off tiny corner of bag. Squeeze bag to drizzle chocolate over marshmallows. Let stand until hardened, about 10 minutes.

1 CUP: Calories 140; Total Fat 6g (Saturated Fat 4g; Trans Fat 0g); Cholesterol 15mg; Sodium 90mg; Total Carbohydrate 18g (Dietary Fiber 0g); Protein 1g EXCHANGES: 1 Starch; 1 Fat CARBOHYDRATE CHOICES: 1

sweet note Betty Crocker® cookie mix provides a simple addition to these delicious caramel cookies—a delightful dessert!

mini cookie collection

PREP TIME: 1 hour 30 minutes *START TO FINISH:* 1 hour 30 minutes [114 MINI COOKIES]

1 pouch (1 lb 1.5 oz) Betty Crocker® chocolate chip, peanut butter or sugar cookie mix

Egg, butter, vegetable oil or water as package directs

Sugar, if needed

Cinnamon, if needed

114 (about 1 cup) miniature semisweet or milk chocolate candy drops for baking (from 10-oz bag), if needed

1 Heat oven to 350°F. Make pouch of cookie mix as directed on package.

2 Shape dough as directed for each kind of cookie, below.

3 Bake 8 to 10 minutes or until edges are light golden brown.

Mini Chocolate Chippers: *Make chocolate chip cookie mix as directed. Drop dough by rounded ½ teaspoonfuls 1 inch apart on ungreased cookie sheet. Bake as directed, above. Cool 1 minute before removing from cookie sheet.*

Mini Peanut Blossom Cookies: *Make peanut butter cookie mix as directed. Shape dough into ½-inch balls; roll in sugar. Place balls 1 inch apart on ungreased cookie sheet. Bake as directed, above. Immediately press miniature chocolate candy drop in top of each cookie. Cool 1 minute before removing from cookie sheet.*

Snicker-Do-Littles: *Make sugar cookie mix as directed. Shape dough into ½-inch balls. Mix 3 tablespoons sugar and 1 teaspoon cinnamon. Roll dough balls in sugar mixture. Place balls 1 inch apart on ungreased cookie sheet. Bake as directed, above. Cool 1 minute before removing from cookie sheet.*

1 COOKIE: Calories 35; Total Fat 2g (Saturated Fat 1g; Trans Fat 0g); Cholesterol 0mg; Sodium 20mg; Total Carbohydrate 4g (Dietary Fiber 0g); Protein 0g EXCHANGES: ½ Fat CARBOHYDRATE CHOICES: 0

sweet note Mini cookies are great for kids' snacks. Pack them in mini snack bags for lunches or snacks. These mini cookies will keep in the freezer for up to 2 months.

salted peanut chews

PREP TIME: 10 minutes *START TO FINISH:* 1 hour [36 BARS]

1 pouch (1 lb 1.5 oz) Betty Crocker® peanut butter cookie mix

3 tablespoons vegetable oil

1 tablespoon water

1 egg

3 cups miniature marshmallows

⅔ cup light corn syrup

¼ cup butter or margarine

2 teaspoons vanilla

1 bag (10 oz) peanut butter chips

2 cups crisp rice cereal

2 cups salted peanuts

1 Heat oven to 350°F. Spray bottom of 13 × 9-inch pan with cooking spray.

2 In large bowl, stir cookie mix, oil, water and egg until soft dough forms. Press dough in pan using floured fingers.

3 Bake 12 to 15 minutes or until set. Immediately sprinkle marshmallows over crust; bake 1 to 2 minutes longer or until marshmallows begin to puff.

4 In 4-quart saucepan, cook corn syrup, butter, vanilla and chips over low heat, stirring constantly, until chips are melted. Remove from heat; stir in cereal and nuts. Immediately spoon cereal mixture evenly over marshmallows. Refrigerate 30 minutes or until firm. For bars, cut into 9 rows by 4 rows.

1 BAR: Calories 220; Total Fat 11g (Saturated Fat 2½g; Trans Fat 0g); Cholesterol 10mg; Sodium 160mg; Total Carbohydrate 25g (Dietary Fiber 1g); Protein 5g EXCHANGES: ½ Starch; 1 Other Carbohydrate; 1½ Fat CARBOHYDRATE CHOICES: 1½

sweet note For a different flavor, try milk chocolate or semi-sweet chocolate chips for the peanut butter chips.

easy monster cookies

PREP TIME: 1 hour *START TO FINISH:* 1 hour [18 COOKIES]

1 pouch (1 lb 1.5 oz) Betty Crocker® chocolate chip cookie mix

1 pouch (1 lb 1.5 oz) Betty Crocker® peanut butter cookie mix

1½ cups quick-cooking oats

1 cup butter or margarine, softened

3 eggs

2 cups candy-coated milk chocolate candies

1 Heat oven to 375°F. In large bowl, stir all ingredients except candies until soft dough forms. Stir in candies.

2 On ungreased cookie sheets, place about ¼ cupfuls dough about 3 inches apart.

3 Bake 12 to 13 minutes or until light golden brown. Cool 2 minutes; remove from cookie sheets. Cool completely. Store in covered container at room temperature.

1 COOKIE: Calories 480; Total Fat 23g (Saturated Fat 12g; Trans Fat 0g); Cholesterol 65mg; Sodium 340mg; Total Carbohydrate 61g (Dietary Fiber 1g); Protein 6g EXCHANGES: 2 Starch; 2 Other Carbohydrate; 4½ Fat CARBOHYDRATE CHOICES: 4

sweet note To make 36 smaller cookies, place 2 heaping tablespoonfuls dough about 2 inches apart on ungreased cookie sheets. Bake 10 to 12 minutes.

double-chocolate caramel-coffee cups

PREP TIME: 30 minutes *START TO FINISH:* 1 hour 10 minutes [36 COOKIE CUPS]

Cookie Cups

1 teaspoon instant espresso coffee granules

1 tablespoon water

1 pouch (1 lb 1.5 oz) Betty Crocker® double chocolate chunk cookie mix

3 tablespoons vegetable oil

1 egg

Topping

1 container (1 lb) Betty Crocker® Rich & Creamy vanilla frosting

2 tablespoons caramel-flavored liqueur

½ cup marshmallow creme

2 tablespoons caramel topping

1 Heat oven to 375°F. Spray 36 miniature muffin cups with cooking spray, or line with paper baking cups. In large bowl, dissolve espresso granules in water. Add cookie mix, oil and egg; stir until soft dough forms. Shape dough into thirty-six 1-inch balls; place in muffin cups.

2 Bake 8 to 9 minutes or until set. Immediately make indentation in center of each cookie with end of wooden spoon to form a cup. Cool 30 minutes. Remove from pan.

3 In small bowl, stir frosting and liqueur until well blended. Gently stir in marshmallow creme. Spoon frosting mixture evenly into each cookie cup. Store covered in refrigerator. Before serving, use fork to drizzle each cookie cup with caramel topping.

1 COOKIE CUP: Calories 130; Total Fat 5g (Saturated Fat 1½g; Trans Fat 1g); Cholesterol 5mg; Sodium 85mg; Total Carbohydrate 20g (Dietary Fiber 0g); Protein 0g EXCHANGES: 1½ Other Carbohydrate; 1 Fat CARBOHYDRATE CHOICES: 1

sweet note Other flavored liqueurs, such as Irish cream liqueur or coffee-flavored liqueur, can be used for the caramel-flavored liqueur.

chocolate-covered strawberry tarts

PREP TIME: 45 minutes *START TO FINISH:* 1 hour 15 minutes [36 TARTS]

1 pouch (1 lb 1.5 oz) Betty Crocker® double chocolate chunk cookie mix

¼ cup vegetable oil

1 egg

2 tablespoons water

⅓ cup strawberry jam

½ cup frozen (thawed) whipped topping

1 cup Betty Crocker® Whipped Strawberry Mist frosting (from 12-oz container)

3 tablespoons miniature semisweet chocolate chips

1 Heat oven to 350°F. Place miniature paper baking cup in each of 36 mini muffin cups.

2 In medium bowl, stir cookie mix, oil, egg and water until soft dough forms. Drop dough by teaspoonfuls into baking cups.

3 Bake 8 to 10 minutes or until edges are set. Gently press end of wooden spoon into bottoms and against sides of baking cups to flatten, being careful not to make holes in dough. Cool completely, about 30 minutes.

4 Spoon ½ teaspoon jam into each cookie cup.

5 In medium bowl, fold whipped topping into frosting until well combined. Spoon frosting mixture into decorating bag fitted with medium star tip, and pipe into the center of each tart. Top with chocolate chips. Store loosely covered.

1 TART: Calories 110; Total Fat 4½g (Saturated Fat 1½g; Trans Fat 0g); Cholesterol 5mg; Sodium 70mg; Total Carbohydrate 17g (Dietary Fiber 0g); Protein 0g EXCHANGES: 1 Other Carbohydrate; 1 Fat CARBOHYDRATE CHOICES: 1

sweet note Create a new holiday tradition with these tarts, reminiscent of chocolate-covered strawberries.

chocolate-cherry glazed cookie bites

PREP TIME: 30 minutes *START TO FINISH:* 50 minutes [24 COOKIES]

1 pouch (1 lb 1.5 oz) Betty Crocker® double chocolate chunk cookie mix

⅓ cup chopped maraschino cherries, drained

⅓ cup vegetable oil

2 tablespoons maraschino cherry juice

1 teaspoon almond extract

1 egg

¾ cup Betty Crocker® Rich & Creamy chocolate frosting (from 1-lb container)

24 maraschino cherries with stems, drained on paper towels (from two 10-oz jars)

1 Heat oven to 350°F. Place miniature paper baking cup in each of 24 miniature muffin cups, or spray with cooking spray. Make cookie dough by blending cookie mix, chopped cherries, oil, cherry juice, almond extract and egg until soft dough forms. Spoon dough into muffin cups, filling each about three-fourths full.

2 Bake 12 to 14 minutes or until dough is set. Cool 20 minutes. Remove from pan. Place cookies on cooling racks.

3 Heat ¾ cup of frosting on High for 30 seconds; stir. Dip tops of cookies into frosting. Allow to set about 1 minute; top each bite with cherry.

1 COOKIE: Calories 160; Total Fat 6g (Saturated Fat 2g; Trans Fat ½g); Cholesterol 10mg; Sodium 115mg; Total Carbohydrate 25g (Dietary Fiber 0g); Protein 1g EXCHANGES: ½ Starch; 1 Other Carbohydrate; 1 Fat CARBOHYDRATE CHOICES: 1½

sweet note Create bite-size fudgy bliss with an easy chocolate cookie mix and a touch of tart cherries.

double-chocolate rocky road bars

PREP TIME: 30 minutes *START TO FINISH:* 3 hours 30 minutes [24 BARS]

Cookie Base

1 pouch (1 lb 1.5 oz) Betty Crocker® double chocolate chunk cookie mix

¼ cup vegetable oil

2 tablespoons water

1 egg

Filling

1 package (8 oz) cream cheese, softened

½ cup granulated sugar

¼ cup butter or margarine, softened

2 tablespoons Gold Medal® all-purpose flour

1 teaspoon vanilla

1 egg

¼ cup chopped pecans

1 cup semisweet chocolate chips (6 oz)

1½ cups miniature marshmallows

Frosting

½ cup butter or margarine

¼ cup unsweetened baking cocoa

⅓ cup milk

3 cups powdered sugar

1 teaspoon vanilla

1 cup chopped pecans

1 Heat oven to 350°F. Spray bottom and sides of 13 × 9-inch pan with cooking spray.

2 In large bowl, stir cookie base ingredients until soft dough forms. Press dough in bottom of pan. Set aside.

3 In large bowl, beat cream cheese, granulated sugar, ¼ cup butter, the flour, 1 teaspoon vanilla and 1 egg with electric mixer on medium speed until smooth. Stir in ¼ cup pecans. Spread over cookie dough base. Sprinkle with chocolate chips.

4 Bake 26 to 28 minutes or until filling is set. Sprinkle evenly with marshmallows. Bake 2 minutes longer.

5 In 2-quart saucepan, melt ½ cup butter over medium heat. Stir in cocoa and milk. Heat to boiling, stirring constantly. Remove from heat. With wire whisk, gradually stir in powdered sugar until well blended. Stir in 1 teaspoon vanilla and 1 cup pecans. Immediately pour over marshmallows, spreading gently to cover. Cool 30 minutes.

6 Refrigerate about 2 hours or until chilled. For bars, cut into 6 rows by 4 rows. Store covered in refrigerator.

1 BAR: Calories 370; Total Fat 20g (Saturated Fat 8g; Trans Fat 1g); Cholesterol 45mg; Sodium 130mg; Total Carbohydrate 45g (Dietary Fiber 1g); Protein 3g EXCHANGES: 1 Starch; 2 Other Carbohydrate; 4 Fat CARBOHYDRATE CHOICES: 3

sweet note Rich double chocolate chunk cookie mix jump-starts a decadent and delicious bar.

chocolate-marshmallow pillows

PREP TIME: 45 minutes *START TO FINISH:* 1 hour 5 minutes [24 COOKIES]

Cookies

1 pouch (1 lb 1.5 oz) Betty Crocker® double chocolate chunk cookie mix

¼ cup vegetable oil

2 tablespoons water

1 egg

⅔ cup chopped pecans

12 large marshmallows, cut in half

Frosting

1 cup semisweet chocolate chips (6 oz)

⅓ cup whipping cream

1 teaspoon butter or margarine

1 teaspoon vanilla

½ cup powdered sugar

1 Heat oven to 350°F. In large bowl, stir cookie mix, oil, water, egg and pecans until soft dough forms.

2 On ungreased cookie sheets, drop dough by rounded tablespoonfuls 2 inches apart.

3 Bake 7 minutes. Remove from oven; immediately press marshmallow half lightly, cut side down, on top of cookie. Bake 1 to 2 minutes longer or just until marshmallows begin to soften. Cool 2 minutes; remove from cookie sheets to cooling racks. Cool completely, about 15 minutes.

4 Meanwhile, in 1-quart nonstick saucepan, melt chocolate chips over low heat, stirring until smooth. Remove from heat. Add whipping cream, butter and vanilla; blend well. Stir in powdered sugar until smooth.

5 Spread frosting over each cooled cookie, covering marshmallow. Let stand until frosting is set.

1 COOKIE: Calories 200; Total Fat 10g (Saturated Fat 3½g; Trans Fat 0g); Cholesterol 15mg; Sodium 100mg; Total Carbohydrate 27g (Dietary Fiber 0g); Protein 1g EXCHANGES: 2 Other Carbohydrate; 2 Fat CARBOHYDRATE CHOICES: 2

sweet note Lightly spray kitchen scissors with cooking spray to make cutting marshmallows easy.

nanaimo cookie bars

PREP TIME: 45 minutes *START TO FINISH:* 2 hours 5 minutes [36 BARS]

Cookie Base

1 pouch (1 lb 1.5 oz) Betty Crocker® double chocolate chunk cookie mix

1 cup graham cracker crumbs

½ cup chopped nut topping or chopped walnuts

½ cup coconut

1 cup butter or margarine, melted

1 egg

Filling

4 cups powdered sugar

4 tablespoons vanilla instant pudding and pie filling mix

⅓ cup butter or margarine, softened

¼ cup milk

Topping

1 bag (12 oz) semisweet chocolate chips (2 cups)

¼ cup butter or margarine

1 Heat oven to 350°F. Line bottom and sides of 13 × 9-inch pan with foil, leaving foil overhanging at 2 opposite sides of pan. In large bowl, stir cookie base ingredients until well mixed. Spread into pan; press lightly. Bake 16 to 18 minutes or until set. Cool completely, about 30 minutes.

2 In another large bowl, stir together powdered sugar and pudding mix. Add ⅓ cup butter and the milk; beat with electric mixer on medium speed until smooth (filling will be very thick). Spoon over cookie base; press evenly to cover. Refrigerate while making topping.

3 In small microwavable bowl, microwave topping ingredients uncovered on High 1 minute to 1 minute 30 seconds, stirring every 30 seconds until melted and smooth. Spread over filling. Refrigerate uncovered until set, about 30 minutes.

4 Use foil to lift bars from pan; pull foil from sides of bars. Cut into 9 rows by 4 rows. Store covered in refrigerator.

1 BAR: Calories 270; Total Fat 14g (Saturated Fat 8g; Trans Fat 0g); Cholesterol 25mg; Sodium 150mg; Total Carbohydrate 34g (Dietary Fiber 0g); Protein 1g EXCHANGES: ½ Starch; 1½ Other Carbohydrate; 3 Fat CARBOHYDRATE CHOICES: 2

sweet note Canadian legend claims that the bar (chocolate crumb base, layer of vanilla, covered in chocolate) originated in Nanaimo, Canada, in the 1950s.

peanut butter–pecan chocolate chip–granola cookies

PREP TIME: 20 minutes *START TO FINISH:* 1 hour 30 minutes [60 COOKIES]

- 1 cup butter, softened
- 1 cup creamy peanut butter
- ¾ cup granulated sugar
- ¾ cup packed brown sugar
- 2 eggs
- 1 teaspoon vanilla
- 2 cups Original Bisquick® mix
- 1¾ cups granola cereal
- 1 cup milk chocolate chips
- 1 cup coarsely chopped pecans

1 Heat oven to 350°F. In large bowl, mix butter, peanut butter, sugars, eggs and vanilla with spoon. Stir in remaining ingredients. On ungreased cookie sheet, drop dough by rounded tablespoonfuls about 2 inches apart.

2 Bake 9 to 11 minutes or until edges are light golden brown (do not overbake). Cool 3 minutes; remove from cookie sheet to cooling rack.

1 COOKIE: Calories 140; Total Fat 8g (Saturated Fat 3½g; Trans Fat 0g); Cholesterol 15mg; Sodium 95mg; Total Carbohydrate 13g (Dietary Fiber 0g); Protein 2g EXCHANGES: ½ Starch; ½ Other Carbohydrate; 1½ Fat CARBOHYDRATE CHOICES: 1

sweet note Use your favorite granola cereal in these cookies.

monster cookies

PREP TIME: 50 minutes *START TO FINISH:* 50 minutes [18 COOKIES]

1¼ cups packed brown sugar

½ cup shortening

2 eggs

2½ cups Original Bisquick® mix

1 cup old-fashioned or quick-cooking oats

1 cup candy-coated chocolate candies

½ cup raisins

½ cup chopped nuts, if desired

1 Heat oven to 375°F. In large bowl, beat brown sugar, shortening and eggs with electric mixer on medium speed, or mix with spoon. Stir in remaining ingredients.

2 On ungreased cookie sheet, drop dough by ¼ cupfuls about 2 inches apart. Flatten to about ½-inch thickness with bottom of glass that has been greased and dipped into granulated sugar.

3 Bake 12 to 16 minutes or until golden brown. Cool 3 minutes; carefully remove from cookie sheet to cooling rack.

1 COOKIE: Calories 270; Total Fat 11g (Saturated Fat 3½g; Trans Fat 1½g); Cholesterol 25mg; Sodium 260mg; Total Carbohydrate 39g (Dietary Fiber 1g); Protein 3g EXCHANGES: 1 Starch; 1½ Other Carbohydrate; 2 Fat CARBOHYDRATE CHOICES: 2½

citrus mini cheesecakes

PREP TIME: 15 minutes *START TO FINISH:* 1 hour 55 minutes [60 SERVINGS]

Crust

1½ cups Original Bisquick® mix

½ cup sugar

1 teaspoon grated lime, lemon or orange peel

⅓ cup firm butter or margarine

Filling

3 packages (8 oz each) cream cheese, softened

1½ cups sugar

2 tablespoons Original Bisquick® mix

1 teaspoon grated lime, lemon or orange peel

1¼ cups milk

3 tablespoons lime, lemon or orange juice

1 teaspoon vanilla

3 eggs

Citrus peel, if desired

1 Heat oven to 375°F. In medium bowl, stir crust ingredients except butter. With pastry blender (or pulling 2 table knives through ingredients in opposite directions), cut in butter until mixture looks like coarse crumbs. Pat on bottom of ungreased 15 × 10-inch pan. Bake 10 minutes.

2 Meanwhile, in large bowl, beat cream cheese, 1½ cups sugar, 2 tablespoons Bisquick mix and 1 teaspoon lime peel with electric mixer on medium speed until blended and fluffy. On low speed, beat in milk, lime juice, vanilla and eggs until blended. Beat on low speed 2 minutes longer. Pour over partially baked crust.

3 Bake 35 to 40 minutes or until knife inserted in center comes out clean. Cool completely, about 1 hour. Refrigerate until ready to serve. For mini cheesecakes, cut into 10 rows by 6 rows. Garnish with citrus peel. Store covered in refrigerator.

1 MINI CHEESECAKE: Calories 100; Total Fat 6g (Saturated Fat 3½g; Trans Fat 0g); Cholesterol 25mg; Sodium 85mg; Total Carbohydrate 9g (Dietary Fiber 0g); Protein 2g
EXCHANGES: ½ Other Carbohydrate; 1½ Fat CARBOHYDRATE CHOICES: ½

sweet note To cut these bars more easily, use a knife dipped in a glass of water. Clean the knife and dip again in water when needed.

sweetie-pie surprise

PREP TIME: 12 minutes *START TO FINISH:* 22 minutes [8 SERVINGS]

⅔ cup powdered sugar

1 package (3 oz) cream cheese, softened

½ teaspoon almond extract

1 egg

1¾ cups Original Bisquick® mix

⅔ cup miniature semisweet chocolate chips

1 can (21 oz) cherry pie filling

¼ cup white baking chips

2 teaspoons shortening

1 Heat oven to 400°F. Stir together powdered sugar, cream cheese, almond extract and egg. Stir in Bisquick mix. Pat dough into 12-inch circle on ungreased cookie sheet.

2 Bake 8 to 10 minutes or until light golden brown. Sprinkle chocolate chips over hot crust. Bake 1 minute longer or until chips are melted; spread evenly. Cool 5 minutes. Gently loosen and transfer to serving plate.

3 Spread pie filling over crust. Heat white baking chips and shortening over low heat until smooth; drizzle over pie filling.

1 SERVING: Calories 421; Total Fat 16g (Saturated Fat 8g; Trans Fat 1g); Cholesterol 40mg; Sodium 385mg; Total Carbohydrate 65g (Dietary Fiber 1 g); Protein 5g EXCHANGES: 1 Starch; 3 Other Carbohydrate; 2½ Fat CARBOHYDRATE CHOICES: 4

sweet notes You'll find that using a fork makes it easy to drizzle the melted white baking chips over the cherry pie filling.

extreme bars

PREP TIME: 10 minutes *START TO FINISH:* 1 hour 30 minutes [25 BARS]

2 cups Original Bisquick® mix

1 cup powdered sugar

½ cup butter or margarine, softened

1 egg

1 package (about 0.13 oz) strawberry-, lemon-, orange- or lime-flavored unsweetened soft drink mix

1 cup Betty Crocker® Rich & Creamy vanilla frosting (from 1-lb container)

Candy sprinkles, fruit-flavored gummy ring-shaped candies, gumdrops or jelly beans, if desired

1 Heat oven to 350°F. In medium bowl, stir Bisquick mix, powdered sugar, butter, egg and drink mix (dry) until dough forms. Pat mixture firmly on bottom of ungreased 8-inch square pan.

2 Bake 14 to 18 minutes or until lightly browned around edges. Cool in pan on wire rack about 1 hour.

3 Spread bars with frosting; sprinkle with candies. For bars, cut into 5 rows by 5 rows.

1 BAR: Calories 150; Total Fat 7g (Saturated Fat 4g; Trans Fat 0g); Cholesterol 20mg; Sodium 170mg; Total Carbohydrate 20g (Dietary Fiber 0g); Protein 0g EXCHANGES: 1½ Other Carbohydrate; 1½ Fat CARBOHYDRATE CHOICES: 1

sweet note Get in the spirit. Choose a drink mix color to match your school or favorite team colors the next time you have a sports potluck.

raspberry truffle tart

PREP TIME: 30 minutes *START TO FINISH:* 4 hours 5 minutes [8 SERVINGS]

1¼ cups Original Bisquick® mix

½ cup powdered sugar

½ cup finely chopped pecans

¼ cup butter or margarine (firm)

1 tablespoon hot water

⅔ cup raspberry preserves, melted

1 cup whipping (heavy) cream

1 package (12 oz) semisweet chocolate chips (2 cups)

2 tablespoons raspberry liqueur, if desired

1 pint raspberries (2 cups)

Whipped cream, if desired

1 Heat oven to 350°F. Grease 9 × 1-inch tart pan with removable bottom, or 9 × 3-inch springform pan. Mix Bisquick, powdered sugar and pecans in medium bowl. Cut in butter, using pastry blender or crisscrossing 2 knives, until mixture looks like fine crumbs. Stir in hot water. Press mixture firmly in bottom of pan.

2 Bake 15 to 20 minutes or until set but not brown. Brush with ⅓ cup of preserves. Cool completely.

3 Heat whipping cream and chocolate chips in 1-quart saucepan over medium heat, stirring constantly, until smooth; remove from heat. Stir in liqueur. Pour over crust; spread evenly. Refrigerate uncovered at least 2 hours until set.

4 Brush remaining ⅓ cup preserves over chocolate layer. Top with raspberries. Refrigerate uncovered at least 15 minutes before serving. Remove side of pan. Cut into wedges. Serve with whipped cream. Store covered in refrigerator.

1 SERVING: Calories 666; Total Fat 40g (Saturated Fat 22g; Trans Fat 1g); Cholesterol 56mg; Sodium 284mg; Total Carbohydrate 79g (Dietary Fiber 4g); Protein 7g
EXCHANGES: 1 Starch; 4 Other Carbohydrate; 7 Fat CARBOHYDRATE CHOICES: 5

sweet note Raspberries are made up of many connected parts, called drupelets, each of which has its own seed. We're most familiar with red raspberries, but this sweet-tart fruit also comes in shades of black and gold.

no-roll sugar cookies

PREP TIME: 55 minutes *START TO FINISH:* 55 minutes [48 COOKIES]

- 4 cups Original Bisquick® mix
- 1½ cups powdered sugar
- ¾ cup butter or margarine, softened
- 1 teaspoon almond extract
- 2 eggs
- 1 cup granulated sugar

1 Heat oven to 400°F. In large bowl, stir all ingredients except granulated sugar until soft dough forms.

2 Shape dough into balls, about 1 inch in diameter; roll in granulated sugar to coat. On ungreased cookie sheets, place balls about 2 inches apart. Flatten balls slightly with bottom of glass.

3 Bake 5 to 6 minutes or until edges are light golden brown. Cool 1 minute; remove from cookie sheets to cooling racks to cool. Store in airtight container.

1 COOKIE: Calories 100; Total Fat 4½g (Saturated Fat 2½g; Trans Fat 0g); Cholesterol 15mg; Sodium 150mg; Total Carbohydrate 14g (Dietary Fiber 0g); Protein 1g
EXCHANGES: ½ Starch; ½ Other Carbohydrate; 1 Fat CARBOHYDRATE CHOICES: 1

pumpkin dessert squares

PREP TIME: 15 minutes *START TO FINISH:* 1 hour 40 minutes [15 SERVINGS]

Base

1½ cups Original Bisquick® mix

½ cup chopped pecans

½ cup butter or margarine, softened

Filling

1 cup sugar

1 can (15 oz) pumpkin (not pumpkin pie mix)

1 can (12 oz) evaporated milk

4 teaspoons pumpkin pie spice

3 eggs

Topping

1 cup Original Bisquick® mix

½ cup packed brown sugar

¼ cup butter or margarine

¾ cup chopped pecans

Whipped cream, if desired

1 Heat oven to 350°F. Spray bottom and sides of 13 × 9-inch pan with cooking spray. In medium bowl, mix 1½ cups Bisquick and ½ cup pecans. Using pastry blender or fork, cut in ½ cup butter until mixture is crumbly. With floured fingers, press mixture in bottom of pan. Bake 10 minutes.

2 Meanwhile, in large bowl, beat filling ingredients with wire whisk until smooth; set aside. In medium bowl, mix 1 cup Bisquick mix and the brown sugar. Using pastry blender or fork, cut in ¼ cup butter until mixture is crumbly. Stir in ¾ cup pecans.

3 Pour filling over hot partially baked base. Sprinkle topping over filling.

4 Bake 50 to 55 minutes or until toothpick inserted in center comes out clean. Cool 30 minutes before cutting into squares. Serve with whipped cream, if desired. Store in refrigerator.

1 SERVING: Calories 370; Total Fat 21g (Saturated Fat 9g; Trans Fat 1g); Cholesterol 75mg; Sodium 350mg; Total Carbohydrate 40g (Dietary Fiber 2g); Protein 5g EXCHANGES: 1½ Starch; 1 Other Carbohydrate; 4 Fat CARBOHYDRATE CHOICES: 2½

sweet note No pumpkin pie spice? Use 2 teaspoons ground cinnamon, 1 teaspoon ground ginger, ½ teaspoon ground allspice and ½ teaspoon ground nutmeg.

candy-topped blossom cookies

PREP TIME: 1 hour 35 minutes *START TO FINISH:* 2 hours 5 minutes [48 COOKIES]

1 can (14 oz) sweetened condensed milk (not evaporated)

1 cup creamy peanut butter

2 cups Original Bisquick® mix

1 teaspoon vanilla

3 tablespoons sugar

48 round chewy caramels in milk chocolate (from 12-oz bag), unwrapped

sweet note If you like, chunky peanut butter can be used instead of the creamy type. The cookies will have a crunchier texture.

1 Heat oven to 375°F. In large bowl, beat condensed milk and peanut butter with electric mixer on medium speed until well blended.

2 Stir in Bisquick mix and vanilla until well blended.

3 Shape dough into forty-eight 1-inch balls. Measure sugar into small bowl. Dip top of each ball into sugar. On ungreased cookie sheets, place balls 2 inches apart.

4 Bake 7 to 9 minutes. Firmly press 1 caramel into center of each cookie. Bake about 1 minute or until chocolate begins to soften and cookie begins to turn light golden brown. Cool 2 to 3 minutes. Remove from cookie sheets to cooling rack. Cool completely, about 30 minutes.

1 SERVING: Calories 110; Total Fat 5g (Saturated Fat 2g; Trans Fat 0g); Cholesterol 0mg; Sodium 110mg; Total Carbohydrate 14g (Dietary Fiber 0g); Protein 2g EXCHANGES: ½ Starch; ½ Other Carbohydrate; 1 Fat CARBOHYDRATE CHOICES: 1

saucepan granola bars

PREP TIME: 10 minutes *START TO FINISH:* 1 hour 35 minutes [48 BARS]

- ½ cup butter or margarine
- 2½ cups Original Bisquick® mix
- 2 cups granola with fruit
- 1 cup packed brown sugar
- ½ cup chopped nuts
- 1 teaspoon vanilla
- 2 eggs

1 Heat oven to 375°F. In 3-quart saucepan, melt butter over low heat. Stir in remaining ingredients until blended. Spoon into ungreased 13 × 9-inch pan; spread evenly.

2 Bake 20 to 25 minutes or until deep golden brown. Cool completely, about 1 hour. For bars, cut into 8 rows by 6 rows.

1 BAR: Calories 90; Total Fat 4½g (Saturated Fat 1½g; Trans Fat 0g); Cholesterol 15mg; Sodium 110mg; Total Carbohydrate 11g (Dietary Fiber 0g); Protein 1g EXCHANGES: ½ Starch; 1 Fat CARBOHYDRATE CHOICES: 1

sweet note Drizzle cooled bars with melted chocolate chips for an extra touch.

lickety-split gingersnaps

PREP TIME: 45 minutes *START TO FINISH:* 1 hour 5 minutes [48 COOKIES]

- 1 cup packed dark brown sugar
- ⅓ cup shortening
- ¼ cup full-flavor (dark) molasses
- 1 egg
- 2½ cups Original Bisquick® mix
- 1½ teaspoons ground allspice
- 1½ teaspoons ground ginger
- 2 tablespoons granulated sugar

1 Heat oven to 375°F. In large bowl, mix brown sugar, shortening, molasses and egg with spoon. Stir in Bisquick mix, allspice and ginger.

2 On work surface sprinkled with Bisquick mix, gently roll dough in Bisquick mix to coat. Divide dough into 4 parts. Shape each part into a roll, ¾ to 1 inch in diameter and about 12 inches long. On large ungreased cookie sheet, place rolls about 2 inches apart. Sprinkle granulated sugar down centers of rolls.

3 Bake 12 to 15 minutes or until set and slightly cracked. Cool on cookie sheet 5 minutes. Cut diagonally into about 1-inch strips. Carefully remove from cookie sheet to cooling rack.

1 COOKIE: Calories 70; Total Fat 2½g (Saturated Fat ½g; Trans Fat 0g); Cholesterol 0mg; Sodium 80mg; Total Carbohydrate 10g (Dietary Fiber 0g); Protein 0g EXCHANGES: ½ Starch; ½ Fat CARBOHYDRATE CHOICES: ½

sweet note For the best flavor, be sure to use spices that are no older than 6 months.

ultimate turtle brownies

PREP TIME: 30 minutes *START TO FINISH:* 3 hours 5 minutes [24 BROWNIES]

- 1 box (1 lb 2.4 oz) Betty Crocker® Original Supreme Premium brownie mix
- Water, vegetable oil and egg called for on brownie mix box
- 36 caramels (from 14-oz bag), unwrapped
- 3 tablespoons whipping cream
- 1⅓ cups semisweet chocolate chunks
- ⅔ cup coarsely chopped pecans

1 Heat oven to 350°F (325°F for dark or nonstick pan). Spray bottom and sides of 9-inch square pan with baking spray with flour.

2 Make brownie mix as directed on box, using pouch of chocolate syrup, water, oil and egg. Spread half of batter in pan. Bake 18 minutes.

3 Meanwhile, in large microwavable bowl, microwave caramels and whipping cream uncovered on High 2 to 3 minutes, stirring occasionally, until smooth.

4 Pour caramel mixture over partially baked brownie; spread to within ¼ inch of edges. Sprinkle with ⅔ cup of the chocolate chunks and ⅓ cup of the pecans. Drop remaining brownie batter by small spoonfuls onto caramel layer. Sprinkle with remaining ⅔ cup chocolate chunks and ⅓ cup pecans.

5 Bake 34 to 37 minutes longer or until center is almost set. Cool 1 hour at room temperature. Cover; refrigerate 1 hour before serving.

6 For brownies, cut into 6 rows by 4 rows. Store covered at room temperature.

1 BROWNIE: Calories 250; Total Fat 11g (Saturated Fat 3g; Trans Fat 0g); Cholesterol 20mg; Sodium 115mg; Total Carbohydrate 36g (Dietary Fiber 1g); Protein 2g EXCHANGES: ½ Starch; 2 Other Carbohydrate; 2 Fat CARBOHYDRATE CHOICES: 2½

sweet note You'll get rave reviews when you tote these caramelicious brownies to your next bake sale or potluck. You can make them the day ahead and store them tightly covered at room temperature so they are ready to go when you are!

mexican brownies

PREP TIME: 30 minutes *START TO FINISH:* 3 hours 30 minutes [16 BROWNIES]

- 1 box (1 lb 2.4 oz) Betty Crocker® Original Supreme Premium brownie mix
- 2 teaspoons ground cinnamon
- Water, vegetable oil and egg called for on brownie mix box
- ⅔ cup semisweet chocolate chips
- ⅓ cup butter or margarine
- ⅔ cup packed brown sugar
- 3 tablespoons milk
- 1½ cups powdered sugar
- ⅔ cup chopped pecans, toasted*

1 Heat oven to 350°F (325°F for dark or nonstick pan). Spray bottom only of 8- or 9-inch square pan with cooking spray.

2 In medium bowl, stir together dry brownie mix and cinnamon. Add pouch of chocolate syrup, water, oil and egg; stir until well blended. Stir in chocolate chips. Spread in pan.

3 Bake as directed on brownie mix box for 8- or 9-inch square pan. Cool completely, about 2 hours.

4 In 2-quart saucepan, melt butter over medium heat. Stir in brown sugar. Heat to boiling, stirring constantly. Reduce heat to low; boil and stir 2 minutes. Stir in milk. Heat to boiling. Remove from heat; cool to lukewarm, about 30 minutes.

5 Gradually beat powdered sugar into brown sugar mixture with wire whisk until blended, then beat until smooth. If frosting becomes too stiff, stir in additional milk, 1 teaspoon at a time. Spread frosting over brownies; sprinkle with pecans.

6 For brownies, cut into 4 rows by 4 rows. Store tightly covered.

1 BROWNIE: Calories 360; Total Fat 16g (Saturated Fat 5g; Trans Fat 0g); Cholesterol 35mg; Sodium 140mg; Total Carbohydrate 53g (Dietary Fiber 1g); Protein 2g EXCHANGES: ½ Starch; 3 Other Carbohydrate; 3 Fat CARBOHYDRATE CHOICES: 3½

* *To toast pecans, bake in ungreased shallow pan in 350°F oven about 10 minutes, stirring occasionally, until golden brown.*

sweet note Lots of cinnamon, caramel and pecans provide the Mexican flair in these decadent brownies.

chocolate chip cookie dough brownies

PREP TIME: 15 minutes *START TO FINISH:* 2 hours 5 minutes [42 BROWNIES]

- 1 box (1 lb 2.4 oz) Betty Crocker® Original Supreme Premium brownie mix
- Water, vegetable oil and egg called for on brownie mix box
- 1 pouch (1 lb 1.5 oz) Betty Crocker® chocolate chip cookie mix
- ½ cup butter or margarine, softened
- 1 egg
- 1 container (1 lb) Betty Crocker® Rich & Creamy chocolate frosting, if desired

1 Heat oven to 350°F (325°F for dark or nonstick pan). Spray bottom only of 13 × 9-inch pan with cooking spray, or grease with shortening. Make brownie mix as directed on box. Spread in pan.

2 Make cookie mix as directed on pouch, using butter and 1 egg. Drop dough by rounded tablespoonfuls evenly onto brownie batter; press down lightly.

3 Bake 42 to 47 minutes or until toothpick inserted 2 inches from side of pan comes out almost clean. Cool on cooling rack 30 minutes. Frost with frosting. For brownies, cut into 7 rows by 6 rows.

1 BROWNIE: Calories 130; Total Fat 6g (Saturated Fat 2½g; Trans Fat 0g); Cholesterol 15mg; Sodium 105mg; Total Carbohydrate 19g (Dietary Fiber 0g); Protein 1g
EXCHANGES: ½ Starch; 1 Other Carbohydrate; 1 Fat CARBOHYDRATE CHOICES: 1

sweet note This is one of those little secrets we know you'll love! Cutting brownies or any bar with a chewy and dense texture is much easier when you use a plastic knife.

chocolate mousse brownie dessert

PREP TIME: 15 minutes *START TO FINISH:* 3 hours 20 minutes [12 SERVINGS]

1 Heat oven to 350°F (325°F for dark or nonstick 13 × 9-inch pan). Grease bottom only of 13 × 9-inch pan or 10-inch springform pan. In large bowl, stir brownie mix, pouch of chocolate syrup, water, oil and 2 eggs until well blended. Spread batter in pan.

2 In 2-quart saucepan, heat ¾ cup whipping cream and the chocolate chips over medium heat, stirring constantly, until chocolate is melted and mixture is smooth; cool slightly. In medium bowl, beat 3 eggs and the granulated sugar with electric mixer on medium speed until foamy; stir into cream-chocolate mixture. Pour evenly over batter.

3 Bake rectangular pan about 44 minutes, springform pan about 1 hour 5 minutes, or until topping is set. Cool completely, about 2 hours. Serve at room temperature, or cover tightly and refrigerate until chilled.

4 In small bowl, beat all whipped cream ingredients with electric mixer on high speed until soft peaks form. Serve dessert with whipped cream. Store in refrigerator.

1 SERVING: Calories 380; Total Fat 18g (Saturated Fat 7g; Trans Fat 0g); Cholesterol 105mg; Sodium 170mg; Total Carbohydrate 51g (Dietary Fiber 2g); Protein 5g EXCHANGES: 1 Starch; 2½ Other Carbohydrate; 3½ Fat CARBOHYDRATE CHOICES: 3½

Dessert

1 box (1 lb 2.4 oz) Betty Crocker® Original Supreme Premium brownie mix

¼ cup water

¼ cup vegetable oil

2 eggs

¾ cup whipping cream

1 cup semisweet chocolate chips (6 oz)

3 eggs

⅓ cup granulated sugar

Chocolate Whipped Cream, if desired

¾ cup whipping cream

3 tablespoons powdered sugar

2 tablespoons unsweetened baking cocoa

sweet note Make it your way! Create butterscotch mousse bars by using butterscotch chips in place of chocolate chips in the mousse layer.

brownie ice cream cake

PREP TIME: 25 minutes *START TO FINISH:* 3 hours 55 minutes [16 SERVINGS]

1 box (1 lb 2.3 oz) Betty Crocker® fudge brownie mix

Water, vegetable oil and eggs called for on brownie mix box

½ gallon (8 cups) vanilla ice cream, slightly softened

1 cup hot fudge topping, warmed if desired

2 tablespoons Betty Crocker® Decorating Decors candy sprinkles

16 red maraschino cherries with stems, drained

1 Heat oven to 350°F. Line two 9-inch round cake pans with foil; grease bottoms only with shortening or cooking spray.

2 Make brownie batter as directed on box. Divide batter evenly between pans. Bake 19 to 22 minutes or until toothpick inserted 2 inches from side of pan comes out almost clean. Cool completely in pans, about 1 hour. Do not remove from pans.

3 Spread slightly softened ice cream evenly on brownies in pans. Freeze at least 2 hours or until ice cream is firm.

4 Remove desserts from pans; remove foil. Place on serving plates. Cut each dessert into 8 wedges. Drizzle each wedge with hot fudge topping. Decorate with candy sprinkles and cherries. Store covered in freezer.

1 SERVING: Calories 380; Total Fat 15g (Saturated Fat 7g; Trans Fat 0g); Cholesterol 40mg; Sodium 230mg; Total Carbohydrate 56g (Dietary Fiber 2g); Protein 4g EXCHANGES: 1 Starch; 2½ Other Carbohydrate; 3 Fat CARBOHYDRATE CHOICES: 4

sweet note Set up a dessert bar with ice cream toppings and syrups as well as extras like fresh strawberries, sliced bananas, chopped nuts and candies.

brownies and chocolate-raspberry fondue

PREP TIME: 20 minutes *START TO FINISH:* 2 hours [16 SERVINGS]

1 box (1 lb 2.4 oz) Betty Crocker® Original Supreme Premium brownie mix

Water, vegetable oil and egg called for on brownie mix box

1 container (1 lb) Betty Crocker® Rich & Creamy chocolate frosting

⅓ cup seedless raspberry preserves

Assorted fresh fruit (orange sections, whole strawberries, banana slices and raspberries) and marshmallows, as desired

1 Heat oven to 350°F (325°F for dark or nonstick pan). Grease bottom only of 8- or 9-inch square pan with cooking spray or shortening. Make brownies as directed on box. Cool completely, about 1 hour. For 49 squares, cut into 7 rows by 7 rows.

2 In microwavable bowl, stir together frosting and preserves. Microwave uncovered on High about 20 seconds or until mixture can be stirred smooth. Pour into fondue pot. Keep warm over low heat, and serve within 1 hour.

3 Spear brownies and fruit with fondue forks; dip in fondue.

1 SERVING (1⁄16 FONDUE MIXTURE, 3 BROWNIES, 1 PIECE EACH ORANGE, STRAWBERRY, BANANA, RASPBERRY): Calories 280; Total Fat 9g (Saturated Fat 2½g; Trans Fat 1½g); Cholesterol 15mg; Sodium 190mg; Total Carbohydrate 49g (Dietary Fiber 1g); Protein 1g EXCHANGES: 1 Starch; 2½ Other Carbohydrate; 1½ Fat CARBOHYDRATE CHOICES: 3

sweet note For easy cutting, line the pan with foil first, before greasing. After baking, lift out the cooled brownies and slice.

brownie peanut chews

PREP TIME: 25 minutes *START TO FINISH:* 2 hours 10 minutes [25 BROWNIES]

Brownies

1 box (1 lb 2.4 oz) Betty Crocker® Original Supreme Premium brownie mix

Water, vegetable oil and egg called for on brownie mix box

2 cups miniature marshmallows

Filling

½ cup light corn syrup

3 tablespoons butter or margarine

1½ teaspoons vanilla

1⅓ cups (8 oz) peanut butter chips

1⅓ cups crisp rice cereal

1⅓ cups salted peanuts

1 Heat oven to 350°F (325°F for dark or nonstick pan). Grease bottom only of 9-inch square pan with cooking spray or shortening. Make brownies as directed on box—except after removing from oven, immediately sprinkle with marshmallows. Bake 1 to 2 minutes longer or until marshmallows just begin to puff.

2 In 3-quart saucepan, heat corn syrup, butter, vanilla and peanut butter chips over medium heat 3 to 4 minutes, stirring constantly, until chips are melted. Remove from heat; stir in cereal and peanuts. Spread evenly over marshmallows. Refrigerate 45 minutes or until firm. For brownies, cut into 5 rows by 5 rows. Store in refrigerator.

1 BROWNIE: Calories 250; Total Fat 11g (Saturated Fat 2½g; Trans Fat 0g); Cholesterol 10mg; Sodium 180mg; Total Carbohydrate 33g (Dietary Fiber 1g); Protein 4g EXCHANGES: 1 Starch; 1 Other Carbohydrate; 2 Fat CARBOHYDRATE CHOICES: 2

sweet note Not a nut lover? Go ahead and leave them out. The bars will be just as gooey and delicious.

peanut butter truffle brownies

PREP TIME: 20 minutes *START TO FINISH:* 2 hours 30 minutes [36 BROWNIES]

1 Heat oven to 350°F. Grease bottom only of 13 × 9-inch pan with shortening or cooking spray. (For easier cutting, line pan with foil, then grease foil on bottom only of pan.)

2 Make and bake brownies as directed on box, using water, oil and eggs. Cool completely, about 1 hour.

3 In medium bowl, beat filling ingredients with electric mixer on medium speed until smooth. Spread mixture evenly over brownie base.

4 In small microwavable bowl, microwave topping ingredients uncovered on High 30 to 60 seconds; stir until smooth. Cool 10 minutes; spread over filling. Refrigerate about 30 minutes or until set.

5 For brownies, cut into 9 rows by 4 rows. Store covered in refrigerator.

1 BROWNIE: Calories 200; Total Fat 12g (Saturated Fat 4½g; Trans Fat 0g); Cholesterol 20mg; Sodium 100mg; Total Carbohydrate 23g (Dietary Fiber 0g); Protein 1g EXCHANGES: 1½ Other Carbohydrate; 2½ Fat CARBOHYDRATE CHOICES: 1½

Brownie Base

1 box (1 lb 2.3 oz) Betty Crocker® fudge brownie mix

Water, vegetable oil and eggs called for on brownie mix box

Filling

½ cup butter or margarine, softened

½ cup creamy peanut butter

2 cups powdered sugar

2 teaspoons milk

Topping

1 cup semisweet chocolate chips

¼ cup butter or margarine, softened

sweet note These brownies are ideal for a dessert buffet. Cut them into bite-size squares and arrange on a decorative platter for serving.

fudgy brownie trifle

PREP TIME: 15 minutes *START TO FINISH:* 5 hours 45 minutes [20 SERVINGS]

1 box (1 lb 2.3 oz) Betty Crocker® fudge brownie mix

Water, vegetable oil and eggs called for on brownie mix box

1 tablespoon instant coffee granules or crystals

1 box (4-serving size) chocolate fudge instant pudding and pie filling mix

2 cups cold milk

1 bag (8 oz) toffee bits

1 container (8 oz) frozen whipped topping, thawed

1 Heat oven to 350°F. Grease bottom only of 13 × 9-inch pan with shortening or cooking spray.

2 Make brownie mix as directed on box, using water, oil and eggs and adding coffee granules. Spread batter in pan. Bake as directed on box. Cool completely, about 1 hour.

3 Cut brownies into 1-inch squares. Place half of the squares in bottom of 3-quart glass bowl. Make pudding mix as directed on box for pudding, using milk. Pour half of the pudding over brownies in bowl. Top with half each of the toffee bits and whipped topping. Repeat with remaining brownies, pudding, toffee bits and whipped topping.

4 Cover; refrigerate at least 4 hours before serving. Store covered in refrigerator.

1 SERVING: Calories 300; Total Fat 15g (Saturated Fat 6g; Trans Fat 0g); Cholesterol 30mg; Sodium 230mg; Total Carbohydrate 38g (Dietary Fiber 1g); Protein 3g EXCHANGES: 1 Starch; 1½ Other Carbohydrate; 3 Fat CARBOHYDRATE CHOICES: 2½

sweet note Trifles are a traditional English dessert originally made with cake or ladyfingers covered with jam and custard and topped with whipped cream. This recipe is a rich chocolaty version with a mild coffee flavor. There's no fruit in this trifle, but you can garnish with fresh strawberries (dipped in chocolate if you like) or raspberries for a pretty finish.

brownie goody bars

PREP TIME: 15 minutes *START TO FINISH:* 2 hours 55 minutes [24 BARS]

1 box (1 lb 2.3 oz) Betty Crocker® fudge brownie mix

Water, vegetable oil and eggs called for on brownie mix box

1 container (12 oz or 1 lb) Betty Crocker® Whipped or Rich & Creamy vanilla frosting

¾ cup salted peanuts, coarsely chopped

3 cups crisp rice cereal

1 cup creamy peanut butter

1 bag (12 oz) semisweet chocolate chips (2 cups)

1 Heat oven to 350°F. Spray bottom only of 13 × 9-inch pan with cooking spray.

2 Make brownie mix as directed on box, using water, oil and eggs. Spread batter into pan.

3 Bake as directed on box. Cool completely.

4 Spread brownies with frosting; sprinkle with peanuts. Refrigerate while making cereal mixture.

5 Into large bowl, measure cereal; set aside. In 1-quart saucepan, melt peanut butter and chocolate chips over low heat, stirring constantly. Pour over cereal in bowl, stirring until evenly coated. Spread over frosted brownies. Cool completely before cutting, about 1 hour.

6 For bars, cut into 6 rows by 4 rows. Store tightly covered at room temperature or in refrigerator.

1 BAR: Calories 370; Total Fat 18g (Saturated Fat 5g; Trans Fat 1g); Cholesterol 10mg; Sodium 160mg; Total Carbohydrate 45g (Dietary Fiber 2g); Protein 4g EXCHANGES: 1 Starch; 2 Other Carbohydrate; 3½ Fat CARBOHYDRATE CHOICES: 3

sweet note These are incredibly rich bars that can be served with a fork. For even more decadence, top off each serving with a drizzle of caramel topping.

brownie pops

PREP TIME: 30 minutes *START TO FINISH:* 2 hours 30 minutes [24 SERVINGS]

- 1 box (1 lb 2.3 oz) Betty Crocker® fudge brownie mix
- Water, vegetable oil and eggs called for on brownie mix box
- 24 craft sticks (flat wooden sticks with round ends)
- 1 cup semisweet chocolate chips (6 oz)
- 2 teaspoons shortening
- Assorted Betty Crocker® Decor Selects decors or sprinkles

1 Heat oven to 350°F. Line 13 × 9-inch pan with foil so foil extends about 2 inches over sides of pan. Spray foil with cooking spray.

2 Make brownie mix as directed on box, using water, oil and eggs. Spread in pan.

3 Bake as directed on box for 13 × 9-inch pan. Cool completely, about 1 hour.

4 Place brownies in freezer for 30 minutes. Remove brownies from pan by lifting foil; peel foil from sides of brownies. Cut brownies into 24 square bars, 6 rows by 4 rows. Gently insert stick into end of each bar, peeling foil from bars. Place on cookie sheet; freeze 30 minutes.

5 In microwavable bowl, microwave chocolate chips and shortening uncovered on High about 1 minute; stir until smooth. If necessary, microwave additional 5 seconds at a time. Dip top one-third to one-half of each brownie into chocolate; sprinkle with decors. Lay flat on waxed paper or foil to dry.

1 BROWNIE POP: Calories 150; Total Fat 6g (Saturated Fat 2g; Trans Fat 0g); Cholesterol 10mg; Sodium 80mg; Total Carbohydrate 24g (Dietary Fiber 0g); Protein 0g EXCHANGES: 1½ Other Carbohydrate; 1 Fat CARBOHYDRATE CHOICES: 1½

sweet note For a little different contrast, use white vanilla baking chips instead of the chocolate chips. Or melt dark and white chocolate for variety. Look for a variety of candy sprinkles at a cake-decorating supply store.

caramel-pecan brownie dessert

PREP TIME: 20 minutes *START TO FINISH:* 5 hours 15 minutes [12 SERVINGS]

- 1 box (1 lb 2.3 oz) Betty Crocker® fudge brownie mix
- ¼ cup water
- ½ cup vegetable oil
- 2 eggs
- 1 cup milk chocolate chips
- ½ cup whipping (heavy) cream
- 20 caramels (from 14-oz bag), unwrapped
- 1 egg, beaten
- 1 cup broken pecans
- ¾ cup whipping (heavy) cream
- 2 tablespoons powdered sugar

1 Heat oven to 350°F (325°F for dark or nonstick pan). Grease bottom and side of 10-inch springform pan with shortening. In medium bowl, stir brownie mix, water, oil and 2 eggs until well blended. Stir in chocolate chips. Spread in pan.

2 Bake 50 to 60 minutes or until puffed in center and toothpick inserted near center comes out clean. Cool completely, about 1 hour.

3 Meanwhile, in 1-quart saucepan, heat ½ cup whipping cream and the caramels over medium heat, stirring frequently, until caramels are melted. Stir small amount of the hot mixture into 1 beaten egg, then stir egg back into mixture in saucepan. Cook over medium heat 2 to 3 minutes, stirring constantly, until thickened. Stir in pecans. Spread over brownies. Refrigerate uncovered at least 3 hours until chilled.

4 Run metal spatula around side of pan to loosen dessert; remove side of pan. Transfer dessert on pan base to serving plate. In chilled small bowl, beat ¾ cup whipping cream and the powdered sugar with electric mixer on high speed until stiff peaks form. Spoon whipped cream in 12 dollops around edge of dessert. Cut into wedges to serve. Store covered in refrigerator.

1 SERVING: Calories 600; Total Fat 38g (Saturated Fat 14g; Trans Fat 0g); Cholesterol 110mg; Sodium 85mg; Total Carbohydrate 57g (Dietary Fiber 3g); Protein 7g
EXCHANGES: 2 Starch; 2 Other Carbohydrate; 7 Fat CARBOHYDRATE CHOICES: 4

sweet note Be sure to taste-test nuts before you use them. Nuts can become rancid quickly, so it's best to store them in an airtight container in the freezer, where they will keep longer.

caramel brownies

PREP TIME: 30 minutes *START TO FINISH:* 3 hours 15 minutes [40 BROWNIES]

- 1 box (1 lb 2.4 oz) Betty Crocker® Original Supreme Premium brownie mix
- ¼ cup vegetable oil
- ¼ cup water
- 2 eggs
- 1 cup coarsely chopped nuts
- 1 cup semisweet chocolate chips (6 oz)
- 25 caramels (from 14-oz bag), unwrapped
- 2 tablespoons milk

1 Heat oven to 350°F (325°F for dark or nonstick pan). Grease bottom only of 13 × 9-inch pan with shortening or cooking spray. In medium bowl, stir brownie mix, pouch of chocolate syrup, oil, water and eggs until well blended. Spread in pan. In small bowl, combine nuts and chocolate chips; sprinkle half of mixture over batter in pan. Set remaining nut mixture aside.

2 Bake 30 minutes. Meanwhile, place caramels and milk in small microwavable bowl; microwave uncovered on High 1½ to 2½ minutes, stirring every minute until caramels are melted.

3 After removing pan from oven, immediately spoon caramel mixture over brownies to within ½ inch of sides; sprinkle with remaining nut mixture. Return to oven and bake an additional 10 minutes until toothpick inserted into brownies 2 inches from side of pan comes out almost clean. Cool completely, about 1½ hours. For brownies, cut into 8 rows by 5 rows. Store covered at room temperature.

1 BROWNIE: Calories 140; Total Fat 6g (Saturated Fat 1½g; Trans Fat 0g); Cholesterol 10mg; Sodium 60mg; Total Carbohydrate 19g (Dietary Fiber 0g); Protein 1g EXCHANGES: ½ Starch; 1 Other Carbohydrate; 1 Fat CARBOHYDRATE CHOICES: 1

sweet note Use your favorite nut for these decadent brownies. For a tropical twist, try macadamia nuts or a cashew-macadamia mix.

black forest brownie dessert

PREP TIME: 20 minutes *START TO FINISH:* 1 hour 20 minutes [6 SERVINGS]

- 1 pouch (10.25 oz) Betty Crocker® fudge brownie mix
- ⅓ cup vegetable oil
- 2 tablespoons water
- 1 egg
- 1 can (21 oz) cherry pie filling
- 2 tablespoons amaretto, if desired
- 1 cup whipping cream
- 1 tablespoon powdered sugar
- ¼ teaspoon unsweetened baking cocoa, if desired

1 Heat oven to 350°F. Spray 9-inch glass pie plate with baking spray with flour.

2 Make brownie mix as directed on pouch, using oil, water and egg. Pour batter into pie plate.

3 Bake 24 to 26 minutes or until toothpick inserted in center comes out almost clean. Cool 30 minutes.

4 In small bowl, stir together pie filling and amaretto. Cut brownie into 6 wedges. Place each wedge on individual serving plate. Spoon about ⅓ cup cherry mixture over each wedge.

5 In medium bowl, beat whipping cream and powdered sugar with electric mixer on high speed until stiff peaks form. Add dollop of whipped cream to each serving. Sprinkle with cocoa.

1 SERVING: Calories 540; Total Fat 28g (Saturated Fat 10g; Trans Fat 1g); Cholesterol 80mg; Sodium 190mg; Total Carbohydrate 70g (Dietary Fiber 3g); Protein 4g
EXCHANGES: 1 Starch; 3½ Other Carbohydrate; 5½ Fat CARBOHYDRATE CHOICES: 4½

sweet note Here's an easy version of the chocolate-cherry torte that originated in Germany's Black Forest region. The original torte uses kirsch, a cherry liqueur, instead of amaretto, and you could substitute cherry liqueur for the amaretto if you like.

chocolate truffle brownie cups

PREP TIME: 15 minutes *START TO FINISH:* 1 hour 35 minutes [42 BROWNIE CUPS]

- 1 box (1 lb 2.3 oz) Betty Crocker® fudge brownie mix
- Water, vegetable oil and eggs called for on brownie mix box
- ⅔ cup whipping cream
- 6 oz semisweet baking chocolate, chopped
- Chocolate candy sprinkles, if desired

1 Heat oven to 350°F. Place mini paper baking cup in each of 42 mini muffin cups.

2 In large bowl, stir brownie mix, water, oil and eggs until well blended. Fill muffin cups about three-quarters full (about 1 tablespoon each) with batter.

3 Bake 19 to 21 minutes or until toothpick inserted into edge of brownie comes out clean. Cool 10 minutes before removing from pan. Cool completely, about 30 minutes.

4 In 1-quart saucepan, heat whipping cream over low heat just until hot but not boiling; remove from heat. Stir in baking chocolate until melted. Let stand about 15 minutes or until mixture coats spoon. (It will become firmer the longer it cools.) Spoon about 2 teaspoons chocolate mixture over each brownie. Sprinkle with candy sprinkles.

1 BROWNIE CUP: Calories 110; Total Fat 6g (Saturated Fat 2g; Trans Fat 0g); Cholesterol 15mg; Sodium 50mg; Total Carbohydrate 14g (Dietary Fiber 0g); Protein 0g EXCHANGES: 1 Other Carbohydrate; 1 Fat CARBOHYDRATE CHOICES: 1

sweet note Here's a nice variation on the original recipe. Just add ½ teaspoon peppermint extract to the brownie batter. Then sprinkle crushed peppermint candies over the chocolate glaze at the end.

cookies ’n cream brownies

PREP TIME: 10 minutes *START TO FINISH:* 1 hour 40 minutes [20 BROWNIES]

1 box (1 lb 2.3 oz) Betty Crocker® fudge brownie mix

¼ cup water

⅔ cup vegetable oil

2 eggs

10 creme-filled chocolate sandwich cookies, crushed (1 cup)

½ container (1-lb size) Betty Crocker® Rich & Creamy chocolate or vanilla frosting (⅔ cup)

5 creme-filled chocolate sandwich cookies, coarsely chopped (⅔ cup)

1 Heat oven to 350°F. Grease bottom only of 13 × 9-inch pan, or spray with cooking spray.

2 Stir brownie mix, water, oil and eggs in medium bowl until well blended. Stir in 1 cup crushed cookies. Spread in pan.

3 Bake 24 to 26 minutes or until toothpick inserted 2 inches from side of pan comes out clean or almost clean. Cool completely, about 1 hour. Frost with frosting. Sprinkle with ⅔ cup chopped cookies. For 20 brownies, cut into 5 rows by 4 rows.

1 BROWNIE: Calories 250; Total Fat 12g (Saturated Fat 2g; Trans Fat 1g); Cholesterol 20mg; Sodium 160mg; Total Carbohydrate 35g (Dietary Fiber 1g); Protein 2g EXCHANGES: ½ Starch; 2 Other Carbohydrate; 2 Fat CARBOHYDRATE CHOICES: 2

sweet note Using a plastic knife when cutting the brownies helps prevent them from sticking to the knife.

german chocolate thumbprints

PREP TIME: 1 hour 30 minutes *START TO FINISH:* 1 hour 30 minutes [42 COOKIES]

1 box Betty Crocker® SuperMoist® German chocolate cake mix

⅔ cup flaked coconut

¼ cup vegetable oil

2 eggs

⅓ cup Betty Crocker® Rich & Creamy coconut pecan frosting (from 1-lb container)

¼ cup flaked coconut, toasted

1 Heat oven to 350°F. In large bowl, mix cake mix, ⅔ cup coconut, the oil and eggs with spoon until dough forms.

2 Shape dough into 1-inch balls; place about 2 inches apart on ungreased cookie sheets. Press thumb into center of each cookie to make indentation, but do not press all the way to the cookie sheet. Fill each indentation with level ¼ measuring teaspoon of the frosting.

3 Bake 8 to 11 minutes or until set. Cool 1 minute; remove from cookie sheets to cooling racks. Sprinkle each with about ¼ teaspoon of the toasted coconut. Cool completely, about 15 minutes.

1 COOKIE: Calories 40; Total Fat 3g (Saturated Fat 1½g; Trans Fat 0g); Cholesterol 10mg; Sodium 25mg; Total Carbohydrate 2g (Dietary Fiber 0g); Protein 0g EXCHANGES: ½ Fat CARBOHYDRATE CHOICES: 0

sweet note For a sparkly finish to these cookies, roll balls of dough in granulated sugar. Instead of topping the baked cookies with toasted coconut, sprinkle with toasted chopped pecans.

mix-easy chocolate chip cookies

PREP TIME: 25 minutes *START TO FINISH:* 1 hour 5 minutes [42 COOKIES]

- 1 box Betty Crocker® SuperMoist® yellow cake mix
- ½ cup butter or margarine, softened
- 1 to 2 tablespoons milk
- 1 teaspoon vanilla
- 1 egg
- ½ cup chopped nuts
- 1 cup semisweet chocolate chips

1 Heat oven to 350°F (325°F for dark or nonstick pans). In large bowl, beat cake mix, butter, 1 tablespoon milk, vanilla and egg with electric mixer on medium speed until smooth, or mix with spoon. Mix in additional 1 tablespoon milk if dough is too dry. Stir in nuts and chocolate chips.

2 Drop dough by slightly less than tablespoonfuls 2 inches apart on ungreased cookie sheets.

3 Bake cookies 10 to 12 minutes or until edges are set (centers will be soft and cookies will be very light in color). Cool 1 minute; remove from cookie sheets to cooling rack. Store covered.

1 COOKIE: Calories 90; Total Fat 5g (Saturated Fat 2½g; Trans Fat 0g); Cholesterol 10mg; Sodium 90mg; Total Carbohydrate 11g (Dietary Fiber 0g); Protein 0g EXCHANGES: ½ Other Carbohydrate; 1 Fat CARBOHYDRATE CHOICES: 1

sweet note For a softer cookie, use only ⅓ cup butter, softened, and 2 eggs; omit milk.

old-fashioned peanut butter cookies

PREP TIME: 1 hour 5 minutes *START TO FINISH:* 1 hour 5 minutes [42 COOKIES]

- 1 package Betty Crocker® SuperMoist® yellow or butter recipe yellow cake mix
- ⅓ cup water
- 1⅓ cups creamy peanut butter
- ⅓ cup butter or margarine, softened
- 1 egg
- 2 tablespoons sugar

1 Heat oven to 375°F (350°F for dark or nonstick pans). In large bowl, beat half of the cake mix, the water, peanut butter, butter and egg with electric mixer on medium speed until smooth, or mix with spoon. Stir in remaining cake mix.

2 On ungreased cookie sheet, drop dough by rounded tablespoonfuls about 2 inches apart. Flatten in crisscross pattern with fork dipped in sugar.

3 Bake 9 to 11 minutes or until golden brown. Cool 1 minute; remove from cookie sheet to cooling rack. Store covered.

1 COOKIE: Calories 110; Total Fat 6g (Saturated Fat 2g; Trans Fat 0g); Cholesterol 10mg; Sodium 125mg; Total Carbohydrate 11g (Dietary Fiber 0g); Protein 2g EXCHANGES: ½ Other Carbohydrate; ½ High-Fat Meat; ½ Fat CARBOHYDRATE CHOICES: 1

sweet note Give a new look to these cookies by pressing the bottom of a cut-crystal glass, a potato masher or a cookie stamp into the dough before baking.

chocolate chip–pecan bars

PREP TIME: 15 minutes *START TO FINISH:* 1 hour 45 minutes [32 BARS]

½ cup butter or margarine, softened

1 package Betty Crocker® SuperMoist® white or yellow cake mix

2 cups pecan halves

⅔ cup butter or margarine

⅔ cup packed brown sugar

1 cup semisweet chocolate chips (6 oz)

sweet note Like walnuts? You could use them instead of the pecans.

1 Heat oven to 350°F (325°F for dark or nonstick pan). In medium bowl, cut ½ cup butter into cake mix, using pastry blender (or pulling 2 table knives through ingredients in opposite directions), until crumbly. Press firmly in bottom of ungreased 13 × 9-inch pan. Bake 13 to 14 minutes or until crust is dry.

2 Sprinkle pecan halves evenly over baked layer. In 2-quart saucepan, heat ⅔ cup butter and the brown sugar to boiling over medium heat, stirring occasionally; boil and stir 1 minute. Spoon mixture evenly over pecans.

3 Bake 13 to 15 minutes or until bubbly and light brown. Sprinkle chocolate chips over warm bars. Cool completely, about 1 hour. For bars, cut into 8 rows by 4 rows.

1 BAR: Calories 200; Total Fat 13g (Saturated Fat 5g; Trans Fat 0g); Cholesterol 15mg; Sodium 140mg; Total Carbohydrate 20g (Dietary Fiber 1g); Protein 1g EXCHANGES: ½ Starch; 1 Other Carbohydrate; 2½ Fat CARBOHYDRATE CHOICES: 1

oatmeal-raisin cookies

PREP TIME: 1 hour *START TO FINISH:* 1 hour [66 COOKIES]

1 box Betty Crocker® SuperMoist® yellow cake mix

½ cup packed brown sugar

½ cup butter or margarine, softened

½ cup shortening

2 tablespoons water

1½ teaspoons ground cinnamon

1 egg

2 cups quick-cooking or old-fashioned oats

1 cup raisins or chopped dates

½ cup chopped nuts, if desired

1 Heat oven to 375°F (350°F for dark or nonstick pans). In large bowl, beat cake mix, brown sugar, butter, shortening, water, cinnamon and egg with electric mixer on medium speed about 1 minute or until smooth. With spoon, stir in oats, raisins and nuts.

2 Drop dough by teaspoonfuls about 2 inches apart onto ungreased cookie sheets; flatten dough slightly with fingers.

3 Bake 9 to 12 minutes (centers will be soft). Cool 1 minute; remove from cookie sheets. Store covered.

1 COOKIE: Calories 80; Total Fat 3½g (Saturated Fat 1½g; Trans Fat 0g); Cholesterol 5mg; Sodium 60mg; Total Carbohydrate 11g (Dietary Fiber 0g); Protein 0g EXCHANGES: ½ Starch; ½ Fat CARBOHYDRATE CHOICES: 1

sweet note Get a jump start on delicious homemade oatmeal cookies with Betty Crocker® cake mix.

chocolate-caramel-oatmeal bars

PREP TIME: 20 minutes *START TO FINISH:* 3 hours 5 minutes [24 BARS]

- 1 jar (12.25 oz) caramel topping (1 cup)
- 1 box Betty Crocker® SuperMoist® yellow cake mix
- ⅔ cup butter or margarine, softened
- 1 egg
- 2 cups quick-cooking oats
- 1½ cups semisweet chocolate chips
- 1 cup chopped walnuts or pecans

1 Heat oven to 350°F (325°F for dark or nonstick pan). Line 13 × 9-inch pan with foil, letting foil hang 2 inches over short ends of pan. Spray foil with cooking spray.

2 In small bowl, mix caramel topping and 1 tablespoon of the cake mix; set aside. In large bowl, beat remaining cake mix, butter and egg with electric mixer on low speed about 1 minute or just until crumbly. Stir in oats, using hands if necessary. Reserve 1 cup oat mixture. Using a piece of plastic wrap on crumb mixture, press remaining oat mixture in bottom of pan; remove plastic wrap. Bake 14 to 18 minutes or until light golden brown.

3 Sprinkle chocolate chips and walnuts over hot crust. Drizzle caramel mixture evenly over chocolate chips and walnuts to within ½ inch of edges. Crumble reserved oat mixture over top.

4 Bake 20 to 25 minutes or until golden brown. Cool completely, about 2 hours. Using foil to lift, remove bars from pan. Remove foil. For bars, cut into 6 rows by 4 rows. Store covered.

1 BAR: Calories 270; Total Fat 13g (Saturated Fat 6g; Trans Fat 0g); Cholesterol 20mg; Sodium 220mg; Total Carbohydrate 36g (Dietary Fiber 2g); Protein 3g EXCHANGES: 1 Starch; 1½ Other Carbohydrate; 2½ Fat CARBOHYDRATE CHOICES: 2½

sweet note Be sure to check your oats to see if they are the quick-cooking kind. Don't use instant oatmeal, which will become mushy when it's baked in dough.

peanutty granola cookies

PREP TIME: 1 hour *START TO FINISH:* 2 hours 5 minutes [32 COOKIES]

1 box Betty Crocker® SuperMoist® butter recipe yellow cake mix

½ cup butter or margarine, softened

2 eggs

4 Nature Valley® Sweet & Salty peanut granola bars (from 7.4-oz box), coarsely chopped

½ cup peanut butter chips (from 10-oz bag)

1½ teaspoons shortening

1 Heat oven to 350°F (325°F for dark or nonstick pan). In large bowl, beat cake mix, butter and eggs with electric mixer on medium speed until smooth. Stir in chopped granola bars. Onto ungreased cookie sheet, drop mixture by tablespoonfuls.

2 Bake 10 to 12 minutes or until set and light golden brown around edges. Let cool on cookie sheet 2 minutes. Remove from cookie sheet to cooling rack. Cool completely, about 30 minutes.

3 In small microwavable bowl, microwave peanut butter chips and shortening uncovered on High 15 seconds; stir. Microwave 15 to 25 seconds longer or until mixture can be stirred smooth. Spoon into small food-storage plastic bag. Cut off tiny corner of bag; squeeze bag to drizzle mixture over cookies. Let stand about 30 minutes or until drizzle is set. Store in airtight container.

1 COOKIE: Calories 120; Total Fat 6g (Saturated Fat 2½g; Trans Fat 0g); Cholesterol 20mg; Sodium 150mg; Total Carbohydrate 16g (Dietary Fiber 0g); Protein 1g EXCHANGES: 1 Other Carbohydrate; 1½ Fat CARBOHYDRATE CHOICES: 1

sweet note If you like the flavor combination of peanut butter and chocolate, substitute chocolate chips for the peanut butter chips.

glazed lemon wedges

PREP TIME: 15 minutes *START TO FINISH:* 1 hour 40 minutes [24 SERVINGS]

Cookies

1 box Betty Crocker® SuperMoist® butter recipe yellow cake mix

⅓ cup butter or margarine, softened

2 tablespoons grated lemon peel

1 egg

Glaze

1 cup powdered sugar

1 teaspoon grated lemon peel

3 tablespoons lemon juice

Garnish

Grated lemon peel, if desired

1 Heat oven to 350°F (325°F for dark or nonstick pans). Spray bottoms and sides of two 8-inch round cake pans with baking spray with flour, or line with foil.

2 In large bowl, beat cake mix, butter, 2 tablespoons lemon peel and the egg with electric mixer on low speed until crumbly. Beat on medium speed until dough forms. Press half of dough in each pan.

3 Bake 17 to 23 minutes or until edges are light golden brown. Cool 10 minutes.

4 In small bowl, mix glaze ingredients until smooth. Spoon glaze over warm shortbread; spread to edges of pans. Cool completely, about 50 minutes. Garnish with lemon peel. Cut each shortbread into 12 wedges. Store loosely covered.

1 COOKIE WEDGE: Calories 110; Total Fat 3½g (Saturated Fat 2g; Trans Fat 0g); Cholesterol 15mg; Sodium 150mg; Total Carbohydrate 20g (Dietary Fiber 0g); Protein 0g
EXCHANGES: 1½ Other Carbohydrate; ½ Fat CARBOHYDRATE CHOICES: 1

sweet note Garnish with grated lemon peel or lemon peel strips. When grating lemon peel, be sure to grate only the yellow part of the skin. The white part, or pith, is very bitter.

spicy pumpkin cookies

PREP TIME: 10 minutes *START TO FINISH:* 1 hour 5 minutes [30 COOKIES]

1 box Betty Crocker® SuperMoist® yellow cake mix

2 teaspoons pumpkin pie spice

1 cup canned pumpkin (not pumpkin pie mix)

¼ cup butter or margarine, softened

½ cup raisins, if desired

1 cup Betty Crocker® Rich & Creamy vanilla frosting (from 1-lb container)

1 Heat oven to 375°F (350°F for dark or nonstick pan). Lightly grease or spray cookie sheet.

2 In large bowl, beat cake mix, pumpkin pie spice, pumpkin and butter with electric mixer on low speed 1 minute. Stir in raisins.

3 On cookie sheet, drop dough by generous tablespoonfuls 2 inches apart.

4 Bake 10 to 13 minutes or until set and light golden brown around edges. Cool 1 to 2 minutes; remove from cookie sheet to cooling rack. Cool completely, about 30 minutes. Frost with frosting. Store loosely covered.

1 COOKIE: Calories 130; Total Fat 4½g (Saturated Fat 2g; Trans Fat ½g); Cholesterol 5mg; Sodium 170mg; Total Carbohydrate 24g (Dietary Fiber 0g); Protein 0g EXCHANGES: 1½ Other Carbohydrate; 1 Fat CARBOHYDRATE CHOICES: 1½

sweet note Sprinkle the tops of the frosted cookies with pumpkin pie spice or ground nutmeg for an extra flavor boost and a special look. If pumpkin pie spice isn't handy, use 1 teaspoon ground cinnamon, ½ teaspoon ground nutmeg and ½ teaspoon ground ginger instead.

fudge crinkles

PREP TIME: 20 minutes *START TO FINISH:* 1 hour 20 minutes [30 COOKIES]

- 1 box Betty Crocker® SuperMoist® devil's food cake mix
- ⅓ cup vegetable oil
- 2 eggs
- 1 teaspoon vanilla
- Powdered sugar

1 Heat oven to 350°F (325°F for dark or nonstick pans). In large bowl, stir dry cake mix, oil, eggs and vanilla with spoon until dough forms.

2 Refrigerate dough 15 to 30 minutes, or as needed for easier handling. Shape dough into 1-inch balls. Roll balls in powdered sugar. On ungreased cookie sheets, place balls about 2 inches apart.

3 Bake 9 to 11 minutes or until set. Cool 1 minute; remove from cookie sheets to cooling rack. Cool completely, about 30 minutes. Store tightly covered.

1 COOKIE: Calories 90; Total Fat 3½g (Saturated Fat 1g; Trans Fat 0g); Cholesterol 15mg; Sodium 125mg; Total Carbohydrate 14g (Dietary Fiber 0g); Protein 1g EXCHANGES: ½ Starch; ½ Other Carbohydrate; ½ Fat CARBOHYDRATE CHOICES: 1

sweet note For an extra flavor treat, stir 1 cup miniature candy-coated chocolate baking bits into the dough. Or instead of rolling the cookies in powdered sugar, dip the tops in chocolate candy sprinkles before baking.

cherries jubilee cheesecake bars

PREP TIME: 20 minutes *START TO FINISH:* 3 hours 5 minutes [36 BARS]

1 box Betty Crocker® SuperMoist® cherry chip cake mix

½ cup butter or margarine, softened

2 packages (8 oz each) cream cheese, softened

1 container (1 lb) Betty Crocker® Rich & Creamy cherry frosting

3 eggs

1 Heat oven to 325°F. In large bowl, beat dry cake mix and butter with electric mixer on low speed until crumbly; reserve 1 cup. Press remaining crumbly mixture in bottom of ungreased 13 × 9-inch pan.

2 In same bowl, beat cream cheese and frosting with electric mixer on medium speed until smooth. Beat in eggs until blended. Pour over crust; sprinkle with reserved crumbly mixture.

3 Bake about 45 minutes (about 42 minutes for dark or nonstick pan) or until set; cool completely. Cover and refrigerate at least 2 hours until chilled. For bars, cut into 6 rows by 6 rows. Store covered in refrigerator.

1 BAR: Calories 170; Total Fat 10g (Saturated Fat 5g; Trans Fat 1g); Cholesterol 40mg; Sodium 180mg; Total Carbohydrate 19g (Dietary Fiber 0g); Protein 1g EXCHANGES: ½ Starch; 1 Other Carbohydrate; 2 Fat CARBOHYDRATE CHOICES: 1

sweet note A dollop of cherry yogurt mixed with whipped topping gives these yummy bars a special finish!

triple-chocolate cherry bars

PREP TIME: 10 minutes *START TO FINISH:* 1 hour 48 minutes [48 BARS]

1 box Betty Crocker® SuperMoist® chocolate fudge cake mix

1 can (21 oz) cherry pie filling

2 eggs, beaten

½ bag (12-oz size) miniature semisweet chocolate chips (1 cup)

1 container (12 oz) Betty Crocker® Whipped chocolate frosting

1 Heat oven to 350°F (325°F for dark or nonstick pan). Grease and flour 15 × 10-inch or 13 × 9-inch pan, or spray with baking spray with flour.

2 In large bowl, gently mix dry cake mix, pie filling, eggs and chocolate chips with rubber scraper; break up any undissolved cake mix by pressing with scraper. Carefully spread in pan.

3 Bake 15 × 10 × 1-inch pan 25 to 30 minutes, 13 × 9-inch pan 35 to 40 minutes, or until toothpick inserted in center comes out clean. Cool completely, about 1 hour. Frost with frosting. For bars, cut into 8 rows by 6 rows.

1 BAR: Calories 100; Total Fat 3g (Saturated Fat 1½g; Trans Fat 0g); Cholesterol 10mg; Sodium 100mg; Total Carbohydrate 17g (Dietary Fiber 0g); Protein 1g EXCHANGES: ½ Starch; ½ Other Carbohydrate; ½ Fat CARBOHYDRATE CHOICES: 1

sweet note A dazzling drizzle of melted white chocolate makes these bars look even more special. Make Triple-Chocolate Strawberry Bars by using strawberry pie filling instead of the cherry.

carrot-spice cookies

PREP TIME: 1 hour *START TO FINISH:* 1 hour 25 minutes [48 COOKIES]

Cookies

1 box Betty Crocker® SuperMoist® carrot cake mix

⅓ cup Gold Medal® all-purpose flour

⅔ cup butter or margarine, melted

2 eggs

1 cup sweetened dried cranberries

Glaze

½ cup Betty Crocker® Rich & Creamy cream cheese frosting (from 1-lb container)

1 Heat oven to 350°F (325°F for dark or nonstick pans). In large bowl, beat cake mix, flour, butter and eggs with electric mixer on low speed 1 minute. Stir in cranberries.

2 On ungreased cookie sheets, drop dough by teaspoonfuls 2 inches apart.

3 Bake 10 to 13 minutes or until edges are set. Immediately remove from cookie sheets to cooling racks. Cool completely, about 10 minutes.

4 In small microwavable bowl, microwave frosting uncovered on Medium (50%) 15 seconds. Drizzle frosting over cookies. Store covered.

1 COOKIE: Calories 80; Total Fat 3½g (Saturated Fat 2g; Trans Fat 0g); Cholesterol 15mg; Sodium 90mg; Total Carbohydrate 12g (Dietary Fiber 0g); Protein 0g EXCHANGES: 1 Other Carbohydrate; ½ Fat CARBOHYDRATE CHOICES: 1

sweet note Regular raisins, golden raisins or dried cherries could be substituted for the cranberries in these tasty cookies.

mix-easy rolled sugar cookies

PREP TIME: 1 hour *START TO FINISH:* 1 hour [48 COOKIES]

1 box Betty Crocker® SuperMoist® white cake mix

½ cup shortening

⅓ cup butter or margarine, softened

1 teaspoon vanilla or ½ teaspoon almond extract or lemon extract

1 egg

Sugar

1 cup Betty Crocker® Rich & Creamy vanilla frosting (from 1-lb container)

Food colors

1 Heat oven to 375°F (350°F for dark or nonstick pan). In large bowl, beat cake mix, shortening, butter, vanilla and egg with electric mixer on low speed 30 seconds, then on high speed 1 minute.

2 Divide dough into 4 equal parts. Roll each part ⅛ inch thick on lightly floured cloth-covered surface with cloth-covered rolling pin. Cut with 2½-inch cookie cutters into desired shapes; sprinkle with sugar. On ungreased cookie sheet, place 2 inches apart.

3 Bake 5 to 7 minutes or until light brown. Cool 1 minute; remove from cookie sheet to cooling rack. In microwavable bowl, microwave frosting uncovered on High 20 to 30 seconds or until melted; stir. Frost cookies. Stir together small amounts of water and food color. Paint colors on freshly frosted cookies, using fine-tip brush, then swirl colors with brush or toothpick to create marble.

1 COOKIE: Calories 110; Total Fat 5g (Saturated Fat 2g; Trans Fat 1g); Cholesterol 10mg; Sodium 100mg; Total Carbohydrate 14g (Dietary Fiber 0g); Protein 0g EXCHANGES: 1 Other Carbohydrate; 1 Fat CARBOHYDRATE CHOICES: 1

sweet note Roll dough to an even thickness by rolling over two wooden dowels or rulers. Use dowels or rulers of the desired thickness, and place them on opposite sides of the dough.

pop art cookies

PREP TIME: 25 minutes *START TO FINISH:* 1 hour 5 minutes [12 COOKIES]

1 pouch (1 lb 1.5 oz) Betty Crocker® sugar cookie mix

⅓ cup butter or margarine, softened

2 tablespoons Gold Medal® all-purpose flour

1 egg

12 craft sticks (flat wooden sticks with round ends)

1 container (1 lb) Betty Crocker® Rich & Creamy frosting (any white variety)

Food colors in desired colors

Assorted candy decorations

1 Heat oven to 375°F. In medium bowl, stir cookie mix, butter, flour and egg until dough forms. Roll dough on floured surface until about ¼ inch thick. Cut with 3-inch round cookie cutter. Place 2 inches apart on ungreased cookie sheet. Carefully insert a wooden stick into side of each cookie.

2 Bake 9 to 11 minutes or until edges are light golden brown. Cool 1 minute before removing from cookie sheet. Cool completely, about 30 minutes.

3 Divide frosting among 4 small bowls. Tint frosting in 3 of the bowls with different color of food color. Reserve some of the tinted frostings for piping on designs. Frost cookies with remaining white and tinted frostings. For piping, place each tinted frosting in small resealable food-storage plastic bag; snip off tiny corner of bag. Pipe frostings on cookies in desired designs. Decorate with candy decorations.

1 COOKIE: Calories 390; Total Fat 18g (Saturated Fat 7g; Trans Fat 4½g); Cholesterol 30mg; Sodium 230mg; Total Carbohydrate 56g (Dietary Fiber 0g); Protein 2g EXCHANGES: 1 Starch; 2½ Other Carbohydrate; 3½ Fat CARBOHYDRATE CHOICES: 4

sweet note Serve cookies from glasses in coordinating colors. Fill the glasses with jelly beans to hold the cookie pops upright.

angel macaroons

PREP TIME: 1 hour *START TO FINISH:* 1 hour [48 COOKIES]

Macaroons

1 box Betty Crocker® white angel food cake mix

½ cup water

1 teaspoon almond extract

1 package (7 oz) flaked coconut (2 cups)

1 tablespoon unsweetened baking cocoa

Glaze

4 teaspoons butter or margarine

4 teaspoons unsweetened baking cocoa

4 teaspoons water

⅔ cup powdered sugar

1 Heat oven to 350°F. Cover cookie sheets with cooking parchment paper or foil. In large (4-quart) glass or metal bowl, beat cake mix, ½ cup water and the almond extract with electric mixer on low speed 30 seconds. On medium speed, beat 1 minute, scraping bowl occasionally. Fold in coconut.

2 Drop half of the mixture by teaspoonfuls about 3 inches apart onto lined cookie sheets.

3 Bake 7 to 9 minutes or until light golden brown around edges. Cool macaroons completely before removing from parchment paper.

4 Meanwhile, stir 1 tablespoon cocoa into remaining mixture. Bake and cool as directed above.

5 In 1-quart saucepan, heat butter, 4 teaspoons cocoa and 4 teaspoons water over low heat, stirring constantly, until butter is melted. Stir in powdered sugar. Drizzle small amount of glaze over each cookie.

1 COOKIE: Calories 60; Total Fat 1½g (Saturated Fat 1g; Trans Fat 0g); Cholesterol 0mg; Sodium 90mg; Total Carbohydrate 11g (Dietary Fiber 0g); Protein 0g EXCHANGES: 1 Other Carbohydrate CARBOHYDRATE CHOICES: 1

sweet note Not an almond fan? Make cool mint macaroons by using mint extract instead of the almond.

triple-ginger bars

PREP TIME: 20 minutes *START TO FINISH:* 2 hours 45 minutes [24 BARS]

1 package Betty Crocker® SuperMoist® white cake mix

½ cup butter or margarine, melted

2 eggs

¼ cup finely chopped crystallized ginger

1 tablespoon grated gingerroot

1 teaspoon ground ginger

2 tablespoons decorating sugar crystals

1 Heat oven to 350°F (325°F for dark or nonstick pan). Grease and lightly flour bottom only of 13 × 9-inch pan, or spray with baking spray with flour.

2 In large bowl, mix cake mix, butter and eggs with spoon until well blended. Stir in remaining ingredients except sugar. Spread batter evenly in pan. Sprinkle with sugar.

3 Bake 18 to 23 minutes or until edges are very light golden brown. Cool completely, about 1 hour. For bars, cut into 6 rows by 4 rows. Store loosely covered.

1 BAR: Calories 130; Total Fat 5g (Saturated Fat 3g; Trans Fat 0g); Cholesterol 35mg; Sodium 170mg; Total Carbohydrate 19g (Dietary Fiber 0g); Protein 1g EXCHANGES: ½ Starch; ½ Other Carbohydrate; 1 Fat CARBOHYDRATE CHOICES: 1

white chocolate–cranberry bars

PREP TIME: 10 minutes *START TO FINISH:* 1 hour 35 minutes [24 BARS]

1 box Betty Crocker® SuperMoist® white cake mix

⅓ cup butter or margarine, melted

2 tablespoons water

2 eggs

1½ cups dried cranberries

1 cup white vanilla baking chips (6 oz)

1 Heat oven to 350°F (325°F for dark or nonstick pan). Grease and lightly flour bottom only of 13 × 9-inch pan, or spray with baking spray with flour.

2 In large bowl, mix cake mix, butter, water and eggs with spoon until dough forms (some dry mix will remain). Stir in cranberries and baking chips. Spread evenly in pan.

3 Bake 22 to 26 minutes or until toothpick inserted in center comes out clean. Cool completely, about 1 hour. For bars, cut into 6 rows by 4 rows. Store loosely covered.

1 BAR: Calories 180; Total Fat 7g (Saturated Fat 4½g; Trans Fat 0g); Cholesterol 25mg; Sodium 180mg; Total Carbohydrate 28g (Dietary Fiber 0g); Protein 2g EXCHANGES: ½ Starch; 1½ Other Carbohydrate; 1½ Fat CARBOHYDRATE CHOICES: 2

citrus biscotti

PREP TIME: 25 minutes *START TO FINISH:* 1 hour 45 minutes [30 COOKIES]

Biscotti

1 box Betty Crocker® SuperMoist® lemon cake mix

½ cup Gold Medal® all-purpose flour

1 tablespoon vegetable oil

2 eggs

2 tablespoons grated lemon peel

1 tablespoon grated lime peel

1 tablespoon grated orange peel

Easy Lemon Glaze

¼ cup Betty Crocker® Rich & Creamy lemon frosting (from 1-lb container)

2 to 4 teaspoons lemon juice

1 Heat oven to 350°F (325°F for dark or nonstick pan). Lightly grease or spray large cookie sheet. In large bowl, mix biscotti ingredients with spoon until dough forms.

2 On cookie sheet, shape dough into 14 × 3-inch rectangle, ½ inch thick. Bake 19 to 25 minutes or until golden brown. Cool on cookie sheet on cooling rack 15 minutes.

3 Cut dough crosswise into ½-inch slices. Arrange slices cut side up on cookie sheet. Bake 7 to 8 minutes or until bottoms are light golden brown; turn slices over. Bake 7 to 8 minutes longer or until bottoms are light golden brown. Cool 5 minutes; remove from cookie sheet to cooling rack. Cool completely, about 15 minutes.

4 In small bowl, mix glaze ingredients until thin enough to drizzle. Drizzle over biscotti. Before stacking biscotti, let stand about 4 hours or until glaze is set. Store loosely covered.

1 COOKIE: Calories 80; Total Fat 1½g (Saturated Fat ½g; Trans Fat 0g); Cholesterol 15mg; Sodium 115mg; Total Carbohydrate 15g (Dietary Fiber 0g); Protein 1g EXCHANGES: 1 Other Carbohydrate; ½ Fat CARBOHYDRATE CHOICES: 1

sweet note Try a cup of a hot citrus-flavored tea with these crisp biscotti—and yes, dunking is allowed!

toasted coconut–almond biscotti

PREP TIME: 20 minutes *START TO FINISH:* 2 hours 20 minutes [24 COOKIES]

1 box Betty Crocker® SuperMoist® white cake mix

¼ cup Gold Medal® all-purpose flour

1 tablespoon vegetable oil

2 eggs

1 cup flaked coconut, toasted

½ cup chopped slivered almonds, toasted

1 cup semisweet chocolate chips (6 oz)

1 tablespoon shortening

1 Heat oven to 350°F (325°F for dark or nonstick pan). In large bowl, mix cake mix, flour, oil and eggs with spoon until dough forms. Stir in coconut and almonds, using hands if necessary.

2 On ungreased cookie sheet, shape dough into 15 × 4-inch rectangle, using greased hands. Bake 21 to 27 minutes or until golden brown. Cool on cookie sheet on cooling rack 15 minutes.

3 Cut rectangle crosswise into ½-inch slices. Place slices, cut sides down, on cookie sheet. Bake 10 to 12 minutes longer or until edges are deep golden brown. Cool 5 minutes; remove from cookie sheet to cooling rack. Cool completely, about 30 minutes.

4 In 1-quart saucepan, heat chocolate chips and shortening over low heat, stirring constantly, until chocolate is melted. Drizzle chocolate over cookies, or dip one end of each cookie into chocolate. Let stand about 30 minutes or until chocolate is set. Store covered.

1 COOKIE: Calories 170; Total Fat 7g (Saturated Fat 3g; Trans Fat 0g); Cholesterol 20mg; Sodium 160mg; Total Carbohydrate 23g (Dietary Fiber 1g); Protein 2g EXCHANGES: ½ Starch; 1 Other Carbohydrate; 1½ Fat CARBOHYDRATE CHOICES: 1½

sweet note To toast coconut and almonds, spread in an ungreased shallow pan. Bake uncovered at 350°F for 5 to 8 minutes, stirring occasionally, until coconut is golden brown and almonds are toasted. Cool completely, about 15 minutes. If using almonds that have been frozen, make sure they are room temperature before toasting so the coconut and almonds toast evenly.

lemon-raspberry cream bars

PREP TIME: 15 minutes *START TO FINISH:* 2 hours 10 minutes [48 BARS]

- 1 box Betty Crocker® SuperMoist® lemon cake mix
- ½ cup butter or margarine, softened
- 2 eggs
- ¾ cup raspberry preserves
- 1 package (8 oz) cream cheese, softened
- 2 tablespoons milk
- 12 oz white chocolate baking bars, chopped
- 2 to 3 teaspoons powdered sugar

1 Heat oven to 350°F (325°F for dark or nonstick pan). Grease bottom only of 15 × 10-inch pan.

2 In large bowl, mix cake mix, butter and eggs with spoon until well blended. With floured fingers, press evenly in pan.

3 Bake 14 to 18 minutes or until light golden brown and toothpick inserted in center comes out clean. Cool 5 minutes. Spread evenly with preserves. Cool 30 minutes.

4 In medium bowl, beat cream cheese and milk with electric mixer on medium speed until smooth; set aside.

5 In 1-quart saucepan, melt white chocolate over low heat, stirring frequently. Add warm melted white chocolate to cream cheese mixture; beat on medium speed until creamy (mixture may look slightly curdled). Carefully spread over preserves. Refrigerate about 1 hour or until set.

6 Sprinkle powdered sugar over top. For bars, cut into 8 rows by 6 rows. Store covered in refrigerator.

1 BAR: Calories 120; Total Fat 6g (Saturated Fat 4g; Trans Fat 0g); Cholesterol 20mg; Sodium 105mg; Total Carbohydrate 15g (Dietary Fiber 0g); Protein 1g EXCHANGES: ½ Starch; ½ Other Carbohydrate; 1 Fat CARBOHYDRATE CHOICES: 1

sweet note Don't be tempted to use reduced-fat cream cheese (Neufchâtel) instead of regular cream cheese. The white chocolate-cream cheese filling may not get firm enough, even when refrigerated.

lemon cookies

PREP TIME: 30 minutes *START TO FINISH:* 45 minutes [30 COOKIES]

1 box Betty Crocker® SuperMoist® lemon cake mix

⅓ cup butter or margarine, softened

¼ cup shortening

1 egg

1 container (12 oz or 1 lb) Betty Crocker® Whipped or Rich & Creamy lemon frosting

1 Heat oven to 375°F (350°F for dark or nonstick pan). In large bowl, beat cake mix, butter, shortening and egg on medium speed about 1 minute or until blended.

2 Onto ungreased cookie sheet, drop dough by rounded tablespoonfuls 2 inches apart.

3 Bake 9 to 12 minutes or until light brown around edges. Cool 1 minute; remove from cookie sheet. Cool completely. Frost with frosting. Store covered.

1 COOKIE: Calories 150; Total Fat 7g (Saturated Fat 2½g; Trans Fat 1g); Cholesterol 10mg; Sodium 150mg; Total Carbohydrate 22g (Dietary Fiber 0g); Protein 0g EXCHANGES: 1½ Other Carbohydrate; 1½ Fat CARBOHYDRATE CHOICES: 1½

sweet note Fun idea! Pick up a lemon-shaped cookie cutter from a cake-decorating supply store or craft store. Make lemon cookies using the rolled cookie directions (see page 258). Your cookies will shape up to their great taste.

lollipop cookies

PREP TIME: 1 hour *START TO FINISH:* 1 hour [22 COOKIES]

1 box Betty Crocker® SuperMoist® golden vanilla cake mix

⅓ cup vegetable oil

2 eggs

20 to 24 craft sticks (flat wooden sticks with round ends)

1 container (1 lb) Betty Crocker® Rich & Creamy frosting (any flavor)

1 Heat oven to 375°F (350°F for dark or nonstick pans). In large bowl, beat cake mix, oil and eggs with electric mixer on low speed until blended.

2 Onto ungreased cookie sheet, drop dough by rounded tablespoonfuls 3 inches apart. Insert wooden stick in edge of dough until tip is in center.

3 Bake 9 to 12 minutes or until light golden brown. Cool 1 minute before removing from cookie sheet. Cool completely, about 30 minutes. Frost and decorate as desired. Store loosely covered.

1 COOKIE: Calories 190; Total Fat 7g (Saturated Fat 1½g; Trans Fat 1g); Cholesterol 20mg; Sodium 190mg; Total Carbohydrate 30g (Dietary Fiber 0g); Protein 1g EXCHANGES: ½ Starch; 1½ Other Carbohydrate; 1½ Fat CARBOHYDRATE CHOICES: 2

chunky chocolate and almond bars

PREP TIME: 20 minutes *START TO FINISH:* 2 hours 35 minutes [48 BARS]

Crust

1 box Betty Crocker® SuperMoist® chocolate fudge cake mix

½ cup butter or margarine, softened

Topping

4 eggs

1 cup dark corn syrup

¼ cup butter or margarine, melted

2 cups salted roasted whole almonds, coarsely chopped

6 oz dark or bittersweet baking chocolate, chopped

1 Heat oven to 350°F (325°F for dark or nonstick pan). Place cake mix in medium bowl. Using pastry blender (or pulling 2 table knives through mixture in opposite directions), cut in ½ cup butter until crumbly. Press firmly in ungreased 13 × 9-inch pan. Bake 12 to 14 minutes or until set.

2 In large bowl, beat eggs, corn syrup and ¼ cup melted butter with whisk until smooth. Stir in almonds and chocolate. Pour over crust.

3 Bake 28 to 34 minutes longer or until golden brown and set. Cool 30 minutes. Refrigerate about 1 hour or until chocolate is firm. For bars, cut into 8 rows by 6 rows. Store covered in refrigerator.

1 BAR: Calories 150; Total Fat 8g (Saturated Fat 3½g; Trans Fat 0g); Cholesterol 25mg; Sodium 130mg; Total Carbohydrate 15g (Dietary Fiber 1g); Protein 2g EXCHANGES: ½ Starch; ½ Other Carbohydrate; 1½ Fat CARBOHYDRATE CHOICES: 1

sweet note Much like the center of a pecan pie, the center of these bars is very moist and may even look raw. Not to worry—that's how they should look.

chapter four

fruit desserts

Perfect Fruit Desserts Every Time

Don't you love trips to the apple orchard and berry farm and the fabulous fruit desserts they inspire? Carry on the baking tradition with these tips for delicious fruit cobblers, crisps, crumbles and more!

Tips from Betty!

- Serve fruit cobblers and crisps the same day they're baked for maximum flavor and quality. They make tasty breakfast items as leftovers, too!
- Use an ovenproof baking dish for fruit desserts like crisps and cobblers. For best results, make sure the fruit is hot before the biscuit topping is added; it will then bake all the way through.
- For unsurpassed freshness and flavor, look for locally grown fruit at groceries, farmers' markets, roadside stands and at community-supported agriculture (CSA) farms. Frequently, consumer information is paired with fruit displays and suggests which varieties are best for baking, cooking, and eating.
- Fresh peaches and plums are plentiful in summer; pears appear in late summer and throughout the fall. Fresh apples are found throughout summer and early fall.
- Fresh berries come into season in midsummer. They're terrific by themselves but also when paired with other fruit in cobblers, crisps, shortcakes and pies.

More Helpful Hints for Fabulous Fruit Pies

- Baking apples come in abundant variety from sweet Beacons to crisp and tart York Imperials. Look for locally grown favorites, which will be especially fresh.
- Try mixing apple varieties in a single pie, combining tart with sweet or crisp with mealy. It may take a bit of trial and error, but this is a great way to personalize a recipe.
- Because apples shrink during baking, a pie may have a gap between the apples and the crust. Use tart, firm apples, layering them so there isn't too much space in between. Cutting larger air slits in the top crust also helps.
- Cut baking time of an apple pie in half by using a microwavable pie plate. Microwave the unbaked apple pie uncovered on High 12 to 14 minutes or until the filling begins to bubble through air slits in the crust. Transfer the pie to a conventional oven (don't preheat), and bake at 450°F 12 to 18 minutes or until the crust is brown and flaky.
- For a yummy berry pie, try berries fresh from the farmers' market or a roadside stand, or pick them fresh at a "pick-it-yourself" farm.

peachy fruit pizza

PREP TIME: 20 minutes *START TO FINISH:* 1 hour 25 minutes [12 SERVINGS]

Crust and Topping

1 box Betty Crocker® SuperMoist® yellow cake mix

½ cup butter or margarine, melted

¼ cup packed brown sugar

1 teaspoon ground cinnamon

½ cup finely chopped nuts, if desired

Filling

1 cup sour cream

1 egg

1 can (29 oz) sliced peaches, drained, patted dry

Glaze, if desired

½ cup powdered sugar

⅛ teaspoon ground cinnamon

2 teaspoons milk

1 Heat oven to 350°F (325°F for dark or nonstick pan).

2 In large bowl, mix cake mix, butter, brown sugar and cinnamon with spoon until crumbly; reserve 1 cup mixture for topping. Press remaining crumbly mixture on bottom and side of ungreased 12-inch pizza pan or in bottom only of ungreased 13 × 9-inch pan.

3 In small bowl, beat sour cream and egg with spoon until blended. Carefully spread over crust. Top with peaches. Sprinkle with reserved crumbly mixture and the nuts.

4 Bake 12-inch pizza pan 29 to 34 minutes, 13 × 9-inch pan 33 to 37 minutes, or until topping is light golden brown and center is set. Cool 30 minutes.

5 In another small bowl, stir all glaze ingredients until consistency of thick syrup, adding additional milk, 1 teaspoon at a time, if necessary. Drizzle glaze over warm pizza. Serve warm or cool. Store covered in refrigerator.

1 SERVING: Calories 290; Total Fat 13g (Saturated Fat 8g; Trans Fat 0g); Cholesterol 50mg; Sodium 340mg; Total Carbohydrate 41g (Dietary Fiber 1g); Protein 2g EXCHANGES: ½ Starch; ½ Fruit; 1½ Other Carbohydrate; 2½ Fat CARBOHYDRATE CHOICES: 3

sweet note For a sweet ending to any meal, serve this fruity pizza with a scoop of vanilla, butter pecan or dulce de leche ice cream.

easy fruit crisp "dump" dessert

PREP TIME: 15 minutes *START TO FINISH:* 1 hour 30 minutes [12 SERVINGS]

1 box Betty Crocker® SuperMoist® yellow cake mix

½ cup butter or margarine, melted

1 can (21 oz) cherry pie filling

1 can (8 oz) crushed pineapple, undrained

1 Heat oven to 350°F (325°F for dark or nonstick pan).

2 In large bowl, stir together cake mix and butter until crumbly; set aside.

3 Spread pie filling and pineapple in ungreased 13 × 9-inch pan. Sprinkle cake mix mixture evenly over fruit.

4 Bake 39 to 46 minutes or until deep golden brown. Cool 30 minutes. Serve warm or cool. Store loosely covered.

1 SERVING: Calories 270; Total Fat 9g (Saturated Fat 6g; Trans Fat 0g); Cholesterol 20mg; Sodium 310mg; Total Carbohydrate 46g (Dietary Fiber 1g); Protein 1g EXCHANGES: 3 Other Carbohydrate; 2 Fat CARBOHYDRATE CHOICES: 3

sweet note Are there members of your family who don't like pineapple? Use two cans of cherry pie filling instead!

tropical fruit bars

PREP TIME: 20 minutes *START TO FINISH:* 3 hours [32 BARS]

1 box Betty Crocker® SuperMoist® yellow cake mix

½ cup butter or margarine, melted

1 egg

1½ cups white vanilla baking chips (from 12-oz bag)

1 bag (7 oz) dried tropical fruit mix

1 cup flaked coconut

1 cup cashew pieces

1 can (14 oz) sweetened condensed milk (not evaporated)

1 Heat oven to 350°F (325°F for dark or nonstick pan).

2 Spray bottom and sides of 13 × 9-inch pan with baking spray with flour.

3 In medium bowl, stir cake mix, butter and egg until mixed. Press in bottom of pan. Sprinkle evenly with baking chips, dried fruit, coconut and cashews. Pour milk evenly over top.

4 Bake 35 to 40 minutes or until edges and center are golden brown. Cool completely, about 2 hours. For bars, cut into 8 rows by 4 rows.

1 BAR: Calories 220; Total Fat 9g (Saturated Fat 6g; Trans Fat 0g); Cholesterol 15mg; Sodium 160mg; Total Carbohydrate 31g (Dietary Fiber 1g); Protein 3g EXCHANGES: 1 Starch; 1 Other Carbohydrate; 1½ Fat CARBOHYDRATE CHOICES: 2

sweet note The tropical fruit mix has dried mango, pineapple and papaya in it. You can use any dried fruit mixture.

peach-pecan cobbler

PREP TIME: 15 minutes *START TO FINISH:* 1 hour 35 minutes [15 SERVINGS]

- ½ cup butter or margarine
- 3 cans (15 oz each) sliced peaches in light syrup, drained, 1 cup syrup reserved
- 1 box Betty Crocker® SuperMoist® yellow cake mix
- 1 teaspoon ground cinnamon
- ⅛ teaspoon ground nutmeg
- 2 eggs
- 1 cup chopped pecans
- 1 tablespoon sugar

1 Heat oven to 350°F (325°F for dark or nonstick pan).

2 In 13 × 9-inch pan, melt butter in oven. Place peach slices on paper towels to absorb liquid.

3 In large bowl, mix cake mix, cinnamon, nutmeg, eggs and 1 cup reserved peach syrup with spoon until well blended. Drop batter by spoonfuls over butter in pan; spread slightly without stirring. Arrange peach slices over batter.

4 Bake 25 minutes. Sprinkle evenly with pecans and sugar. Bake 10 to 15 minutes longer or until edges are deep golden brown and center springs back when touched lightly in center. Cool 30 minutes. Serve warm or cool.

1 SERVING: Calories 270; Total Fat 13g (Saturated Fat 5g; Trans Fat 0g); Cholesterol 45mg; Sodium 260mg; Total Carbohydrate 35g (Dietary Fiber 2g); Protein 2g EXCHANGES: ½ Starch; ½ Fruit; 1½ Other Carbohydrate; 2½ Fat CARBOHYDRATE CHOICES: 2

sweet note A deliciously sweet fruit cobbler is the source of controversy? Yes! Some believe true cobbler is made with a cakelike or rich biscuit topping, while others insist a pie crust topping be used. Either way, this comfort food disappears fast.

brownie 'n berries dessert pizza

PREP TIME: 20 minutes *START TO FINISH:* 2 hours 50 minutes [16 SERVINGS]

1 box (1 lb 2.3 oz) Betty Crocker® fudge brownie mix

Water, vegetable oil and eggs called for on brownie mix box

1 package (8 oz) cream cheese, softened

⅓ cup sugar

½ teaspoon vanilla

2 cups sliced fresh strawberries

1 cup fresh blueberries

1 cup fresh raspberries

½ cup apple jelly

1 Heat oven to 350°F. Grease bottom only of 12-inch pizza pan with shortening or cooking spray.

2 In medium bowl, stir brownie mix, water, oil and eggs until well blended. Spread in pan.

3 Bake 24 to 26 minutes or until toothpick inserted 2 inches from side of pan comes out clean or almost clean. Cool completely, about 1 hour.

4 In small bowl, beat cream cheese, sugar and vanilla with electric mixer on medium speed until smooth. Spread mixture evenly over brownie base. Arrange berries over cream cheese mixture. Stir jelly until smooth; brush over berries. Refrigerate about 1 hour or until chilled.

5 Cut into wedges. Store covered in refrigerator.

1 SERVING: Calories 320; Total Fat 15g (Saturated Fat 4½g; Trans Fat 0g); Cholesterol 40mg; Sodium 170mg; Total Carbohydrate 44g (Dietary Fiber 1g); Protein 2g EXCHANGES: ½ Starch; ½ Fruit; 2 Other Carbohydrate; 3 Fat CARBOHYDRATE CHOICES: 3

sweet note For easy cleanup, bake the brownie in a 12-inch disposable foil pizza pan. Slide the pan onto a cookie sheet when you remove the brownie from the oven. Place the brownie dessert on a tray when you take it to the table.

easy fruit cookie tarts

PREP TIME: 50 minutes *START TO FINISH:* 1 hour 30 minutes [16 TARTS]

4 cups Original Bisquick® mix

⅔ cup sugar

⅔ cup butter or margarine, softened

2 eggs

1 package (3 oz) cream cheese, softened

⅓ cup sugar

1 teaspoon vanilla

¾ cup whipping (heavy) cream

2 cups assorted cut-up fresh fruit

2 tablespoons apple jelly, melted

1 Heat oven to 375°F.

2 Stir Bisquick, ⅔ cup sugar, the butter and eggs in large bowl until soft dough forms. Pat dough into sixteen 3-inch circles on ungreased cookie sheets.

3 Bake 8 to 10 minutes or until edges just begin to brown. Remove from cookie sheet to wire rack. Cool completely, about 30 minutes.

4 Beat cream cheese, ⅓ cup sugar and the vanilla in small bowl with electric mixer on low speed until smooth. Beat in whipping cream on high speed until stiff peaks form. Spread over tarts to within ¼ inch of edges. Place fruit on top; brush with jelly. Store covered in refrigerator.

1 TART: Calories 316 ; Total Fat 18g (Saturated Fat 10g; Trans Fat 2g); Cholesterol 68mg; Sodium 456mg; Total Carbohydrate 36g (Dietary Fiber 1g); Protein 4g EXCHANGES: 1 Starch; 1 Other Carbohydrate; 3 Fat CARBOHYDRATE CHOICES: 2½

sweet note Keep a stash of these cookie tarts in the freezer just waiting to be thawed, frosted and enjoyed! We use apple jelly because of its light, golden color, but you could also try apricot and peach.

southern apple crumble

PREP TIME: 20 minutes *START TO FINISH:* 1 hour 20 minutes [9 SERVINGS]

Filling

3 large apples, peeled, coarsely chopped (about 3 cups)

½ cup granulated sugar

¼ cup packed brown sugar

1 to 2 teaspoons ground cinnamon

¼ cup cold butter or margarine, cut into small pieces

Topping

1 pouch (1 lb 1.5 oz) Betty Crocker® oatmeal cookie mix

½ cup butter or margarine, melted

½ cup chopped pecans

1 Heat oven to 300°F. Spray bottom and sides of 8-inch square (2-quart) glass baking dish with cooking spray. In large bowl, toss filling ingredients. Spread mixture in baking dish.

2 In same large bowl, stir cookie mix and melted butter until crumbly. Sprinkle over filling.

3 Bake 40 minutes. Remove from oven; sprinkle with pecans. Bake 15 to 20 minutes longer or until topping is golden brown. Serve warm or at room temperature.

1 SERVING: Calories 480; Total Fat 22g (Saturated Fat 10g; Trans Fat ½g); Cholesterol 40mg; Sodium 320mg; Total Carbohydrate 67g (Dietary Fiber 2g); Protein 5g
EXCHANGES: 1½ Starch; 3 Other Carbohydrate; 4 Fat CARBOHYDRATE CHOICES: 4½

sweet note Use fresh peaches for the apples for a juicy peach crumble.

peach crisp

PREP TIME: 10 minutes *START TO FINISH:* 40 minutes [6 SERVINGS]

1 pouch (1 lb 1.5 oz) Betty Crocker® oatmeal cookie mix

½ cup cold butter

5 cups frozen sliced peaches, thawed and drained, or 1 can (29 oz) sliced peaches, drained

1 Heat oven to 375°F.

2 In large bowl, place cookie mix. Cut in butter, using pastry blender or fork, until mixture looks like coarse crumbs.

3 In ungreased 8-inch square baking dish or 2-quart round casserole, place peaches. Sprinkle cookie mixture over peaches.

4 Bake 25 to 30 minutes or until topping is golden brown. Serve warm or cool.

1 SERVING: Calories 650; Total Fat 19g (Saturated Fat 10g; Trans Fat ½g); Cholesterol 40mg; Sodium 440mg; Total Carbohydrate 113g (Dietary Fiber 5g); Protein 7g EXCHANGES: 2 Starch; 1 Fruit; 4½ Other Carbohydrate; 3½ Fat CARBOHYDRATE CHOICES: 7½

sweet note Top this yummy dessert with vanilla or cinnamon ice cream or with sweetened whipped cream.

strawberries and cream dessert squares

PREP TIME: 30 minutes *START TO FINISH:* 2 hours 30 minutes [20 SERVINGS]

Crust

- 1 pouch (1 lb 1.5 oz) Betty Crocker® sugar cookie mix
- ½ cup butter or margarine, softened
- 1 egg

Filling

- 1 cup white vanilla baking chips (6 oz)
- 1 package (8 oz) cream cheese, softened

Topping

- 4 cups sliced fresh strawberries
- ½ cup sugar
- 2 tablespoons cornstarch
- ⅓ cup water
- 10 to 12 drops red food color, if desired

1 Heat oven to 350°F. Spray bottom only of 15 × 10- or 13 × 9-inch pan with cooking spray.

2 In large bowl, stir cookie mix, butter and egg until soft dough forms. Press evenly in bottom of pan.

3 Bake 15 to 20 minutes or until light golden brown. Cool completely, about 30 minutes.

4 In small microwavable bowl, microwave baking chips uncovered on High 45 to 60 seconds or until chips are melted and can be stirred smooth. In medium bowl, beat cream cheese with electric mixer on medium speed until smooth. Stir in melted chips until blended. Spread mixture over crust. Refrigerate while making topping.

5 In small bowl, crush 1 cup of the strawberries. In 2-quart saucepan, mix sugar and cornstarch. Stir in crushed strawberries and ⅓ cup water. Cook over medium heat, stirring constantly, until mixture boils and thickens. Stir in food color. Cool 10 minutes. Gently stir in the remaining 3 cups strawberries. Spoon topping over filling. Refrigerate 1 hour or until set; serve within 4 hours. Store covered in refrigerator.

1 SERVING: Calories 270; Total Fat 13g (Saturated Fat 8g; Trans Fat 1g); Cholesterol 35mg; Sodium 150mg; Total Carbohydrate 34g (Dietary Fiber 0g); Protein 3g EXCHANGES: 1 Starch; 1 Other Carbohydrate; 2½ Fat CARBOHYDRATE CHOICES: 2

sweet note Strawberries are available most times of the year. Look for those that are bright red with green caps still attached. They should look fresh and have no signs of mold or decay.

candied apple tart

PREP TIME: 15 minutes *START TO FINISH:* 35 minutes [10 SERVINGS]

- 2 cups Original Bisquick® mix
- ⅔ cup whipping (heavy) cream
- 2 tablespoons granulated sugar
- 4 cups thinly sliced apples (about 4 medium)
- ¼ cup Original Bisquick® mix
- ⅓ cup packed brown sugar
- 1 tablespoon firm butter or margarine
- ¾ teaspoon ground cinnamon
- About 2 tablespoons cinnamon apple jelly

1 Heat oven to 425°F.

2 In medium bowl, stir 2 cups Bisquick mix, the whipping cream and granulated sugar until soft dough forms; shape into a ball. Pat dough in ungreased 12-inch pizza pan. Spread apples over dough.

3 In small bowl, mix ¼ cup Bisquick mix, the brown sugar, butter and cinnamon with fork until crumbly; sprinkle over apples. Cover edge of dough with 2-inch strip of aluminum foil to prevent excessive browning.

4 Bake 5 minutes; remove foil. Bake 10 to 15 minutes longer or until edge is deep golden brown. Heat jelly until melted; drizzle over tart.

1 SERVING: Calories 245; Total Fat 11g (Saturated Fat 5g; Trans Fat 1g); Cholesterol 22mg; Sodium 354mg; Total Carbohydrate 36g (Dietary Fiber 1g); Protein 3g EXCHANGES: 1 Starch; ½ Fruit; 1 Other Carbohydrate; 2 Fat CARBOHYDRATE CHOICES: 2½

sweet note There's no need to peel the apples for this recipe. The apple peel adds color to the dessert. If a caramel apple tart appeals to you and your family, just omit the cinnamon apple jelly and drizzle with caramel topping.

puffy pancake with fruit

PREP TIME: 10 minutes *START TO FINISH:* 45 minutes [8 SERVINGS]

2/3 cup water

1/4 cup butter or margarine

1 cup Original Bisquick® mix

4 eggs

1 to 2 cans (21 oz each) fruit pie filling, any flavor

1 Heat oven to 400°F.

2 Generously grease 13 × 9-inch baking dish or pan. Heat water and butter to boiling in 2-quart saucepan. Add Bisquick all at once. Stir vigorously over low heat about 1 minute or until mixture forms a ball; remove from heat.

3 Beat in eggs, two at a time, with spoon; beat until smooth and glossy after each addition. Spread in pan (do not spread up sides).

4 Bake 30 to 35 minutes or until puffed and dry in center. Immediately spread pie filling over pancake. Cut into rectangles; serve immediately.

1 SERVING: Calories 230; Total Fat 11g (Saturated Fat 5g; Trans Fat 1/2g); Cholesterol 120mg; Sodium 260mg; Total Carbohydrate 30g (Dietary Fiber 1g); Protein 5g
EXCHANGES: 1/2 Starch; 1 1/2 Other Carbohydrate; 1 1/2 Fat CARBOHYDRATE CHOICES: 2

sweet note Add variety to this showy pancake by combining two different fruit fillings. Strawberries and blueberries, apples and pears, the possibilities are endless!

cinnamon-peach cobbler

PREP TIME: 15 minutes *START TO FINISH:* 40 minutes [12 SERVINGS]

Peach Mixture

¼ cup butter or margarine

½ cup sugar

2 tablespoons cornstarch

2 teaspoons ground cinnamon

½ teaspoon ground nutmeg

2 teaspoons vanilla

½ teaspoon lemon extract

2 jars (24.5 oz each) sliced peaches in light syrup, drained, 1½ cups syrup reserved

Topping

2 cups Bisquick Heart Smart® mix

3 tablespoons sugar

¼ teaspoon ground cinnamon

½ cup milk

1 tablespoon butter or margarine, melted

1 Heat oven to 400°F.

2 In 4-quart saucepan, heat ¼ cup butter, ½ cup sugar and the cornstarch over medium heat 1 minute, stirring constantly, until butter is melted. Stir in 2 teaspoons cinnamon, the nutmeg, vanilla, lemon extract and peaches with reserved syrup. Heat to boiling; boil 1 minute, stirring occasionally. Pour into ungreased 13 × 9-inch (3-quart) glass baking dish.

3 In medium bowl, stir Bisquick mix, 2 tablespoons of the sugar, ¼ teaspoon cinnamon, the milk and 1 tablespoon melted butter until soft dough forms. Drop dough by heaping tablespoonfuls over hot peach mixture. Sprinkle with the remaining 1 tablespoon sugar.

4 Bake 20 to 25 minutes or until peach mixture is bubbly around edges and topping is golden brown. Serve warm.

1 SERVING: Calories 250; Total Fat 6g (Saturated Fat 3g; Trans Fat 0g); Cholesterol 15mg; Sodium 210mg; Total Carbohydrate 44g (Dietary Fiber 2g); Protein 2g EXCHANGES: ½ Starch; 1 Fruit; 1½ Other Carbohydrate; 1 Fat CARBOHYDRATE CHOICES: 3

sweet note Add a little extra decadence by topping servings of this dessert with frozen yogurt.

white chocolate–berry bread pudding

PREP TIME: 30 minutes *START TO FINISH:* 10 hours 10 minutes [12 SERVINGS]

Pudding

4½ cups Original Bisquick® mix

1⅓ cups milk

¾ cup grated white chocolate baking bars

⅔ cup sugar

3½ cups milk

1½ cups whipping cream

2 tablespoons butter or margarine, melted

1 tablespoon vanilla

4 eggs

1 cup frozen unsweetened raspberries (do not thaw)

1 cup frozen unsweetened blueberries (do not thaw)

Berry Sauce and Garnish

⅓ cup sugar

2 tablespoons Original Bisquick® mix

1 cup frozen unsweetened raspberries (do not thaw)

1 cup frozen unsweetened blueberries (do not thaw)

½ cup water

Fresh berries, if desired

1 Heat oven to 450°F. Butter bottom and sides of 13 × 9-inch (3-quart) glass baking dish.

2 In large bowl, stir 4½ cups Bisquick mix and 1⅓ cups milk with spoon until soft dough forms. Drop dough by heaping tablespoonfuls onto ungreased large cookie sheet. Bake 8 to 10 minutes or until golden. Cool on cooling rack, about 30 minutes.

3 Break up biscuits into random-size pieces; spread in baking dish. Sprinkle with grated baking bars. In large bowl, beat ⅔ cup sugar, 3½ cups milk, the whipping cream, butter, vanilla and eggs with electric mixer on low speed until blended. Pour over biscuits in baking dish. Cover and refrigerate at least 8 hours but no longer than 24 hours.

4 Heat oven to 350°F. Stir 1 cup frozen raspberries and 1 cup frozen blueberries into biscuit mixture. Bake uncovered about 1 hour or until top is golden brown and toothpick inserted in center comes out clean.

5 In 1-quart saucepan, place ⅓ cup sugar and 2 tablespoons Bisquick mix. Stir in 1 cup frozen raspberries, 1 cup frozen blueberries and the water. Cook over medium heat, stirring constantly, until mixture thickens and boils. Boil and stir 1 minute; remove from heat. Serve pudding warm topped with sauce. Garnish with fresh berries. Store in refrigerator.

1 SERVING: Calories 551; Total Fat 28g (Saturated Fat 14g; Trans Fat 2g); Cholesterol 128mg; Sodium 770mg; Total Carbohydrate 68g (Dietary Fiber 2g); Protein 11g EXCHANGES: 3½ Starch; 1 Fruit; 4 Fat CARBOHYDRATE CHOICES: 4½

sweet note In this recipe, drop biscuits rather than rolled biscuits are made to give a crusty brown surface to the pudding.

chocolate-cherry dessert

PREP TIME: 10 minutes *START TO FINISH:* 30 minutes [8 SERVINGS]

- ⅔ cup powdered sugar
- ½ teaspoon almond extract
- 1 egg
- 1 package (3 oz) cream cheese, softened
- 1¾ cups Original Bisquick® mix
- ⅔ cup miniature semisweet chocolate chips
- 1 can (21 oz) cherry pie filling
- ¼ cup white baking chips
- 2 teaspoons shortening

1 Heat oven to 400°F. Mix powdered sugar, almond extract, egg and cream cheese in medium bowl. Stir in Bisquick. Roll or pat dough into 12-inch circle on ungreased cookie sheet. Flute edge if desired. Bake 8 to 10 minutes or until crust is light golden brown.

2 Sprinkle chocolate chips over hot crust. Bake about 1 minute or until chips are melted; spread evenly. Cool 5 minutes. Gently loosen and transfer to serving plate.

3 Spread pie filling over chocolate. Heat white baking chips and shortening over low heat, stirring frequently, until smooth; drizzle over pie filling.

1 SERVING: Calories 421; Total Fat 16g (Saturated Fat 8g; Trans Fat 1g); Cholesterol 39mg; Sodium 386mg; Total Carbohydrate 65g (Dietary Fiber 1g); Protein 5g EXCHANGES: 4 Starch; 2½ Fat CARBOHYDRATE CHOICES: 4

sweet note If you're making this for your sweetheart, pat the dough into a large heart shape before baking and topping it. You'll find that using a fork makes it easy to drizzle the melted white baking chips over the cherry pie filling.

cherry-raspberry chocolate cobbler

PREP TIME: 10 minutes *START TO FINISH:* 40 minutes [8 SERVINGS]

- 1 can (21 oz) cherry pie filling
- ½ teaspoon almond extract
- 2 cups fresh raspberries
- ¾ cup chocolate ice cream
- ½ cup bittersweet chocolate chips
- 1 cup Original Bisquick® mix
- 3 tablespoons sliced almonds

1 Heat oven to 375°F. In medium bowl, mix pie filling and extract; fold in raspberries. Spread in ungreased 8-inch square pan. Bake 15 minutes.

2 Meanwhile, in medium microwavable bowl, microwave ice cream and chocolate chips on High about 1 minute 30 seconds, stirring every 30 seconds, until smooth. Add Bisquick mix; mix well. Let stand until fruit is done baking.

3 Drop dough into 8 mounds (about 3 tablespoons each) on hot fruit. Sprinkle each mound with almonds. Bake 15 to 18 minutes longer or until chocolate topping is just set. Serve warm.

1 SERVING: Calories 260; Total Fat 8g (Saturated Fat 3½g; Trans Fat ½g); Cholesterol 0mg; Sodium 200mg; Total Carbohydrate 44g (Dietary Fiber 4g); Protein 3g EXCHANGES: ½ Starch; ½ Fruit; 2 Other Carbohydrate; 1½ Fat CARBOHYDRATE CHOICES: 3

sweet note Bittersweet chocolate chips are not as sweet as the more common semisweet chocolate chips. You can find them next to the other chocolate chips.

harvest fruit compote cobbler

PREP TIME: 25 minutes *START TO FINISH:* 1 hour 15 minutes [6 SERVINGS]

Compote

3 medium baking apples (1½ lb), peeled, cut into ½-inch slices (3 cups)

3 medium slightly ripe, firm Bartlett pears (1½ lb), peeled, cut into ½-inch slices (3 cups)

½ cup dried apricot halves, cut in half

½ cup dried plums, cut in half

½ cup packed brown sugar

2 tablespoons Original Bisquick® mix

2 tablespoons finely chopped crystallized ginger

¼ teaspoon ground cloves

Topping

1½ cups Original Bisquick® mix

⅓ cup milk

¼ cup granulated sugar

½ teaspoon ground ginger

¼ cup butter or margarine, melted

1 tablespoon coarse sugar

1 Heat oven to 375°F.

2 In large bowl, mix compote ingredients. Spoon into ungreased 8-inch square (2-quart) glass baking dish.

3 Bake uncovered 25 minutes. Meanwhile, in same bowl, mix all topping ingredients except coarse sugar, using rubber spatula or spoon, until dough forms. Drop dough by spoonfuls over top of hot compote. Sprinkle with coarse sugar.

4 Bake 25 to 30 minutes or until fruit is tender and topping is golden brown and baked throughout.

1 SERVING: Calories 470; Total Fat 12g (Saturated Fat 6g; Trans Fat 1½g); Cholesterol 20mg; Sodium 470mg; Total Carbohydrate 86g (Dietary Fiber 5g); Protein 4g EXCHANGES: 1 Starch; 1 Fruit; 3½ Other Carbohydrate; 2½ Fat CARBOHYDRATE CHOICES: 6

sweet note In this recipe, use pears that are a bit ripe but still firm. If they are too ripe, they'll cook more quickly than the apples and be mushy at the end of baking.

summer fruit crisp

PREP TIME: 15 minutes *START TO FINISH:* 1 hour 10 minutes [6 SERVINGS]

- 6 medium red or purple plums, sliced (about 5 cups)
- ½ cup sugar
- 3 tablespoons cornstarch
- ½ cup crushed gingersnap cookie crumbs (about 15 cookies)
- ½ cup chopped walnuts
- ½ cup Original Bisquick® mix
- ¼ cup butter or margarine, softened
- ¼ cup sugar

1 Heat oven to 350°F. Spray 8-inch square (2-quart) glass baking dish with cooking spray.

2 In large bowl, stir plums, ½ cup sugar and the cornstarch until combined. Spread in baking dish.

3 In medium bowl, mix cookie crumbs, walnuts, Bisquick mix, butter and ¼ cup sugar with fork until crumbly. Sprinkle over plum mixture.

4 Bake 45 to 55 minutes or until mixture is hot and bubbly and topping is lightly browned. Serve warm.

1 SERVING: Calories 410; Total Fat 17g (Saturated Fat 6g; Trans Fat 1g); Cholesterol 20mg; Sodium 260mg; Total Carbohydrate 60g (Dietary Fiber 3g); Protein 4g EXCHANGES: 1 Starch; 1 Fruit; 2 Other Carbohydrate; 3½ Fat CARBOHYDRATE CHOICES: 4

sweet note Be sure to serve this plum crisp warm with a big scoop of vanilla ice cream. Crushed cinnamon-sugar graham crackers can be substituted for the gingersnap cookie crumbs.

impossibly easy french apple dessert squares

PREP TIME: 25 minutes *START TO FINISH:* 1 hour 50 minutes [15 SERVINGS]

Streusel

1 cup Original Bisquick® mix

½ cup packed brown sugar

¼ cup butter or margarine

¾ cup chopped nuts

Fruit Mixture

6 cups sliced peeled tart apples (6 medium)

2 teaspoons ground cinnamon

½ teaspoon ground nutmeg

1 cup Original Bisquick® mix

1 cup granulated sugar

1 cup milk

2 tablespoons butter or margarine, melted

4 eggs, beaten

sweet note Apple varieties that would be good for this recipe include Cortland, Rome Beauty, McIntosh, Granny Smith and Jonathan.

1 Heat oven to 350°F. Spray 13 × 9-inch pan with cooking spray.

2 In medium bowl, mix 1 cup Bisquick mix and the brown sugar. Cut in ¼ cup butter, using pastry blender (or pulling 2 table knives through ingredients in opposite directions), until crumbly. Stir in nuts; set aside.

3 In large bowl, mix apples, cinnamon and nutmeg; spoon into pan. In medium bowl, stir remaining ingredients until well blended. Pour mixture over apples. Sprinkle with streusel.

4 Bake 45 to 55 minutes or until knife inserted in center comes out clean and top is golden brown. Cool 30 minutes or until set before cutting into squares. Store in refrigerator.

1 SERVING: Calories 290; Total Fat 12g (Saturated Fat 5g; Trans Fat 1g); Cholesterol 70mg; Sodium 280mg; Total Carbohydrate 39g (Dietary Fiber 2g); Protein 4g EXCHANGES: 1 Starch; 1½ Other Carbohydrate; 2½ Fat CARBOHYDRATE CHOICES: 2½

easy cherry and peach clafoutis

PREP TIME: 15 minutes *START TO FINISH:* 55 minutes [8 SERVINGS]

- 1 can (14.5 oz) pitted tart red cherries in water, well drained
- 1 can (15.25 oz) sliced peaches in syrup, drained
- ⅓ cup slivered almonds
- ⅔ cup Original Bisquick® mix
- ½ cup granulated sugar
- 1 cup milk
- 1½ teaspoons vanilla
- 3 eggs
- 1 teaspoon powdered sugar

1 Heat oven to 350°F.

2 Spray 10-inch round shallow baking dish with cooking spray. Evenly distribute cherries, peaches and almonds in baking dish.

3 In medium bowl, beat Bisquick mix, granulated sugar, milk, vanilla and eggs with electric mixer on medium speed 2 minutes. Pour over fruit mixture.

4 Bake 35 to 40 minutes or until knife inserted in center comes out clean. Sprinkle with powdered sugar. Serve warm.

1 SERVING: Calories 230; Total Fat 6g (Saturated Fat 1½g; Trans Fat 0g); Cholesterol 80mg; Sodium 170mg; Total Carbohydrate 37g (Dietary Fiber 2g); Protein 5g
EXCHANGES: ½ Fruit; 2 Other Carbohydrate; ½ Fat CARBOHYDRATE CHOICES: 2½

sweet note Use fresh seasonal fruits such as raspberries, rhubarb, cherries, peaches or other fruits in place of the canned fruits.

blueberry-peach cobbler with walnut biscuits

PREP TIME: 30 minutes *START TO FINISH:* 1 hour 40 minutes [6 SERVINGS]

1 Heat oven to 400°F.

2 In medium bowl, stir together fruit mixture ingredients; let stand 10 minutes to allow sugar to pull juices from peaches. Transfer to ungreased 8-inch square (2-quart) glass baking dish.

3 Bake uncovered about 10 minutes or until fruit is bubbling. Remove from oven; stir. Bake 10 to 12 minutes longer or until bubbly around edges (fruit must be hot in middle so biscuit topping bakes completely).

4 Meanwhile, in medium bowl, stir all biscuit topping ingredients except 2 teaspoons milk and coarse sugar until firm dough forms. Drop dough by 6 spoonfuls onto warm fruit mixture. Brush dough with 2 teaspoons milk. Sprinkle with coarse sugar.

5 Bake 25 to 30 minutes or until biscuits are deep golden brown and bottom of center biscuit is no longer doughy. Cool 10 minutes on cooling rack. Serve warm.

1 SERVING: Calories 380; Total Fat 15g (Saturated Fat 4g; Trans Fat 1g); Cholesterol 10mg; Sodium 300mg; Total Carbohydrate 55g (Dietary Fiber 4g); Protein 5g EXCHANGES: 1½ Starch; 1 Fruit; 1 Other Carbohydrate; 3 Fat CARBOHYDRATE CHOICES: 3½

sweet note If fresh fruit is unavailable, it's easy to substitute frozen fruit. Use 1 cup frozen blueberries and 2 bags (16 ounces each) frozen sliced peaches instead. Thaw the frozen fruit before using.

Fruit Mixture

8 medium fresh peaches (about 2 lb), peeled, each cut into 6 wedges

1 cup fresh blueberries

1 tablespoon cornstarch

½ cup granulated sugar

1 tablespoon lemon juice

¼ teaspoon ground cinnamon

Dash salt

Cobbler Topping

1 cup Original Bisquick® mix

¼ teaspoon ground nutmeg

2 tablespoons milk

2 tablespoons butter or margarine, softened

2 tablespoons granulated sugar

⅔ cup chopped walnuts

2 teaspoons milk, if desired

1 tablespoon coarse sugar

creamy fruit tarts

PREP TIME: 30 minutes *START TO FINISH:* 1 hour 12 minutes [6 TARTS]

- 1 cup Original Bisquick® mix
- 2 tablespoons sugar
- 1 tablespoon butter or margarine, softened
- 2 packages (3 oz each) cream cheese, softened
- ¼ cup sugar
- ¼ cup sour cream
- 1½ cups assorted sliced fresh fruit or berries
- ⅓ cup apple jelly, melted

1 Heat oven to 375°F.

2 In medium bowl, stir Bisquick mix, 2 tablespoons sugar, the butter and 1 package cream cheese in small bowl until dough forms a ball.

3 Divide dough into 6 parts. Press each part of the dough on bottom and ¾ inch up side in each of 6 tart pans, 4¼ × 1 inch, or 10-ounce custard cups. Place on cookie sheet.

4 Bake 10 to 12 minutes or until light brown. Cool in pans on wire rack, about 30 minutes. Remove tart shells from pans.

5 In a small bowl, beat remaining package cream cheese, ¼ cup sugar and the sour cream until smooth. Spoon into tart shells, spreading over bottoms. Top each with about ¼ cup fruit. Brush with jelly.

1 SERVING: Calories 320; Total Fat 16g (Saturated Fat 8g; Trans Fat 1g); Cholesterol 40mg; Sodium 359mg; Total Carbohydrate 43g (Dietary Fiber 2g); Protein 4g EXCHANGES: 1 Starch; 1 Other Carbohydrate; 3 Fat CARBOHYDRATE CHOICES: 3

sweet note Use your imagination when choosing fruit for these tarts. Try sliced strawberries, kiwifruit, peaches or nectarines. Whole fruits such as raspberries, blueberries or blackberries are nice, too.

strawberry-banana crepes

PREP TIME: 25 minutes *START TO FINISH:* 25 minutes [12 SERVINGS]

Crepes

1 cup Original Bisquick® mix

¾ cup milk

2 eggs

Filling

1½ cups whipping cream

¼ cup sugar

2 to 3 bananas, sliced

1 pint (2 cups) fresh strawberries, sliced, or 1 box (10 oz) frozen strawberries, partially thawed

¼ cup chopped walnuts

1 In small bowl, stir all crepe ingredients until blended. Grease 6- or 7-inch skillet with shortening or cooking spray; heat over medium-high heat. For each crepe, pour 2 tablespoons batter into skillet; rotate skillet until batter covers bottom. Cook until golden brown. Gently loosen edge with metal spatula; turn and cook other side until golden brown. Stack crepes as you remove them from skillet, placing waxed paper between each. Keep crepes covered to prevent them from drying out.

2 In chilled medium bowl, beat whipping cream and sugar with electric mixer on high speed until stiff. Spoon about 3 tablespoons whipped cream down center of each crepe; top with 4 or 5 banana slices. Roll up; top each crepe with whipped cream, strawberries and walnuts.

1 SERVING: Calories 220; Total Fat 14g (Saturated Fat 7g; Trans Fat ½g); Cholesterol 70mg; Sodium 150mg; Total Carbohydrate 19g (Dietary Fiber 1g); Protein 4g EXCHANGES: 1 Starch; ½ Other Carbohydrate; 2½ Fat CARBOHYDRATE CHOICES: 1

sweet notes Use raspberries, blueberries, blackberries or a combination. All will be delicious in these sweet crepes.

Crepes can be frozen up to 3 months. Stack cool unfilled crepes with waxed paper between each. Wrap in foil or place in an airtight plastic freezer bag; label and freeze. Thaw at room temperature about 1 hour or in refrigerator 6 to 8 hours.

chocolate-strawberry crumble

PREP TIME: 15 minutes *START TO FINISH:* 1 hour 30 minutes [16 SERVINGS]

- 2 cans (21 oz each) strawberry pie filling
- 1 box (10 oz) frozen strawberries in syrup, thawed
- 1 box Betty Crocker® SuperMoist® devil's food cake mix
- ¾ cup butter or margarine, softened
- ½ cup chopped walnuts
- Vanilla ice cream, if desired

1 Heat oven to 350°F (325°F for dark or nonstick pan).

2 In ungreased 13 × 9-inch pan, pour pie filling and strawberries; stir gently to mix.

3 In large bowl, beat cake mix and butter with electric mixer on low speed until crumbly. Crumble over fruit mixture. Sprinkle with walnuts.

4 Bake 40 to 45 minutes or until bubbly around edges and top is set. Cool at least 30 minutes. Serve warm with ice cream.

1 SERVING: Calories 260; Total Fat 11g (Saturated Fat 6g; Trans Fat 0g); Cholesterol 20mg; Sodium 280mg; Total Carbohydrate 39g (Dietary Fiber 2g); Protein 2g EXCHANGES: 1 Starch; 1½ Other Carbohydrate; 2 Fat CARBOHYDRATE CHOICES: 2½

sweet note If you prefer, you can substitute yellow cake mix for the devil's food. For mixed-berry crumble, use a can of raspberry pie filling in place of one of the cans of strawberry filling.

pear-raisin pie

PREP TIME: 35 minutes *START TO FINISH:* 1 hour 5 minutes [8 SERVINGS]

Streusel Topping

⅔ cup quick-cooking oats

½ cup Original Bisquick® mix

⅓ cup packed brown sugar

¼ cup firm butter or margarine

Crust

1 cup Original Bisquick® mix

¼ cup butter or margarine, softened

2 tablespoons boiling water

Filling

½ cup pineapple juice

½ cup raisins

1 tablespoon cornstarch

⅛ teaspoon ground nutmeg

⅛ teaspoon ground ginger

4 cups sliced peeled pears (about 3 medium)

1 Heat oven to 375°F.

2 In small bowl, mix oats, ½ cup Bisquick mix and the brown sugar. Cut in ¼ cup firm butter with fork or pastry blender until mixture is crumbly; set aside.

3 In medium bowl, mix 1 cup Bisquick mix and ¼ cup softened butter. Add boiling water; stir vigorously until very soft dough forms. In ungreased 9-inch glass pie plate, press dough firmly, using fingers dusted with Bisquick mix and bringing dough onto rim of pie plate. Flute edge if desired.

4 In 2-quart saucepan, mix pineapple juice, raisins, cornstarch, nutmeg and ginger. Cook over medium heat, stirring constantly, until mixture thickens and boils. Boil and stir 1 minute; remove from heat. Stir in pears. Spoon into pie plate. Sprinkle with streusel topping.

5 Bake 25 to 30 minutes or until crust and topping are light golden brown.

1 SERVING: Calories 360; Total Fat 15g (Saturated Fat 8g; Trans Fat 1g); Cholesterol 30mg; Sodium 360mg; Total Carbohydrate 51g (Dietary Fiber 4g); Protein 4g EXCHANGES: 2 Starch; ½ Fruit; 1 Other Carbohydrate; 2½ Fat CARBOHYDRATE CHOICES: 3½

sweet note Pears rock hard? To speed up the ripening process, place them in a paper bag with an apple. Pierce the bag in several places with the tip of a knife, and leave at room temperature. Serve this streusel-topped pie warm topped with slices of Cheddar cheese cut into pear or heart shapes.

chocolate chip–cherry cobbler

PREP TIME: 15 minutes *START TO FINISH:* 50 minutes [6 SERVINGS]

1 can (21 oz) cherry pie filling

2 tablespoons orange juice

½ teaspoon almond extract

1½ cups Original Bisquick® mix

½ cup whipping cream

1 tablespoon sugar

1 tablespoon butter or margarine, softened

¼ cup miniature semisweet chocolate chips

½ teaspoon sugar

Chocolate syrup, if desired

1 Heat oven to 350°F.

2 In 1½-quart casserole, mix pie filling, orange juice and almond extract. Microwave uncovered on High about 4 minutes or until bubbly around edge; stir.

3 In medium bowl, mix remaining ingredients except ½ teaspoon sugar with spoon until stiff dough forms. Drop dough by 6 spoonfuls (about ¼ cup each) onto warm pie filling. Sprinkle ½ teaspoon sugar over dough.

4 Bake 30 to 35 minutes or until topping is golden brown. Serve warm, drizzled with chocolate syrup.

1 SERVING: Calories 350; Total Fat 15g (Saturated Fat 7g; Trans Fat 1g); Cholesterol 25mg; Sodium 450mg; Total Carbohydrate 50g (Dietary Fiber 2g); Protein 4g EXCHANGES: 1 Starch; 2½ Other Carbohydrate; 3 Fat CARBOHYDRATE CHOICES: 3

sweet note For a little more sparkle, sprinkle with 1 tablespoon coarse white sparkling sugar instead of the ½ teaspoon regular granulated sugar.

chocolate-strawberry shortcakes

PREP TIME: 15 minutes *START TO FINISH:* 1 hour 45 minutes [6 SERVINGS]

- 1 quart (4 cups) fresh strawberries, sliced
- ½ cup sugar
- 2 cups Original Bisquick® mix
- ⅓ cup unsweetened baking cocoa
- 2 tablespoons sugar
- ⅔ cup milk
- 2 tablespoons butter or margarine, melted
- ⅓ cup miniature semisweet chocolate chips
- 1½ cups frozen (thawed) whipped topping

1. In medium bowl, toss strawberries and ½ cup sugar until coated. Let stand 1 hour.
2. Heat oven to 375°F. Spray cookie sheet with cooking spray.
3. In medium bowl, stir Bisquick mix, cocoa, 2 tablespoons sugar, the milk and butter until soft dough forms. Stir in chocolate chips. Drop dough by about ⅓ cupfuls onto cookie sheet.
4. Bake 12 to 15 minutes or until tops of shortcakes appear dry and cracked. Cool 15 minutes. Using serrated knife, split warm shortcakes. Fill and top with strawberries and whipped topping.

1 SERVING: Calories 460; Total Fat 17g (Saturated Fat 10g; Trans Fat 1½g); Cholesterol 15mg; Sodium 540mg; Total Carbohydrate 69g (Dietary Fiber 5g); Protein 6g EXCHANGES: 2 Starch; 1 Fruit; 1½ Other Carbohydrate; 3 Fat CARBOHYDRATE CHOICES: 4½

sweet note For the chocolate lovers in the family, sprinkle additional miniature chocolate chips over tops of the shortcakes before serving.

cranberry-apple shortcakes

PREP TIME: 40 minutes *START TO FINISH:* 55 minutes [6 SERVINGS]

Cranberry-Apple Filling

2 cups cranberries

⅓ cup apple juice

2 cups thinly sliced peeled cooking apples (1 to 2 medium)

⅔ cup sugar

½ cup apple juice

1 tablespoon cornstarch

Shortcakes

2½ cups Original Bisquick® mix

½ cup milk

3 tablespoons sugar

3 tablespoons butter or margarine, melted

Garnish, if desired

Whipped topping

1 In 2-quart saucepan, heat cranberries and ⅓ cup apple juice to boiling. Stir in apples; reduce heat. Simmer uncovered about 5 minutes or until apples are softened. In small bowl, mix remaining filling ingredients; stir into cranberry mixture. Cook, stirring constantly, until mixture thickens and boils. Boil and stir 1 minute; remove from heat. (Filling can be served warm or cool.)

2 Heat oven to 425°F. In medium bowl, mix all shortcake ingredients until soft dough forms. On surface lightly dusted with Bisquick mix, gently roll dough in Bisquick mix to coat. Knead 8 to 10 times. Roll ½ inch thick. Cut with 3-inch round cutter dipped in Bisquick mix. Place on ungreased cookie sheet.

3 Bake 10 to 12 minutes or until golden brown. Split shortcakes horizontally. Fill and top shortcakes with filling. Top with whipped topping.

1 SERVING: Calories 450; Total Fat 14g (Saturated Fat 6g; Trans Fat 1½g); Cholesterol 15mg; Sodium 660mg; Total Carbohydrate 76g (Dietary Fiber 3g); Protein 5g EXCHANGES: 1½ Starch; ½ Fruit; 3 Other Carbohydrate; 2½ Fat CARBOHYDRATE CHOICES: 5

sweet note Replace the apple juice with cranberry juice for a tangy filling. For a fun fall dessert, use a large apple-shaped cookie cutter to cut out shortcakes, and garnish filled shortcakes with a fresh mint leaf.

fruity oat shortcakes

PREP TIME: 20 minutes *START TO FINISH:* 30 minutes [6 SERVINGS]

- 2 cups Original Bisquick® mix
- ⅓ cup quick-cooking oats
- 3 tablespoons packed brown sugar
- ½ cup milk
- 3 tablespoons butter or margarine, melted
- 2 medium firm pears, peeled and cut into 1-inch pieces
- 1 cup fresh or frozen cranberries
- ½ cup orange juice
- ¼ teaspoon ground cinnamon
- 1 can (21 oz) apricot pie filling

1 Heat oven to 425°F.

2 In large bowl, mix Bisquick mix, oats, brown sugar, milk and butter until soft dough forms. Drop dough by 6 spoonfuls onto ungreased cookie sheet. Sprinkle with additional brown sugar and oats if desired.

3 Bake 8 to 10 minutes or until light golden brown.

4 In 2-quart saucepan, heat pears, cranberries, orange juice and cinnamon to boiling; reduce heat. Simmer uncovered 3 to 4 minutes, stirring occasionally, just until cranberries pop. Stir in pie filling. Split warm shortcakes; fill and top with fruit mixture.

1 SERVING: Calories 440; Total Fat 13g (Saturated Fat 5g; Trans Fat 1g); Cholesterol 15mg; Sodium 550mg; Total Carbohydrate 76g (Dietary Fiber 5g); Protein 5g EXCHANGES: 1½ Starch; 3½ Other Carbohydrate; 2½ Fat CARBOHYDRATE CHOICES: 5

sweet note Shortcakes make a fun do-it-yourself dessert. Let your family make their own and add as much filling as they like. Don't forget the whipped cream!

pecan-cinnamon shortcakes with bananas and dulce de leche

PREP TIME: 20 minutes *START TO FINISH:* 1 hour 15 minutes [4 SERVINGS]

1¼ cups Original Bisquick® mix

2 tablespoons sugar

¼ cup finely chopped pecans

½ teaspoon ground cinnamon

½ cup whipping (heavy) cream

½ teaspoon sugar

1 cup whipping (heavy) cream

4 tablespoons dulce de leche (caramelized sweetened condensed milk), from 13.4-oz can

2 ripe bananas, cut into ¼-inch slices

4 teaspoons grated chocolate

1 Heat oven to 350°F. In medium bowl, mix Bisquick mix, 2 tablespoons sugar, the pecans and cinnamon. Add ½ cup cream; stir until soft dough forms.

2 On ungreased cookie sheet, drop dough by ¼ cupfuls 2 inches apart; pat into rounds, about ¾ inch thick. Sprinkle tops with ½ teaspoon sugar.

3 Bake 16 to 18 minutes or until light golden brown. Remove from cookie sheet to cooling rack; cool completely.

4 In chilled large deep bowl, beat 1 cup cream with electric mixer on high speed until soft peaks form. Cover; refrigerate until serving time.

5 Using a serrated knife, carefully slice shortcakes in half horizontally. Place bottom halves on 4 dessert plates; spread each with 1 tablespoon dulce de leche. Top each with ½ sliced banana, 3 tablespoons whipped cream and ½ teaspoon grated chocolate. Cover with top halves of shortcakes. Top each with 3 tablespoons whipped cream and ½ teaspoon grated chocolate. Serve immediately.

1 SERVING: Calories 640; Total Fat 40g (Saturated Fat 21g; Trans Fat 2½g); Cholesterol 105mg; Sodium 510mg; Total Carbohydrate 63g (Dietary Fiber 3g); Protein 7g EXCHANGES: 2 Starch; 2 Other Carbohydrate; 8 Fat CARBOHYDRATE CHOICES: 4

sweet note Find dulce de leche in a can next to other canned milks in the baking aisle in the grocery store.

plum and walnut crisp

PREP TIME: 15 minutes *START TO FINISH:* 1 hour 10 minutes [6 SERVINGS]

6 medium red or purple plums, sliced (about 5 cups)

½ cup sugar

3 tablespoons cornstarch

½ cup crushed gingersnap cookies (about 15 cookies)

½ cup chopped walnuts

½ cup Original Bisquick® mix

¼ cup butter or margarine, softened

¼ cup sugar

Ice cream, if desired

1 Heat oven to 350°F. Spray 8-inch square (2-quart) glass baking dish with cooking spray.

2 In large bowl, stir plums, ½ cup sugar and the cornstarch until combined. Spread in baking dish.

3 In medium bowl, mix crushed cookies, walnuts, Bisquick mix, butter and ¼ cup sugar with fork until crumbly. Sprinkle over plum mixture.

4 Bake 45 to 55 minutes or until mixture is hot and bubbly and topping is lightly browned. Serve warm, with ice cream if desired.

1 SERVING: Calories 410; Total Fat 17g (Saturated Fat 6g; Trans Fat 1g); Cholesterol 20 mg; Sodium 260mg; Total Carbohydrate 60g (Dietary Fiber 3g); Protein 4g EXCHANGES: 1 Starch; 1 Fruit; 2 Other Carbohydrate; 3½ Fat CARBOHYDRATE CHOICES: 4

sweet note Crushed cinnamon-sugar graham crackers can be substituted for the gingersnap cookies.

upside-down cherry-pear cake

PREP TIME: 15 minutes *START TO FINISH:* 1 hour 30 minutes [9 SERVINGS]

- 1 can (21 oz) cherry pie filling
- 1 can (15 oz) pear halves, drained
- ¾ cup slivered almonds
- ¼ cup butter or margarine, melted
- 1 cup sugar
- 1 cup Original Bisquick® mix
- ¼ teaspoon ground cinnamon
- 2 eggs
- 1 quart (4 cups) vanilla ice cream

1 Heat oven to 350°F. Grease 8-inch square (2-quart) glass baking dish. Spread cherry pie filling in baking dish. Arrange pear halves, cut side up, over pie filling. Bake about 20 minutes or until filling is hot.

2 Meanwhile, in food processor or blender, cover and process almonds until finely ground. In medium bowl, mix butter, sugar, Bisquick mix, almonds, cinnamon and eggs with spoon.

3 Spoon batter over hot pie filling and pears. Bake 40 to 45 minutes or until cherries are bubbly and toothpick inserted in center of cake comes out clean. Let stand 10 minutes.

4 Run sharp knife around edges of baking dish to loosen. Place heatproof serving plate upside down onto baking dish; turn plate and dish over. Let dish remain over cake a few minutes so topping can drizzle over cake. Serve warm with ice cream.

1 SERVING: Calories 370; Total Fat 14g (Saturated Fat 6g; Trans Fat ½g); Cholesterol 60mg; Sodium 240mg; Total Carbohydrate 54g (Dietary Fiber 3g); Protein 5g EXCHANGES: ½ Starch; 3 Other Carbohydrate; ½ High-Fat Meat; 2 Fat CARBOHYDRATE CHOICES: 3½

sweet note This easy-to-make dessert can also be prepared with apple or blueberry pie filling.

cherry-chocolate pudding cake

PREP TIME: 10 minutes *START TO FINISH:* 55 minutes [18 SERVINGS]

1 Heat oven to 350°F (325°F for dark or nonstick pan). Mix brown sugar, ⅓ cup cocoa and the hot water in ungreased 13 × 9-inch pan until sugar is dissolved.

2 Stir Bisquick mix, granulated sugar, ¼ cup cocoa, the oil, almond extract and eggs in large bowl until blended. Stir in pie filling. Spoon batter over cocoa mixture in pan.

3 Bake 35 to 45 minutes or until top springs back when touched lightly. Serve warm with ice cream.

1 SERVING: Calories 230; Total Fat 6g (Saturated Fat 1½g; Trans Fat ½g); Cholesterol 25mg; Sodium 180mg; Total Carbohydrate 42g (Dietary Fiber 1g); Protein 2g
EXCHANGES: 1 Starch; 2 Other Carbohydrate; 1 Fat CARBOHYDRATE CHOICES: 3

sweet note Make this satisfying comfort-food favorite simply irresistible with a scoop of vanilla ice cream or a spoonful of whipped cream.

- 1 cup packed brown sugar
- ⅓ cup unsweetened baking cocoa
- 2 cups hot water
- 2 cups Original Bisquick® mix
- 1 cup granulated sugar
- ¼ cup unsweetened baking cocoa
- ¼ cup vegetable oil
- 1 teaspoon almond extract
- 2 eggs
- 1 can (21 oz) cherry pie filling
- Ice cream or whipped cream, if desired

fresh fruit tart

PREP TIME: 25 minutes *START TO FINISH:* 1 hour 15 minutes [12 SERVINGS]

1 box Betty Crocker® SuperMoist® lemon cake mix

½ cup butter or margarine, softened

1 egg

3 containers (6 oz each) Yoplait® Original 99% Fat Free lemon burst or French vanilla yogurt

1 box (4-serving size) vanilla instant pudding and pie filling mix

3 cups sliced fruits, berries and/or mandarin orange segments

3 tablespoons apricot preserves

1 cup fresh raspberries

1 Heat oven to 375°F (350°F for dark or nonstick pan). Grease 12-inch pizza pan or bottom only of 13 × 9-inch pan with shortening or cooking spray.

2 In large bowl, mix cake mix, butter and egg with spoon until crumbly. Press on bottom of pan.

3 Bake 14 to 18 minutes or until set. Cool completely, about 30 minutes.

4 In medium bowl, beat yogurt and dry pudding mix with electric mixer on medium speed until blended. Spoon over baked layer. Smooth surface with rubber spatula. Arrange fruit on yogurt mixture.

5 Heat preserves over medium heat until melted; brush over fruit. Mound raspberries in center. Serve immediately, or refrigerate up to 24 hours. Store covered in refrigerator.

1 SERVING: Calories 300; Total Fat 7g (Saturated Fat 4½g; Trans Fat 0g); Cholesterol 35mg; Sodium 450mg; Total Carbohydrate 56g (Dietary Fiber 2g); Protein 3g
EXCHANGES: 1 Starch; 2½ Other Carbohydrate; 1½ Fat CARBOHYDRATE CHOICES: 4

sweet note In a hurry? A 21-ounce can of blueberry, cherry or apple filling can be substituted for the fruit, preserves and raspberries. Spoon the pie filling to within 1 inch of the edge of the yogurt mixture.

grilled summer cobbler

PREP TIME: 15 minutes *START TO FINISH:* 45 minutes [8 SERVINGS]

1¼ cups Original Bisquick® mix

½ cup sugar

½ cup milk

¼ cup butter or margarine

1 medium nectarine, sliced (1 cup)

1 cup fresh blueberries

¼ cup sugar

½ teaspoon ground cinnamon

1 Heat gas or charcoal grill.

2 Meanwhile, in medium bowl, mix Bisquick mix, ½ cup sugar and the milk; beat 30 seconds.

3 In 9-inch round foil cake pan, melt butter on grill over medium heat. Pour batter over butter in pan. Top with nectarine and blueberries. Sprinkle with ¼ cup sugar and the cinnamon.

4 Cover grill; cook about 30 minutes or until toothpick inserted in center comes out clean.

1 SERVING: Calories 230; Total Fat 9g (Saturated Fat 4½g; Trans Fat 1g); Cholesterol 15mg; Sodium 280mg; Total Carbohydrate 36g (Dietary Fiber 1g); Protein 2g EXCHANGES: ½ Starch; 2 Other Carbohydrate; 1½ Fat CARBOHYDRATE CHOICES: 2½

sweet note Blackberries can be substituted for the blueberries, and a peach can be used for the nectarine. After the cobbler is baked, move the pan to the side of the grill to keep it warm.

carrot-raisin bars

PREP TIME: 10 minutes *START TO FINISH:* 1 hour 40 minutes [48 BARS]

1 box Betty Crocker® SuperMoist® carrot cake mix

½ cup vegetable oil

¼ cup water

2 eggs

¾ cup raisins

½ cup chopped nuts

1 container (1 lb) Betty Crocker® Rich & Creamy cream cheese frosting

1 Heat oven to 350°F (325°F for dark or nonstick pan). Grease and flour, or spray with baking spray with flour, bottom and sides of 15 × 10-inch pan.

2 In large bowl, mix cake mix, oil, water and eggs with spoon. Stir in raisins and nuts. Spread evenly in pan.

3 Bake 18 to 24 minutes (25 to 29 minutes for dark or nonstick pan) or until bars spring back when touched lightly in center. Cool completely, about 1 hour. Spread with frosting. For bars, cut into 8 rows by 6 rows. Store loosely covered at room temperature.

1 SERVING: Calories 120; Total Fat 6g (Saturated Fat 1g; Trans Fat ½g); Cholesterol 10mg; Sodium 85mg; Total Carbohydrate 16g (Dietary Fiber 0g); Protein 1g EXCHANGES: ½ Starch; ½ Other Carbohydrate; 1 Fat CARBOHYDRATE CHOICES: 1

five-ingredient rhubarb squares

PREP TIME: 15 minutes *START TO FINISH:* 1 hour 25 minutes [16 SERVINGS]

- 1 box Betty Crocker® SuperMoist® yellow cake mix
- 1 cup cold butter or margarine, cut into small pieces
- 1¾ cups sugar
- 3 eggs
- 4 cups sliced fresh rhubarb
- Whipped cream, if desired

1 Heat oven to 350°F (325°F for dark or nonstick pan). Reserve 2 tablespoons of the cake mix. In large bowl, cut butter into remaining cake mix, using pastry blender (or pulling 2 table knives through ingredients in opposite directions), until crumbly. In bottom of ungreased 13 × 9-inch pan, pat 2¼ cups of the mixture (if mixture is sticky, lightly flour hands). Reserve remaining crumbly mixture for topping. Bake 15 minutes. Remove from oven.

2 In large bowl, beat reserved 2 tablespoons cake mix, the sugar and eggs with electric mixer on medium speed until creamy. Stir in rhubarb. Pour over partially baked crust. Sprinkle remaining crumbly mixture over top.

3 Bake 45 to 55 minutes longer or until golden brown and center is set. Cool slightly before serving. Serve warm or cold with whipped cream. Store covered in refrigerator.

1 SERVING: Calories 290; Total Fat 11g (Saturated Fat 6g; Trans Fat 0g); Cholesterol 65mg; Sodium 270mg; Total Carbohydrate 46g (Dietary Fiber 1g); Protein 2g EXCHANGES: ½ Starch; ½ Fruit; 2 Other Carbohydrate; 2 Fat CARBOHYDRATE CHOICES: 3

sweet note If fresh rhubarb isn't available, use 4 cups frozen (slightly thawed) rhubarb (from two 16-oz bags).

strawberry trifle

PREP TIME: 15 minutes *START TO FINISH:* 3 hours 48 minutes [16 SERVINGS]

- 1 box Betty Crocker® SuperMoist® white cake mix
- Water, vegetable oil and egg whites called for on cake mix box
- 2 boxes (4-serving size each) vanilla instant pudding and pie filling mix
- 4 cups milk
- 2 bags (16 oz each) frozen strawberries in light syrup, thawed
- 1½ cups frozen (thawed) whipped topping
- ¼ cup slivered almonds, toasted

1 Heat oven to 350°F (325°F for dark or nonstick pan).

2 Make and bake cake as directed on box for 13 × 9-inch pan. Run knife around sides of pan to loosen cake. Cool completely, about 1 hour.

3 While cake is cooling, in large bowl, beat pudding mixes into milk with wire whisk about 2 minutes or until blended.

4 Cut or tear cake into 1-inch pieces. In 3½-quart glass trifle bowl, arrange half the pieces, cutting pieces to fit shape of bowl. Pour half of the thawed strawberries (with syrup) over cake; spread with 2 cups of the pudding. Place remaining cake pieces on pudding and around edge of bowl. Top with remaining strawberries and pudding. Cover; refrigerate at least 2 hours until chilled.

5 Spread whipped topping over top of trifle. Sprinkle with almonds. Store covered in refrigerator up to 12 hours.

1 SERVING: Calories 300; Total Fat 10g (Saturated Fat 3½g; Trans Fat 0g); Cholesterol 5mg; Sodium 330mg; Total Carbohydrate 48g (Dietary Fiber 1g); Protein 5g EXCHANGES: 1 Starch; 2 Other Carbohydrate; 2 Fat CARBOHYDRATE CHOICES: 3

sweet note Mix and match to take an ordinary clear glass bowl uptown! Create a pedestal serving dish for a buffet. To make, turn a small bowl upside down and attach sturdy double-sided tape or sticky wax to the bottom. Then place the trifle bowl on the "pedestal" for a dramatic presentation. It's easiest if you match the dishes before making the trifle.

three-berry trifle

PREP TIME: 15 minutes *START TO FINISH:* 2 hours 50 minutes [12 SERVINGS]

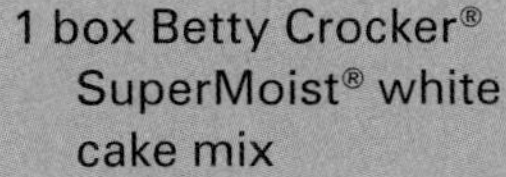

Water, vegetable oil and egg whites called for on cake mix box

1 pint (2 cups) blueberries

1 pint (2 cups) raspberries

1 pint (2 cups) strawberries, halved

⅓ cup granulated sugar

¼ cup raspberry-flavored liqueur or cranberry-raspberry juice

1 cup whipping cream

2 tablespoons powdered sugar

1 Heat oven to 350°F (325°F for dark or nonstick pan). Make and bake cake as directed on box for 13 × 9-inch pan. Run knife around sides of pan to loosen cake. Cool completely, about 1 hour.

2 While cake is cooling, in medium bowl, gently mix berries, granulated sugar and raspberry liqueur.

3 In chilled large bowl, beat whipping cream and powdered sugar with electric mixer on high speed until stiff peaks form.

4 Cut or tear cake into 1-inch pieces. In 3-quart glass trifle bowl, arrange half the pieces. Spoon half of the berry mixture over cake; top with half of the whipped cream. Repeat layers. Cover; refrigerate at least 1 hour before serving. Garnish with additional berries if desired. Store covered in refrigerator up to 12 hours.

1 SERVING: Calories 330; Total Fat 14g (Saturated Fat 6g; Trans Fat 0g); Cholesterol 20mg; Sodium 290mg; Total Carbohydrate 47g (Dietary Fiber 3g); Protein 3g EXCHANGES: 1 Starch; 2 Other Carbohydrate; 2½ Fat CARBOHYDRATE CHOICES: 3

sweet note Spread the fruit layers all the way to the edges of the trifle bowl so that the colors will be visible when the trifle is assembled.

chapter five

decorated desserts

Fabulous Finishing Touches

It's easy to turn a basic cake into a showstopper! Here are some irresistible ideas to make your cakes look as good as they taste.

Simple Additions

Create chocolate cutouts: Melt a 4-ounce bar of sweet cooking chocolate or 4 ounces of semisweet baking chocolate. Spread the melted chocolate over the outside bottom of an 8-inch square pan. Refrigerate until firm; bring to room temperature. Use cookie cutters in desired shapes and sizes to make cutouts. Refrigerate until ready to place on the cake.

Garnish with chocolate curls: Place a bar or block of chocolate on a sheet of waxed paper; let stand in a warm place for 15 minutes. Press a vegetable parer firmly against the bar of chocolate and pull the parer toward you in long, thin strokes to make curls. Transfer each curl carefully with a wooden pick to avoid breaking.

Dust with powdered sugar, cinnamon or cocoa: Place a paper doily or stencil on top of a frosted or unfrosted cake. Shake powdered sugar generously through a sieve over the doily; carefully remove doily. Try cocoa mixed with powdered sugar for added color variation.

Embellish with fresh flowers: Place fresh flowers in floral tubes. Poke the tubes right into the cake top. Remove the containers before slicing the cake.

Frosting Flourishes

Thread it: Frost the cake with a fluffy frosting. Dip a piece of white sewing thread in liquid food color; stretching it taut, press into frosting. Repeat, using a new thread for each color.

Go geometric: Pour melted chocolate or chocolate syrup over the top of a frosted layer cake, beginning with a small circle in the center and encircling with larger circles 1 inch apart. Alternately, draw a spatula or knife from the center outward and from the outside inward 8 times.

Make waves: Use the tines of a fork to make wave designs in the frosting.

On the wedge: Mark the top and sides of a frosted layered cake into 8 equal wedges and panels. Sprinkle candies over alternate wedges and press onto alternate side panels.

Pick your own pattern: Draw a design on a frosted cake, or dip a cookie cutter in food color and press it into the frosting. Fill in the design with crushed candies, colored sugar or chopped nuts.

almond petits fours

PREP TIME: 45 minutes *START TO FINISH:* 1 hour 45 minutes [58 SERVINGS]

Cake

1 package Betty Crocker® SuperMoist® white cake mix

Water, vegetable oil and egg whites called for on cake mix box

1 teaspoon almond extract

Almond Glaze

1 bag (2 lb) powdered sugar

½ cup water

½ cup corn syrup

2 teaspoons almond extract

1 to 3 teaspoons hot water

Decoration

Assorted colors Betty Crocker® decorating icing (in 4.25-oz tubes), fresh edible flowers, or purchased candy flowers

1 Heat oven to 350°F (325°F for dark or nonstick pans). Spray bottoms only of about 58 mini muffin cups with baking spray with flour.

2 Make cake batter as directed on box, adding 1 teaspoon almond extract with the water. Divide batter evenly among muffin cups, filling them about half full. (If using one pan, refrigerate batter while baking other cakes; wash pan before filling with additional batter.)

3 Bake 10 to 15 minutes or until toothpick inserted in center comes out clean. Cool 5 minutes; remove from pan to cooling rack. Cool completely, about 30 minutes.

4 Place cooling rack on cookie sheet or waxed paper to catch glaze drips. In 3-quart saucepan, stir powdered sugar, ½ cup water, the corn syrup and 2 teaspoons almond extract. Heat over low heat, stirring frequently, until sugar is dissolved; remove from heat. Stir in hot water, 1 teaspoon at a time, until glaze is pourable. Turn each mini cake on cooling rack so top side is down. Pour about 1 tablespoon glaze over each cake, letting glaze coat the sides. Let stand 15 minutes.

5 With decorating icing, pipe designs on cakes, or garnish cakes with flowers just before serving. Store loosely covered.

1 PETIT FOUR: Calories 110; Total Fat 1½g (Saturated Fat 0g; Trans Fat 0g); Cholesterol 0mg; Sodium 60mg; Total Carbohydrate 24g (Dietary Fiber 0g); Protein 0g EXCHANGES: ½ Starch; 1 Other Carbohydrate CARBOHYDRATE CHOICES: 1½

sweet note These petits fours are great for themed parties like a baby shower or going-away party. Pipe one individual letter on each cake to spell out "It's A Girl!" or "Bon Voyage."

sweetheart cake

PREP TIME: 15 minutes *START TO FINISH:* 1 hour 58 minutes [12 SERVINGS]

1 box Betty Crocker® SuperMoist® white cake mix

Water, vegetable oil and egg whites called for on cake mix box

1 container (12 oz) Betty Crocker® Whipped fluffy white frosting

Red food color

sweet note Gently press miniature chocolate chips into the sides of this frosted cake for that extra-special touch.

1 Heat oven to 350°F (325°F for dark or nonstick pans). Grease or lightly spray bottoms only of one 8-inch round and one 8-inch square pan.

2 In large bowl, beat cake mix, water, oil and egg whites with electric mixer on low speed 30 seconds, then on medium speed 2 minutes, scraping bowl occasionally. Pour batter into pans.

3 Bake square pan 25 to 29 minutes, round pan 29 to 34 minutes, or until toothpick inserted in center comes out clean. Cool 10 minutes; remove from pans. Cool completely, about 1 hour.

4 Cut round cake in half. Put square cake on tray with one point toward you. Place cut side of each half against one of the top sides of square cake to make a heart as shown in diagram, attaching pieces with small amount of frosting.

5 Tint frosting with a few drops food color. Frost cake with frosting. Store loosely covered.

1 SERVING: Calories 330; Total Fat 14g (Saturated Fat 3½g; Trans Fat 2g); Cholesterol 0mg; Sodium 310mg; Total Carbohydrate 48g (Dietary Fiber 0g); Protein 2g EXCHANGES: 1 Starch; 2 Other Carbohydrate; 2½ Fat CARBOHYDRATE CHOICES: 3

Cutting and Assembling Sweetheart Cake

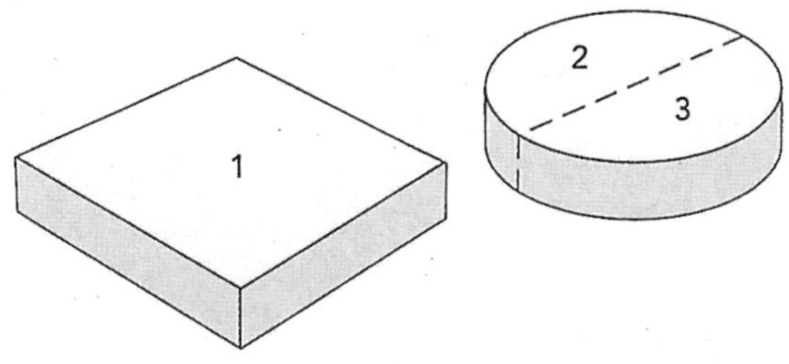

Cut round cake in half.

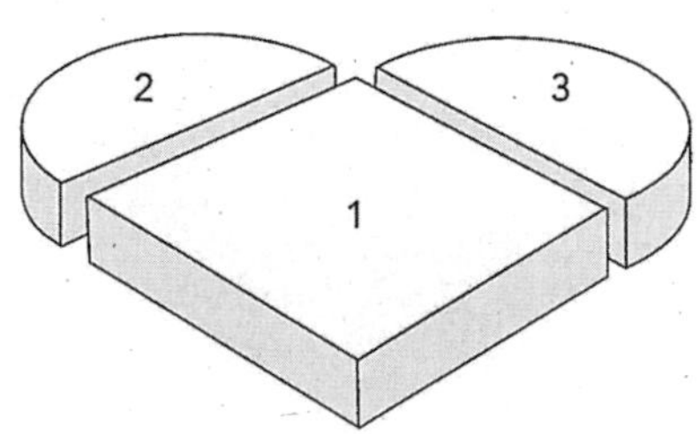

Place cut edges of cake halves against sides of square cake to form heart.

heart and flowers cake

PREP TIME: 25 minutes *START TO FINISH:* 2 hours 13 minutes [16 SERVINGS]

1 box Betty Crocker® SuperMoist® cake mix (any flavor)

Water, vegetable oil and eggs called for on cake mix box

1½ containers (1 lb or 12 oz each) Betty Crocker® Rich & Creamy or Whipped frosting (any flavor)

Assorted gumdrops

Candied orange slices, if desired

1 Heat oven to 350°F (325°F for dark or nonstick pans). Make, bake and cool cake as directed on box—except use one 8-inch round pan and one 8-inch square pan. Check square pan for doneness about 2 minutes before round pan.

2 Cut round cake in half. Place cut sides against sides of square cake to form heart shape, attaching pieces with small amount of frosting. (See diagram on page 320.)

3 Spread frosting on cake. Make gumdrop flowers with assorted gumdrops: Flatten gumdrops with rolling pin. Cut out small petal-shaped flowers. Pinch flower in center to make it 3-dimensional. Cut out gumdrop leaves and stems. Arrange gumdrop flowers on cake. Arrange candied orange slices to form butterfly wings and butterfly body. Store loosely covered.

1 SERVING: Calories 340; Total Fat 15g (Saturated Fat 3g; Trans Fat 2½g); Cholesterol 40mg; Sodium 290mg; Total Carbohydrate 51g (Dietary Fiber 0g); Protein 1g
EXCHANGES: ½ Starch; 3 Other Carbohydrate; 3 Fat CARBOHYDRATE CHOICES: 3½

sweet note Keep extra sugar handy when working with gumdrops to use if they get sticky.

mother's day hat cake

PREP TIME: 30 minutes *START TO FINISH:* 3 hour 45 minutes [16 SERVINGS]

1 box Betty Crocker® SuperMoist® cake mix (any flavor)

Water, vegetable oil and eggs called for on cake mix box

2 containers (1 lb or 12 oz each) Betty Crocker® Rich & Creamy or Whipped frosting (any flavor)

Ribbon and edible flowers (dianthus, pansies, violas)

1 Heat oven to 350°F (325°F for dark or nonstick pans). Bake and cool cake as directed on box—except use one 8-inch round pan and one 9-inch round pan. For easier handling, refrigerate or freeze cake 30 to 60 minutes or until firm.

2 Cut 6-inch circle out of waxed paper; place on 8-inch layer. Cut cake around circle with small knife to make 6-inch round layer; place on 9-inch layer, attaching pieces with small amount of frosting. Frost with a thin layer of frosting. Refrigerate or freeze 30 to 60 minutes to set frosting.

3 Frost cake. Trim hat with ribbon and flowers. Store loosely covered in refrigerator.

1 SERVING: Calories 380; Total Fat 16g (Saturated Fat 3½g; Trans Fat 3g); Cholesterol 35mg; Sodium 300mg; Total Carbohydrate 58g (Dietary Fiber 0g); Protein 1g EXCHANGES: ½ Starch; 3½ Other Carbohydrate; 3 Fat CARBOHYDRATE CHOICES: 4

sweet note Children of all ages will enjoy making this dessert—and sharing it with mom! Just make sure they don't burn themselves while using the hot oven.

guitar cake

PREP TIME: 30 minutes *START TO FINISH:* 2 hours 25 minutes [15 SERVINGS]

1 box Betty Crocker® SuperMoist® yellow cake mix

Water, vegetable oil and eggs called for on cake mix box

Tray or cardboard, 19 × 11 inches, covered with wrapping paper and plastic food wrap or foil

1 Heat oven to 350°F (325°F for dark or nonstick pan). Grease bottom and sides of 13 × 9-inch pan with shortening or cooking spray.

2 Make and bake cake mix as directed on box for 13 × 9-inch pan. Cool 10 minutes. Run knife around sides of pan to loosen cake; remove from pan to cooling rack. Cool completely, about 1 hour. Refrigerate or freeze cake about 1 hour or until firm.

3 Using serrated knife, cut rounded top off cake to level surface; place cake cut side down. Cut 9 × 2-inch strip of cake as shown in

diagram for guitar neck. Cut body of guitar from remaining cake. Place pieces on tray.

4 Place ½ cup frosting in small bowl. Stir in 4 to 6 drops green food color. Into remaining vanilla frosting, stir 6 drops yellow food color. Attach guitar neck to body with small amount of frosting. Frost guitar neck with a thin layer of green frosting and frost top and sides of guitar body with a thin layer of yellow frosting to seal in crumbs. Refrigerate or freeze cake 30 to 60 minutes to set frosting. Frost entire cake with same colors.

5 Press 3 gumdrops on each side of neck for tuning pegs. On neck, draw crosswise lines with decorating gel, 1 inch apart, for frets. Place wafer cookie on center of body. Place tart and tangy candies around wafer cookie. Place stick of gum 1 inch under wafer cookie. Place licorice on neck for strings. Press remaining gumdrops into frosting below gum stick. Store loosely covered.

1 SERVING (CAKE AND FROSTING ONLY): Calories 350; Total Fat 15g (Saturated Fat 3g; Trans Fat 2½g); Cholesterol 40mg; Sodium 290mg; Total Carbohydrate 52g (Dietary Fiber 0g); Protein 1g EXCHANGES: ½ Starch; 3 Other Carbohydrate; 3 Fat CARBOHYDRATE CHOICES: 3½

- 1 to 1½ containers (1 lb each) Betty Crocker® Rich & Creamy vanilla frosting
- Green and yellow food colors
- 10 small gumdrops
- 1 tube (0.68 oz) Betty Crocker® orange decorating gel
- 1 thin chocolate wafer cookie
- 18 tart and tangy round candies
- 1 stick gum
- Pull-and-peel red licorice

Cutting and Assembling Guitar Cake

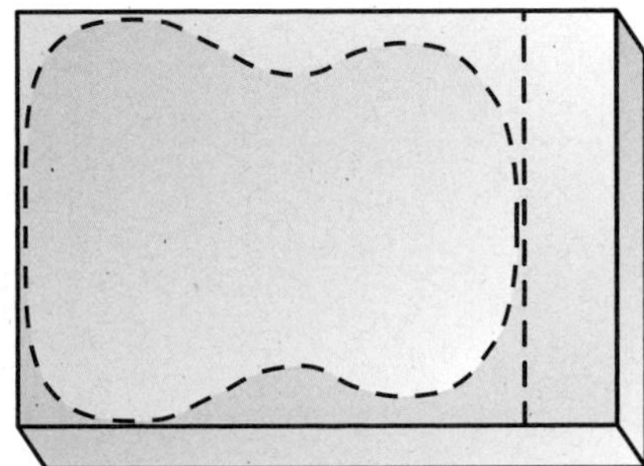

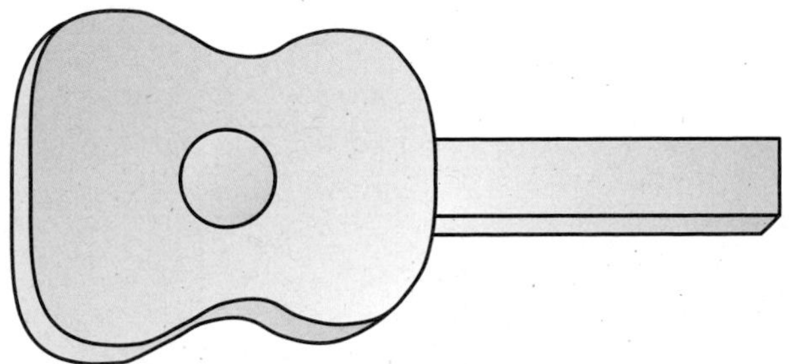

sailboat cake

PREP TIME: 40 minutes *START TO FINISH:* 3 hours 30 minutes [14 SERVINGS]

- 1 box Betty Crocker® SuperMoist® yellow cake mix
- Water, vegetable oil and eggs called for on cake mix box
- 2 containers (1 lb each) Betty Crocker® Rich & Creamy vanilla frosting
- Yellow or brown food color
- Tray or cardboard, 20 × 18 inches, covered with foil
- 2 pull-and-peel cherry licorice twists (from 14-oz package)
- 1 roll Betty Crocker® Fruit Roll-Ups® chewy fruit snack (from 5-oz box)
- Ring-shaped hard candies
- Tiny star candies
- Miniature candy-coated chocolate baking bits

1 Heat oven to 350°F (325°F for dark or nonstick pans). Grease bottom and sides of 13 × 9-inch pan, or spray with baking spray with flour. Make and bake cake as directed on box for 13 × 9-inch pan. Cool 10 minutes; remove from pan to cooling rack. Cool completely, about 1 hour. Refrigerate or freeze cake 1 hour until firm.

2 Cut cake as shown in diagram. Arrange pieces to form sailboat on tray. Tint 1⅓ cups of the frosting with yellow or brown food color for hull. To "crumb-coat" cake, spread thin layer of white frosting over top and sides of sails, and thin layer of tinted frosting over top and sides of hull to seal crumbs. Refrigerate or freeze cake 30 to 60 minutes.

3 Frost entire cake with remaining frosting. Cut licorice pieces to desired length for mast; place near edge of longest sail. To create top flag, spread thin layer of frosting on small piece of aluminum foil. Unroll and remove wrapper from fruit snack roll; press onto frosting-coated foil. Using kitchen scissors, cut

into flag shape. Secure flag to mast with small amount of frosting. Use candy for portholes, or decorate as desired. Store loosely covered.

1 SERVING: Calories 460; Total Fat 19g (Saturated Fat 4g; Trans Fat 4g); Cholesterol 45mg; Sodium 370mg; Total Carbohydrate 69g (Dietary Fiber 0g); Protein 2g EXCHANGES: 1 Starch; 3½ Other Carbohydrate; 3½ Fat CARBOHYDRATE CHOICES: 4½

sweet note Purchase nautical theme wrapping paper to cover a large tray or piece of sturdy cardboard. Then cover the entire tray in plastic food storage wrap. This makes an attractive display for your sailboat cake.

Cutting and Assembling Sailboat Cake

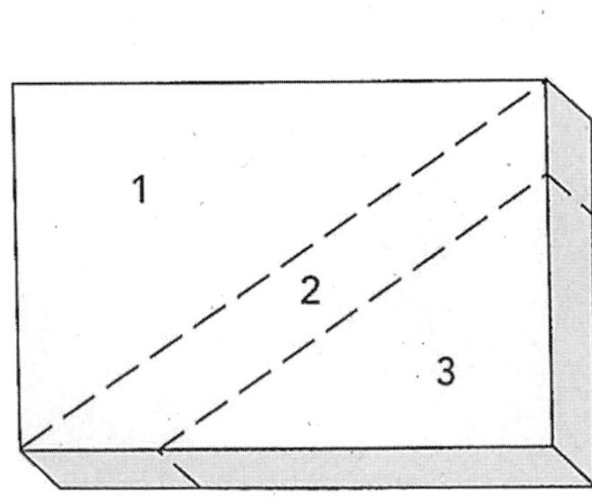

Cut cake diagonally into 3 pieces

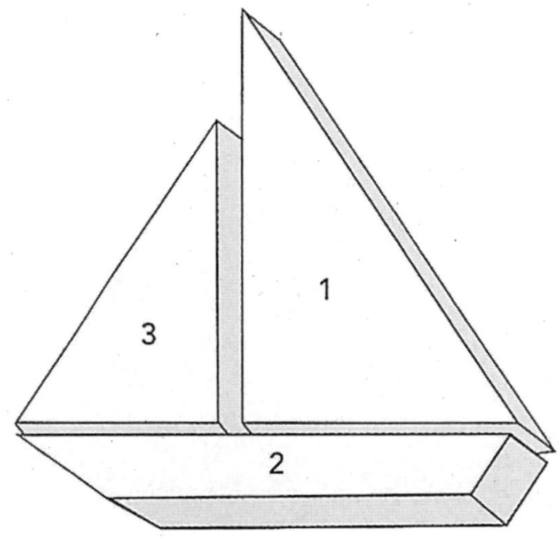

Arrange pieces to form sailsboat, leaving space between sails for mast

bunny cupcakes

PREP TIME: 30 minutes *START TO FINISH:* 1 hour 45 minutes [24 CUPCAKES]

1 box Betty Crocker® SuperMoist® yellow or white cake mix

Water, vegetable oil and eggs or egg whites called for on cake mix box

Pink food color

2 containers (12 oz each) Betty Crocker® Whipped fluffy white frosting

5 large marshmallows

Pink sugar

Candy decorations and sprinkles, as desired

1 Heat oven to 350°F (325°F for dark or nonstick pans). Make and bake cake mix as directed on box for 24 cupcakes. Cool in pans 10 minutes; remove from pans to cooling rack. Cool completely, about 30 minutes.

2 Stir a few drops pink food color into 1 container of frosting. Frost cupcakes with pink frosting.

3 Spoon 1 heaping teaspoonful white frosting on center of each cupcake. To make ears, cut each marshmallow crosswise into 5 pieces with kitchen scissors. Using scissors, cut through center of each marshmallow piece to within ¼ inch of edge. Separate to look like bunny ears; press 1 side of cut edges into pink sugar, flattening slightly. Arrange on each of the white frosting mounds. Use candy decorations and sprinkles to make eyes, nose and whiskers. Store loosely covered.

1 CUPCAKE (CAKE AND FROSTING ONLY): Calories 240; Total Fat 12g (Saturated Fat 3g; Trans Fat 2g); Cholesterol 25mg; Sodium 170mg; Total Carbohydrate 33g (Dietary Fiber 0g); Protein 1g EXCHANGES: ½ Starch; 1½ Other Carbohydrate; 2½ Fat CARBOHYDRATE CHOICES: 2

sweet note You're just a hop away from making deliciously sweet bunny cupcakes. Cake mix and ready-to-spread frosting make it extra easy.

chirping chick cupcakes

PREP TIME: 30 minutes *START TO FINISH:* 1 hour 45 minutes [24 CUPCAKES]

1 box Betty Crocker® SuperMoist® yellow or white cake mix

Water, vegetable oil and eggs or egg whites called for on cake mix box

2 containers (12 oz each) Betty Crocker® Whipped fluffy white frosting

Yellow food color

24 orange jelly beans

48 small orange candies

1. Heat oven to 350°F (325°F for dark or nonstick pans). Make and bake cake as directed on box for 24 cupcakes. Cool completely.
2. Frost cupcakes with 1 container of frosting.
3. Stir a few drops yellow food color into other container of frosting. Spoon 1 heaping teaspoonful yellow frosting on center of each cupcake. To make beak, cut orange jelly bean lengthwise to within ⅛ inch of end; spread apart slightly. Press into yellow frosting. Add orange candies for eyes. Store loosely covered.

1 CUPCAKE (CAKE AND FROSTING ONLY): Calories 260; Total Fat 12g (Saturated Fat 3g; Trans Fat 2g); Cholesterol 25mg; Sodium 170mg; Total Carbohydrate 37g (Dietary Fiber 0g); Protein 1g EXCHANGES: ½ Starch; 2 Other Carbohydrate; 2½ Fat CARBOHYDRATE CHOICES: 2½

sweet note For a more two-dimensional design, smear the frosting onto each cupcake with the back of your spoon and lay jelly bean pieces and orange candies flat.

treasure chest cake

PREP TIME: 35 minutes *START TO FINISH:* 4 hours 30 minutes [15 SERVINGS]

1 box Betty Crocker® SuperMoist® chocolate fudge cake mix

1 cup water

Vegetable oil and eggs called for on cake mix box

Tray, 24 × 20 inches, covered with wrapping paper and plastic food wrap or foil

Yellow and orange paste food colors

1 container (1 lb) Betty Crocker® Rich & Creamy creamy white frosting

Pull-and-peel red licorice

Foil-covered chocolate coins

Candy necklaces

Round hard candies

Gummy ring, halved

1 Heat oven to 350°F (325°F for dark or nonstick pan). Spray bottom only of 13 × 9-inch pan with baking spray with flour. Make and bake cake mix as directed on box for 13 × 9-inch pan—except use 1 cup water, the oil and eggs. Cool 10 minutes; remove from pan to cooling rack. Cool completely, about 1 hour.

2 From center of cake, cut one 3-inch crosswise strip (see diagram). Cut the strip diagonally in half to make two 9-inch triangular wedges. (Discard 1 cake wedge or reserve for another use.)

3 On tray, place a 9 × 5-inch cake piece. Stir food colors into frosting to make golden yellow. Spread 1 tablespoon of frosting on 1 edge of triangular wedge of cake. Attach wedge, frosting side down, to 9 × 5-inch cake piece on tray, placing wedge along top edge of larger cake piece. Freeze all cake pieces 1 hour.

4 Spread 1 tablespoon of frosting on top edge of triangular wedge of cake. Attach remaining 9 × 5-inch cake piece to cake wedge to

look like partially opened treasure chest. To seal crumbs, frost cake with a thin layer of frosting. Refrigerate or freeze 30 to 60 minutes to set frosting. Spread remaining frosting evenly over entire cake. Pull fork through frosting to look like wood grain.

5 Use pull-and-peel licorice to make handles and straps. Fill chest with chocolate coins, candy necklaces, and other hard candies. Add gummy ring half for clasp. Store loosely covered.

1 SERVING (CAKE AND FROSTING ONLY): Calories 400; Total Fat 25g (Saturated Fat 4½g; Trans Fat 2g); Cholesterol 40mg; Sodium 330mg; Total Carbohydrate 43g (Dietary Fiber 0g); Protein 2g EXCHANGES: ½ Starch; 2½ Other Carbohydrate; 5 Fat CARBOHYDRATE CHOICES: 3

sweet note This treasure chest can be turned into a jewelry box for a princess party. Tint the frosting pink, and use colorful hard candies for gems and strings of candy for necklaces.

Cutting and Assembling Treasure Chest Cake

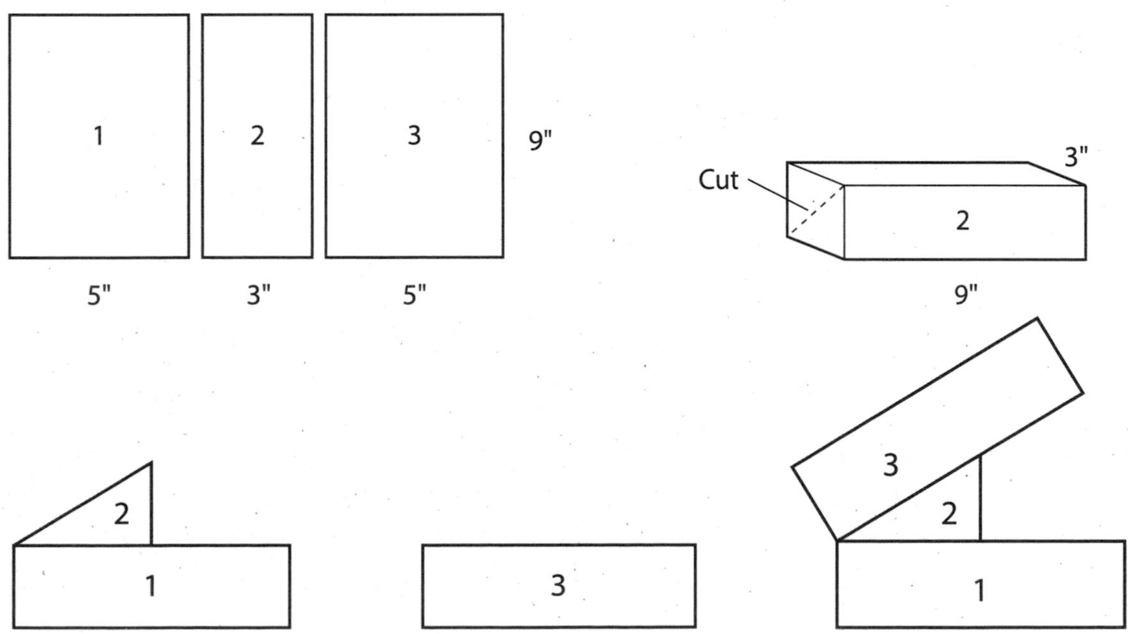

butterfly cake

PREP TIME: 40 minutes *START TO FINISH:* 3 hours 35 minutes [8 SERVINGS]

Cake

1 box Betty Crocker® SuperMoist® yellow cake mix

Water, vegetable oil and eggs called for on cake mix box

Platter, tray or foil-covered cardboard (about 10 × 10 inches)

Frosting and Decorations

1 container (1 lb) Betty Crocker® Rich & Creamy vanilla frosting

1 candy stick (8 to 10 inches long)

Food color (in desired colors)

Betty Crocker® decorating gel (from 0.68-oz tube) in any color

Decorating sugar crystals (any color)

8 jelly beans

Small round candy decorations

1 Heat oven to 350°F (325°F for dark or nonstick pans). Grease bottoms and sides of two 8- or 9-inch round pans with shortening or cooking spray. Make, bake and cool cakes as directed on box for 8- or 9-inch rounds. Wrap and freeze 1 layer for later use. Freeze remaining layer 45 minutes before cutting to reduce crumbs.

2 Cut off rounded top of cake to make flat surface; place cake cut side down. Cut cake in half crosswise; cut each half into ⅓ and ⅔ pieces (as shown in diagram). Place cake pieces on platter to form butterfly. Gently separate cake pieces to form wings.

3 Reserve ½ cup frosting; set aside. Spread top and sides of cake with thin layer of frosting to seal in crumbs. Refrigerate or freeze 30 to 60 minutes to set frosting. Frost cake with remaining frosting. Place candy stick between cake pieces for butterfly body.

Cutting and Assembling Butterfly Cake

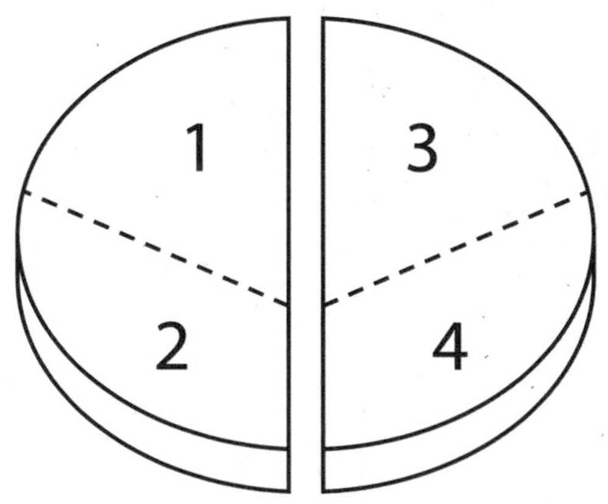

4 Stir food color into reserved frosting until well blended. Spread over cake in desired pattern on wings. Outline wing patterns with gel. Sprinkle with sugar crystals. Place jelly beans on corners of wings. Decorate butterfly with candy decorations.

1 SERVING (CAKE AND FROSTING ONLY): Calories 400; Total Fat 17g (Saturated Fat 3½g; Trans Fat 3½g); Cholesterol 40mg; Sodium 320mg; Total Carbohydrate 60g (Dietary Fiber 0g); Protein 1g EXCHANGES: ½ Starch; ½ Other Carbohydrate; 3½ Fat CARBOHYDRATE CHOICES: 4

sweet note Turn the leftover cake layer into a trifle! Cut leftover cake into 1-inch cubes and layer them with chocolate pudding and fresh strawberries in a large glass bowl. Top with whipped cream.

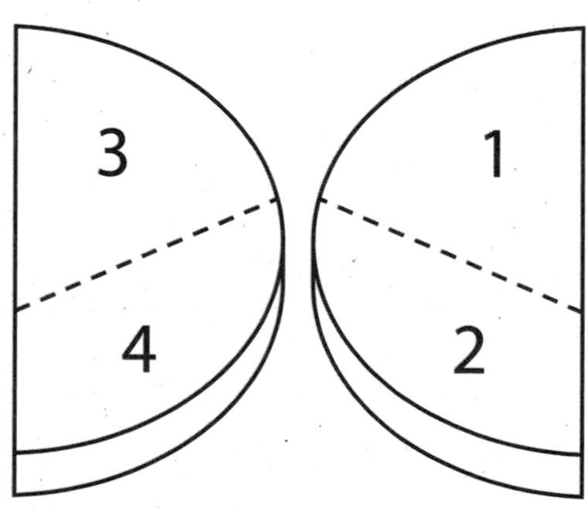

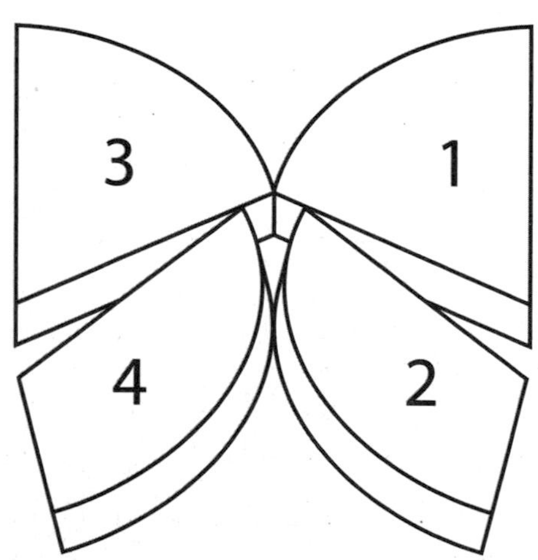

new year's cake

PREP TIME: 45 minutes *START TO FINISH:* 3 hours [30 SERVINGS]

- 2 boxes (1 lb 2.25 oz each) Betty Crocker® SuperMoist® chocolate fudge cake mix
- Water, vegetable oil and eggs called for on cake mix box
- Tray or cardboard, 16 × 16 inches, covered
- 2 containers (1 lb each) Betty Crocker® Rich & Creamy milk chocolate frosting
- 1 cup white vanilla baking chips
- Decorating bag with tips

1 Heat oven to 350°F (325°F for dark or nonstick pans). Grease bottoms and sides of four 8-inch square pans with shortening or cooking spray. In large bowl, mix both cake mixes with water, oil and eggs for both mixes as directed on box. Divide batter among pans (about 2⅓ cups for each pan). Refrigerate 2 pans of batter while 2 pans bake.

2 Bake 2 pans at a time, following times on cake mix box for 8-inch round pans. Cool 10 minutes; remove from pans to wire racks. Cool completely, about 30 minutes.

3 Cut off domed top from each cake so layers will be flat when stacked. On tray, place 1 cake; spread with ⅓ cup frosting. Top with second cake; spread with ⅓ cup frosting. Top with third cake; spread with ⅓ cup frosting.

4 Cut fourth cake into star shape. Place on top of stacked cakes. Freeze 1 hour.

5 In small microwavable bowl, microwave white baking chips uncovered on High 1 minute, stirring after 30 seconds, until softened; stir until smooth. Pour into decorating bag with writing tip. On piece of foil, cooking parchment paper or waxed paper, pipe stars, letters or other shapes; refrigerate until firm.

6 Spread remaining chocolate frosting over entire stacked cake. Decorate with white stars, letters and shapes.

1 SERVING: Calories 310; Total Fat 15g (Saturated Fat 4½g; Trans Fat 2g); Cholesterol 30mg; Sodium 370mg; Total Carbohydrate 44g (Dietary Fiber 2g); Protein 3g EXCHANGES: 3 Other Carbohydrate; 2½ Fat CARBOHYDRATE CHOICES: 3

just bugging you cupcakes

PREP TIME: 20 minutes *START TO FINISH:* 2 hours 35 minutes [30 CUPCAKES]

1 box Betty Crocker® SuperMoist® cake mix (any nonswirl flavor)

Water, vegetable oil and eggs called for on cake mix box

30 flat-bottom ice cream cones

1 container (12 oz) Betty Crocker® Whipped frosting (any flavor)

Assorted candies and cookies, if desired

1 Heat oven to 350°F. Make cake batter as directed on box. Fill 12 cones about half full of batter. Stand cones in muffin pan. Refrigerate any leftover batter until ready to fill and bake remaining cones.

2 Bake 21 to 26 minutes or until toothpick carefully inserted in center comes out clean. Cool completely, about 1 hour.

3 Spread with frosting. Decorate with candies and cookies to create bugs and butterflies. Use small cookies or licorice candies for bodies, miniature candy-coated chocolate baking bits for eyes and small pieces of licorice for legs and antennae. Store loosely covered.

1 CUPCAKE CONE: Calories 160; Total Fat 7g (Saturated Fat 2g; Trans Fat 1g); Cholesterol 20mg; Sodium 125mg; Total Carbohydrate 22g (Dietary Fiber 0g); Protein 1g
EXCHANGES: ½ Starch; 1 Other Carbohydrate; 1½ Fat CARBOHYDRATE CHOICES: 1½

sweet note Look for colorful ice cream cones for extra fun! Use chocolate chips or colored candy sprinkles for quick and easy decorations.

picnic pals

PREP TIME: 1 hour *START TO FINISH:* 2 hours 10 minutes [24 CUPCAKES]

- 1 box Betty Crocker® SuperMoist® cake mix (any flavor)
- Water, vegetable oil and eggs called for on cake mix box
- 1 container (12 oz) Betty Crocker® Whipped fluffy white or vanilla frosting
- Assorted gumdrops and candies
- Betty Crocker® Fruit by the Foot® chewy fruit snack rolls (any variety)
- 1 tube (0.68 oz) Betty Crocker® black decorating gel

1 Heat oven to 350°F (325°F for dark or nonstick pans). Place paper baking cup in each of 24 regular-size muffin cups.

2 Make and bake cake mix as directed on box for 24 cupcakes. Cool in pans 10 minutes; remove from pans to cooling rack. Cool completely, about 30 minutes.

3 Frost cupcakes with frosting. Decorate with whole or cut-up gumdrops, candies, cut-up or thinly rolled fruit snacks and gel to look like ladybugs, bumblebees, butterflies, caterpillars and beetles.

1 CUPCAKE: Calories 180; Total Fat 9g (Saturated Fat 2g; Trans Fat 1g); Cholesterol 25mg; Sodium 150mg; Total Carbohydrate 24g (Dietary Fiber 0g); Protein 1g EXCHANGES: 1 Starch; ½ Other Carbohydrate; 1½ Fat CARBOHYDRATE CHOICES: 1½

sweet note When cutting gumdrops, dip the knife or kitchen scissors into water to keep from sticking.

watermelon slices cake

PREP TIME: 30 minutes *START TO FINISH:* 1 hour 45 minutes [16 SERVINGS]

- 1 box Betty Crocker® SuperMoist® white cake mix
- Water, vegetable oil and egg whites called for on cake mix box
- 1 package (0.13 oz) cherry-flavored or other red-colored unsweetened soft drink mix
- ½ cup miniature semisweet chocolate chips
- 1 container (12 oz) Betty Crocker® Whipped fluffy white frosting
- Green and red food colors
- ⅔ cup green jelly beans
- 2 tablespoons miniature semisweet chocolate chips

1 Heat oven to 350°F (325°F for dark or nonstick pans). Grease bottoms only of two 8- or 9-inch round cake pans with shortening or cooking spray. In large bowl, beat cake mix, water, oil, egg whites and drink mix with electric mixer on low speed 30 seconds; beat on medium speed 2 minutes, scraping bowl occasionally. (Batter will be lumpy.) Stir in ½ cup chocolate chips. Pour into pans.

2 Bake as directed on box for 8- or 9-inch round pans. Cool 10 minutes. Remove from pans. Cool completely, about 1 hour.

3 In small bowl, stir 1 cup of the frosting with 10 to 12 drops green food color. Stir 10 to 12 drops red food color into remaining frosting. Frost sides of cakes with green frosting; press green jelly beans into frosting. Frost tops of cakes with red frosting; press 2 tablespoons chocolate chips into frosting for seeds. If desired, cut cakes crosswise in half and arrange "slices" randomly on tray. To serve, cut into wedges. Store loosely covered at room temperature.

1 SERVING: Calories 320; Total Fat 12g (Saturated Fat 4g; Trans Fat 1½ g); Cholesterol 0mg; Sodium 240mg; Total Carbohydrate 50g (Dietary Fiber 0g); Protein 2g EXCHANGES: 1 Starch; 2 Other Carbohydrate; 2½ Fat CARBOHYDRATE CHOICES: 3

sweet note Use mini chips to make sure there are lots of chips and that they stay distributed in the cake.

surprise cupcake cones

PREP TIME: 40 minutes *START TO FINISH:* 1 hour 25 minutes [18 CUPCAKES]

- 1 box Betty Crocker® SuperMoist® yellow cake mix
- Water, vegetable oil and eggs called for on cake mix box
- 1 cup candy-coated chocolate candies
- 18 flat-bottom ice cream cones
- 3 containers (12 oz each) Betty Crocker® Whipped strawberry frosting
- ¼ cup Betty Crocker® candy decors

1 Heat oven to 350°F (325°F for dark or nonstick pans). Place paper baking cup in each of 18 regular-size muffin cups; place mini paper baking cup in each of 18 mini muffin cups. Make cake batter as directed on box. Spoon batter evenly into regular and mini muffin cups.

2 Bake mini cupcakes 10 to 14 minutes, regular cupcakes 15 to 20 minutes (18 to 24 minutes for dark or nonstick pan), or until toothpick inserted in center comes out clean. Remove from pans to cooling racks. Cool completely, about 30 minutes.

3 If ice cream cone holder is unavailable, make a holder for the cones by tightly covering the tops of 2 empty square or rectangular pans (at least 2 to 2½ inches deep) with heavy-duty foil. With sharp knife, cut 18 "stars" in foil, 3 inches apart, by making slits about 1 inch long.

4 Place about 2 teaspoons candies in each ice cream cone. Remove paper cups from cupcakes. For each cone, frost top of 1 regular cupcake with frosting; turn upside down onto a cone. Frost bottom (now the top) of cupcake. Place mini cupcake upside down on frosted regular cupcake; frost side of regular cupcake and entire mini cupcake completely (it's easiest to frost from the cone toward the top). Sprinkle with candy decors. Push cone through foil opening in cone holder; the foil will keep it upright. Store loosely covered.

1 CUPCAKE CONE: Calories 490; Total Fat 23g (Saturated Fat 7g; Trans Fat 3½g); Cholesterol 35mg; Sodium 250mg; Total Carbohydrate 68g (Dietary Fiber 0g); Protein 2g EXCHANGES: ½ Starch; 4 Other Carbohydrate; 4½ Fat CARBOHYDRATE CHOICES: 4½

sweet note If the strawberry frosting is not available, tint Betty Crocker® Rich & Creamy vanilla frosting a light pink with red food color. For extra pizzazz, top each "cone" with a maraschino cherry.

goin' fishin' cupcakes

PREP TIME: 5 minutes *TOTAL TIME:* 2 hours 31 minutes [24 CUPCAKES]

Cupcakes

1 box Betty Crocker® SuperMoist® devil's food cake mix

Water, vegetable oil and eggs called for on cake mix box

1 container (1 lb) Betty Crocker® Rich & Creamy vanilla or butter cream frosting

Blue food color

Fishing Poles

24 cocktail straws

24 pieces dental floss

24 Betty Crocker® Shark Bites® chewy fruit snacks (2 to 3 pouches)

1 Heat oven to 350°F (325°F for dark or nonstick pans). Make, bake and cool cake as directed on box for 24 cupcakes.

2 Stir together frosting and 2 or 3 drops food color. Frost cupcakes with blue frosting; pull up on frosting, using metal spatula, so frosting looks like waves.

3 To make fishing poles, cut each straw to make one 3-inch piece. Cut dental floss into 3½-inch lengths. Attach piece of dental floss to end of each straw, using needle, to look like fish line. Attach 1 fruit snack to end of each piece of dental floss. Decorate each cupcake with a fishing pole. Store loosely covered.

1 CUPCAKE: Calories 190; Total Fat 9g (Saturated Fat 2g; Trans Fat 1g); Cholesterol 25mg; Sodium 200mg; Total Carbohydrate 28g (Dietary Fiber 0g); Protein 1g EXCHANGES: ½ Starch; 1½ Other Carbohydrate; 1½ Fat CARBOHYDRATE CHOICES: 2

sweet note Keep the party theme going by serving blue raspberry punch with "fishy" ice cubes. Place 1 Shark Bites® chewy fruit snack in each section of an ice-cube tray. Fill with ginger ale or water and freeze until solid.

dalmation cupcakes

PREP TIME: 10 minutes *START TO FINISH:* 1 hour 15 minutes [24 CUPCAKES]

2 packages (3 oz each) cream cheese, softened

⅓ cup sugar

1 egg

1 cup miniature or regular semisweet chocolate chips

1 box Betty Crocker® SuperMoist® devil's food cake mix

1¼ cups water

⅓ cup vegetable oil

3 eggs

1 container (1 lb or 12 oz) Betty Crocker® Rich & Creamy or Whipped vanilla frosting

½ cup miniature or regular semisweet chocolate chips

1 Heat oven to 350°F (325°F for dark or nonstick pans). Place paper baking cup in each of 24 regular-size muffin cups.

2 In medium bowl, beat cream cheese, sugar and 1 egg with electric mixer on medium speed until smooth. Stir in 1 cup chocolate chips; set aside.

3 In large bowl, beat cake mix, water, oil and 3 eggs on low speed 30 seconds. Beat on medium speed 2 minutes. Divide batter among muffin cups (¼ cup in each). Top each with 1 heaping teaspoon cream cheese mixture.

4 Bake 21 to 27 minutes or until tops spring back when touched lightly. Cool in pans 10 minutes. Remove from pans to cooling racks. Cool completely, about 30 minutes.

5 Frost with frosting. Sprinkle with ½ cup chocolate chips. Store loosely covered in refrigerator.

1 CUPCAKE: Calories 270; Total Fat 13g (Saturated Fat 5g; Trans Fat 1g); Cholesterol 45mg; Sodium 220mg; Total Carbohydrate 37g (Dietary Fiber 1g); Protein 2g EXCHANGES: 1 Starch; 1½ Other Carbohydrate; 2½ Fat CARBOHYDRATE CHOICES: 2½

sweet note How about a Dalmatian-themed party? Serve cupcakes with chocolate chip ice cream, play "pin the spot on the dog," and send kids home with a "doggie bag" full of dog-themed treats and prizes.

ball game cupcakes

PREP TIME: 35 minutes *START TO FINISH:* 1 hour 55 minutes [24 CUPCAKES]

1 cup miniature semisweet chocolate chips

1 box Betty Crocker® SuperMoist® yellow cake mix

1 cup water

⅓ cup vegetable oil

3 eggs

1 container (1 lb) Betty Crocker® Rich & Creamy vanilla frosting

Assorted colors Betty Crocker® decorating icing (in 4.25-oz tubes) or Betty Crocker® Easy Flow decorating icing (in 6.4-oz cans)

Assorted food colors

1 Heat oven to 350°F (325°F for dark or nonstick pans). Place paper baking cup in each of 24 regular-size muffin cups. In small bowl, toss chocolate chips with 1 tablespoon of the cake mix. In large bowl, beat remaining cake mix, water, oil and eggs with electric mixer on low speed 30 seconds, then on medium speed 2 minutes, scraping bowl occasionally. Stir in coated chocolate chips. Divide batter evenly among muffin cups, filling each about two-thirds full.

2 Bake 20 to 26 minutes or until toothpick inserted in center comes out clean. Cool 10 minutes; remove from pan to wire rack. Cool completely, about 30 minutes. Decorate as desired below. Store cupcakes loosely covered at room temperature.

Baseballs: *Frost cupcakes with vanilla frosting. With black, red or blue icing, pipe 2 arches on opposite sides of cupcakes, curving lines slightly toward center. Pipe small lines from each arch to resemble stitches on a baseball.*

Basketballs: *Color frosting with yellow and red food colors to make orange; frost cupcakes. With black icing, pipe line across center of cupcake. On either side, pipe an arch that curves slightly toward center line.*

Soccer Balls: *Frost cupcakes with vanilla frosting. With black icing, pipe a pentagon shape in the center of cupcake, piping a few rows of icing into center of pentagon. Pipe lines from pentagon to edge of cupcake to resemble seams. With toothpick or spatula, spread black icing in center of pentagon to fill in the entire shape.*

Tennis Balls: *Color frosting with yellow and green food colors to make tennis-ball yellow; frost cupcakes. With white icing, pipe curved design to resemble tennis balls.*

1 CUPCAKE: Calories 270; Total Fat 13g (Saturated Fat 4½g; Trans Fat 2g); Cholesterol 25mg; Sodium 200mg; Total Carbohydrate 38g (Dietary Fiber 0g); Protein 2g
EXCHANGES: ½ Starch; 2 Other Carbohydrate; 2½ Fat CARBOHYDRATE CHOICES: 2½

sweet note Arrange cupcakes on green "grass." To make grass, shake 1 cup coconut and 3 drops green food color in tightly covered jar until evenly tinted.

mini cupcake mortarboards

PREP TIME: 30 minutes *START TO FINISH:* 50 minutes [60 MINI CUPCAKES]

- 1 box Betty Crocker® SuperMoist® cake mix (any nonswirl flavor)
- Water, vegetable oil and eggs called for on cake mix box
- 1 box (4.5 oz) Betty Crocker® Fruit by the Foot® chewy fruit snack rolls (any flavor) or shoestring licorice
- 1 container (1 lb) Betty Crocker® Rich & Creamy vanilla frosting
- Food color
- 60 square shortbread cookies, from two 10-oz packages
- 60 candy-coated chocolate or fruit-flavored candies

1 Heat oven to 350°F (325°F for dark or nonstick pans). Place miniature paper baking cups in 24 mini muffin cups, 1¾ × 1 inch. Make cake batter as directed on box. Fill cups two-thirds full of batter (about 1 rounded tablespoon each). Refrigerate remaining batter.

2 Bake 10 to 15 minutes or until toothpick inserted in center comes out clean; cool. Repeat with remaining batter. (Leave paper baking cups on cupcakes so mortarboards are quicker and easier to make and more portable to serve.)

3 To make tassels: Cut sixty 2½-inch lengths from fruit snack rolls. Cut each into several strips up to ½ inch from 1 end. Roll uncut end between fingertips to make tassels. Or cut several pieces of shoestring licorice into 2½-inch lengths.

4 Tint frosting with food color to match paper baking cups. Frost bottoms of cookies. Place 1 candy on center of each. For each mortarboard, place small dollop of frosting on bottom of cupcake; top with cookie. Press uncut end of fruit snack or 3 or 4 pieces of licorice into frosted cookie next to candy. Store loosely covered.

1 MINI CUPCAKE: Calories 130; Total Fat 6g (Saturated Fat 2½g; Trans Fat 0g); Cholesterol 10mg; Sodium 100mg; Total Carbohydrate 18g (Dietary Fiber 0g); Protein 0g
EXCHANGES: ½ Starch; ½ Other Carbohydrate; 1 Fat CARBOHYDRATE CHOICES: 1

sweet note Make this fun, delicious dessert to honor your graduate!

angel food flag cake

PREP TIME: 45 minutes *START TO FINISH:* 4 hours 30 minutes [16 SERVINGS]

- 1 package Betty Crocker® white angel food cake mix
- 1¼ cups cold water
- 3 cups fresh or frozen unsweetened (thawed and drained) raspberries
- 3 tablespoons sugar
- 3 tablespoons seedless red raspberry jam, melted
- 1 container (8 oz) frozen whipped topping, thawed (3 cups)
- 2 cups fresh or frozen (thawed and drained) blueberries

1 Move oven rack to middle position. Heat oven to 350°F (325°F for dark or nonstick pans).

2 Beat cake mix and water in extra-large glass or metal bowl with electric mixer on low speed 30 seconds; beat on medium speed 1 minute. Pour into 2 ungreased 9 × 5-inch loaf pans, or 3 ungreased 8½ × 4½-inch loaf pans.

3 Bake 9-inch pans 35 to 45 minutes, 8½-inch pans 28 to 38 minutes, or until top is dark golden brown and cracks feel very dry and not sticky. Do not underbake. Immediately turn each pan on its side on heatproof surface and let rest until completely cool. Run knife around edges; remove from pans.

4 Line each same loaf pan with plastic wrap, allowing wrap to extend over edges. Place raspberries, sugar and jam in food processor; cover and process, using 3 quick on-and-off motions, until coarsely chopped. Cut each loaf cake horizontally into 4 slices, using serrated or electric knife. Place 1 slice in bottom of each pan; spread 3 tablespoons of the raspberry mixture over each. Top with another slice of cake. Repeat with remaining raspberry mixture and cake slices. Cover with plastic wrap and refrigerate at least 2 hours until chilled.

5 To remove loaves easily from pans, place serving plate upside down on top of pan; turn pan upside down onto plate. Remove pan and plastic wrap. Cut each loaf crosswise into 8 slices, using serrated or electric knife. Serve with whipped topping and blueberries.

1 SERVING: Calories 168; Total Fat 2g (Saturated Fat 2g; Trans Fat 0g); Cholesterol 0mg; Sodium 239mg; Total Carbohydrate 33g (Dietary Fiber 2g); Protein 3g EXCHANGES: 1 Starch; 2 Other Carbohydrate; ½ Fat CARBOHYDRATE CHOICES: 2

sweet note Angel food cake is lower in fat than most other sweets. Why? Angel food cake is made with egg whites and no added fats. Egg whites contain only about 20 of a whole egg's 75 calories.

tie-dyed cupcakes

PREP TIME: 15 minutes *START TO FINISH:* 1 hour 25 minutes [24 CUPCAKES]

1 box Betty Crocker® SuperMoist® white or yellow cake mix

Water, vegetable oil and egg whites called for on cake mix box

1 container (9 oz) Betty Crocker® Parlor Perfect™ confetti sprinkles

1 Heat oven to 350°F (325°F for dark or nonstick pans). Place paper baking cup in each of 24 regular-size muffin cups.

2 Make cake as directed on box for 24 cupcakes—except fill muffin cups half full; top each with ¼ teaspoon sprinkles. Top with remaining batter; sprinkle each with ½ teaspoon sprinkles.

3 Bake as directed on box for cupcakes. Cool in pans 10 minutes; remove from pans to cooling rack. Cool completely, about 30 minutes.

1 CUPCAKE: Calories 170; Total Fat 7g (Saturated Fat 2½g; Trans Fat 0g); Cholesterol 0mg; Sodium 160mg; Total Carbohydrate 25g (Dietary Fiber 0g); Protein 2g EXCHANGES: ½ Starch; 1 Other Carbohydrate; 1½ Fat CARBOHYDRATE CHOICES: 1½

sweet note The brightly colored sprinkles melt into the cupcake batter, making a tie-dyed look inside and on top. Top vanilla ice cream with the same sprinkles to carry the color throughout the dessert.

stars and stripes cupcakes

PREP TIME: 45 minutes *START TO FINISH:* 1 hour 40 minutes [24 CUPCAKES]

Cupcakes

1 box Betty Crocker® SuperMoist® white cake mix

¾ cup water

1 cup sour cream

⅓ cup vegetable oil

½ teaspoon almond extract

3 eggs

1 jar (10 oz) maraschino cherries (about 38 cherries), drained, finely chopped and patted dry

Glaze

3 cups powdered sugar

3 tablespoons water

2 tablespoons light corn syrup

½ teaspoon almond extract

Decoration

24 blue candy stars

Betty Crocker® red decorating icing (from 4.25-oz tube)

1 Heat oven to 375°F (350°F for dark or nonstick pans). Place paper baking cup in each of 24 regular-size muffin cups.

2 In large bowl, beat cake mix, water, sour cream, oil, ½ teaspoon almond extract and the eggs with electric mixer on low speed 30 seconds. Beat on medium speed 2 minutes, scraping bowl occasionally. Stir in cherries. Divide batter evenly among muffin cups, filling each about two-thirds full.

3 Bake 18 to 22 minutes or until toothpick inserted in center comes out clean. Remove from pan to cooling racks. Cool completely, about 30 minutes.

4 Meanwhile, in medium bowl, beat powdered sugar, water, corn syrup and ½ teaspoon almond extract with electric mixer on medium speed until smooth. Spoon over cupcakes, using back of spoon to spread. Let stand 10 minutes.

5 Place 1 candy star on each cupcake. Using writing tip, pipe icing in wavy stripes on each cupcake to resemble flag.

1 CUPCAKE: Calories 200; Total Fat 5g (Saturated Fat 1½g; Trans Fat 0g); Cholesterol 30mg; Sodium 150mg; Total Carbohydrate 37g (Dietary Fiber 0g); Protein 1g EXCHANGES: ½ Starch; 2 Other Carbohydrate; 1 Fat CARBOHYDRATE CHOICES: 2½

sweet note When making the glaze, start with 3 tablespoons water; if the glaze is too stiff, add 1 teaspoon water at a time until the glaze is spreadable. Look for red paper baking cups at kitchen specialty stores or wherever cake-decorating supplies are sold.

pull-apart turtle cupcakes

PREP TIME: 30 minutes *START TO FINISH:* 2 hours [24 CUPCAKES]

1 box Betty Crocker® SuperMoist® yellow or devil's food cake mix

Water, vegetable oil and eggs called for on cake mix box

1 container (1 lb) Betty Crocker® Rich & Creamy vanilla frosting

Green food color

1 container (1 lb) Betty Crocker® Rich & Creamy chocolate frosting

4 green candy-coated chocolate candies

4 brown miniature candy-coated chocolate candies, if desired

1 piece red string licorice

1 green licorice twist, cut in half

1 Heat oven to 350°F (325°F for dark or nonstick pans). Place paper baking cup in each of 24 regular-size muffin cups. Make and bake cake mix as directed on box for cupcakes, using water, oil and eggs. Cool 10 minutes; remove from pan to cooling racks. Cool completely, about 30 minutes.

2 In small bowl, mix vanilla frosting and green food color until desired shade. Place ¼ cup green frosting and ¼ cup chocolate frosting in separate small resealable plastic freezer bags; seal bags. Cut small tip from corner of each bag; set aside.

3 On each of 2 large serving trays, arrange 12 cupcakes as shown in diagram. Frost shell of one turtle with chocolate frosting. Frost head and feet with green frosting. (Push cupcakes together slightly to frost entire turtle, not just individual cupcakes.) Pipe green frosting on chocolate shell to create

Assembling Pull-Apart Turtle Cupcakes

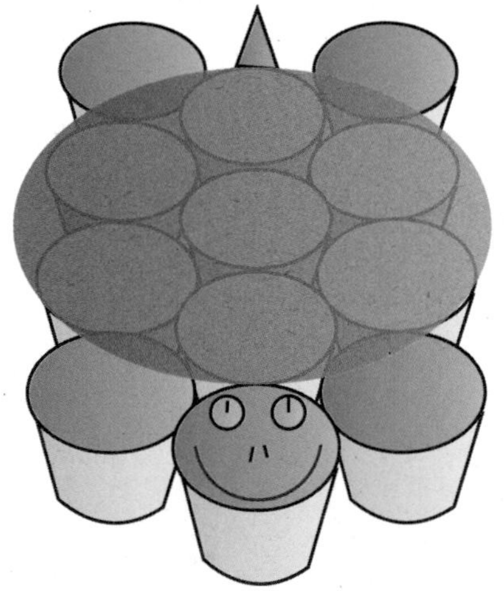

turtle design. Add 2 candies for eyes; add pupils with chocolate frosting. Add nostrils with chocolate frosting or miniature chocolate candies. Add red string licorice for mouth (trimming to fit) and green licorice for tail.

4 Frost remaining cupcakes with green frosting for shell and chocolate frosting for head and feet. Pipe chocolate frosting on green shell to create turtle design. Add 2 candies for eyes; add pupils with chocolate frosting. Add nostrils with green frosting or miniature chocolate candies. Add red string licorice for mouth (trimming to fit) and green licorice for tail. Store loosely covered.

1 CUPCAKE: Calories 270; Total Fat 10g (Saturated Fat 2½g; Trans Fat 2½g); Cholesterol 25mg; Sodium 240mg; Total Carbohydrate 43g (Dietary Fiber 0g); Protein 1g
EXCHANGES: 3 Other Carbohydrate; 2 Fat CARBOHYDRATE CHOICES: 3

sweet note You can vary the cake mix to suit your taste. Just follow the directions on the box for amounts of water, oil and eggs. For each cake, push cupcakes together slightly and frost entire turtle.

jungle animal cupcakes

PREP TIME: 1 hour 45 minutes *START TO FINISH:* 2 hours 45 minutes [24 CUPCAKES]

Cupcakes and Frosting

1 box Betty Crocker® SuperMoist® yellow or devil's food cake mix

Water, vegetable oil and eggs called for on cake mix box

1¼ cups Betty Crocker® Rich & Creamy chocolate frosting (from 1-lb container)

Black food color

2½ cups Betty Crocker® Rich & Creamy vanilla frosting (from two 1-lb containers)

Yellow and red food colors

Lion Decorations

1½ cups caramel popcorn

12 brown miniature candy-coated chocolate baking bits

12 pretzel sticks

12 pieces Cheerios® cereal (any flavor)

Tiger Decorations

12 brown miniature candy-coated chocolate baking bits

12 orange chewy fruit-flavored gumdrops (not sugar coated), cut in half crosswise, top halves discarded

1 Heat oven to 350°F (325°F for dark or nonstick pans). Place paper baking cup in each of 24 regular-size muffin cups. Make and bake cake mix as directed on box for 24 cupcakes. Cool in pans 10 minutes; remove from pans to cooling rack. Cool completely, about 30 minutes. Decorate cupcakes to make 6 lions, 6 tigers, 6 monkeys and 6 zebras.

2 In small bowl, mix ½ cup chocolate frosting with black food color to make black frosting. Place in resealable plastic freezer bag; cut small tip off 1 corner of bag. Use black frosting to decorate lions, tigers, monkeys and zebras (steps 3 through 7).

3 Lions and tigers: In medium bowl, mix 1 cup vanilla frosting with enough yellow and red food colors to make orange. In small bowl, mix 1 tablespoon orange frosting with 3 tablespoons white vanilla frosting to make lighter orange for muzzles. Frost 12 cupcakes with darker orange frosting. For muzzle, spread or pipe small circle of lighter orange frosting on each cupcake.

4 For lions, place caramel corn around edges of cupcakes for mane. For eyes, add brown baking bits. For whiskers, break about ½-inch pieces off each end of pretzel sticks and insert in cupcakes. For ears, add cereal pieces. Using black frosting, pipe on mouth and nose.

5 For tigers, use black frosting to pipe on stripes, nose and mouth. For eyes, add brown baking bits. For ears, add gumdrop halves.

6 Monkeys: Frost 6 cupcakes with chocolate frosting. In small bowl, mix 1 tablespoon chocolate frosting and 2 tablespoons vanilla frosting to make light brown. For muzzle, spread or pipe circle of light brown on each cupcake that starts in middle and extends to edge; pipe small tuft of hair on opposite edge. For each eye, attach brown baking bit to marshmallow half with frosting; place on cupcakes. With black frosting, pipe on nose and mouth. For ears, add mints.

7 Zebras: Cut small horizontal slit in top of 6 cupcakes near edge of paper cup. Insert edge of vanilla wafer cookie into each slit to create elongated face, adding small amount of vanilla frosting to cookie before inserting to help stick. Frost cupcakes with vanilla frosting. For muzzles, frost cookies with black frosting. With black frosting, pipe on stripes and mane. Add brown baking bits for nostrils and eyes. For ears, add black gumdrop halves, cut sides down.

1 CUPCAKE (CUPCAKE AND FROSTING ONLY): Calories 290; Total Fat 12g (Saturated Fat 3g; Trans Fat 2½g); Cholesterol 25mg; Sodium 240mg; Total Carbohydrate 43g (Dietary Fiber 0g); Protein 1g EXCHANGES: ½ Starch; 2½ Other Carbohydrate; 2½ Fat CARBOHYDRATE CHOICES: 3

sweet note Lions and tigers, oh my! Create a jungle of decorating activities by making kids' favorite animals.

Monkey Decorations

12 brown miniature candy-coated chocolate baking bits

6 miniature marshmallows, cut in half crosswise, pieces flattened

12 small round chocolate-covered creamy mints

Zebra Decorations

6 round vanilla wafer cookies

24 brown miniature candy-coated chocolate baking bits

6 black chewy licorice-flavored gumdrops (not sugar coated), cut in half vertically

spooky kooky cupcakes

PREP TIME: 40 minutes *START TO FINISH:* 2 hours 10 minutes [24 CUPCAKES]

1 box Betty Crocker® SuperMoist® devil's food cake mix

Water, vegetable oil and eggs called for on cake mix box

1 container (1 lb) Betty Crocker® Rich & Creamy creamy white frosting

1 tube (0.68 oz) Betty Crocker® black decorating gel

1 cup assorted small candies (tiny jelly beans, candy corn, etc.)

1 Heat oven to 350°F (325°F for dark or nonstick pans). Place paper baking cup in each of 24 regular-size muffin cups.

2 Make, bake and cool cake mix as directed on box for 24 cupcakes.

3 To decorate each cupcake, spoon about 1 tablespoonful frosting on top of each. With back of spoon, spread frosting into shape of lightbulb to look like skeleton head. While frosting is still wet, decorate with gel and candies to make skeleton face.

1 CUPCAKE (CAKE AND FROSTING ONLY): Calories 190; Total Fat 9g (Saturated Fat 2g; Trans Fat 1g); Cholesterol 25mg; Sodium 200mg; Total Carbohydrate 27g (Dietary Fiber 0g); Protein 1g EXCHANGES: ½ Starch; 1½ Other Carbohydrate; 1½ Fat CARBOHYDRATE CHOICES: 2

sweet note Assorted candies can include tiny jelly beans, candy corn and other colorful or black candies. Candy shops and grocery stores featuring bulk candy allow fun choices in small amounts for tasty decorations!

witchly cupcakes

PREP TIME: 40 minutes *START TO FINISH:* 2 hours 10 minutes [24 CUPCAKES]

1 box Betty Crocker® SuperMoist® cake mix (any flavor)

Water, vegetable oil and eggs called for on cake mix box

1 container (1 lb) Betty Crocker® Rich & Creamy vanilla frosting

8 drops green food color

Assorted candies (black licorice twists, candy corn, candy-coated peanut butter candies)

1 tube (0.68 oz) Betty Crocker® black decorating gel

1. Heat oven to 350°F (325°F for dark or nonstick pans). Place paper baking cup in each of 24 regular-size muffin cups. Make and bake cake mix as directed on box for 24 cupcakes. Cool in pans 10 minutes; remove from pans to cooling rack. Cool completely, about 30 minutes.
2. Tint frosting with green food color. Cut licorice twists lengthwise in half; cut each half crosswise into various lengths.
3. Frost cupcakes with frosting. Arrange licorice pieces on each cupcake for hat, candy corn for nose and peanut butter candies for eyes. Make pupils of eyes with black gel.

1 CUPCAKE: Calories 240; Total Fat 9g (Saturated Fat 2g; Trans Fat 1g); Cholesterol 25mg; Sodium 200mg; Total Carbohydrate 37g (Dietary Fiber 0g); Protein 1g EXCHANGES: 1 Starch; 1½ Other Carbohydrate; 1½ Fat CARBOHYDRATE CHOICES: 2½

sweet note Cake mix, ready-to-spread frosting and candies make witchly cupcakes anything but scary.

spiderweb cupcakes

PREP TIME: 20 minutes *START TO FINISH:* 1 hour 10 minutes [24 CUPCAKES]

1 box Betty Crocker® SuperMoist® devil's food cake mix

Water, vegetable oil and eggs called for on cake mix box

1 container (1 lb) Betty Crocker® Rich & Creamy vanilla frosting

3 drops red food color

4 to 5 drops yellow food color

1 tube (0.68 oz) Betty Crocker® black decorating gel

48 large black gumdrops

1 Heat oven to 350°F (325°F for dark or nonstick pans). Place paper baking cup in each of 24 regular-size muffin cups. Make, bake and cool cake mix as directed on box for 24 cupcakes.

2 Tint frosting with red and yellow food colors to make orange frosting. Spread frosting over tops of cupcakes.

3 Squeeze circles of decorating gel on each cupcake; pull knife through gel from center outward to make web. To make each spider, roll out 1 gumdrop and cut out 8 strips for legs; place another gumdrop on top. Place spider on cupcake. Store loosely covered at room temperature.

1 CUPCAKE (CAKE AND FROSTING ONLY): Calories 190; Total Fat 9g (Saturated Fat 2g; Trans Fat 1g); Cholesterol 25mg; Sodium 200mg; Total Carbohydrate 27g (Dietary Fiber 0g); Protein 1g EXCHANGES: ½ Starch; 1½ Other Carbohydrate; 1½ Fat CARBOHYDRATE CHOICES: 2

sweet note Turn these into Holly Wreath Cupcakes by using green-tinted frosting instead of orange. Squeeze circles of red decorating gel on each cupcake, and decorate with small red cinnamon candy "berries."

autumn leaf cupcakes

PREP TIME: 45 minutes *START TO FINISH:* 1 hour 30 minutes [24 CUPCAKES]

1 box Betty Crocker® SuperMoist® devil's food cake mix

Water, vegetable oil and eggs called for on cake mix box

½ cup semisweet chocolate chips, melted

½ cup butterscotch chips, melted

1 container (1 lb) Betty Crocker® Rich & Creamy chocolate frosting

1 Heat oven to 350°F (325°F for dark or nonstick pans). Place paper baking cup in each of 24 regular-size muffin cups. Make and bake cake mix as directed on box for 24 cupcakes, using water, oil and eggs. Cool 10 minutes; remove from pans to cooling racks. Cool completely, about 30 minutes.

2 Meanwhile, place 12-inch sheet of waxed paper on cookie sheet; mark an 8-inch square on waxed paper. Alternately place spoonfuls of melted chocolate and butterscotch on waxed paper. With small spatula, swirl together for marbled effect, spreading to an 8-inch square. Refrigerate until firm, about 30 minutes.

3 Remove from refrigerator; let stand about 10 minutes or until slightly softened. Use 1½-inch leaf cookie cutter to make 24 leaf cutouts. Carefully remove cutouts from paper with spatula; place on another waxed paper–lined cookie sheet. Refrigerate until firm, about 5 minutes.

4 Frost cupcakes. Garnish with leaf cutouts. Store loosely covered in refrigerator.

1 CUPCAKE: Calories 230; Total Fat 11g (Saturated Fat 3½g; Trans Fat 1g); Cholesterol 25mg; Sodium 210mg; Total Carbohydrate 31g (Dietary Fiber 0g); Protein 2g
EXCHANGES: ½ Starch; 1½ Other Carbohydrate; 2 Fat CARBOHYDRATE CHOICES: 2

sweet note Use your favorite flavor Betty Crocker® SuperMoist® cake mix for the cupcakes.

thanksgiving turkey cupcakes

PREP TIME: 45 minutes *START TO FINISH:* 2 hours [24 CUPCAKES]

- 1 box Betty Crocker® SuperMoist® yellow cake mix
- 1¼ cups water
- ¼ cup vegetable oil
- 3 eggs
- ¾ cup creamy peanut butter
- 1 container (1 lb) Betty Crocker® Rich & Creamy chocolate frosting
- 4 oz vanilla-flavored candy coating (almond bark)
- 4 oz semisweet baking chocolate
- 24 Hershey's® Kisses® Brand milk chocolates, unwrapped

1 Heat oven to 350°F (325°F for dark or nonstick pans). Place paper baking cup in each of 24 regular-size muffin cups.

2 In large bowl, beat cake mix, water, oil, eggs and peanut butter with electric mixer on low speed 30 seconds, then on medium speed 2 minutes, scraping bowl occasionally. Divide batter evenly among muffin cups, filling each about two-thirds full.

3 Bake 18 to 23 minutes or until toothpick inserted in center comes out clean. Cool in pans 10 minutes; remove from pans to cooling rack. Cool completely, about 30 minutes. Frost cupcakes with frosting.

4 Line cookie sheet with waxed paper. In separate small microwavable bowls, microwave candy coating and baking chocolate uncovered on High 30 to 60 seconds, stirring every 15 seconds, until melted and smooth. Place coating and chocolate in separate resealable food-storage plastic bags; snip off tiny corner of each bag. Pipe coating and chocolate into feather shapes onto waxed paper, about 3 inches long and 2½ inches wide. Refrigerate coating and chocolate about 5 minutes until set.

5 When set, peel feathers off waxed paper and insert into cupcakes. Place milk chocolate candy on each cupcake for head of turkey. Store loosely covered.

1 CUPCAKE: Calories 300; Total Fat 16g (Saturated Fat 6g; Trans Fat 1g); Cholesterol 30mg; Sodium 230mg; Total Carbohydrate 35g (Dietary Fiber 1g); Protein 4g
EXCHANGES: 1½ Starch; 1 Other Carbohydrate; 3 Fat CARBOHYDRATE CHOICES: 2

sweet note To make the turkey feathers even more colorful, stir a small amount of red and yellow food color into the melted white candy coating to make it orange.

football cupcake pull-aparts

PREP TIME: 40 minutes *START TO FINISH:* 1 hour 45 minutes [24 CUPCAKES]

1 box Betty Crocker® SuperMoist® yellow cake mix

Water, vegetable oil and eggs called for on cake mix box

2 containers (1 lb each) Betty Crocker® Rich & Creamy chocolate frosting

½ cup candy-coated chocolate candies

1 tube (4.25 oz) Betty Crocker® white decorating icing

1 Heat oven to 350°F (325°F for dark or nonstick pans). Place paper baking cup in each of 24 regular-size muffin cups.

2 Make and bake cake mix as directed on box for 24 cupcakes. Cool in pans 10 minutes; remove from pans to cooling rack. Cool completely, about 30 minutes.

3 Spoon frosting into decorating bag with large star tip (size #5). Arrange cupcakes in football shape using 15 of the 24 cupcakes. Pipe thick lines of frosting over football-cupcake shape. Using spatula, spread frosting over cupcakes. Pipe decorative border of chocolate frosting around edge of football. Sprinkle decorative border with candy-coated chocolate candies. Pipe laces with white icing. Frost and decorate remaining cupcakes as desired, and serve alongside football. Store loosely covered.

1 CUPCAKE (CAKE AND FROSTING ONLY): Calories 260; Total Fat 11g (Saturated Fat 3g; Trans Fat 2g); Cholesterol 25mg; Sodium 240mg; Total Carbohydrate 38g (Dietary Fiber 0g); Protein 1g EXCHANGES: ½ Starch; 2 Other Carbohydrate; 2 Fat CARBOHYDRATE CHOICES: 2½

sweet note Get in the team spirit! Use candy-coated chocolate candies that match your team colors.

Assembling Football Cupcake Pull-Aparts

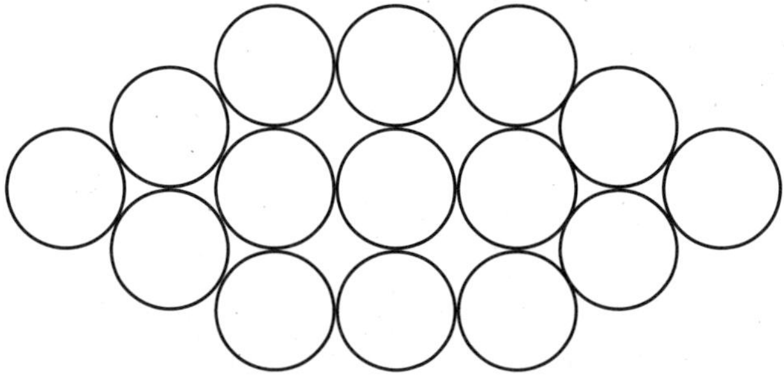

Arrange cupcakes according to diagram shown (1-2-3-3-3-2-1).
Tip: Start in the middle with the two vertical lines or three cupcakes each.
Work your way out to the end on each side.

team color cupcake poppers

PREP TIME: 45 minutes *START TO FINISH:* 1 hour 15 minutes [30 SERVINGS]

1 box Betty Crocker® Super Moist® white cake mix

Water, vegetable oil and egg whites called for on cake mix box

2 teaspoons red liquid food color*

2 cups Betty Crocker® Whipped fluffy white frosting (from two 12-oz containers)

1 Heat oven to 350°F (325°F for dark or nonstick pans). Spray 60 mini muffin cups with cooking spray. Make cake batter as directed on box, adding food color to batter.

2 Fill each muffin cup with 1 level measuring tablespoon batter.

3 Bake 11 to 14 minutes or until toothpick inserted in center comes out clean. Cool 5 minutes in pans; remove from pans to cooling rack. Cool completely, about 10 minutes.

4 Assemble each popper using 2 mini cupcakes. Cut tops off each cupcake horizontally (save bottoms for another use). Spread or pipe about 1 tablespoon frosting on cut side of 1 cupcake top. Make a sandwich by placing cut side of second cupcake top on frosting; press lightly. Repeat with remaining cupcake tops. Store loosely covered.

**To make blue cupcake poppers, add 2 teaspoons royal blue food color paste and a toothpickful of violet food color paste to cake batter instead of red liquid food color.*

1 POPPER: Calories 140; Total Fat 6g (Saturated Fat 1½g; Trans Fat 1g); Cholesterol 0mg; Sodium 125mg; Total Carbohydrate 20g (Dietary Fiber 0g); Protein 1g EXCHANGES: ½ Starch; 1 Other Carbohydrate; 1 Fat CARBOHYDRATE CHOICES: 1

sweet note Follow directions on food color package to make your favorite team colors.

reindeer cupcakes

PREP TIME: 20 minutes *START TO FINISH:* 1 hour 45 minutes [24 CUPCAKES]

- 1 box Betty Crocker® SuperMoist® cake mix (any nonswirl flavor)
- Water, vegetable oil and eggs called for on cake mix box
- 1 container (1 lb) Betty Crocker® Rich & Creamy chocolate frosting
- Betty Crocker® chocolate sprinkles
- 24 large pretzel twists
- 24 miniature marshmallows
- 24 small red gumdrops
- 24 red cinnamon candies

1. Heat oven to 350°F (325°F for dark or nonstick pans). Place paper baking cup in each of 24 regular-size muffin cups. Make, bake and cool cake mix as directed on box for 24 cupcakes.
2. Frost cupcakes with frosting. Sprinkle chocolate sprinkles over tops of cupcakes.
3. For each cupcake, cut pretzel twist in half; arrange on cupcake for reindeer antlers. Cut miniature marshmallow in half; arrange on cupcake for eyes. Center gumdrop below marshmallow halves for nose. Place red cinnamon candy below gumdrop for mouth. Store loosely covered.

1 CUPCAKE: Calories 270; Total Fat 10g (Saturated Fat 2½g; Trans Fat 1g); Cholesterol 25mg; Sodium 430mg; Total Carbohydrate 44g (Dietary Fiber 1g); Protein 3g
EXCHANGES: ½ Starch; 2½ Other Carbohydrate; 2 Fat CARBOHYDRATE CHOICES: 3

sweet note Bake these festive cupcakes in holiday-themed baking cups for even more holiday spirit!

snowman cupcakes

PREP TIME: 45 minutes *START TO FINISH:* 2 hours [24 CUPCAKES]

1 box Betty Crocker® SuperMoist® white cake mix

Water, vegetable oil and egg whites called for on cake mix box

1 container (12 oz) Betty Crocker® Whipped fluffy white frosting

White decorator sugar crystals

1 bag (16 oz) large marshmallows

Pretzel sticks

Betty Crocker® Fruit by the Foot® chewy fruit snack rolls, any red or orange flavor

Assorted candies (such as gumdrops, gummy ring candies, peppermint candies, chocolate chips, pastel mint chips, candy decors, string licorice)

1 Heat oven to 350°F (325°F for dark or nonstick pans). Place paper baking cup in each of 24 regular-size muffin cups. Make, bake and cool cake mix as directed on box for 24 cupcakes.

2 Set aside ¼ cup frosting. Frost cupcakes with remaining frosting. Sprinkle frosting with sugar crystals. Stack 2 or 3 marshmallows on each cupcake, using ½ teaspoon frosting between marshmallows to attach.

3 For arms, break pretzel sticks into pieces 1½ inches long. Press 2 pieces into marshmallow on each cupcake. Cut 1-inch mitten shapes from fruit snack. Attach mittens to pretzels. For scarf, cut fruit snack into 6 × ¼-inch piece; wrap and tie around base of top marshmallow. For hat, stack candies, using frosting to attach. For earmuff, use piece of string licorice and candies, using frosting to attach. For faces and buttons, attach desired candies with small amount of frosting. Store loosely covered.

1 CUPCAKE (CAKE AND FROSTING ONLY): Calories 160; Total Fat 7g (Saturated Fat 2g; Trans Fat 1g); Cholesterol 0mg; Sodium 160mg; Total Carbohydrate 24g (Dietary Fiber 0g); Protein 1g EXCHANGES: ½ Starch; 1 Other Carbohydrate; 1½ Fat CARBOHYDRATE CHOICES: 1½

sweet note Make your own snow creatures! There are lots of clever ways that snow people can be decorated; check your pantry for colorful candies you might have on hand.

bonus chapter

50 gluten-free desserts

Our Gluten-Free Story

Betty Crocker is proud to offer a variety of gluten-free mixes for cakes, cookies and brownies. The recipes in this chapter were tested with these gluten-free mixes, such as Betty Crocker® Gluten Free devil's food cake mix, which can be found in any grocery store.

Why Go Gluten Free?

Not long ago, two of our co-workers found themselves in the gluten-free world. Linc was diagnosed with celiac disease, and Colleen's family switched to the diet for her son's well-being. Their experiences opened our eyes to the challenges families face following the diet. It's hard to be different, especially when it affects sweet moments with friends and family. No one wants to miss sharing a birthday cake or see their child have to turn down a homemade cookie from a buddy after a game. We hope we can help by bringing you these mixes and recipes for gluten-free desserts that look and taste like the treats you've been longing to share. Finally, Betty Crocker® Gluten Free!

—The Betty Crocker® Baking Team

What You Should Know about Gluten Sensitivity

What Is Gluten?

Gluten is a protein naturally found in certain grains such as wheat, barley, rye and some oats. Foods that are made with these grains also contain gluten—that includes foods like bagels, breads, cakes, cereals, cookies, crackers, pasta, pizza and more.

Who Should Avoid Gluten?

About three million Americans suffer from a serious medical condition called celiac disease. For someone with this disease, eating gluten-containing foods causes damage to the lining of the small intestine (where foods go after they have been eaten and digested). This damage makes it very difficult for the body to absorb nutrients from foods. Over time this damage can lead to malnourishment and possibly other complications. While there is no cure for celiac disease, the good news is that eating gluten free is the best way to prevent further damage to the small intestine. Some people avoid gluten due to a sensitivity to it, while others make a personal choice to avoid it.

Knowing What to Look For: Reading Labels

The best way to know if a product is gluten free is to read the ingredients label. To determine if a product contains gluten, there are five main words you need to know:

- Wheat
- Barley
- Rye
- Malt
- Oats

Looking for any of these five words will help you identify products that contain gluten. Always read labels to be sure each recipe ingredient is gluten free. Ingredients can change over time, so checking the ingredients label every time is the most accurate way to identify what is in a food or beverage product. After you have read the label and determined that the product does not contain these obvious sources of gluten, you may always contact the manufacturer to confirm.

Studies suggest that pure oats that are not mixed with wheat, barley or rye consumed in moderation can be tolerated by most people with celiac disease. Check with your health care provider to find out if this is right for you.

Q&A: Gluten Free Mixes

Q: What products are available gluten free from Betty Crocker®?

- Betty Crocker® Gluten Free yellow cake mix
- Betty Crocker® Gluten Free devil's food cake mix
- Betty Crocker® Gluten Free brownie mix
- Betty Crocker® Gluten Free chocolate chip cookie mix

Q: Are the Betty Crocker® Gluten Free dessert mixes made in a gluten-free processing facility?

Yes.

Q: Is Betty Crocker® frosting gluten free?

All flavors of Betty Crocker ready-to-spread frosting are labeled "gluten free."

Q: Are the Betty Crocker® Gluten Free dessert mixes kosher? Why is there an unusual-looking symbol on the package?

Yes. The Betty Crocker® Gluten Free dessert mixes are all kosher pareve. The symbol on the box may look different from what you're used to because the mixes are made and kosher certified in Canada.

Q: Do you give back to the celiac community?

Yes. We sponsor both the Celiac Disease Foundation and the Celiac Sprue Association.

Q: Do Betty Crocker® Gluten Free dessert mixes participate in the Box Tops for Education® program?

Yes. Now you have another way to collect for your favorite school!

Q: Where can I buy Betty Crocker® Gluten Free dessert mixes?

They are now available in traditional grocery stores nationwide. If you can't find them at your local store, please ask the manager to start carrying them!

fresh baked is best

Baked goods make from gluten-free ingredients and Betty Crocker mixes will taste best when eaten the day they are baked. However, these products freeze well. Wrap small amounts in airtight containers. When you're ready to serve, thaw only what you need.

brownie ganache torte with raspberries

PREP TIME: 15 minutes *START TO FINISH:* 1 hour 55 minutes [12 SERVINGS]

- 1 box (16 oz) Betty Crocker® Gluten Free brownie mix
- ¼ cup butter, melted
- 2 eggs
- ⅓ cup whipping cream
- ½ cup semisweet chocolate chips
- 1 cup fresh raspberries or sliced strawberries

1 Heat oven to 350°F. Spray bottom only of 8-inch springform pan with cooking spray without flour.

2 In medium bowl, stir brownie mix, butter and eggs until well blended. Spread in pan.

3 Bake 26 to 29 minutes or until toothpick inserted 2 inches from side of pan comes out almost clean; cool 10 minutes. Run knife around edge of pan to loosen; remove side of pan. Cool completely, about 1 hour.

4 In 1-quart saucepan, heat whipping cream over medium-low heat until hot. Remove from heat; stir in chocolate chips until melted and smooth. Let stand 15 minutes to thicken. Carefully pour chocolate mixture onto top center of brownie; spread just to edge. Cut into wedges. Serve with raspberries.

1 SERVING: Calories 270; Total Fat 11g (Saturated Fat 7g; Trans Fat 0g); Cholesterol 55mg; Sodium 110mg; Total Carbohydrate 38g (Dietary Fiber 1g); Protein 2g EXCHANGES: 1 Starch; 1½ Other Carbohydrate; 2 Fat CARBOHYDRATE CHOICES: 2½

sweet note In addition to the fresh raspberries, top these fudgy wedges with a dollop of whipped cream and a few toasted slivered almonds. Spectacular!

peppermint patty brownies

PREP TIME: 20 minutes *START TO FINISH:* 2 hours [16 BROWNIES]

- 1 box (16 oz) Betty Crocker® Gluten Free brownie mix
- Butter and eggs as called for on brownie box
- ½ cup sweetened condensed milk
- 1½ teaspoons peppermint extract
- 2½ to 3 cups gluten-free powdered sugar
- 1 cup Betty Crocker® Rich & Creamy chocolate frosting (from 1-lb container)

1 Heat oven to 350°F (325°F for dark or nonstick pan). Line 8- or 9-inch square pan with aluminum foil; grease bottom of pan with shortening. Make and bake brownies as directed on box, using butter and eggs, for 8- or 9-inch square pan. Cool 1 hour.

2 In medium bowl, stir together sweetened condensed milk and peppermint extract. Beat in enough powdered sugar on low speed of electric mixer until blended and slightly crumbly. Turn mixture onto surface sprinkled with powdered sugar. Knead lightly to form a smooth ball. Pat mixture evenly over top of brownies.

3 Spread frosting over brownies. To serve, remove brownies from pan by lifting on aluminum foil; transfer to cutting board. With long sharp knife, cut into squares, 4 rows by 4 rows.

1 BROWNIE: Calories 320; Total Fat 9g (Saturated Fat 4½g; Trans Fat 1g); Cholesterol 35mg; Sodium 140mg; Total Carbohydrate 59g (Dietary Fiber 0g); Protein 2g EXCHANGES: 1 Starch; 3 Other Carbohydrate; 1½ Fat CARBOHYDRATE CHOICES: 4

sweet note Turn a simple pan of brownies into a festive holiday treat with an easy peppermint filling and frosting—all gluten free!

mexican chocolate brownies

PREP TIME: 15 minutes *START TO FINISH:* 2 hours 15 minutes [16 BROWNIES]

- 3 cups Cinnamon Chex® cereal
- 3 tablespoons packed brown sugar
- ¼ teaspoon baking soda
- ¼ cup butter or margarine, melted
- 1 box (16 oz) Betty Crocker® Gluten Free brownie mix
- ¼ cup butter or margarine, melted
- 2 eggs

1 Heat oven to 350°F (325°F for dark or nonstick pan). Spray bottom only of 8-inch square pan with cooking spray without flour. Place cereal in resealable food-storage plastic bag; seal bag and crush with rolling pin to make about 1½ cups.

2 In medium bowl, mix cereal, brown sugar and baking soda; stir in ¼ cup melted butter until well mixed. Reserve ⅓ cup cereal mixture for topping. Press remaining cereal mixture evenly in bottom of pan. Bake 5 minutes. Cool 5 minutes.

3 Meanwhile, in medium bowl, stir brownie mix, ¼ cup melted butter and the eggs until well blended. Drop batter by small spoonfuls over baked layer. Carefully spread over baked layer; sprinkle with reserved ⅓ cup cereal mixture.

4 Bake 30 to 34 minutes or until brownies look dry and set. (Brownies will be soft; do not use toothpick test.) Cool completely, about 1½ hours. For brownies, cut into 4 rows by 4 rows. Store tightly covered.

1 BROWNIE: Calories 190; Total Fat 6g (Saturated Fat 3g; Trans Fat 0g); Cholesterol 35mg; Sodium 150mg; Total Carbohydrate 33g (Dietary Fiber 0g); Protein 2g EXCHANGES: 1 Starch; 1 Other Carbohydrate; 1 Fat CARBOHYDRATE CHOICES: 2

sweet note Jazz up Betty Crocker® Gluten Free brownie mix with Cinnamon Chex® cereal, creating a classic Mexican-flavored combo with added crunch.

peanut butter truffle brownies

PREP TIME: 20 minutes *START TO FINISH:* 2 hours 30 minutes [16 BROWNIES]

Brownie Base

1 box (16 oz) Betty Crocker® Gluten Free brownie mix

Butter and eggs called for on brownie mix box

Filling

¼ cup butter, softened

¼ cup gluten-free creamy peanut butter

1 cup gluten-free powdered sugar

1 teaspoon milk

Topping

1 cup semisweet chocolate chips

¼ cup butter

1 Heat oven to 350°F (325°F for dark or nonstick pan). Make and bake brownie mix as directed on box, using butter, eggs and any of the pan choices—except line pan with foil, then grease foil on bottom only for easier removal. Cool completely, about 1 hour.

2 In medium bowl, stir filling ingredients until smooth. Spread mixture evenly over brownie base.

3 In small microwavable bowl, microwave topping ingredients uncovered on High 30 to 60 seconds. Stir until smooth; cool 10 minutes. Spread over filling. Refrigerate about 30 minutes or until set. Store covered in refrigerator.

1 BROWNIE: Calories 290; Total Fat 16g (Saturated Fat 9g; Trans Fat 0g); Cholesterol 50mg; Sodium 135mg; Total Carbohydrate 33g (Dietary Fiber 1g); Protein 3g EXCHANGES: 2 Other Carbohydrate; ½ High-Fat Meat; 2½ Fat CARBOHYDRATE CHOICES: 2

sweet note Looking for a delicious dessert made using Betty Crocker® Gluten Free brownie mix? Then check out these peanut butter truffle brownies with semisweet chocolate chips topping.

turtle brownies

PREP TIME: 20 minutes *TOTAL TIME:* 2 hours [16 BROWNIES]

- 1 box (16 oz) Betty Crocker® Gluten Free brownie mix
- Butter and eggs called for on brownie mix box
- 25 caramels, unwrapped
- 2 tablespoons whipping cream
- 1 cup semisweet chocolate chips
- ½ cup coarsely chopped pecans

1 Heat oven to 350°F (325°F for dark or nonstick pan). Grease bottom of 8- or 9-inch square pan. In medium bowl, stir together brownie mix, butter and eggs until blended. Spread two-thirds of batter in pan. Bake 10 minutes.

2 Meanwhile, in medium microwavable bowl, microwave caramels and whipping cream uncovered on High 1 to 2 minutes, stirring every 30 seconds, until smooth. Drizzle caramel evenly over partially baked brownie. Sprinkle with half the chocolate chips and half the pecans. Drop remaining brownie batter by small spoonfuls onto caramel layer. Sprinkle with remaining chocolate chips and pecans.

3 Bake 20 to 25 minutes longer or until top of brownie looks dry. Cool completely before cutting. Cut into squares, 4 rows by 4 rows.

1 BROWNIE: Calories 300; Total Fat 13g (Saturated Fat 6g; Trans Fat 0g); Cholesterol 35mg; Sodium 120mg; Total Carbohydrate 43g (Dietary Fiber 1g); Protein 3g EXCHANGES: 1 Starch; 2 Other Carbohydrate; 2½ Fat CARBOHYDRATE CHOICES: 3

sweet note To easily cut and remove bars from the pan, cool at room temperature 1 hour. Then refrigerate 30 minutes to 1 hour. Cut and store at room temperature.

tom-and-jerry brownies

PREP TIME: 25 minutes *START TO FINISH:* 2 hours [16 BROWNIES]

1 box (16 oz) Betty Crocker® Gluten Free brownie mix

Butter and eggs called for on brownie mix box

4 oz (half of 8-oz package) cream cheese, softened

¼ cup granulated sugar

2 teaspoons brandy or 1 teaspoon gluten-free brandy extract

½ teaspoon ground nutmeg

1 egg yolk

Gluten-free powdered sugar, if desired

1 Heat oven to 375°F (350°F for dark or nonstick pan). Make brownie mix as directed on box, using butter, eggs and any of the pan choices. Spread half of batter in pan.

2 In small bowl, stir remaining ingredients except powdered sugar until smooth. Drop cream cheese mixture by spoonfuls onto brownie batter. Spoon remaining brownie batter over cream cheese mixture. With knife, swirl cream cheese mixture through brownie batter for marbled design.

3 Bake 30 to 35 minutes or until toothpick inserted 2 inches from side of pan comes out clean or almost clean. Cool completely, about 1½ hours. Sprinkle with powdered sugar. For 16 brownies, cut into 4 rows by 4 rows. Store covered in refrigerator.

1 BROWNIE: Calories 170; Total Fat 8g (Saturated Fat 4½g; Trans Fat 0g); Cholesterol 55mg; Sodium 95mg; Total Carbohydrate 22g (Dietary Fiber 0g); Protein 2g EXCHANGES: ½ Starch; 1 Other Carbohydrate; 1½ Fat CARBOHYDRATE CHOICES: 1½

sweet note Betty Crocker® Gluten Free brownie mix and cream cheese turn into a delicious bar reminiscent of the popular Tom-and-Jerry drink.

brownie 'n berries dessert pizza

PREP TIME: 20 minutes *START TO FINISH:* 2 hours 40 minutes [12 SERVINGS]

1 box (16 oz) Betty Crocker® Gluten Free brownie mix

Butter and eggs called for on brownie mix box

1 package (8 oz) cream cheese, softened

⅓ cup sugar

½ teaspoon gluten-free vanilla

2 cups sliced fresh strawberries

1 cup fresh blueberries

1 cup fresh raspberries

½ cup apple jelly

1 Heat oven to 350°F (325°F for dark or nonstick pan). Grease bottom only of 12-inch pizza pan with cooking spray without flour or shortening.

2 In large bowl, stir brownie mix, butter and eggs until well blended. Spread in pan.

3 Bake 18 to 20 minutes or until toothpick inserted 2 inches from side of pan comes out clean or almost clean. Cool completely, about 1 hour.

4 In small bowl, beat cream cheese, sugar and vanilla with electric mixer on medium speed until smooth. Spread mixture evenly over brownie base. Arrange berries over cream cheese mixture. Stir jelly until smooth; brush over berries. Refrigerate about 1 hour or until chilled. Cut into wedges. Store covered in refrigerator.

1 SERVING: Calories 310; Total Fat 13g (Saturated Fat 7g; Trans Fat 0g); Cholesterol 65 mg; Sodium 160 mg; Total Carbohydrate 44g (Dietary Fiber 2g); Protein 3g EXCHANGES: ½ Starch; ½ Fruit; 2 Other Carbohydrate; 2½ Fat CARBOHYDRATE CHOICES: 3

sweet note Want to wow a chocolate-craving crowd? Make a sweet dessert pizza topped with a creamy layer and tart berries.

crunchy fudge cookies

PREP TIME: 40 minutes *START TO FINISH:* 40 minutes [24 COOKIES]

Cookies

1 box (16 oz) Betty Crocker® Gluten Free brownie mix

3 cups Cinnamon Chex® cereal

⅓ cup water

1 egg, slightly beaten

2 teaspoons gluten-free vanilla

¼ cup miniature semisweet chocolate chips

Glaze

¾ cup gluten-free powdered sugar

⅛ to ¼ teaspoon ground cinnamon

3 teaspoons milk

1 Heat oven to 350°F (325°F for dark or nonstick pans). Spray cookie sheets with cooking spray without flour.

2 In large bowl, mix cookie ingredients with spoon until blended. Drop dough by rounded measuring tablespoonfuls about 2 inches apart onto cookie sheets.

3 Bake 10 to 12 minutes or until set. Cool 2 minutes; remove from cookie sheet to cooling rack. Cool 10 minutes before glazing.

4 In small bowl, mix powdered sugar and cinnamon. Stir in milk until smooth. If necessary, add additional milk 1 teaspoon at a time until glaze reaches drizzling consistency. Drizzle cookies with glaze.

1 COOKIE: Calories 130; Total Fat 2½g (Saturated Fat 1g; Trans Fat 0g); Cholesterol 10mg; Sodium 70mg; Total Carbohydrate 25g (Dietary Fiber 0g); Protein 1g EXCHANGES: ½ Starch; ½ Fat CARBOHYDRATE CHOICES: 1½

sweet note Enjoy a great-tasting fudgy cookie with a cinnamon twist made with gluten-free brownie mix and cereal.

fudgy brownie trifle

PREP TIME: 15 minutes *START TO FINISH:* 5 hours 45 minutes [10 SERVINGS]

- 1 box (16 oz) Betty Crocker® Gluten Free brownie mix
- Butter and eggs called for on brownie mix box
- 1 teaspoon instant coffee granules
- 4 snack-size containers (4 oz each) gluten-free chocolate pudding
- 1 cup frozen (thawed) whipped topping
- 1 cup toffee bits

1 Heat oven to 350°F (325°F for dark or nonstick pan). Grease bottom only of 8-inch square pan with shortening or cooking spray without flour. Make brownie mix as directed on box, using butter and eggs; stir in coffee granules. Spread in pan. Bake as directed on box. Cool completely, about 1 hour.

2 Cut brownies into 1-inch squares. In bottom of 2-quart glass bowl, place half of the brownie squares. Pour 2 containers of the pudding over brownies in bowl. Top with half each of the whipped topping and toffee bits. Repeat with remaining brownies, pudding, whipped topping and toffee bits.

3 Cover; refrigerate at least 4 hours before serving. Store covered in refrigerator.

1 SERVING: Calories 470; Total Fat 22g (Saturated Fat 13g; Trans Fat 1g); Cholesterol 90mg; Sodium 230mg; Total Carbohydrate 64g (Dietary Fiber 1g); Protein 4g
EXCHANGES: ½ Starch; 4 Other Carbohydrate; 4½ Fat CARBOHYDRATE CHOICES: 4

sweet note Indulgent gluten-free dessert? Layer gluten-free brownies, whipped cream and chocolate for a gluten-free celebration.

pumpkin–chocolate chip cookies

PREP TIME: 30 minutes *START TO FINISH:* 1 hour [36 COOKIES]

¾ cup canned pumpkin (not pumpkin pie mix)

¼ cup butter, softened (not melted)

1 teaspoon gluten-free vanilla

1 egg

1 box (19 oz) Betty Crocker® Gluten Free chocolate chip cookie mix

½ cup raisins, if desired

¼ teaspoon ground cinnamon

Gluten-free powdered sugar, if desired

1 Heat oven to 350°F (325°F for dark or nonstick pans). Grease cookie sheets with shortening.

2 In large bowl, stir pumpkin, butter, vanilla and egg until blended. Stir in cookie mix, raisins and cinnamon until soft dough forms. Drop dough by rounded tablespoonfuls 2 inches apart on cookie sheets.

3 Bake 10 to 12 minutes or until almost no indentation remains when lightly touched in center and edges are golden brown. Immediately remove from cookie sheet to cooling rack. Cool completely, about 15 minutes. Sprinkle with powdered sugar.

1 COOKIE: Calories 80; Total Fat 2½g (Saturated Fat 1½g; Trans Fat 0g); Cholesterol 10mg; Sodium 80mg; Total Carbohydrate 13g (Dietary Fiber 0g); Protein 0g EXCHANGES: 1 Other Carbohydrate; ½ Fat CARBOHYDRATE CHOICES: 1

sweet note Betty Crocker® Gluten Free chocolate chip cookie mix, pumpkin and a pinch of spice bake into yummy homemade cookies.

decadent double chocolate-cherry cookies

PREP TIME: 1 hour 10 minutes *START TO FINISH:* 1 hour 30 minutes [32 COOKIES]

1 box (19 oz) Betty Crocker® Gluten Free chocolate chip cookie mix

1 box (4-serving size) gluten-free chocolate instant pudding and pie filling mix

1 cup dried cherries

½ cup coarsely chopped pecans

½ cup butter, melted

2 eggs

1 teaspoon gluten-free vanilla

1 cup semisweet chocolate chips (6 oz)

¼ cup whipping cream

1 Heat oven to 350°F (325°F for dark or nonstick pans). In large bowl, mix dry cookie mix, dry pudding mix, cherries and pecans. Add melted butter, eggs and vanilla; stir until soft dough forms.

2 Drop dough by rounded measuring tablespoonfuls onto ungreased cookie sheets; flatten slightly. Bake 9 to 11 minutes or until set. Cool 2 minutes; remove from cookie sheet to cooling rack. Cool completely.

3 Meanwhile, in small microwavable bowl, microwave chocolate chips and cream uncovered on High 30 to 45 seconds; stir until smooth. Spoon generous teaspoonful on each cookie; spread over cookies. Allow chocolate to set until firm, about 1 hour.

1 COOKIE: Calories 190; Total Fat 8g (Saturated Fat 4g; Trans Fat 0g); Cholesterol 25mg; Sodium 150mg; Total Carbohydrate 26g (Dietary Fiber 0g); Protein 2g EXCHANGES: 1 Starch; 1 Other Carbohydrate; 1½ Fat CARBOHYDRATE CHOICES: 2

sweet note These cookies will surprise you and your guests, and nobody will ever know they are gluten free!

ooey-gooey rocky road bars

PREP TIME: 10 minutes *START TO FINISH:* 2 hours 35 minutes [24 BARS]

½ cup butter, softened
1 egg
1 teaspoon gluten-free vanilla
1 box (19 oz) Betty Crocker® Gluten Free chocolate chip cookie mix
2 cups semisweet chocolate chips
½ cup chopped toasted pecans
3 cups miniature marshmallows

1 Heat oven to 350°F (325°F for dark or nonstick pan). Spray bottom only of 13 × 9-inch pan with cooking spray without flour. In large bowl, mix butter, egg and vanilla until blended. Stir in cookie mix until soft dough forms. Press dough evenly in pan.

2 Bake 20 to 25 minutes or until top is golden brown and center puffs slightly. Immediately sprinkle chocolate chips over crust. Let stand 3 to 5 minutes or until chocolate begins to melt. Gently spread chocolate evenly over crust.

3 Set oven control to broil. Sprinkle nuts and marshmallows over melted chocolate. Broil with top 5 to 6 inches from heat 20 to 30 seconds or until marshmallows are toasted. (Watch closely; marshmallows will brown quickly.) Cool 30 to 45 minutes to serve warm or cool completely, about 2 hours. For bars, cut into 6 rows by 4 rows. Store tightly covered.

1 BAR: Calories 250; Total Fat 12g (Saturated Fat 6g; Trans Fat 0g); Cholesterol 20mg; Sodium 140mg; Total Carbohydrate 33g (Dietary Fiber 1g); Protein 2g EXCHANGES: ½ Starch; 1½ Other Carbohydrate; 2½ Fat CARBOHYDRATE CHOICES: 2

sweet note Turn Betty Crocker® Gluten Free chocolate chip cookie mix into an indulgent dessert-bar cookie.

peanut butter–chocolate chip bars with chocolate frosting

PREP TIME: 15 minutes *START TO FINISH:* 1 hour 35 minutes [16 BARS]

1 box (19 oz) Betty Crocker® Gluten Free chocolate chip cookie mix

⅓ cup butter, softened

⅓ cup gluten-free peanut butter

1 teaspoon gluten-free vanilla

1 egg

1 cup Betty Crocker® Rich & Creamy chocolate frosting (from 1-lb container)

1 Heat oven to 350°F (325°F for dark or nonstick pan). Grease bottom only of 8- or 9-inch square pan.

2 In medium bowl, stir together cookie mix, butter, peanut butter, vanilla and egg with spoon until soft dough forms (dough will be crumbly). Pat dough into pan. Bake 18 to 22 minutes or until edges are dry and golden brown. Run knife around inside edge of pan. Cool on wire rack about 1 hour.

3 Spread frosting over bars. Cut into squares, 4 rows by 4 rows.

1 BAR: Calories 280; Total Fat 12g (Saturated Fat 5g; Trans Fat 1g); Cholesterol 25mg; Sodium 260mg; Total Carbohydrate 40g (Dietary Fiber 0g); Protein 3g EXCHANGES: 1 Starch; 1½ Other Carbohydrate; 2½ Fat CARBOHYDRATE CHOICES: 2½

sweet note Whip up delicious dessert bars using gluten-free chocolate chip cookie mix.

chocolate-marshmallow pillows

PREP TIME: 45 minutes *START TO FINISH:* 1 hour [30 COOKIES]

Cookies

½ cup butter, softened

1 egg

1 box (19 oz) Betty Crocker® Gluten Free chocolate chip cookie mix

⅔ cup chopped pecans

15 large marshmallows, cut in half

Frosting

1 cup semisweet chocolate chips (6 oz)

⅓ cup whipping cream

1 teaspoon butter

1 teaspoon gluten-free vanilla

½ cup gluten-free powdered sugar

1 Heat oven to 350°F (325°F for dark or nonstick pans). In medium bowl, stir ½ cup butter and the egg until blended. Stir in cookie mix until soft dough forms. Stir in pecans. Onto ungreased cookie sheets, drop dough by rounded tablespoonfuls about 3 inches apart.

2 Bake 8 minutes. Remove from oven; immediately press marshmallow half lightly, cut side down, on top of each cookie. Bake 1 to 2 minutes longer or just until marshmallows begin to soften. Cool 2 minutes; remove from cookie sheets to cooling racks. Cool completely, about 15 minutes.

3 Meanwhile, in medium microwavable bowl, microwave chocolate chips uncovered on High about 1 minute, stirring until smooth. Add whipping cream, 1 teaspoon butter and the vanilla; blend well. Stir in powdered sugar until smooth.

4 Spread frosting over each cooled cookie, covering marshmallow. Let stand until frosting is set.

1 COOKIE: Calories 180; Total Fat 9g (Saturated Fat 4½g; Trans Fat 0g); Cholesterol 20mg; Sodium 115mg; Total Carbohydrate 24g (Dietary Fiber 0g); Protein 1g EXCHANGES: 1 Starch; ½ Other Carbohydrate; 1½ Fat CARBOHYDRATE CHOICES: 1½

sweet note Looking for a delicious cookie recipe made using Betty Crocker® Gluten Free chocolate chip cookie mix? Then check out this chocolate-marshmallow pillows recipe that's ready in an hour—perfect for a dessert.

chocolate chip–ice cream dessert

PREP TIME: 30 minutes *START TO FINISH:* 3 hours 55 minutes [15 SERVINGS]

1 box (19 oz) Betty Crocker® Gluten Free chocolate chip cookie mix

½ cup butter, softened

1 egg

1 bottle (7.25 oz) gluten-free chocolate topping that forms hard shell

1 container (1.5 quarts) chocolate chip ice cream (6 cups)

1 Heat oven to 350°F (325°F for dark or nonstick pan). In large bowl, stir cookie mix, butter and egg until soft dough forms. On ungreased cookie sheet, make 5 cookies by dropping dough by tablespoonfuls. Bake 8 to 10 minutes or until edges are golden brown. Cool 2 minutes; remove from cookie sheet to cooling rack.

2 Meanwhile, using moistened fingers (dough will be sticky), press remaining dough in ungreased 13 × 9-inch pan. Bake 16 to 18 minutes or until set. Cool completely, about 30 minutes.

3 Spread ⅓ cup of the chocolate topping over cooled baked crust. Freeze 10 to 15 minutes or until chocolate is set. Meanwhile, remove ice cream from freezer to soften.

4 Spread softened ice cream evenly over chocolate-topped crust. Crumble 5 baked cookies; sprinkle over ice cream layer. Drizzle remaining chocolate topping over cookie crumbs. Cover; freeze 2 hours or overnight.

5 To serve, let stand at room temperature 10 minutes before cutting. For serving pieces, cut into 5 rows by 3 rows. Store covered in freezer.

1 SERVING: Calories 400; Total Fat 21g (Saturated Fat 12g; Trans Fat 0g); Cholesterol 55mg; Sodium 260mg; Total Carbohydrate 51g (Dietary Fiber 0g); Protein 4g EXCHANGES: 1½ Starch; 2 Other Carbohydrate; 4 Fat CARBOHYDRATE CHOICES: 3½

sweet note Love ice cream shop cakes? Try this tasty homemade version made easily with a cookie mix.

caramel-coffee fondue

PREP TIME: 20 minutes *START TO FINISH:* 20 minutes [8 SERVINGS]

¼ cup water

1 tablespoon instant coffee crystals

1 can (14 oz) sweetened condensed milk

1 bag (14 oz) caramels, unwrapped

½ cup coarsely chopped pecans

2 apples (1 Braeburn, 1 Granny Smith), cut into ½-inch slices

2 cups fresh pineapple chunks

½ baked Betty Crocker® Gluten Free yellow cake mix, cut into 1-inch cubes (about 4 cups)

1 In 2-quart nonstick saucepan, heat water over high heat until hot. Dissolve coffee crystals in water.

2 Add milk, caramels and pecans to coffee. Heat over medium-low heat, stirring frequently, until caramels are melted and mixture is hot. Pour mixture into fondue pot and keep warm.

3 Arrange apples, pineapple and cake on serving plate. Use skewers or fondue forks to dip into fondue.

1 SERVING: Calories 560; Total Fat 13g (Saturated Fat 4½g; Trans Fat 1g); Cholesterol 30mg; Sodium 330mg; Total Carbohydrate 101g (Dietary Fiber 2g); Protein 8g EXCHANGES: 1 Starch; 4½ Other Carbohydrate; 1½ Fat CARBOHYDRATE CHOICES: 7

easy monster cookies

PREP TIME: 10 minutes *START TO FINISH:* 40 minutes [24 COOKIES]

½ cup butter, softened

½ cup gluten-free peanut butter

1 egg

1 box (19 oz) Betty Crocker® Gluten Free chocolate chip cookie mix

¾ cup candy-coated milk chocolate candies

½ cup Rice Chex® cereal

1 Heat oven to 350°F (325°F for dark or nonstick pans). In large bowl, stir butter, peanut butter and egg until blended. Stir in cookie mix until soft dough forms. Stir in candies and cereal, breaking cereal apart as dough is stirred.

2 Onto ungreased cookie sheets, drop dough by rounded tablespoonfuls about 3 inches apart.

3 Bake 11 to 13 minutes or until edges are light golden brown. Cool at least 2 minutes; remove from cookie sheets. Cool completely before storing in airtight container.

1 COOKIE: Calories 200; Total Fat 10g (Saturated Fat 4½g; Trans Fat 0g); Cholesterol 20mg; Sodium 170mg; Total Carbohydrate 25g (Dietary Fiber 0g); Protein 2g EXCHANGES: ½ Starch; 1 Other Carbohydrate; 2 Fat CARBOHYDRATE CHOICES: 1½

cookie-brownie bars

PREP TIME: 20 minutes *START TO FINISH:* 1 hour 55 minutes [24 BARS]

Cookie

1 box (19 oz) Betty Crocker® Gluten Free chocolate chip cookie mix

½ cup butter, softened

1 teaspoon gluten-free vanilla

1 egg

Brownie

1 box (16 oz) Betty Crocker® Gluten Free brownie mix

¼ cup butter, melted

2 eggs

1 Heat oven to 350°F (325°F for dark or nonstick pan). Grease bottom only of 13 × 9-inch pan with shortening or cooking spray without flour.

2 In medium bowl, stir cookie ingredients until soft dough forms. Drop dough by rounded tablespoonfuls onto bottom of pan.

3 In another medium bowl, stir brownie ingredients until well blended. Drop batter by tablespoonfuls evenly between mounds of cookie dough.

4 Bake 30 to 35 minutes or until cookie portion is golden brown. Cool completely, about 1 hour. For 24 bars, cut into 6 rows by 4 rows.

1 BAR: Calories 180; Total Fat 7g (Saturated Fat 4g; Trans Fat 0g); Cholesterol 30mg; Sodium 140mg; Total Carbohydrate 26g (Dietary Fiber 0g); Protein 1g EXCHANGES: ½ Starch; 1 Other Carbohydrate; 1½ Fat CARBOHYDRATE CHOICES: 2

sweet note Betty Crocker® Gluten Free chocolate chip cookie mix and brownie mix stir up into a delicious new dessert bar.

chocolate chip cookie cheesecake

PREP TIME: 20 minutes *START TO FINISH:* 5 hours 30 minutes [16 SERVINGS]

Crust

1 box (19 oz) Betty Crocker® Gluten Free chocolate chip cookie mix

Butter, gluten-free vanilla and egg as called for on cookie mix box

Filling

3 packages (8 oz each) cream cheese, softened

1¼ cups sugar

2 teaspoons gluten-free vanilla

4 eggs

½ cup miniature chocolate chips

1 Heat oven to 325°F. For crust, make cookies as directed on box using butter, vanilla and egg—except press dough into bottom and 1 inch up side of 10-inch springform pan. Set aside.

2 For filling, in large bowl, beat cream cheese and sugar on low speed of electric mixer 30 seconds or until blended. Beat in vanilla and eggs, one at a time. Stir in chocolate chips. Pour into pan.

3 Bake 1 hour to 1 hour 15 minutes or until puffed and light golden brown. Turn oven off; let cake stand in oven 15 minutes with door open at least 4 inches. Remove from oven; run knife around inside edge of pan. Cool on wire rack. Refrigerate leftovers.

1 SERVING: Calories 460; Total Fat 26g (Saturated Fat 15g; Trans Fat ½g); Cholesterol 130mg; Sodium 350mg; Total Carbohydrate 50g (Dietary Fiber 0g); Protein 6g EXCHANGES: 1 Starch; 2½ Other Carbohydrate; ½ High-Fat Meat; 4 Fat CARBOHYDRATE CHOICES: 3

holiday layer bars

PREP TIME: 15 minutes *START TO FINISH:* 1 hour 55 minutes [36 BARS]

1 box (19 oz) Betty Crocker® Gluten Free chocolate chip cookie mix

½ cup butter, softened

1 egg

1 cup white vanilla baking chips (6 oz)

1¼ cups flaked coconut

½ cup chopped red or green candied cherries

¾ cup chopped cashews

1 can (14 oz) sweetened condensed milk (not evaporated)

1 Heat oven to 350°F (325°F for dark or nonstick pan). Line bottom of 13 × 9-inch pan with foil; spray with cooking spray without flour. In large bowl, stir cookie mix, butter and egg until soft dough forms. Press dough in bottom of pan. Bake 10 minutes.

2 Sprinkle baking chips, coconut, cherries and cashews evenly over partially baked crust. Pour condensed milk evenly over mixture.

3 Bake 25 to 35 minutes longer or until light golden brown, covering edges with strips of foil if necessary to prevent excessive browning. Cool completely, about 1 hour. For bars, cut into 6 rows by 6 rows.

1 BAR: Calories 200; Total Fat 10g (Saturated Fat 6g; Trans Fat 0g); Cholesterol 15mg; Sodium 120mg; Total Carbohydrate 25g (Dietary Fiber 0g); Protein 2g EXCHANGES: ½ Starch; 1 Other Carbohydrate; 2 Fat CARBOHYDRATE CHOICES: 1½

pumpkin streusel cheesecake bars

PREP TIME: 45 minutes *START TO FINISH:* 3 hours 50 minutes [24 BARS]

- 1 box Betty Crocker® Gluten Free yellow cake mix
- ½ cup finely chopped pecans
- ½ cup butter, softened
- 2 packages (8 oz each) cream cheese, softened
- 1 cup sugar
- 1 cup canned pumpkin (not pumpkin pie mix)
- 1 tablespoon pumpkin pie spice
- 2 tablespoons whipping cream
- 2 eggs

1 Heat oven to 350°F (325°F for dark or nonstick pan). In medium bowl, stir together cake mix and pecans. With pastry blender or fork, cut in butter until mixture is crumbly. Reserve 1 cup mixture for topping. In bottom of ungreased 13 × 9-inch pan, press remaining mixture. Bake 10 minutes.

2 In large bowl, beat cream cheese and sugar with electric mixer on medium speed until smooth. Add remaining ingredients; beat until well blended. Pour over warm crust. Sprinkle with reserved topping.

3 Bake about 35 minutes or until center is set. Cool 30 minutes. Refrigerate about 2 hours or until chilled. For bars, cut into 6 rows by 4 rows. Store covered in refrigerator.

1 BAR: Calories 230; Total Fat 13g (Saturated Fat 7g; Trans Fat 0g); Cholesterol 50mg; Sodium 190mg; Total Carbohydrate 26g (Dietary Fiber 0g); Protein 2g EXCHANGES: ½ Starch; 1 Other Carbohydrate; 2½ Fat CARBOHYDRATE CHOICES: 2

sweet note No need to say no to dessert while on a gluten-free diet. Try our spicy pumpkin bars made with Betty Crocker® Gluten Free cake mix.

sugar cookies

PREP TIME: 40 minutes *START TO FINISH:* 40 minutes [18 COOKIES]

1 box Betty Crocker® Gluten Free yellow cake mix

½ cup butter, softened

1 teaspoon gluten-free vanilla

1 egg

Colored sugar

1 Heat oven to 350°F (325°F for dark or nonstick pans). In large bowl, stir all ingredients except colored sugar with spoon until dough forms.

2 Shape dough by teaspoonfuls into balls. On ungreased cookie sheets, place balls 2 inches apart. Flatten with bottom of glass dipped in colored sugar.

3 Bake 9 to 11 minutes or until set. Cool 2 minutes; carefully remove from cookie sheets to cooling racks.

1 COOKIE: Calories 140; Total Fat 5g (Saturated Fat 3½g; Trans Fat 0g); Cholesterol 25mg; Sodium 170mg; Total Carbohydrate 21g (Dietary Fiber 0g); Protein 1g EXCHANGES: 1 Starch; ½ Other Carbohydrate; 1 Fat CARBOHYDRATE CHOICES: 1½

sweet note Yes! A gluten-free sugar cookie at last! Thanks to an awesome gluten-free cake mix.

apple streusel cheesecake bars

PREP TIME: 20 minutes *START TO FINISH:* 3 hours 30 minutes [24 BARS]

1 box Betty Crocker® Gluten Free yellow cake mix

½ cup cold butter

2 packages (8 oz each) cream cheese, softened

½ cup sugar

1 teaspoon gluten-free vanilla

1 egg

1 can (21 oz) apple pie filling

½ teaspoon ground cinnamon

⅓ cup chopped walnuts

1 Heat oven to 350°F (325°F for dark or nonstick pan). Spray bottom and sides of 13 × 9-inch pan with cooking spray without flour.

2 Place cake mix in large bowl. With pastry blender or fork, cut in butter until mixture is crumbly and coarse. Reserve 1½ cups crumb mixture; press remaining crumbs in bottom of pan. Bake 10 minutes.

3 Meanwhile, in large bowl, beat cream cheese, sugar, vanilla and egg with electric mixer on medium speed until smooth.

4 Spread cream cheese mixture evenly over partially baked crust. In medium bowl, mix pie filling and cinnamon. Spoon evenly over cream cheese mixture. Sprinkle reserved crumbs over top. Sprinkle with walnuts.

5 Bake 35 to 40 minutes longer or until light golden brown. Cool about 30 minutes. Refrigerate to chill, about 2 hours. For bars, cut into 6 rows by 4 rows. Store covered in refrigerator.

1 BAR: Calories 230; Total Fat 12g (Saturated Fat 6g; Trans Fat 0g); Cholesterol 40mg; Sodium 190mg; Total Carbohydrate 28g (Dietary Fiber 0g); Protein 2g EXCHANGES: 1½ Other Carbohydrate; ½ Milk; 1½ Fat CARBOHYDRATE CHOICES: 2

sweet note Challenged with a sweet tooth on a gluten-free diet? Try our yummy apple bars thanks to Betty Crocker® Gluten Free cake mix.

easy grasshopper bars

PREP TIME: 20 minutes *START TO FINISH:* 1 hour 15 minutes [36 BARS]

Bars

1 box Betty Crocker® Gluten Free devil's food cake mix

⅓ cup vegetable oil

2 tablespoons water

1 egg

Frosting

1 container (1 lb) Betty Crocker® Rich & Creamy cream cheese frosting

¼ teaspoon mint extract

3 to 4 drops green food color

Glaze

1 oz unsweetened baking chocolate

1 tablespoon butter

1 Heat oven to 350°F (325°F for dark or nonstick pan). Spray bottom only of 13 × 9-inch pan with cooking spray without flour. In large bowl, stir bar ingredients until soft dough forms. Press dough in bottom of pan. Bake 15 minutes. Cool about 10 minutes.

2 In frosting container, stir in mint extract and food color. Spread over bars.

3 In small microwavable bowl, microwave glaze ingredients uncovered on High 30 seconds; stir until smooth. Drizzle over frosting. Refrigerate 30 minutes or until set. For bars, cut into 6 rows by 6 rows.

1 BAR: Calories 120; Total Fat 5g (Saturated Fat 1g; Trans Fat ½g); Cholesterol 5mg; Sodium 95mg; Total Carbohydrate 19g (Dietary Fiber 0g); Protein 0g EXCHANGES: ½ Starch; 1 Other Carbohydrate; 1 Fat CARBOHYDRATE CHOICES: 1

sweet note Chocolate drizzle and cool minty cream cheese frosting top indulgent chocolate bars. *Mmm!*

harvest pumpkin-spice bars

PREP TIME: 15 minutes *START TO FINISH:* 2 hours 40 minutes [49 BARS]

1 Heat oven to 350°F (325°F for dark or nonstick pan). Lightly grease bottom and sides of 15 × 10-inch pan with shortening or cooking spray without flour.

2 In large bowl, beat all bar ingredients except raisins with electric mixer on low speed 30 seconds, then on medium speed 2 minutes, scraping bowl occasionally. Stir in raisins. Spread in pan.

3 Bake 20 to 25 minutes or until light brown. Cool completely in pan on cooling rack, about 2 hours.

4 Spread frosting over bars. Sprinkle with walnuts. For bars, cut into 7 rows by 7 rows. Store in refrigerator.

1 BAR: Calories 90; Total Fat 3½g (Saturated Fat 1½g; Trans Fat ½g); Cholesterol 20mg; Sodium 85mg; Total Carbohydrate 14g (Dietary Fiber 0g); Protein 0g EXCHANGES: ½ Starch; ½ Other Carbohydrate; ½ Fat CARBOHYDRATE CHOICES: 1

sweet note You'll fall in love with these pumpkin bars! They have a light texture, are full of cinnamon, ginger, raisins and nuts and are topped with cream cheese frosting.

Bars

1 box Betty Crocker® Gluten Free yellow cake mix

1 can (15 oz) pumpkin (not pumpkin pie mix)

½ cup butter, softened

¼ cup water

2 teaspoons ground cinnamon

½ teaspoon ground ginger

¼ teaspoon ground cloves

3 eggs

1 cup raisins, if desired

Frosting

1 container (1 lb) Betty Crocker® Rich & Creamy cream cheese frosting

¼ cup chopped walnuts, if desired

lemon lover's cupcakes with lemon buttercream frosting

PREP TIME: 20 minutes *START TO FINISH:* 1 hour 20 minutes [12 CUPCAKES]

Cupcakes

1 box Betty Crocker® Gluten Free yellow cake mix

⅔ cup water

½ cup butter, melted

3 eggs, beaten

2 tablespoons grated lemon peel

Frosting

2 cups gluten-free powdered sugar

¼ cup butter, softened

2 to 3 tablespoons fresh lemon juice

1 teaspoon grated lemon peel

1 Heat oven to 350°F (325°F for dark or nonstick pan). Place paper baking cup in each of 12 regular-size muffin cups.

2 In large bowl, stir cake mix, water, ½ cup melted butter, the eggs and lemon peel just until dry ingredients are moistened. Divide batter evenly among muffin cups.

3 Bake 18 to 23 minutes or until toothpick inserted in center comes out clean. Cool 10 minutes; remove from pan to cooling rack. Cool completely, about 30 minutes.

4 In medium bowl, beat powdered sugar, ¼ cup butter and 1 tablespoon of the lemon juice with electric mixer on low speed until mixed. Add remaining lemon juice, 1 teaspoon at a time, until creamy and smooth. Beat in 1 teaspoon peel. Frost cupcakes with frosting.

1 CUPCAKE: Calories 330; Total Fat 13g (Saturated Fat 8g; Trans Fat 0g); Cholesterol 85mg; Sodium 290mg; Total Carbohydrate 51g (Dietary Fiber 0g); Protein 2g
EXCHANGES: ½ Starch; 3 Other Carbohydrate; 2½ Fat CARBOHYDRATE CHOICES: 3½

sweet note Stir up Betty Crocker® Gluten Free yellow cake mix with fresh lemon to create delicious cupcakes.

pineapple upside-down cake

PREP TIME: 15 minutes *START TO FINISH:* 1 hour 30 minutes [9 SERVINGS]

- ¼ cup butter
- ⅔ cup packed brown sugar
- 2 tablespoons light corn syrup
- 9 slices pineapple in juice (from 16-oz can), drained
- 9 maraschino cherries, drained
- 1 box Betty Crocker® Gluten Free yellow cake mix
- ½ cup butter, softened
- ⅔ cup water
- 2 teaspoons gluten-free vanilla
- 3 eggs

1 Heat oven to 350°F (325°F for dark or nonstick pan). In 9-inch square pan, melt ¼ cup butter in oven. Stir in brown sugar and corn syrup; spread evenly in pan. Arrange pineapple slices on brown sugar mixture. Place cherry in center of each pineapple slice.

2 In large bowl, beat cake mix, ½ cup butter, water, vanilla and eggs with electric mixer on low speed 30 seconds, then on medium speed 2 minutes, scraping bowl occasionally. Pour batter over pineapple and cherries.

3 Bake 38 to 43 minutes or until surface is golden brown and toothpick inserted in center comes out clean. Immediately run knife around side of pan to loosen cake. Place heatproof serving plate upside down onto pan; turn plate and pan over. Leave pan over cake 5 minutes so brown sugar topping can drizzle over cake. Remove pan; cool 30 minutes. Serve warm or cool. Store covered in refrigerator.

1 SERVING: Calories 440; Total Fat 17g (Saturated Fat 10g; Trans Fat ½g); Cholesterol 110mg; Sodium 390mg; Total Carbohydrate 68g (Dietary Fiber 0g); Protein 3g EXCHANGES: 1 Starch; ½ Fruit; 3 Other Carbohydrate; 3½ Fat CARBOHYDRATE CHOICES: 4½

sweet note Whip up Betty Crocker® Gluten Free yellow cake mix to create a delicious fruit-topped dessert.

celebration trifle

PREP TIME: 30 minutes *START TO FINISH:* 3 hours 30 minutes [10 SERVINGS]

- 1 box Betty Crocker® Gluten Free yellow cake mix
- Water, butter, gluten-free vanilla and eggs as called for on cake mix box
- ½ cup granulated sugar
- ¼ cup cornstarch
- 2 cups milk
- 2 eggs, lightly beaten
- 2 tablespoons butter
- 1 teaspoon gluten-free vanilla
- ¾ cup whipping cream
- ¼ cup raspberry-flavored liqueur, brandy or apple juice concentrate, thawed
- 2 cups raspberries or sliced strawberries
- 2 mangoes, peeled and cut up
- ½ cup sweetened coconut, toasted

1 Heat oven to 350°F (325°F for dark or nonstick pan). Grease bottom only of 8- or 9-inch square pan. Make and bake cake as directed on box using water, butter, vanilla and eggs. Run knife around sides of pan to loosen cake. Cool 1 hour. Cut cake into 1-inch pieces; set aside.

2 Meanwhile, in 2-quart heavy saucepan, stir together sugar and cornstarch; stir in milk. Cook and stir over medium heat until thickened and bubbly. In medium bowl, beat 2 eggs with wire whisk just until blended. Gradually stir 1 cup hot milk mixture into egg mixture, whisking constantly, until combined. Pour milk and egg mixture back into saucepan. Return to medium heat. Cook, stirring constantly, 1 to 2 minutes longer, or until thick and bubbly. Remove from heat. Stir in butter and vanilla. Press plastic wrap on filling to prevent a tough layer from forming on top. Refrigerate at least 1 hour.

3 In medium bowl, whip cream until stiff peaks form. Fold whipped cream into pudding mixture until combined.

4 In large bowl or trifle bowl, place half of the cake pieces. Brush or sprinkle half the liqueur over cake. Spoon half the berries, half the mangoes and half the coconut over cake. Spread half the pudding mixture over coconut. Repeat with remaining cake, liqueur, berries, mangoes and coconut. Cover; refrigerate at least 1 hour before serving. Garnish with additional fruit and coconut, if desired. Refrigerate any remaining trifle.

1 SERVING: Calories 480; Total Fat 23g (Saturated Fat 14g; Trans Fat ½g); Cholesterol 160mg; Sodium 380mg; Total Carbohydrate 58g (Dietary Fiber 2g); Protein 7g EXCHANGES: 2 Starch; 1 Fruit; 1 Other Carbohydrate; 4½ Fat CARBOHYDRATE CHOICES: 4

sweet note Make a sweet statement with this fabulous and fruity trifle with an easy homemade pastry cream.

banana cupcakes with browned butter frosting

PREP TIME: 20 minutes *START TO FINISH:* 1 hour 25 minutes [17 CUPCAKES]

Cupcakes

- 1 box Betty Crocker® Gluten Free yellow cake mix
- 1 cup mashed ripe bananas (2 medium)
- ⅓ cup butter, melted
- ⅓ cup water
- 3 eggs, beaten
- 2 teaspoons gluten-free vanilla

Frosting

- ⅓ cup butter
- 3 cups gluten-free powdered sugar
- 1 teaspoon gluten-free vanilla
- 3 to 4 tablespoons milk

1 Heat oven to 350°F. Place paper baking cups in each of 17 regular-size muffin cups. In large bowl, stir cupcake ingredients just until dry ingredients are moistened. Spoon batter evenly into muffin cups.

2 Bake 16 to 18 minutes or until toothpick inserted in center comes out clean. Remove from pan to cooling rack. Cool completely, about 30 minutes.

3 In 1-quart saucepan, heat ⅓ cup butter over medium heat just until light brown, stirring occasionally. (Watch carefully because butter can burn quickly.) Remove from heat. Cool slightly, about 5 minutes.

4 In medium bowl, beat browned butter, powdered sugar, 1 teaspoon vanilla and enough milk until smooth and spreadable. Spread frosting over cooled cupcakes.

1 CUPCAKE: Calories 270; Total Fat 8g (Saturated Fat 5g; Trans Fat 0g); Cholesterol 55mg; Sodium 200mg; Total Carbohydrate 46g (Dietary Fiber 0g); Protein 2g EXCHANGES: ½ Starch; 2½ Other Carbohydrate; 1½ Fat CARBOHYDRATE CHOICES: 3

sweet note Ripe bananas? Mix them with Betty Crocker® Gluten Free yellow cake mix and create delicious homemade cupcakes.

carrot cake

PREP TIME: 15 minutes *START TO FINISH:* 1 hour 55 minutes [12 SERVINGS]

Cake

1 box Betty Crocker® Gluten Free yellow cake mix

⅔ cup water

½ cup butter, softened

½ teaspoon ground cinnamon

¼ teaspoon ground nutmeg

2 teaspoons gluten-free vanilla

3 eggs

1 cup finely shredded carrots (2 medium)

¼ cup finely chopped pecans or walnuts

Frosting

4 oz (half of 8-oz package) cream cheese, softened

2 tablespoons butter

½ teaspoon gluten-free vanilla

1 to 3 teaspoons milk

2 cups gluten-free powdered sugar

¼ cup coconut, if desired

1 Heat oven to 350°F (325°F for dark or nonstick pan). Grease bottom only of 8- or 9-inch square pan with shortening, or spray with cooking spray without flour.

2 In large bowl, beat cake mix, water, ½ cup butter, cinnamon, nutmeg, 2 teaspoons vanilla and eggs on low speed 30 seconds. Beat on medium speed 2 minutes, scraping bowl occasionally. With spoon, stir in carrots and pecans. Spread in pan.

3 Bake 36 to 41 minutes for 8-inch pan, 33 to 38 minutes for 9-inch pan, or until toothpick comes out clean. Cool completely, about 1 hour.

4 In large bowl, beat cream cheese, 2 tablespoons butter, ½ teaspoon vanilla and 1 teaspoon milk with electric mixer on low speed until smooth. Gradually beat in powdered sugar, 1 cup at a time, until smooth and spreadable. If frosting is too thick, beat in more milk, a few drops at a time. Stir in coconut. Spread frosting over cake.

1 SERVING: Calories 420; Total Fat 16g (Saturated Fat 9g; Trans Fat 0g); Cholesterol 90mg; Sodium 310mg; Total Carbohydrate 66g (Dietary Fiber 0g); Protein 3g EXCHANGES: 1 Starch; 3½ Other Carbohydrate; 3 Fat CARBOHYDRATE CHOICES: 4½

sweet note Finely shredding the carrot and finely chopping the nuts spreads their goodness through the whole cake and makes it easier to cut, too.

marble cake

PREP TIME: 20 minutes *START TO FINISH:* 2 hours 20 minutes [12 SERVINGS]

Yellow Cake

1 box Betty Crocker® Gluten Free yellow cake mix

½ cup butter, softened

⅔ cup water

2 teaspoons gluten-free vanilla

3 eggs

Devil's Food Cake

1 box Betty Crocker® Gluten Free devil's food cake mix

½ cup butter, softened

1 cup water

3 eggs

Chocolate Frosting

3 cups gluten-free powdered sugar

⅓ cup butter, softened

2 teaspoons gluten-free vanilla

3 oz unsweetened baking chocolate, melted, cooled

3 to 4 tablespoons milk

1 Heat oven to 350°F (325°F for dark or nonstick pans). Grease bottoms only of two 8- or 9-inch round cake pans with shortening or cooking spray without flour.

2 In large bowl, beat yellow cake ingredients with electric mixer on low speed 30 seconds, then on medium speed 2 minutes, scraping bowl occasionally. Set aside.

3 In another large bowl, beat devil's food cake ingredients on low speed 30 seconds, then on medium speed 2 minutes, scraping bowl occasionally.

4 Spoon yellow and devil's food batters alternately into pans, dividing evenly. Cut through batters with table knife in zigzag pattern for marbled design.

5 Bake 40 to 45 minutes or until toothpick inserted in center comes out clean. Cool in pans on cooling racks 15 minutes. Remove from pans. Cool completely, top sides up, about 1 hour.

6 In medium bowl, beat powdered sugar and ⅓ cup butter with spoon or electric mixer on low speed until blended. Stir in 2 teaspoons vanilla and the chocolate. Gradually beat in just enough milk to make frosting smooth and spreadable.

7 On serving plate, place 1 cake, rounded side down (trim rounded side if necessary so cake rests flat). Spread with ¼ cup frosting. Top with second cake, rounded side up. Frost side and top of cake with remaining frosting.

1 SERVING: Calories 490; Total Fat 21g (Saturated Fat 12g; Trans Fat ½g); Cholesterol 120mg; Sodium 430mg; Total Carbohydrate 70g (Dietary Fiber 1g); Protein 4g EXCHANGES: 1½ Starch; 3 Other Carbohydrate; 4 Fat CARBOHYDRATE CHOICES: 4½

sweet note Butter is recommended for the success of this recipe.

valentine confetti cupcakes

PREP TIME: 25 minutes *START TO FINISH:* 1 hour 30 minutes [16 CUPCAKES]

- 1 box Betty Crocker® Gluten Free devil's food cake mix
- Water, butter and eggs called for on cake mix box
- 1 container (12 oz) Betty Crocker® Whipped fluffy white frosting
- 1 box (4.5 oz) Betty Crocker® Fruit by the Foot® strawberry chewy fruit snack
- Decorative paper scissors
- Heart-shape paper punch

1 Heat oven to 350°F (325°F for dark or nonstick pan). Place paper baking cup in each of 16 regular-size muffin cups. Make cake mix as directed on box, using water, butter and eggs. Divide batter evenly among muffin cups.

2 Bake 15 to 20 minutes or until toothpick inserted in center comes out clean. Cool 10 minutes; remove from pan to cooling rack. Cool completely, about 30 minutes.

3 Frost cupcakes with frosting. Cut some of the wrapped fruit snacks with decorative scissors into 1 × ¼-inch strips for streamers and punch heart shapes from some; remove wrappers. Arrange streamers and hearts on each cupcake.

1 CUPCAKE: Calories 290; Total Fat 12g (Saturated Fat 6g; Trans Fat 1½g); Cholesterol 55mg; Sodium 240mg; Total Carbohydrate 42g (Dietary Fiber 0g); Protein 2g
EXCHANGES: 1 Starch; 2 Other Carbohydrate; 2 Fat CARBOHYDRATE CHOICES: 3

sweet note Whip up a batch of gluten-free cupcakes and decorate them with fun snips of fruit snack.

chocolate-hazelnut dream torte

PREP TIME: 30 minutes *START TO FINISH:* 2 hours 10 minutes [10 SERVINGS]

⅔ cup whole hazelnuts

1 box Betty Crocker® Gluten Free devil's food cake mix

1 cup water

½ cup butter, softened

3 eggs

1 can (14 oz) sweetened condensed milk (not evaporated)

2 squares (1 oz each) white chocolate, chopped

1 teaspoon gluten-free vanilla

1 Heat oven to 350°F. Place hazelnuts in single layer in shallow baking pan. Toast hazelnuts 8 to 10 minutes or until golden brown and aromatic. Transfer hot nuts to several thicknesses of paper towels. Rub hazelnuts together to remove skins. Let cool. In food processor or blender, grind half of the hazelnuts finely. Chop remaining hazelnuts; set aside.

2 Generously grease bottom only of 8- or 9-inch round pan. (Lower oven temperature to 325°F if using dark or nonstick pan.)

3 In large bowl, beat ground hazelnuts, cake mix, water, butter and eggs on low speed of electric mixer 30 seconds, then on medium speed 2 minutes, scraping bowl occasionally. Pour into pan. Bake 43 to 48 minutes or until toothpick inserted in center comes out clean. Cool 10 minutes; run knife around inside edge of pan; remove from pan to wire rack. Cool completely.

4 In small heavy saucepan, heat sweetened condensed milk and white chocolate over medium heat until chocolate melts. Cook and stir over medium-low heat about 7 to 10 minutes longer or just until thickened. Remove from heat; cool 10 minutes. Stir in vanilla.

5 Cut cooled cake in half horizontally. Place bottom layer, cut side up, on serving plate; spread half the white chocolate mixture over cake; sprinkle with half the chopped hazelnuts. Top with remaining cake half, cut side down. Spread remaining white chocolate mixture over top (some may drip down side). Sprinkle with remaining hazelnuts. Refrigerate any remaining cake.

1 SERVING: Calories 490; Total Fat 23g (Saturated Fat 11g; Trans Fat 0g); Cholesterol 105mg; Sodium 380mg; Total Carbohydrate 63g (Dietary Fiber 2g); Protein 7g EXCHANGES: 1 Starch; 3 Other Carbohydrate; ½ High-Fat Meat; 4 Fat CARBOHYDRATE CHOICES: 4

sweet note Delight hazelnut lovers with this decadent torte filled and topped with white chocolate glaze.

cappuccino flats

PREP TIME: 1 hour *10 minutes* *START TO FINISH:* 3 hours 40 minutes [40 COOKIES]

- 2 cups Bisquick® Gluten Free mix
- 1 teaspoon ground cinnamon
- 1 tablespoon instant coffee granules or crystals
- 1 teaspoon hot water
- 1 cup butter, softened
- ½ cup granulated sugar
- ½ cup packed brown sugar
- 1 egg
- 2 oz unsweetened baking chocolate, melted and cooled
- 1¼ cups semisweet chocolate chips
- ⅓ cup shortening

1 In small bowl, mix Bisquick mix and cinnamon. In another small bowl, dissolve coffee granules in water. In large bowl, beat butter, granulated sugar, brown sugar, egg and dissolved coffee with electric mixer on low speed until blended. Add melted chocolate and Bisquick mixture; mix just until soft dough forms. Refrigerate 1 hour.

2 Place half the dough on 16-inch length of waxed paper. Use waxed paper to shape dough into a roll, 5 inches long and 2 inches in diameter. Wrap in waxed paper. Repeat with remaining half of dough. Refrigerate about 1 hour or until firm.

3 Heat oven to 300°F. Cut dough into ¼-inch slices with sharp knife. On ungreased cookie sheet, place slices 1 inch apart.

4 Bake 9 to 10 minutes or until set. Cool 5 minutes on cookie sheet. Carefully remove to cooling rack. Cool 30 minutes before dipping.

5 In small shallow microwavable bowl, microwave chocolate chips and shortening uncovered on High about 1 minute or until softened; stir until smooth. Dip half of each cookie into chocolate, allowing excess to drip back into dish. Place on waxed paper; let stand about 30 minutes or until chocolate is set.

1 COOKIE: Calories 140; Total Fat 8g (Saturated Fat 4½g; Trans Fat 0g); Cholesterol 20mg; Sodium 105mg; Total Carbohydrate 14g (Dietary Fiber 0g); Protein 1g EXCHANGES: ½ Starch; ½ Other Carbohydrate; 1½ Fat CARBOHYDRATE CHOICES: 1

better-than-almost-anything cake

PREP TIME: 20 minutes *START TO FINISH:* 3 hours [9 SERVINGS]

- 1 box Betty Crocker® Gluten Free devil's food cake mix
- Water, butter and eggs called for on cake mix box
- 1 jar (12.25 oz) caramel topping
- 1 cup frozen (thawed) whipped topping
- ½ cup toffee bits

1 Heat oven to 350°F (325°F for dark or nonstick pan). Make and bake cake mix as directed on box, using water, butter, eggs and any of the pan choices.

2 With handle of wooden spoon, poke top of warm cake every ½ inch. Drizzle caramel topping evenly over top of cake; let stand until absorbed into cake. Cover; refrigerate about 2 hours or until chilled.

3 Spread whipped topping over top of cake. Sprinkle with toffee bits. Store covered in refrigerator.

1 SERVING: Calories 520; Total Fat 21g (Saturated Fat 13g; Trans Fat ½g); Cholesterol 115mg; Sodium 520mg; Total Carbohydrate 80g (Dietary Fiber 1g); Protein 4g
EXCHANGES: 1½ Starch; 4 Other Carbohydrate; 4 Fat CARBOHYDRATE CHOICES: 5

sweet note The combination of rich ingredients produces a decadent, caramel-soaked cake that's sure to be a hit!

chocolate-orange cake

PREP TIME: 15 minutes *START TO FINISH:* 2 hours [12 SERVINGS]

Cake

1 box Betty Crocker® Gluten Free devil's food cake mix

½ cup butter, softened

1 cup orange juice

3 eggs

1 tablespoon grated orange peel

Frosting

2 cups gluten-free powdered sugar

¼ cup butter, softened

1 to 2 tablespoons orange juice

1 teaspoon grated orange peel

Additional orange peel or mandarin orange segments, if desired

1 Heat oven to 350°F (325°F for dark or nonstick pan). Grease bottom only of 8- or 9-inch square pan. In large bowl, beat cake ingredients on low speed 30 seconds. Beat on medium speed 2 minutes. Pour into pan.

2 Bake 44 to 49 minutes for 8-inch pan, 38 to 43 minutes for 9-inch pan, until toothpick inserted in center comes out clean. Cool completely, about 1 hour.

3 In medium bowl, beat powdered sugar, ¼ cup butter and 1 tablespoon of the orange juice with electric mixer on low speed until mixed. Add remaining orange juice, 1 teaspoon at a time, until creamy and smooth. Beat in 1 teaspoon orange peel. Spread frosting on cooled cake. Garnish with orange peel or mandarin orange segments.

1 SERVING: Calories 340; Total Fat 14g (Saturated Fat 8g; Trans Fat 0g); Cholesterol 85mg; Sodium 300mg; Total Carbohydrate 52g (Dietary Fiber 1g); Protein 2g EXCHANGES: ½ Starch; 3 Other Carbohydrate; 2½ Fat CARBOHYDRATE CHOICES: 3½

sweet note Whip up a delicious cake with an orange accent using Betty Crocker® Gluten Free devil's food cake mix.

zucchini–devil's food snack cake

PREP TIME: 15 minutes *START TO FINISH:* 1 hour 5 minutes [12 SERVINGS]

Cake

1 box Betty Crocker® Gluten Free devil's food cake mix

½ cup butter, softened

1 cup shredded unpeeled zucchini (about 1 medium)

½ teaspoon ground cinnamon

⅛ teaspoon ground cloves

⅓ cup water

3 eggs

Streusel

¼ cup packed brown sugar

2 tablespoons butter, softened

¼ cup chopped walnuts or pecans

1 Heat oven to 350°F (325°F for dark or nonstick pan). Grease bottom only of 8- or 9-inch square pan with shortening or cooking spray.

2 Reserve ¼ cup cake mix for streusel; set aside. In large bowl, beat remaining cake mix, ½ cup butter, zucchini, cinnamon, cloves, water and eggs on low speed 30 seconds, then on medium speed 2 minutes, scraping bowl occasionally. Spread in pan.

3 In small bowl, mix reserved ¼ cup cake mix and streusel ingredients with fork until mixture is crumbly. Sprinkle over batter.

4 Bake 44 to 49 minutes for 8-inch pan, 38 to 43 minutes for 9-inch pan, until toothpick inserted in center comes out clean. Serve warm or cool.

1 SERVING: Calories 270; Total Fat 13g (Saturated Fat 7g; Trans Fat 0g); Cholesterol 80mg; Sodium 290mg; Total Carbohydrate 35g (Dietary Fiber 1g); Protein 3g EXCHANGES: ½ Starch; 2 Other Carbohydrate; 2½ Fat CARBOHYDRATE CHOICES: 2

sweet note Whip up a sweet snack using Betty Crocker® Gluten Free devil's food cake mix.

eggnog breakfast cake

PREP TIME: 30 minutes *START TO FINISH:* 2 hours 10 minutes [10 SERVINGS]

- 1 box Betty Crocker® Gluten Free yellow cake mix
- ⅔ cup milk
- ½ cup butter, softened
- 1½ teaspoons rum extract
- 1 teaspoon gluten-free vanilla
- ¼ teaspoon ground nutmeg
- 3 eggs
- ¼ cup Betty Crocker® Rich & Creamy vanilla frosting (from 1-lb container)
- ⅓ cup chopped pecans

1 Heat oven to 350°F (325°F for dark or nonstick pan). Grease bottom only of 8- or 9-inch round or square pan. Beat cake mix, milk, butter, extracts, nutmeg and eggs in large bowl on low speed 30 seconds, then on medium speed 2 minutes, scraping bowl occasionally. Pour into pan.

2 Bake 33 to 41 minutes or until toothpick inserted in center comes out clean. Cool 10 minutes. Run knife around inside edge of pan. Cool 30 minutes longer.

3 Heat frosting in microwavable bowl 10 to 15 seconds or until easy to drizzle. Drizzle frosting over cake; sprinkle with pecans.

1 SERVING: Calories 320; Total Fat 15g (Saturated Fat 7g; Trans Fat 1g); Cholesterol 90mg; Sodium 330mg; Total Carbohydrate 43g (Dietary Fiber 0g); Protein 4g EXCHANGES: 1 Starch; 2 Other Carbohydrate; 3 Fat CARBOHYDRATE CHOICES: 3

sweet note For an indulgent treat, use candied pecans. Just make sure they're labeled gluten free.

chocolate chip–cherry cobbler

PREP TIME: 15 minutes *START TO FINISH:* 55 minutes [6 SERVINGS]

Fruit Mixture

- 1 can (21 oz) cherry pie filling
- 2 tablespoons orange juice
- ½ teaspoon almond extract

Topping

- 1 cup Bisquick® Gluten Free mix
- 1 cup whipping cream
- 2 tablespoons sugar
- 2 tablespoons butter, softened
- ¼ cup miniature semisweet chocolate chips
- ½ teaspoon sugar

1 Heat oven to 350°F. In ungreased 1½-quart casserole, mix fruit mixture ingredients. Microwave uncovered on High about 4 minutes or until bubbly around edge; stir.

2 In medium bowl, mix all topping ingredients except ½ teaspoon sugar with spoon until stiff dough forms. Drop dough by 6 spoonfuls (about ¼ cup each) onto warm fruit mixture. Sprinkle ½ teaspoon sugar over dough.

3 Bake 35 to 40 minutes or until topping is golden brown. Serve warm.

1 SERVING: Calories 480; Total Fat 19g (Saturated Fat 11g; Trans Fat ½g); Cholesterol 55mg; Sodium 270mg; Total Carbohydrate 75g (Dietary Fiber 3g); Protein 3g EXCHANGES: 2 Starch; 3 Other Carbohydrate; 3½ Fat CARBOHYDRATE CHOICES: 5

sweet note Looking for a fruit dessert? Then check out this cherry cobbler recipe using Bisquick® Gluten Free mix that can be ready in less than an hour.

snickerdoodles

PREP TIME: 50 minutes *START TO FINISH:* 50 minutes [30 COOKIES]

2 eggs
1 cup sugar
¼ cup butter, softened
¼ cup shortening
2 cups Bisquick® Gluten Free mix
¼ cup sugar
2 teaspoons ground cinnamon

1 Heat oven to 375°F (325°F for dark or nonstick pans). In large bowl, mix eggs, 1 cup sugar, the butter and shortening. Stir in Bisquick mix until dough forms.

2 In small bowl, mix ¼ cup sugar and the cinnamon. Shape dough into 1¼-inch balls. (If dough feels too soft for shaping into balls, put dough in freezer for 10 to 15 minutes.) Roll balls in sugar-cinnamon mixture; place 2 inches apart on ungreased cookie sheets.

3 Bake 10 to 12 minutes or until set. Immediately remove from cookie sheets to cooling racks.

1 COOKIE: Calories 100; Total Fat 3½g (Saturated Fat 1½g; Trans Fat 0g); Cholesterol 20mg; Sodium 105mg; Total Carbohydrate 15g (Dietary Fiber 0g); Protein 1g EXCHANGES: ½ Starch; ½ Other Carbohydrate; ½ Fat CARBOHYDRATE CHOICES: 1

sweet note Bisquick® Gluten Free mix is the champ that creates a tasty gluten-free version of a classic cinnamon and sugar cookie.

peanut blossoms

PREP TIME: 30 minutes *START TO FINISH:* 1 hour 50 minutes [48 COOKIES]

½ cup granulated sugar

½ cup packed brown sugar

½ cup gluten-free peanut butter

¼ cup shortening

¼ cup butter, softened

1 egg

1½ cups Bisquick® Gluten Free mix

¼ cup granulated sugar

48 Hershey's® Kisses® Brand milk chocolates, unwrapped

1 In large bowl, mix ½ cup granulated sugar, the brown sugar, peanut butter, shortening, butter and egg. Stir in Bisquick mix. Cover; refrigerate 1 hour or until firm.

2 Heat oven to 375°F (325°F for dark or nonstick pans). In small bowl, place ¼ cup granulated sugar. Shape dough into 1-inch balls; roll in granulated sugar. On ungreased cookie sheets, place balls 2 inches apart.

3 Bake 8 to 10 minutes or until light golden brown. Immediately top each cookie with 1 milk chocolate candy, pressing down firmly so cookie cracks around edge. Remove from cookie sheets to cooling racks.

1 COOKIE: Calories 100; Total Fat 5g (Saturated Fat 2g; Trans Fat 0g); Cholesterol 10mg; Sodium 65mg; Total Carbohydrate 12g (Dietary Fiber 0g); Protein 1g EXCHANGES: ½ Starch; ½ Other Carbohydrate; 1 Fat CARBOHYDRATE CHOICES: 1

sweet note Try our Bisquick® Gluten Free mix cookie recipe. It's a take on a classic peanut butter and chocolate candy cookie recipe.

holiday toffee bars

PREP TIME: 15 minutes *START TO FINISH:* 1 hour 15 minutes [32 BARS]

- 1 cup butter, softened
- 1 cup packed brown sugar
- 1 teaspoon gluten-free vanilla
- 1 egg yolk
- 2 cups Bisquick® Gluten Free mix
- 1 cup milk chocolate chips
- ½ cup chopped nuts, if desired

1 Heat oven to 350°F (325°F for dark or nonstick pan). Spray 13 × 9-inch pan with cooking spray without flour. In large bowl, mix butter, brown sugar, vanilla and egg yolk. Stir in Bisquick mix. Press in pan.

2 Bake 20 to 25 minutes or until very light brown (crust will be soft). Immediately sprinkle chocolate chips on hot crust; let stand about 5 minutes or until chocolate is soft. Spread chocolate evenly; sprinkle with nuts. Cool 30 minutes in pan on cooling rack. For bars, cut into 8 rows by 4 rows.

1 BAR: Calories 140; Total Fat 8g (Saturated Fat 4½g; Trans Fat 0g); Cholesterol 25mg; Sodium 130mg; Total Carbohydrate 16g (Dietary Fiber 0g); Protein 1g EXCHANGES: ½ Starch; ½ Other Carbohydrate; 1½ Fat CARBOHYDRATE CHOICES: 1

sweet note Bisquick® Gluten Free mix makes giving gluten-free cookies not only possible but delicious.

chocolate crinkles

PREP TIME: 1 hour 20 minutes *START TO FINISH:* 4 hours 20 minutes [72 COOKIES]

½ cup vegetable oil

4 oz unsweetened baking chocolate, melted, cooled

2 cups granulated sugar

2 teaspoons gluten-free vanilla

4 eggs

2½ cups Bisquick® Gluten Free mix

½ cup gluten-free powdered sugar

1 In large bowl, mix oil, chocolate, granulated sugar and vanilla. Stir in eggs, one at a time. Stir in Bisquick mix until dough forms. Cover; refrigerate at least 3 hours.

2 Heat oven to 350°F (325°F for dark or nonstick pans). Grease cookie sheets with shortening or cooking spray without flour. Drop dough by teaspoonfuls into powdered sugar; roll around to coat and shape into balls. Place about 2 inches apart on cookie sheets.

3 Bake 10 to 12 minutes or until almost no imprint remains when touched lightly in center. Immediately remove from cookie sheets to cooling racks.

1 COOKIE: Calories 60; Total Fat 2g (Saturated Fat 0g; Trans Fat 0g); Cholesterol 10mg; Sodium 50mg; Total Carbohydrate 10g (Dietary Fiber 0g); Protein 0g EXCHANGES: ½ Other Carbohydrate; ½ Fat CARBOHYDRATE CHOICES: ½

sweet note Bisquick® Gluten Free mix creates a classic chocolate crinkle cookie kissed with powdered sugar.

impossibly easy french apple pie

PREP TIME: 25 minutes *START TO FINISH:* 1 hour 15 minutes [6 SERVINGS]

Filling

3 cups thinly sliced peeled apples (3 medium)

1 teaspoon ground cinnamon

¼ teaspoon ground nutmeg

½ cup Bisquick® Gluten Free mix

½ cup granulated sugar

½ cup milk

2 tablespoons butter or margarine, melted

3 eggs

Streusel

⅓ cup Bisquick® Gluten Free mix

⅓ cup chopped nuts

¼ cup packed brown sugar

3 tablespoons firm butter or margarine

1 Heat oven to 325°F. Spray 9-inch glass pie plate with cooking spray without flour. In medium bowl, mix apples, cinnamon and nutmeg; place in pie plate.

2 In medium bowl, stir remaining filling ingredients until well blended. Pour over apple mixture in pie plate. In small bowl, mix all streusel ingredients, using fork, until crumbly; sprinkle over filling.

3 Bake 45 to 50 minutes or until knife inserted in center comes out clean. Store in refrigerator.

1 SERVING: Calories 380; Total Fat 17g (Saturated Fat 8g; Trans Fat 0g); Cholesterol 135mg; Sodium 300mg; Total Carbohydrate 49g (Dietary Fiber 2g); Protein 6g EXCHANGES: 1½ Starch; 2 Other Carbohydrate; 3 Fat CARBOHYDRATE CHOICES: 3

sweet note Gluten-free apple pie? Try our tasty version thanks to Bisquick® Gluten Free mix.

russian tea cakes

PREP TIME: 1 hour *START TO FINISH:* 1 hour 25 minutes [48 COOKIES]

1 cup butter, softened

½ cup gluten-free powdered sugar

1 teaspoon gluten-free vanilla

1 egg

2¼ cups Bisquick® Gluten Free mix

¾ cup finely chopped nuts

⅔ cup gluten-free powdered sugar

1 Heat oven to 400°F (375°F for dark or nonstick pans). In large bowl, mix butter, ½ cup powdered sugar, the vanilla and egg. Stir in Bisquick mix and nuts until dough holds together.

2 Shape dough into 1-inch balls. On ungreased cookie sheets, place balls about 1 inch apart.

3 Bake 9 to 11 minutes or until set but not brown. Immediately remove from cookie sheets to cooling racks. Cool slightly.

4 Roll warm cookies in powdered sugar; place on cooling racks to cool completely. Roll in powdered sugar again.

1 COOKIE: Calories 80; Total Fat 5g (Saturated Fat 2½g; Trans Fat 0g); Cholesterol 15mg; Sodium 90mg; Total Carbohydrate 8g (Dietary Fiber 0g); Protein 0g EXCHANGES: ½ Starch; 1 Fat CARBOHYDRATE CHOICES: ½

sweet note These buttery melt-in-your-mouth cookie balls go by many names in recipe collections, including Mexican Wedding Cakes. They always contain finely chopped nuts and are twice rolled in powdered sugar. This holiday favorite is one of Betty's Best!

ultimate cutout cookies

PREP TIME: 55 minutes *START TO FINISH:* 55 minutes [18 COOKIES]

½ cup gluten-free powdered sugar

1 package (3 oz) cream cheese, softened

⅓ cup butter, softened

3 tablespoons shortening

1 teaspoon gluten-free vanilla

1 egg yolk

1½ cups Bisquick® Gluten Free mix

Additional gluten-free powdered sugar for work surface

1 container (1 lb) Betty Crocker® Rich & Creamy vanilla frosting, if desired

1 Heat oven to 375°F (325°F for dark or nonstick pans). Lightly grease cookie sheets with shortening or cooking spray without flour. In large bowl, stir ½ cup powdered sugar, cream cheese, butter, shortening, vanilla and egg yolk with spoon until well blended. Stir in Bisquick mix until dough forms.

2 On work surface sprinkled with additional powdered sugar, roll half of dough at a time to ¼-inch thickness. Cut with cookie cutters. Use metal spatula to transfer cookie cutouts to cookie sheets, placing cutouts about 1 inch apart.

3 Bake 6 to 8 minutes or until edges are light golden brown. Cool 2 minutes; carefully remove from cookie sheets to cooling racks. Cool completely, about 15 minutes. Spread frosting on cookies.

1 COOKIE: Calories 120; Total Fat 8g (Saturated Fat 3½g; Trans Fat ½g); Cholesterol 25mg; Sodium 140mg; Total Carbohydrate 11g (Dietary Fiber 0g); Protein 1g EXCHANGES: ½ Starch; 1½ Fat CARBOHYDRATE CHOICES: 1

sweet note You can enjoy sugar cookies and still be gluten free thanks to Bisquick® Gluten Free mix.

apple crisp

PREP TIME: 15 minutes *START TO FINISH:* 1 hour [12 SERVINGS]

Apples

6 large tart cooking apples, thinly sliced

1 teaspoon ground cinnamon

Topping

1 box Betty Crocker® Gluten Free yellow cake mix

½ cup chopped nuts

½ cup butter, softened

1 teaspoon ground cinnamon

1 egg, beaten

Ice cream, if desired

1 Heat oven to 350°F (325°F for dark or nonstick pan). In large bowl, toss apples and 1 teaspoon cinnamon. Spread apples evenly in ungreased 13 × 9-inch pan.

2 In large bowl, mix cake mix and nuts. With pastry blender or fork, cut in butter until crumbly. Add 1 teaspoon cinnamon and the egg; mix well. Sprinkle evenly over apples.

3 Bake about 45 minutes or until topping is light brown. Serve warm with ice cream.

1 SERVING: Calories 300; Total Fat 11g (Saturated Fat 5g; Trans Fat 0g); Cholesterol 40mg; Sodium 250mg; Total Carbohydrate 46g (Dietary Fiber 2g); Protein 2g EXCHANGES: 1 Starch; ½ Fruit; 1½ Other Carbohydrate; 2 Fat CARBOHYDRATE CHOICES: 3

sweet note Try our yummy gluten-free apple crisp thanks to Betty Crocker® Gluten Free cake mix.

strawberry shortcakes

PREP TIME: 10 minutes *START TO FINISH:* 1 hour 25 minutes [6 SHORTCAKES]

- 4 cups (1 qt) strawberries, sliced
- ¼ cup sugar
- 2⅓ cups Bisquick® Gluten Free mix
- ¼ cup sugar
- ⅓ cup butter or margarine
- ¾ cup milk
- 3 eggs, beaten
- ½ teaspoon gluten-free vanilla
- ¾ cup whipping cream, whipped

1 In small bowl, mix strawberries and ¼ cup sugar; set aside.

2 Heat oven to 425°F. Grease cookie sheet. In medium bowl, combine Bisquick mix and ¼ cup sugar; cut in butter with pastry blender or fork. Stir in milk, eggs and vanilla. Drop by 6 spoonfuls onto cookie sheet.

3 Bake 10 to 12 minutes or until light golden brown. Cool 5 minutes. With serrated knife, split shortcakes; fill and top with strawberries and whipped cream.

1 SHORTCAKE: Calories 520; Total Fat 24g (Saturated Fat 13g; Trans Fat 1g); Cholesterol 170mg; Sodium 650mg; Total Carbohydrate 67g (Dietary Fiber 3g); Protein 8g
EXCHANGES: 1½ Starch; 2 Fruit; 1 Other Carbohydrate; ½ High-Fat Meat; 4 Fat
CARBOHYDRATE CHOICES: 4½

sweet note Bisquick® Gluten Free mix makes it easy for you to enjoy a classic dessert—strawberry shortcake.

impossibly easy coconut pie

PREP TIME: 10 minutes *START TO FINISH:* 1 hour [8 SERVINGS]

- 3 eggs
- 1¾ cups milk
- ¼ cup butter, melted
- 1½ teaspoons gluten-free vanilla
- 1 cup flaked or shredded coconut
- ¾ cup sugar
- ½ cup Bisquick® Gluten Free mix

1 Heat oven to 350°F. Grease 9-inch glass pie plate with shortening or cooking spray without flour.

2 In large bowl, stir together all ingredients until blended. Pour into pie plate.

3 Bake 45 to 50 minutes or until golden brown and knife inserted in the center comes out clean. Store any remaining pie covered in refrigerator.

1 SERVING: Calories 260; Total Fat 13g (Saturated Fat 8g; Trans Fat 0g); Cholesterol 100mg; Sodium 180mg; Total Carbohydrate 32g (Dietary Fiber 0g); Protein 4g
EXCHANGES: ½ Starch; 1½ Other Carbohydrate; 2½ Fat CARBOHYDRATE CHOICES: 2

sweet note Enjoy this impossibly easy pie made using Bisquick® Gluten Free mix that can be ready in an hour.

key lime yogurt pie

PREP TIME: 25 minutes *START TO FINISH:* 2 hours 55 minutes [8 SERVINGS]

Crust

1 cup Bisquick® Gluten Free mix

5 tablespoons cold butter

3 tablespoons water

Filling

2 tablespoons cold water

1 tablespoon fresh lime juice

1½ teaspoons unflavored gelatin

4 oz (half of 8-oz package) cream cheese, softened

3 containers (6 oz each) Yoplait® Light Thick & Creamy Key lime pie yogurt

½ cup frozen (thawed) whipped topping

2 teaspoons grated lime peel

Whipped topping, if desired

Grated lime peel, if desired

1 Heat oven to 425°F. Grease 9-inch glass pie plate with shortening or cooking spray without flour. In medium bowl, place Bisquick mix. Cut in butter with pastry blender or fork (or pulling 2 table knives through mixture in opposite directions), until mixture looks like fine crumbs. Stir in water; shape into ball with hands. Press dough in bottom and up side of pie plate.

2 Bake 10 to 12 minutes or until lightly browned. Cool completely, about 30 minutes.

3 In 1-quart saucepan, mix 2 tablespoons cold water and the lime juice. Sprinkle gelatin on lime juice mixture; let stand 1 minute. Heat over low heat, stirring constantly, until gelatin is dissolved. Cool slightly, about 2 minutes.

4 In medium bowl, beat cream cheese with electric mixer on medium speed until smooth. Add yogurt and lime juice mixture; beat on low speed until well blended.

5 Fold in whipped topping and lime peel. Pour into crust. Refrigerate until set, about 2 hours. Garnish with whipped topping and grated lime peel. Cover and refrigerate any remaining pie.

1 SERVING: Calories 220; Total Fat 13g (Saturated Fat 8g; Trans Fat 0g); Cholesterol 35mg; Sodium 300mg; Total Carbohydrate 22g (Dietary Fiber 0g); Protein 4g EXCHANGES: 1 Starch; ½ Other Carbohydrate; 2½ Fat CARBOHYDRATE CHOICES: 1½

sweet note Purchase Key limes and garnish each serving with a lime slice nestled in the whipped topping.

index by ingredient

<u>Underscored</u> page references indicate boxed text. **Boldfaced** page references indicate photographs.

d

f

g

h

i

l

m

n

o

p

r

recipes by mix

Underscored page references indicate boxed text. **Boldfaced** page references indicate photographs.

d

l

conversion chart

These equivalents have been slightly rounded to make measuring easier.

Volume Measurements

U.S.Imperial	*Metric U.S.*	*Metric*
¼ tsp	–	1 ml
½ tsp	–	2 ml
1 tsp	–	5 ml
1 Tbsp	–	15 ml
2 Tbsp (1 oz)	1 fl oz	30 ml
¼ cup (2 oz)	2 fl oz	60 ml
⅓ cup (3 oz)	3 fl oz	80 ml
½ cup (4 oz)	4 fl oz	120 ml
⅔ cup (5 oz)	5 fl oz	160 ml
¾ cup (6 oz)	6 fl oz	180 ml
1 cup (8 oz)	8 fl oz	240 ml

Weight Measurements

U.S.	*Metric*
1 oz	30 g
2 oz	60 g
4 oz (¼ lb)	115 g
5 oz (⅓ lb)	145 g
6 oz	170 g
7 oz	200 g
8 oz (½ lb)	230 g
10 oz	285 g
12 oz (¾ lb)	340 g
14 oz	400 g
16 oz (1 lb)	455 g
2.2 lb	1 kg

Length Measurements

¼"	0.6 cm
½"	1.25 cm
1"	2.5 cm
2"	5 cm
4"	11 cm
6"	15 cm
8"	20 cm
10"	25 cm
12" (1')	30 cm

Pan Sizes

U.S.	*Metric*
8" cake pan	20 × 4 cm sandwich or cake tin
9" cake pan	23 × 3.5 cm sandwich or cake tin
11" × 7" baking pan	28 × 18 cm baking tin
13" × 9" baking pan	32.5 × 23 cm baking tin
15" × 10" baking pan	38 × 25.5 cm baking tin (Swiss roll tin)
1½ qt baking dish	1.5 liter baking dish
2 qt baking dish	2 liter baking dish 325°
2 qt rectangular baking dish	30 × 19 cm baking dish
9" pie plate	22 × 4 or 23 × 4 cm pie plate
7" or 8" springform pan	18 or 20 cm springform or loose-bottom cake tin
9" × 5" loaf pan	23 × 13 cm or 2 lb narrow loaf tin or pâté tin

Temperatures

Fahrenheit	*Centigrade*	*Gas*
140°	60°	–
160°	70°	–
180°	80°	–
225°	105°	¼
250°	120°	½
275°	135°	1
300°	150°	2
160°	3	
350°	180°	4
375°	190°	5
400°	200°	6
425°	220°	7
450°	230°	8
475°	245°	9
500°	260°	–